*The ritual lament in
Greek tradition*

The ritual lament in Greek tradition

MARGARET ALEXIOU

Lecturer in Byzantine and Modern Greek
University of Birmingham

Cambridge University Press

Published by the Syndics of the Cambridge University Press
Bentley House, 200 Euston Road, London NW1 2DB
American Branch: 32 East 57th Street, New York, N.Y. 10022

© Cambridge University Press 1974

Library of Congress Catalogue Card Number: 72–97879

ISBN: 0 521 20226 4

Printed in Great Britain
at the University Printing House, Cambridge
(Brooke Crutchley, University Printer)

To the memory of
JESSIE GRAHAM STEWART
and
ΔΗΜΗΤΡΗ ΑΛΕΞΊΟΥ

Contents

Contents

Contents

Plates

(between pp. 128 and 129)

1 Athens, National Museum no. 450, from Pikrodaphne. Athenian black-figure *loutrophóros* amphora, by the Sappho painter, *c.* 500 B.C.

2a Crete, Heraklion Historical Museum no. 285. Panel-painting by an unknown Cretan artist, early seventeenth century, formerly in the Mone Sabbathiana. The *thrênos* is a local Cretan version of a type similar to the Lampardos *thrênos*, *c.* 1600, Athens, Byzantine Museum no. 352.

2b Athens, Byzantine Museum no. 580. Panel-painting, 1699.

3a From the region of Kozani, western Macedonia. Photograph by A. N. Devteraios, Ἐπετηρὶς τοῦ Κέντρου Ἐρεύνης Ἑλληνκῆς Λαογραφίας, 18–19 (1965–6), 258.

3b From Monastiraki, Vonitsa. Photograph by S. D. Peristeris, *ibid.* 348.

4a and b From Aetos Xiromerou, Aitoloakarnania. Photographs by G. N. Aikaterinidis, *ibid.* 20–1 (1967–8), 344 and 345.

I wish to thank Dr A. A. M. Bryer for his assistance with Plate 2, and Mr T. Christidis for his assistance with Plates 3 and 4.

Preface

My purpose in this book is to study the ritual lament as it evolved and developed throughout Greek tradition, indicating how poets of different ages were able to draw on a common fund of ideas, themes and formulae, frequently investing an old and well-established convention with a new significance and contributing something of their own. At the same time, since the practice of ritual lamentation is attested in both ancient and medieval sources, and remains to this day part of a living folk tradition, whose survival depends not on individuals but on the collective participation of a community, we may also perceive how the lament has retained its vitality and spontaneity, while absorbing many features from its literary past. It is this dynamic interaction between learned and popular poetry which makes the study of Greek tradition so rewarding and exciting when seen as a whole.

This raises the question of continuity in Greek culture, which has long been debated both within Greece and outside. The ardour and acrimony which the discussion has sometimes aroused in both adherents and contestants derive from a subjective and one-sided approach. Continuity needs to be clearly defined and demonstrated within a specific context, if it is to be a meaningful concept. It is not a value judgement: it cannot imply the superiority or originality of those features which can be traced from antiquity to the present day; nor can it preclude the influence of other cultures. Many features of the lament which are discussed in the course of this book can be paralleled in the literary and vernacular tradition of other peoples. But since the written records of the Greek language can be traced, without a significant break, from the second millennium B.C. to the present, and since the lament is among the oldest recorded types of song, we have an exceptionally long perspective in which to study its growth and its treatment in both learned and vernacular literature. The methodological problems involved in such a study are complex and diverse. To those who might object that ancient poetry cannot be treated as valid evidence of prevailing beliefs and practices, I would reply, first, that it is not my intention to reconstruct, for example, from the laments of ancient tragedy how ordinary people lamented their dead in classical Athens, but rather to indicate those features which belong to a common tradition. Literary evidence, properly used in conjunction with other sources, can afford valuable insight into the conventions of lamentation in antiquity. To deny its validity would be as mistaken as to dismiss the evidence of a vase-painting or a funerary inscription on the grounds that the former is an art form and the latter a convention.

More specific problems are those which arise from the disparate nature of our sources. For antiquity, in addition to the evidence of literature, I have drawn on the funerary inscriptions, especially those of the Hellenistic and Greco-Roman periods, as indicative of an essentially more popular and less literary convention. For those inscriptions first published elsewhere but included in Peek's *Griechische Vers-Inschriften*, the reader is referred to his collection for the sake of convenience and ease of reference. For the Byzantine period, our knowledge of lamentation is drawn from a diverse range of sources: the literary lament is found in learned poetry and prose – reflecting, on the whole, a conscious preservation of old forms – as well as in religious and vernacular poetry, where a diversity of new influences is apparent. Other sources of information include patristic writings, saints' lives, chronicles and histories. As for the modern lament, I have restricted my study to folk tradition, although the literary material is no less rich and plentiful, because it is only through the folk lament that the continuity (as opposed to literary preservation) of specific features can be demonstrated. Further, our knowledge of the ritual customs and beliefs associated with lamentation is much fuller for the present period than at any other time, and can throw valuable light on cultural and social factors which have contributed to the process of evolution and continuity. Here, it should be stressed that the study of folk song requires an essentially different approach from that of literary criticism. The task of collecting folk songs in Greece was pioneered last century, without modern technical aids, and without the application of the principle and method of F. J. Child in this country, who published all known variants of each song. Nikolaos Politis, who compares his task to that of the textual critic in the introduction to his collection of Greek folk songs in 1914, is too philological in approach, since the process of continuity, variation and selection which is part of the definition of folk song precludes the literary concept of one original, authentic version of a song, of which variants are corruptions requiring *recensio*, if not *emendatio*. But whatever their shortcomings, it is thanks to the collections of the nineteenth and early twentieth centuries that some of the best of Greek folk tradition has been preserved. They should not be rejected, but used together with the more fully documented material now available.

Absolute consistency in the transliteration of Greek words and names – if, indeed, it has ever been achieved – is precluded in this book by the changes in the pronunciation of the Greek language from antiquity to the present. I have attempted to achieve some sort of general uniformity by avoiding, where convention permits, Latinised forms of classical and Byzantine names. In transliterating modern demotic words and names I have tried to approximate to the modern pronunciation (hence Politis, not Polites). For medieval Greek, I have observed the conventional non-Latinised spelling for learned words and names (e.g. Niketas Choniates, not Nikitas Choniatis), but the modern form for names current in vernacular literature (e.g. Digenis Akritas, not Digenes Acrites). I have had to infringe this principle where modern or early vernacular words are also discussed in an ancient context, or with reference to their etymology, so as to avoid confusing the reader with two forms of the same word: hence I write *thrênos*, not *thrînos*; *paregoriá*, not *parigoriá*, regardless of the change in pronunciation. As for the spelling of modern Greek in the texts cited, I have followed the rules for vowels and word division (though not always for accentuation) laid down by M. Triandafyllidis in his *Modern Greek Grammar*, since to retain the spelling of texts as published by each editor would create an impossible barrier for those readers who are familiar with Greek but not with the vagaries of modern Greek spelling.

Finally, a few words about the plan of this book. I have not followed the obvious course of discussing the ancient, Byzantine and modern material in three separate sections, since to do so would have involved unnecessary repetition, and would also have obscured the thread of continuity in my treatment of particular themes. Part I therefore defines the relation between lament and ritual, demonstrating how the survival of the lament as a living form has depended on the complex collective ritual of which it is a part. Chapter 1 describes the ritual occasions for lamentation in antiquity, and discusses possible causes for the legislation restricting funerary rites in the sixth and fifth centuries B.C. Chapter 2 indicates how some pagan elements were gradually absorbed into the ritual of the Orthodox church, while pagan forms of lamentation persisted among the people. Chapter 3 assesses the extent to which features of ancient and Byzantine ritual have survived today. Part II is an attempt to classify and analyse the main types and forms of lament. In chapter 4 aspects of the ancient laments for gods and heroes are examined and compared with the Byzantine and modern laments of the Virgin for Christ, and with some modern seasonal laments. Chapter 5 traces the growth of a tradition of historical laments for the fall or destruction of cities – a tradition which was readily adaptable to new calamities while retaining old conventions and formulae. Chapter 6 examines some distinctions in the various types of laments and songs to the dead, drawing partly on an analysis of terminology and etymology, and partly on the evidence of literature and modern folk songs. Part III is a detailed study of the structure and thought, conventions and imagery, which are shown to be traditional to the lament thoughout its history. Chapter 7 analyses the use of three-part form, dialogue and refrain, and illustrates how in the best of the laments, the style is not external to but dependent upon the structure and thought. In chapter 8 several conventions, themes and formulae are traced from ancient literary laments and funerary inscriptions through Byzantine learned and vernacular poetry to the modern folk songs. Chapter 9 studies the use of imagery in the lament, and concludes that continuity, both in form and content, has depended not on the static conservation of established patterns, but on the poetic rehandling of traditional beliefs and practices which have remained alive among the people.

For generous help and valuable suggestions at various stages of my work on this book I wish to thank Mr S. J. Papastavrou, Mr J. S. Morrison, Professor G. A. Megas, Professor G. Spyridakis and Professor D. S. Loukatos. I am especially grateful to those people in the villages of Thessaly and Macedonia who provided me with information and allowed me to record their laments, and to Mrs Vasiliki Papayianni, without whose assistance I could not have undertaken my field work. For valued discussions on different aspects of my subject I wish to thank colleagues in the University of Birmingham and elsewhere, in particular Professor R. F. Willetts and Mr A. L. Vincent. Sincere thanks are also due to the Syndics and staff of the Cambridge University Press for their expert and patient assistance. My warmest thanks go to my father, George Thomson and to my husband for their constant encouragement and critical advice.   M. A.

Birmingham, February 1973

PART I
LAMENT AND RITUAL

Problems and method

The lament for the dead is essentially functional. It is only one part of a complex tradition of ritual customs and beliefs. To understand the nature of its development in Greek tradition, and to determine the extent of its continuity from ancient to modern times, it must therefore be studied not in isolation but as an integral part of the ritual to which it belongs.

This raises several problems. First, the interpretation of much of the ancient material is still in dispute, largely because of insufficient evidence and the differing kinds of sources available. Second, while there is no lack of evidence for the Byzantine and modern periods, it has not yet been systematically collected and studied. Third, the method and approach required for the study of funeral ritual are not the same as those required for the study of the lament. For these reasons I shall not attempt to give a full account of the funeral ritual, but rather try to determine the relation between lamentation and ritual in ancient, Byzantine and modern tradition. I have drawn primarily on the evidence of the laments themselves, supplementing it with other literary sources and with some epigraphical and archaeological material. In doing so I have tried not to oversimplify the divergences of practice and belief which existed within the ancient world and which still exist today.

The recent book *Greek Burial Customs* by Donna Kurtz and John Boardman, which comprises a primarily archaeological survey of the ancient material, unfortunately appeared while my own book was in the final stages of preparation, and I have consequently been unable to make use of it as fully as I should have wished.

As for modern Greek, a substantial amount of material has been collected and published in somewhat scattered form in the numerous regional and national folklore periodicals of Greece. Where possible I have drawn also on my own field work, which was conducted in Thessaly in 1963 and in western Macedonia in 1966. Since most of the funerals I was able to attend were for people whose relatives were personally known to me, I felt unable to record from the actuality of a funeral. Nor is it easy to persuade people to sing laments at other times, because of the emotional strain it causes and because of their fear of evil consequences. The value of my field work lies not so much in the intrinsic merits of the laments I recorded as in the greater insight which it afforded me into the composition and performance of the lament and into its meaning for the people today.

1
Tradition and change in antiquity

μή μ' ἄκλαυτον ἄθαπτον ἰὼν ὄπιθεν καταλείπειν,
νοσφισθείς, μή τοί τι θεῶν μήνιμα γένωμαι.　　　　*Od.* 11.72–3

Don't abandon me, don't leave me behind, unwept and unburied,
lest I become a visitation upon you from the gods.

The first soul to greet Odysseus on his visit to the Underworld was
that of Elpenor, who had been left unwept and unburied in Circe's
house after falling from the roof in a drunken stupor. His warning
words indicate that lamentation and burial were two inseparable aspects
of the same thing, the γέρας θανόντων (privilege of the dead).[1] Fear of
the wrath of the dead or of the gods arising from the neglect of these
duties is a recurrent theme in the laments throughout antiquity, and
especially in tragedy. In the long *kommós* performed at Agamemnon's
tomb in Aeschylus' *Choephori*, Elektra cried out in horror at her mother's
crime: she dared to bury Agamemnon without the ceremony due to
a king, and without mourning.[2] This connection between lamentation
and burial can be understood more specifically by considering some
aspects of the actual procedure at the funeral.

Wake, funeral procession and burial

The lament was by no means just a spontaneous outbreak of grief.
It was carefully controlled in accordance with the ritual at every stage.
To weep for someone who was still alive, however great the probability
of his death, was a bad omen. This was something Andromache forgot
when she called her serving-women to join her dirge for Hector after
he had taken leave:[3]

αἱ μὲν ἔτι ζωὸν γόον Ἕκτορα ᾧ ἐνὶ οἴκῳ.   *Il.* 6.500

They wept for Hector in his own house, although he was still alive.

Sokrates sent his wife away before he drank the hemlock so that he could die quietly, and when his closest friends could not control their grief at the moment of death he rebuked them, saying that the dying should pass away in peace.[4] This was because dying involved the struggle of the soul to break loose, known as ψυχορραγεῖν. It could not depart easily if some vow had remained unfulfilled, or if close ties and family obligations were left behind.[5] In Plato's view it was the sinful soul which was reluctant to depart from life.[6] But in Euripides' *Alkestis*, which is described by the scholiast as a popular story orally transmitted,[7] it seems that the fight with death was given a more concrete interpretation: Herakles challenged Thanatos to a fight and rescued Alkestis' soul just as it was being snatched away.[8] Whatever the exact form of this 'struggle of the soul', it was a time of danger, at which, according to a tradition preserved by Plato, the *daímon* appointed to look after each man during his lifetime endeavoured to lead away his soul.[9]

As soon as the moment of dying was over, the body was prepared for the *próthesis*, or wake. In the early period it was a grand, public occasion, probably taking place out of doors. But after the restrictive legislation of the sixth and fifth centuries it was held indoors, or at least in the courtyard within the household.[10] First the eyes and mouth were closed by the next of kin, and the body was washed, anointed and dressed by the women of the house, usually in white, but sometimes in the case of an unmarried or newly married person in wedding attire.[11] It was then laid on a bier, with a mattress, pillow and cover, with the feet placed towards the door or street.[12] Sometimes it was strewn with wild marjoram, celery and other herbs, believed to ward off evil spirits, then laid on vine, myrtle or laurel leaves. The head, which at this stage was uncovered, was decorated with garlands of laurel and celery.[13] At the door stood a bowl of water brought from outside for the purification of all who came into contact with the corpse, and ointment vessels were placed under the bier.[14] Later writers mention the custom of hanging a branch of cypress over the door to warn passers-by of the presence of the dead.[15]

All was now ready for the *próthesis* to begin. Its ritual importance from earliest times is attested by the Homeric poems and by several geometric and archaic vase-paintings, although its relative infrequency on vase-paintings of the fifth and fourth centuries may suggest some decline in its importance during the classical period.[16]

It was at the *próthesis* that the formal lamentation of the dead began. Paintings on Attic and Athenian funerary plaques and vases give a detailed picture of the scene: the father waits at some distance to greet the guests who are arriving to pay their last respects and to take part in the funeral procession.[17] Meanwhile the kinswomen stand round the bier, the chief mourner, either mother or wife, at the head, and the others behind.[18] Other women, possibly professional mourners, are sometimes grouped on the other side, but it is rare to find men, unless they are close relatives, as father, brother or son.[19]

The ritual formality of the men, who enter in procession usually from the right with their right arm raised in a uniform gesture, contrasts sharply with the wild ecstasy of the women, who stand round the bier in varying attitudes and postures.[20] The chief mourner usually clasps the head of the dead man with both hands, while the others may try to touch his hand, their own right hand stretched over him.[21] Most frequently both hands are raised above the head, sometimes beating the head and visibly pulling at their loosened hair.[22] One painting shows the hair actually coming out.[23]

These details are important. The raising of the arms, which can be traced back to Mycenean painted *lárnakes* (coffins) and to the earliest vases of the Dipylon period, is perhaps the most frequent and the most ancient, although its precise origin and significance are unknown.[24] The other gestures are no less a part of the ritual: Andromache leads off the dirge at Hector's *próthesis* by laying her hands around his head, and Achilles laments by laying his hand on Patroklos' breast.[25] Orestes regards this stretching-out of the hand as an essential ritual gesture which he was unable to carry out at Agamemnon's funeral.[26] And the violent tearing of the hair, face and clothes were not acts of uncontrolled grief, but part of the ritual indispensable to lamentation throughout antiquity.[27]

The archaeological and literary evidence, taken together, makes it clear that lamentation involved movement as well as wailing and singing. Since each movement was determined by a pattern of ritual, frequently accompanied by the shrill music of the *aulós* (reed-pipe), the scene must have resembled a dance, sometimes slow and solemn, sometimes wild and ecstatic.[28]

The duration of the *próthesis* varied. Hector's body was burned on the ninth day.[29] Solon stipulated that the *ekphorá* (funeral procession) should take place on the third, and this seems to have remained customary throughout antiquity.[30] Attic vase-paintings confirm that in the geometric and archaic periods the *ekphorá* had been a magnificent, public affair, with the bier carried on a waggon and drawn by two horses, followed by kinswomen, professional mourners and armed men.[31]

Was there any lamentation at this stage? One black-figure *kýathos* shows a lament with *aulós* accompaniment performed at the *ekphorá*.[32] And the universal insistence of the restrictive legislation that silence should be maintained indicates that originally there had been some lamentation, although the words suggest wailing rather than a formal dirge.[33] Similarly the injunction in the Gambreion laws that women's clothes should not be torn shows that it had been customary for the ritual rending of garments to continue.[34]

An Attic black-figure *loutrophóros* from about 500 B.C. shows the coffin with the body of the dead man being laid into the grave: two men are underneath, stretching out their hands to receive it, while two on either side are lowering it in; behind come the women, lamenting.[35] The laws from Delphi forbid wailing during the *ekphorá* but permit it at the tomb, limiting only the numbers taking part.[36]

Offerings at the tomb

Offerings at the tomb were made on the third, ninth and thirtieth days, after one year, and on certain festivals to propitiate the spirits of the dead.[37] References to *tà tríta* and *tà énata* (third-day and ninth-day rites) are frequent in ancient sources, but none makes it clear whether they were reckoned from death or burial. On the whole the former would appear the most probable, in which case *tà tríta* would have followed immediately after burial.[38]

The scene at the tomb is frequently depicted on vase-paintings, especially on Athenian white-figure *lékythoi*, and towards the middle of the fifth century it becomes more common than the scenes of *próthesis* and *ekphorá*. Here the archaeological material affords an invaluable supplement to the literary and epigraphical evidence, which is plentiful but rarely explicit.[39]

First the mourner dedicated a lock of hair, together with *choaí*, a libation of wine, oils and perfumes. These were always accompanied by a prayer.[40] Then came the *enagísmata*, or offerings to the dead, which included milk, honey, water, wine, celery, *pélanon* (a mixture of meal, honey and oil) and *kóllyba* (the first-fruits of the crops and dried and fresh fruits).⁴¹ Even after bull-sacrifice had been forbidden by Solon, it was usual to sacrifice animals – sheep, lambs, kids, birds and fowl – 'according to ancient custom', and bull-sacrifice was permitted on special occasions, for example, to honour the Marathon dead.⁴² All victims were killed over the *eschára* (trench) so that the blood might run into the earth to appease the souls of the dead.⁴³

The offerings were part of the feast due to the dead, the meal being burnt as a holocaust.⁴⁴ On the vase-paintings the mourner can be seen at the tomb with her *lékythoi*, containing oil, wine and perfumes, and wide baskets and cloth bundles with various kinds of food. Besides food and drink, offerings might include *auloí*, lyres, ribbons, garlands and robes, as well as torches and lamps which were kept alight on the graves.⁴⁵

Offerings were never made in silence. The vase-paintings show the mourners approaching with their gifts: there are not usually more than two, one always a woman and on foot, sometimes followed by a man who enters from the right on horseback or on foot, leading his horse.⁴⁶ The woman then lays her offerings on the tomb and begins her supplication, either kneeling down in earnest prayer with her right arm outstretched, or standing with the right arm in the same position and the left tearing her loosened hair.⁴⁷ They are the same ritual gestures as were customary at the *próthesis*, and they seem to have continued for some time, since usually when the mourner arrives she is closely wrapped in a dark-coloured robe, her head covered;⁴⁸ but when the supplication has begun in earnest she is shown with hair loose, or newly shorn, with one or both shoulders bared.⁴⁹

Perhaps the more ecstatic attitude of the mourner at the tomb can be explained by the nature of the ritual. The *próthesis* was a formal affair, with a large number of people grouped round the bier in more or less set positions. Lamentation at the tomb on the other hand was at once more restricted and more personal, involving the direct communication between the relatives and the dead. If the offerings were to be successful, a more passionate invocation, with ritual gestures, was necessary, as the following poorly spelt inscription from Notion (first century A.D.) vividly describes:

ἔτρεχεν ἡ νάννη καὶ σχείζει τόν γε χιτῶνα,
ἔτρεχε κἡ μήτηρ καὶ ἵστατο ἥ γε τυπητόν.　　　Peek 1159.9–10

Her aunt ran up and tore her cloak; her mother ran up too,
and began the beating of the breast.

There was also an underlying sense of fear of the harm the dead might inflict on the living if not fully satisfied. Tendance was the same as appeasement. That is why even Clytemnestra sent mourners with offerings and libations to the tomb of Agamemnon.[50]

There was another reason for the importance attached to the ritual at the tomb: by burying the dead in the earth and making offerings of fruit, grain and flowers it was believed that the earth could be repaid for the gift of life, since earth was nurse and mother of all things, and so fertility could be promoted. As one fifth-century inscription from Attica expresses it:

θρεφθὲς δ' ἐν χθονὶ τῆιδε θάνεν...   Peek 697.5

He died in the earth where he was nourished.

This idea, implicit in many of the laments from tragedy, is expressed in formulaic form from the fifth century on, as in another Attic inscription (fourth to third centuries B.C.):[51]

ἐκ γαίας βλαστὼν γαῖα πάλιν γέγονα   *Ibid.* 1702.2

Having sprung from the earth, earth I have become once more.

Since the earth was so closely associated with the dead, it was natural that the mourner should appeal first to her to receive the offerings and convey them to the dead.[52] In the later inscriptions and in the more literary epigrams of the Palatine Anthology, the earth may even be requested to remember past services, and to treat the dead kindly in return:[53]

Γαῖα φίλη, τὸν πρέσβυν 'Αμύντιχον ἔνθεο κόλποις,
    πολλῶν μνησαμένη τῶν ἐπὶ σοὶ καμάτων.
καὶ γὰρ ἀεὶ πρέμνον σοι ἀνεστήριξεν ἐλαίης...
ἀνθ' ὧν σὺ πρηεῖα κατὰ κροτάφου πολιοῖο
    κεῖσο καὶ εἰαρινὰς ἀνθοκόμει βοτάνας.   *AP* 7.321.1–3, 7–8

Dear Earth, take to your breast the old Amyntichos,
    and remember his many toils for your sake.
In you he always firmly set the stem of the olive-tree...
so in return, lie gently round his aged head,
    and dress yourself in flowers of spring.

An old idea, rooted in fertility magic of great antiquity, has been given new life and vigour with new poetic forms.

The period of mourning varied considerably in different parts of Greece and at different times in the same part.[54] After the burial came a series of purification rites, which involved the thorough cleansing of the house and household objects with sea-water and hyssop, and the ritual washing in clean water of the women most closely related to the dead, who were considered unclean. Finally came the ritual meal, known as *kathédra* and *perídeipnon*, shared by all the dead man's relatives around the hearth of his house.[55]

Kinswomen and strangers

In the classical period the main responsibility for lamentation rested with the next of kin, particularly the women. But throughout antiquity there persisted the custom of hiring or compelling strangers to lament at funerals. In the *Iliad*, Trojan women, captives in the Greek camp, are forced to lament for Patroklos.[56] The Spartan Helots were made to lament at the funeral of a king, and so were the Messenians.[57] Under the Erythraian tyrants the citizens themselves, together with their wives and children, were whipped until they screamed and tore their flesh.[58] Nor was the custom unknown in classical Athens: Aeschylus refers to 'unhired grief', and it must have been common enough for Plato to have thought it necessary in his *Laws* to forbid 'hired songs', usually performed by Carian women at funerals.[59]

The practice was not confined to the Greeks. It was as prevalent among the more civilised Chinese, Egyptians and Romans as among more primitive peoples, and it survives today among the Greeks and other Balkan peoples, in Asia Minor and in Spain.[60] This makes it difficult to believe, with Martin Nilsson, that originally only the next of kin had taken part in the lament, and that the practice of hiring mourners began with civilisation, when improvisation was considered inadequate.[61]

It would be impossible to recover the precise origins of the practice. But some aspects of its development in Greece are important in determining both the nature of the obligation towards the dead and the kinship groups on which it devolved.

A good starting point is terminology. Words often provide useful historical evidence because they are an unconscious reflection of the connections between concepts belonging to a more primitive stage of social development. Such a word is the Greek for funeral, κηδεία, which can also mean *alliance* or *parenthood*. Its root form κῆδος means *concern*, and in the plural *funeral rites* or *family feeling*. The verb κηδεύω means *to tend* (a bride or a corpse), or *to contract an alliance by marriage*, and the noun κηδεστής means *relation-in-law*. Why is tendance of the dead so directly linked with relationship by marriage?

Analysing the meaning of the word *kadestás* in the Gortyn Code, R. F. Willetts draws attention to the fact that in classical literature a single term, *kedestés*, was used to denote the general concept of relation by marriage as well as the more specific categories of son-in-law, father-in-law and brother-in-law. Plato uses it generically, and in Crete it could also include the heiress' mother and the mother's brothers.[62] He argues that the explanation lies in the conditions of family relationship in Crete, known to have differed from those of the more advanced states in that they were closer to tribal custom, and that the rule of tribal endogamy was normally applied. Relationship in the *génos*, or clan, was based on well-defined intermarrying groups and was therefore determined not by the family as we know it but by a series of continuously intermarrying collateral groups. Although Cretan society of the historical period was founded on the *oîkos*, or family, as a unit within the *génos*, many traces of the older system survive, especially in the terminology. Besides *kadestás*, the Code uses the word *epibállontes*, kinsmen in any degree, members of the same *génos* but not of the same *oîkos*.[63] It is likely, Willetts argues, that these *kadestaí* and *epibállontes* were two intermarrying groups, each with mutual obligations entailing both the protection of marriage rights and the care of funeral ritual. In a Cretan law of the early fifth century it is apparently the *kadestaí* who carry the corpse from the house to the grave, while another law of slightly later date stipulates that the *epibállontes* carry out the appropriate lustration after the funeral.[64] Originally both kinsmen and relations by marriage had well-defined obligations towards the dead, and this can be supported by a considerable body of comparative evidence.[65]

If it had once been the duty of the *kedestaí* to take charge of some of the ritual, then the otherwise obscure connection between tendance of the dead and relationship by marriage can be explained historically.[66] Can the practice of hiring or compelling strangers to mourn and tend the corpse be a relic of this earlier stage, when such duties were performed not by the next of kin but by the intermarrying group? Again terminology affords some clues, although a definite answer is precluded by the nature of the evidence.

Two of the commonest words for *lament* are *thrênos* and *góos*. Although used with little distinction of meaning by classical writers, Homeric usage shows some differentiation. *Thrênos* occurs only twice. In the *Odyssey* the pitiful wailing of the Ocean Nymphs, who are kinswomen, is sharply contrasted with the ordered, antiphonal lament of the Muses sung at Achilles' *próthesis*:

Lament and ritual

ἀμφὶ δέ σ᾿ ἔστησαν κοῦραι ἁλίοιο γέροντος
οἴκτρ᾿ ὀλοφυρόμεναι, περὶ δ᾿ ἄμβροτα εἵματα ἕσσαν.
Μοῦσαι δ᾿ ἐννέα πᾶσαι ἀμειβόμεναι ὀπὶ καλῇ
θρήνεον· ἔνθα κεν οὔ τιν᾿ ἀδάκρυτόν γ᾿ ἐνόησας
Ἀργείων· τοῖον γὰρ ὑπώρορε Μοῦσα λίγεια.   *Od.* 24.58–62

The daughters of the old sea-god stood round you,
weeping bitterly, and laid upon you the immortal garments.
Then the nine Muses sang laments, each responding in sweet
tones. None of the Argives could restrain his tears, stirred forth
so strongly by the Muse's shrill-voiced song.

In the *Iliad* the distinction emerges even more clearly in the account of
Hector's *próthesis* between the *thrênos* of the professional mourners,
which was a proper song, and the *góos* of the kinswomen, which was
merely wailed:

παρὰ δ᾿ εἷσαν ἀοιδοὺς
θρήνων ἐξάρχους, οἵ τε στονόεσσαν ἀοιδὴν
οἱ μὲν δὴ θρήνεον, ἐπὶ δὲ στενάχοντο γυναῖκες.
τῇσιν δ᾿ Ἀνδρομάχη λευκώλενος ἦρχε γόοιο.   *Il.* 24.720–3

They brought in singers,
leaders of the dirges, who sang laments
in mournful tune, while the women wailed in chorus.
White-armed Andromache led their keening.

Only the laments of the kinswomen – Andromache, Hekabe and Helen
– are given in full, and it is these we are interested in from a literary
point of view. Yet the mourning for Hector clearly involved more than
a string of solos followed by a refrain of keening: there are two groups
of mourners, professional singers and kinswomen. The singers begin
with a musical *thrênos*, answered by a refrain of cries, and then the lament
is taken up by the three next of kin, each singing a verse in turn and
followed by another refrain of cries. Their verses are an answer to the
lamentation of the professional singers.

Independent support for this interpretation of the early *thrênos* as the
lament especially composed and performed at the funeral by non-kinsmen
comes from Plutarch's account of Solon's legislation restricting funeral
rites, in his *Life of Solon*: 'He [Solon] forbade laceration of cheeks,
singing of set dirges and lamentation at other people's tombs' (21.4).
Here θρηνεῖν πεποιημένα, or *set dirges*, implies a polished composition,
and the close connection between this and the limitation of the right to
mourn to kinswomen only is a further indication that the *thrênos* was

12

Tradition and change in antiquity

not originally performed by the next of kin. This might also explain why the *thrênos* was the particular kind of lament to be developed artistically by the lyric poets.[67]

As for the *góos*, it is by far the most frequent term in Homer for all the laments which are given in full. These have two features in common: first that they are improvisations inspired by the grief of the occasion, and second that they are all sung by the dead man's relations or close friends.[68]

This points to the origin of the lament in the antiphonal singing of two groups of mourners, strangers and kinswomen, each singing a verse in turn and followed by a refrain sung in unison. In Homer the antiphonal element is becoming obscured, and even the refrain has been reduced to a perfunctory formula. In the aristocratic period the choral ode was developed in the form of the *thrênos* and the soloist dispensed with altogether, but in tragedy the older form was re-established in the *kommós*, which is clearly defined by Aristotle as a tragic lament in dialogue form between chorus and actors.[69] The long *kommós* in Aechylus' *Choephoroi* (306–478) is just such an antiphonal lament between Orestes and Elektra, who are Agamemnon's next of kin, and the chorus of libation-bearers, probably Trojan captives, who are slaves in the palace and have been ordered by Clytemnestra to take part in the lamentation.

Reference has already been made to Nilsson's view that the antiphonal lament developed out of the solo and refrain after the inadequacy of the improvisations of the next of kin had given rise to the establishment of groups of professional mourners. It implies that antiphony and the use of strange mourners belong to an advanced rather than a primitive stage of development. But first, none of the Homeric *góoi* provides the slightest evidence for the 'inadequacies of the next of kin': on the contrary, these are given in full, whereas the *thrênoi* are mentioned only twice and in passing. Second, the Oriental lament, which Nilsson himself considers a possible forerunner of the Greek, was definitely performed by two groups singing antiphonally.[70]

This analysis of the early use of *thrênos* and *góos* therefore complements the evidence of the kinship terminology. Both antiphony and the role of the *kedestaí* can be shown by usage and terminology to be extremely ancient. In ancient Greek the antiphonal performance could be explained by the twin roles of the next of kin, collateral relations of the same *génos*, and the relations by marriage, collateral members of the opposite *génos*, each responsible for specified formalities of ritual and lamentation. When this older system of relationship was superseded, the duties of tendance passed from the relations-in-law to other non-kinsmen, who were either compelled or hired for the purpose. The origin of the practice in tribal relationship might also explain its strong ritual character and its tenacity throughout antiquity.

The legislation on funeral rites and lamentation

In its origins and early development the lament was an integral part of the funeral ritual. What was the purpose of the legislation restricting lamentation and ritual? Did it result in a break in tradition and a tendency for the lament to lose its ritual significance and become a mere literary convention?

The question is complex, and raises many issues which cannot be thoroughly investigated here. But it may be helpful to bring some of them forward for discussion, since in this way the lament can be seen in a historical perspective, as a phenomenon which could affect social and political life. It also provides an opportunity to touch on the fundamental problem of how continuity of tradition is affected in times of upheaval.

Archaeology, epigraphy and literature all bear witness to the importance attached to funeral ritual in the societies of prehistoric and archaic Greece. The monumental *thóloi* and chamber tombs of the Mycenean period, designed for the whole *génos*, show traces of elaborate burial customs and rich offerings of gifts and utensils which cannot be paralleled in later times.[71] For the geometric and archaic periods the large amphorae and the early funerary plaque series illustrate the grandeur of the *ekphorá*. According to Cicero it was Kekrops, legendary founder of Athens, who initiated the full pomp and ceremony of funerals there.[72] And the fact that from the sixth century on so many laws were passed restricting funeral ritual is itself proof of its previous significance, regarded as somehow harmful and offensive to the newer societies. What are the implications of the strength of these funerary practices in the archaic period, and why was it decided to forbid them?

The evidence is both epigraphic and literary. Since the literary evidence, even when it is late, is so closely supported by the epigraphic, it can be accepted as authentic. The earliest laws known to us in detail are those of Solon, described in Plutarch's *Life of Solon* and in a speech attributed to Demosthenes. According to Plutarch Solon's legislation arose as a direct result of the Kylon affair: the blood-feud which followed Megakles' massacre of Kylon and his fellow conspirators, after they had failed in their attempted *coup d'état* and had taken refuge at one of the city's most sacred altars, left a deep mark on Athenian society. Descendants of the two families were in continual strife some thirty years later, in Solon's time.⁷³ Legislating under these circumstances, Solon is said to have been influenced by Epimenides of Crete, who had enacted similar legislation in Phaistos and had come to Athens in order to help. Thanks to Solon the barbaric excesses for which women were chiefly responsible were brought to an end.

What is meant by 'forbidding everything disorderly and excessive in women's festivals, processions and funeral rites', as Plutarch says? No woman was to carry to the grave for burial with the dead more than three garments, one obol's worth of food and drink, or a basket of more than one cubit's length. There was to be no procession by night except by lighted coach, no singing of set dirges and no wailing of other dead. Bull-sacrifice was also forbidden. No one was to walk about other people's graves unaccompanied, and all offenders were to be punished by *gynaikonómoi*, officials specially appointed to deal with women's affairs.⁷⁴ The two aspects of the legislation emphasised most are the strict curtailing of the offerings at the grave and the limitation of the right to mourn to kinswomen only.

Demosthenes, who claims to be quoting the actual words of Solon's law, supplements Plutarch's account in the following details: the wake was to take place indoors and be over by sunrise.⁷⁵ Again, it was an attempt to turn what had been a public ceremony held outside into a private affair attracting as little attention as possible. The only women permitted to follow the body and weep at the graveside were those 'within the degree of cousins' children', and even they were to keep behind the men. Whether they did or not was another matter: the vase-paintings suggest that the letter of the law was disregarded on this point.

The next law comes from Ioulis in the island of Keos, dating from the second half of the fifth century, but probably a new formulation of earlier legislation.⁷⁶ Since contact between Athens and Keos had been maintained through the vermilion trade, it is possible that this law owes something to Solon's. It may also have been connected with the anti-oligarchic movement in Keos which saw Bakchylides exiled between 468 and 459.

The main points are the same as at Athens. The maximum allowance for offerings was rather more generous, but all vessels had to be taken home afterwards. The same applied to the bier and the covers. The motive for the removal of such objects is less likely to have been economy than a desire to prevent the setting up of a permanent mark on the grave which would have made it a place of worship. The *ekphorá* was to take place in silence, and, in order to facilitate this, once more the women were ordered to stand behind the men. Numbers were more strictly limited than at Athens: only five women, all within the degree of cousins' children, were permitted in addition to the immediate family of the dead man's wife, mother, sisters and daughters.

One feature not mentioned in Solon's law is the ban on *triekóstia* (monthly observances) which included the depositing of *kallýsmata* (sweepings from the house) on the grave. Monthly observances were not exclusive to funerals: offerings of food and sweepings from the house, containing all kinds of refuse (including human excreta), were customarily taken by the women every month and left at the crossroads. They were known as 'Hekate's suppers'. Their purpose was apotropaic, to warn off evil spirits, and the monthly occurrence together with their association with Hekate suggests an origin in primitive moon magic.[77] After a funeral their function was apparently to purge the pollution in the household of the deceased. Perhaps the law was trying to put a stop to these primitive practices controlled by the women and replace them with other more hygienic methods of purification.[78]

Part of the social and religious legislation of the priestly clan of the Labyadai at Delphi is also concerned with funeral practice.[79] It dates from the end of the fifth century, but the opening phrase suggests that it was a reformulation of an earlier law. New features include the specification in money value of the offerings permitted, and mention of a fifty drachma fine for disobedience. Regulations for the *ekphorá* are exact and strict: the corpse must be closely veiled and carried in silence, and must not be laid down and wailed for *at the turnings in the road*[80] or outside other people's houses. There were to be no set dirges and no lamenting at the tomb of 'those long dead'. All mourners were to go straight home after the burial except for the *homéstioi*, a new term meaning 'those at the same hearth'. Wailing and set dirges were forbidden on the customary days after burial and after one year, but offerings were permitted.

From the third century B.C. there is a law from Gambreion in Asia Minor which is sufficiently different to be considered independent of the earlier legislation:[81] it contains none of the restrictions on expense and numbers, and the time limit for mourning is more generous, three months for men and four for women. It specifies that the dress worn by women at funerals should be dark, not the usual white, and that it should not be torn. Women are selected as the chief offenders, and are to be punished for disobedience by the *gynaikonómoi* with exclusion from the state festival of the Thesmophoria and from sacrifice to any god for a period of ten years. The injunction for the women to 'take part in the processions written in the law' after the official period of mourning is over may reflect an attempt to replace the importance of funeral rites in the religious life of the women with something else.

The last group of inscriptions comes from the Pontos in the fourth century B.C., from Nisyros in the third and from Brindisi in the second to first: all make it an offence for women to bury their dead within the temple precincts.[82] One of the motives for these laws may have been to discourage families from setting up their tombs as places of worship.

The remaining literary evidence may be summarised as follows: according to Plutarch, Lykourgos, legendary lawgiver at Sparta, removed the curse of pollution by allowing the dead to be buried within the city precincts and curbed excess by stipulating that the dead be buried in a single scarlet robe and laid only on olive leaves. Only soldiers killed in war might have their names inscribed on their tombs, and all mourning was to end after eleven days.[83] According to Diodoros, Gelon of Syracuse also forbade expensive funerals.[84] Cicero mentions Pittakos of Lesbos as legislating against the lamentation of other dead, and refers to further restrictive legislation at Athens, passed both 'some time after' Solon's laws and during the rule of Demetrios of Phaleron towards the end of the fourth century.[85] Finally, the preamble to laws from Katana purporting to be by the lawgiver Charondas (sixth century B.C.) includes the restriction of funeral rites.[86]

It emerges from this summary of the evidence that the restrictions originated in the more advanced city states where a new society, often culminating in democracy, was establishing itself. The exception is Sparta. But in Sparta, as nowhere else in Greece, full pomp and ceremony were maintained for the funeral of kings, so that restriction was selective, not general.[87] By taking such a step in good time, along with other social and economic measures, Lykourgos was able to forestall the rise of all-powerful noble families who might challenge both the position of the kings and the limitations imposed on economic and political developments.

If we consider the legislation passed before the end of the fifth century, we shall see that although the details vary, the main points are essentially the same. First, the curbing of extravagance indicates that the laws were aimed primarily at the rich, not the poor. Second, the limitation of the right to mourn to the immediate kin suggests a changing emphasis from clan to family. Third, the restrictions on women point to their former prominence in funerals, now considered undesirable. Fourth, the ban on ritual likely to attract attention implies that funerals could arouse dangerous sentiments among the people.

Two main causes for this legislation have been suggested. First, that it was part of an economy drive, and second, that it was designed to curb popular superstition.[88] Both need clearer definition. Who was economising on what and on whom? Why should the lawgivers in these societies, where plenty of money was spent on the reorganisation of religious festivals, the building of temples, theatres and public works, be so concerned about expensive funerals, especially as it was not state money anyway? And some of the things forbidden did not cost anything, such as laceration of the cheeks and bewailing of the dead. Nor was it a rationalist attempt to curb superstition. At the same time as the restrictive legislation, hero worship was officially introduced, highly organised and receiving full support from the Delphic oracle. This often involved the same beliefs and practices as for the dead.

Let us look at the situation in Athens a little more closely, since evidence elsewhere is too fragmentary to present a complete picture. These restrictive measures should not be seen in isolation from other reforms of the sixth century, the general aims of which are fairly clear. It is possible that the restriction of funeral rites was part of an attempt to break down the hold of the aristocratic clan cults. Aristotle says that the democratic trend was to reduce the number of such cults and to throw them open to the public, and that this trend was begun in the age of the tyrants.[89] It is not hard to see why this might have been necessary, since the basis of the aristocratic clan cults was worship of a real or legendary founder: ritual had important associations with cult and could therefore be used to increase religious and political power. Possibly we have here an explanation for the ban on *thrênoi*. In the choral form in which they were performed by professional singers, they were part of the clan cult. Simonides, the first poet known to have composed choral *thrênoi*, wrote them all for wealthy families outside his native Keos, for the court of the Skopadai in Thessaly, and for Antiochos of the Aleuadai in Larisa.[90] It has been plausibly suggested that the small number of these *thrênoi* to survive is due to the restrictive legislation.[91]

As for the replacement of clan cults by state cults and hero worship, it was Drakon, in 620 B.C., who first strengthened hero worship in

Attica; and in doing so he did not introduce anything new or extraneous to Greek religion, but revived and extended what had long been popular in local tradition.[92] In the course of the sixth century these reforms were intensified. Solon reorganised the old, local cult groups known as *orgeônes* and *thíasoi*, with admission by initiation and adoption instead of by birth, and with the local hero instead of the clan ancestor at the centre of the cult.[93] He does not seem to have interfered directly with the aristocratic cults, but his restrictions on funeral rites were probably designed to limit their scale and influence. Another step of the utmost significance in this connection was his probable transformation of the *genésia* from a private and sumptuous festival held on the anniversary of a man's death into a general and public Festival of the Dead held on a fixed calendar date and open to the whole people.[94]

Reforms such as these accord with Solon's moderate tactics, which sought not to alienate the aristocracy but to achieve a compromise and modify excess. Further, Epimenides, on whose advice Solon had formulated his restrictive legislation, was famous for his religious reforms in Crete, and it seems likely that one of the consequences of these reforms was the adaptation of older ritual arts to newer forms and purposes.[95] It was at about the same time that the first steps in introducing the mystery religions in Athens were taken. Under the tyrant Peisistratos and his sons, both hero worship and the mysteries were incorporated into state religion, a process which can be documented by some epigraphic evidence.[96] The final step was taken by Kleisthenes, who in the course of his democratic reforms at the end of the sixth century renamed the old tribes and phratries after heroes, discarding the old clan names. It was a political move of prime importance, as Herodotos points out.[97]

These reforms therefore involved a gradual transfer of ritual, and of all the emotive feeling attached to it, from the ancestor of the clan cult to the hero of the state cult. The same athletic contests, rich sacrifices and offerings, choral *enkómia* and *thrênoi*, tragic choruses and lamentation, persisted. But they were no longer exclusive to aristocratic clan cults dependent on birth.[98] They were part of a public festival open to all: the mysteries promised happiness to all initiates in afterlife, irrespective of birth or wealth; while for the less sophisticated, the cult of heroes' shrines remained a safeguard against pestilence, defeat in war and failure of crops.[99]

In view of the generally democratic nature of these reforms it is not surprising to find in the restrictions on funeral rites traces of another equally important motive, the consolidation of private property and of the right of a son to inherit – of the rights of the family as opposed to those of the *génos*. It was pointed out by Bruck that the limitation of offerings to the dead restricts the amount of wealth to be buried with the ancestor in his tomb and increases the amount to be inherited. This restrictive tendency must have begun much earlier, because the archaic tombs show no traces of the vast deposits of wealth which are to be found in Mycenean times. The struggle between ancestor worship and family property developed more gradually and less acutely in Greece than elsewhere; but just because the main conflict had been resolved before, developments in the sixth century were more far-reaching.[100]

In the aristocratic period, the customary law of intestate succession was followed. Male descendants in every degree were considered to be the natural and legal heirs; there was no law of primogeniture. If a man died without heirs, his estate passed to collaterals and their descendants. An extinct household therefore passed to the next of kin, who absorbed the property into their own.[101] The old law protected not the *oîkos* but the *génos*. The system dated back to patriarchal society, where landed estates were held in common by the *génos*, large groups of three or four generations related to a common ancestor, who lived and worked on the same undivided soil.[102] In Athens, with the growing independence of the family (*oîkos*) as the new socio-economic unit of the city state, a struggle arose between the concentrative tendencies of the clan and the autonomous inclinations of the family; and this conflict was only resolved by means of state imposition of new legislation. Solon's laws on inheritance and property, the first known to us in detail, consisted of testamentary adoption, whereby in default of male heirs the testator adopted a son who perpetuated the family household and kept its *sacra* alive. Thus collaterals or ascendants were prevented from inheriting and the concentrative tendencies of the clan were curtailed. As Plutarch says, formerly 'money and property went to the clan, but under Solon's law it became possible for a childless man to leave his property to anyone he liked, and so for the first time a man's goods became his own possession'.[103]

There is evidence that throughout Greek antiquity the right to inherit was directly linked with the right to mourn. Within the clan system the duty of maintaining the clan founder in his old age and of tending his grave after death devolved on all descendants down to the fourth generation, as far as his great-grandsons, who inherited the property in equal shares.[104] Even after the breakdown of the clan system, the link between inheritance and mourning survived. Laws from Gortyn in fifth-century Crete stipulate that an adopted heir cannot partake of the property of his adoptive father unless he undertakes the sacred duties of the house of the deceased.[105] In Athens of the fifth and fourth centuries it was the same. Isaios asks in one of his speeches, 'Is it not a most unholy thing if a man, without having done any of the customary rites due to the dead, yet expects to take the inheritance of the dead man's property?' (4.19). In another speech, he describes how the quarrel over Kiron's estate began before he was even buried, when two claimants presented themselves at his wake on the day after he died in order to take charge of the body and of funeral expenses (8.21–4). The suspicion that their eagerness was due less to piety than to the initial advantage they believed they would gain in claiming the inheritance is confirmed when we hear of the sordid quarrel which broke out between them at the graveside. Finally, the implication behind Demosthenes' speech *Against Makartatos* is that by taking part in the *ekphorá* for Hagnias, Makartatos' mother and Theopompos' wife are laying false claims on Hagnias' inheritance (43.79–80). If the right to mourn was so closely linked with the right to inherit until the end of the fourth century, it is not hard to understand why the funeral legislation so persistently restricts the care of the dead to the immediate kin: only those 'within the degree of first cousins and their children' were permitted because only they in future were to have any claim on the inheritance.[106]

It remains to explain why the women were so hard hit by the restrictive legislation. From earliest times the main responsibility for funeral ritual and lamentation had rested with them:[107] they were therefore in control of something which in the archaic period had played a vital part in the religious and social life of the clan, and it may be suspected that they gained access in this way to decisions about property. If the family, based on father-right, was to be established as the basic unit of society, then the power of women in religious and family affairs must be stopped, and they must be made to play a more secondary role at funerals. Restrictions on women are another sign of incipient democracy. But perhaps in consolation for their lost privileges they were given at the same time an important part in the Thesmophoria and the Eleusinian mysteries, where they were safely under state control.[108]

Perhaps there was a further motive: the women, by wailing, lacerating themselves and holding ceremonies in public, were attracting attention which might amount to a social menace, not only indecent but dangerous. In the inflammable atmosphere of the blood feud between the families of Megakles and Kylon that was still raging in Solon's time, what more effective way could there be to stir up feelings of revenge than the incessant lamentation at the tomb by large numbers of women for 'those long dead'?

These exaggerated displays, which included the use of professional mourners, must have excited a state of frenzy. This coincides exactly with the role of women in cases of vengeance. Although the act itself rested with the men, unless there was no male survivor, the women maintained the consciousness for the need to take revenge by constant lamentation and invocation at the tomb. Literary examples include Aeschylus' *Choephoroi*, where Elektra starts, hesitant even to pray for revenge, but by the end of the long *kommós* she is transformed, crying out for blood like a savage wolf.[109] In this play, as in Sophokles' *Elektra*, it is clear that Orestes was brought up by another to contemplate the deed of matricide, and was even in need of reassurance at the last minute, whereas Elektra had roused herself to such a pitch of frenzy by means of her passionate invocations that she was ready to do the deed herself. Finally, the dirge is always strongest where the law of vendetta flourishes, as in Sicily or Mani today. The restrictions imposed on women in funeral ritual might well have been designed to end internecine strife between clans by removing the responsibility for punishment in cases of homicide from clan to state, as Plutarch implies himself by connecting them with the Kylon affair and with Drakon's homicide laws. It is significant to note that the homicide laws restrict the initiative in prosecution to those who are 'within the degree of cousins' children', that is, to the same relatives who were considered legal heirs and were permitted to lament at the dead man's funeral.[110]

How effective, then, was the restrictive legislation? On the surface it does not appear to have changed substantially the character of funeral ritual. Vase-paintings throughout the fifth century, the sumptuary laws of Demetrios of Phaleron and the comments made by Plato in his *Laws* at the end of the fourth century, Lucian's caustic satire in the second century A.D., and many other sources, point not only to extreme conservatism in such matters but also to the return and revival of many practices which had been forbidden.[111] At the same time it is probable that the early legislation was successful in its fundamental anti-aristocratic aims. There was a gradual transformation in the function and nature of funeral ritual, in accordance with the social changes which had taken place, and the aristocratic hold on these traditions, together with the privileges which they entailed, was broken down.

As for the relation between ritual and lament, it is possible to detect a change in emphasis from the public lamentation at the grander ceremonies of *próthesis* and *ekphorá* to a more personal kind of lamentation at the tomb. At the beginning of the fifth century the funerary epigram was elaborated into more than a mere statement of the fact of death, expressing a more intimate contact of mourner and dead. This coincides with the introduction of the *epitáphios lógos* as a public tribute to those deserving special honour and the discarding of the choral *thrênos*.[112]

But it was only a change in emphasis. Even in its most highly developed literary form, the lament retained something of its ritual connections, because lamentation and funeral ritual never became a purely private affair. Moreover in the more backward, rural districts, where the restrictive legislation failed to penetrate, tradition must have continued much as it always had done.

This uneven development enabled the poets of the classical period to draw on an extremely rich and varied tradition, which they refined and developed but never completely ignored. At the same time it ensured the survival and proliferation of many local practices which might otherwise have disappeared.[113] This factor became increasingly important after the breakdown of the city state, with the unification of the Greek world under the Hellenistic, Roman and Byzantine Empires.

2
From paganism to Christianity

We have seen in the first chapter how the function and purpose of the lament changed in accordance with the historical developments of antiquity. What was the impact of the economic, social and religious upheavals which accompanied the decline of the ancient world and the rise of Byzantium? Was there not an inevitable transformation by Christianity of all the most characteristic features of something so essentially pagan as funeral ritual and lamentation?

The transition from paganism to Christianity took place very gradually and unevenly in late antiquity and in the early Byzantine world. The Hellenistic expansion which had begun in the third century B.C. had carried Greek culture far beyond the boundaries of Greece itself, but in doing so it had opened the way for a new influx of mystic cults from the East. Byzantium was heir to all these. Some idea of the confusion in popular religion soon after the founding of Constantinople in A.D. 324 can be gained from the anonymous magic incantations of the period, many of which have been preserved on papyrus.[1] Among the intellectuals there was a more conscious fusion of pagan and Christian beliefs and doctrines, beginning with Clement of Alexandria and Origen and culminating in the late Gnostic and Neoplatonic writers.

For the first two centuries of the Byzantine Empire, official policy towards paganism was cautious and tolerant. Even after the closing of the Athenian Academy in 529 by Justinian, its philosophers were permitted to remain within the Empire without becoming Christians. It was during this period that Christianity absorbed a great many pagan elements, numerous ancient cult sites being transformed into Christian shrines of similar association.[2] But the process was neither immediate nor exhaustive. At the turn of the fourth and fifth centuries the religion, customs, language and laws observed in the towns and villages of Greece appear to have changed little since antiquity, while in the countryside the survival of pagan ritual is referred to in various sources from the seventh to the twelfth centuries.[3]

These conditions favoured the survival of the ritual lament. Throughout the Byzantine period the correct observation of funeral ritual was a matter of concern for people at all levels of society, as can be understood from the homilies of the Christian fathers, and from works such as the Emperor Konstantinos Porphyrogennetos' *de Cerimoniis* (tenth century), or from the curious handbook entitled *de Ordine Sepulturae*, written *c.* 1420 by Symeon, Archbishop of Thessaloniki.

The evidence for the survival of the ritual lament is plentiful, but it needs to be handled with caution, since it comes mainly from homilies, chronicles and commentaries, where pagan survivals are mentioned only with disapproval. It cannot always be taken as a true reflection of popular tradition.

The struggle of the soul

The ritual began as soon as it was clear that death was imminent. The first task, the sweeping of the house (not unlike the custom which had been forbidden in the legislation from Keos in antiquity), was observed, according to one tradition, at the death of the Virgin herself.[4] Then came the ψυχορράγημα as the struggle of the soul was now known. John Chrysostom (*c.* 347–407), Archbishop at Antioch and at Constantinople, gives a vivid account of what was seen by the soul at this moment. It might also be taken for an echo of Plato's description in the *Phaedo*, were it not for the fact that he refers explicitly to popular belief:

> That is why you can hear the common people tell of fearful
> sights and dreadful visions at this moment...because the soul
> is forcing herself down, reluctant to be torn away from the
> body and unable to bear the sight of the approaching angels.
>
> Migne 58.532[5]

The reason for the soul's fear of the host of *ángeloi* and *daímones* is that it sees 'the hostile forces standing there, account-books in hand, shouting accusations and trying to snatch it away' (*ibid.* 60.727).[6]

The full terror of this moment is graphically captured by Makarios (fourth century), one of the early ascetics from Egypt, in what he calls 'A Dreadful Story which Appals the Mind'. Near Heaven, angels are busily flying up and down, guiding the souls of the dead past the judgement barriers which separate them from Paradise. Suddenly a host of black, insect-like creatures appear and try to snatch the souls away to Hell. The angels resist, and all are saved except for one sinful soul, which fails to pass the formidable Barrier of Prostitution and Adultery. Angels and devils argue fiercely about the desirability of saving it, and the dispute is only decided by the propitious intervention of the soul's guardian spirit, who has been busy making sure that all was ready at the tomb. This ἄγγελος ὁ ἀπὸ τοῦ βαπτίσματος δοθεὶς αὐτῷ εἰς παραφυλακήν (angel appointed at baptism to guard him), who is exactly parallel to Plato's ὁ ἑκάστου δαίμων ὅσπερ ζῶντα εἰλήχει (*daimon* to whom each man is allotted during his lifetime), assures both sides of the man's sincere death-bed repentance, and so the soul is acquitted, much to the annoyance of the devils.[7] The idiomatic style of this cautionary tale suggests a popular origin.

Another belief which expresses the physical terror of dying is that the dying man's soul was weighed on the scales of justice. Commenting on a line in Euripides, Eustathios of Thessaloniki (twelfth century) refers to the phrase εἰς τὰ τοῦ ῞Αιδου κεῖσθαι ζυγά (to lie on Hades' scales) as synonymous with dying in popular speech.[8] Three centuries later we find the same idea in one of the many popular dialogues between Man and Charon, written in the vernacular. Charon says threateningly:

Ζύγι κρατῶ στὸ χέρι μου τῆς ἐλεημοσύνης
γιὰ νὰ ζυάσω τά 'καμες...   Moravcsik *SBN* (1931) III.33–4

In my hand I hold the scales of Mercy,
to weigh out what you've done...

It is also incorporated into the funeral service of the Orthodox Church:

'Ελεήσατέ με, ἄγγελοι πανάγιοι...οὐκ ἔχω γε ἔργον ἀγαθὸν
ἀντισταθμίζειν τὸν ζυγὸν τῶν φαύλων πράξεων.   Spyridakis 97

Have mercy upon me, all-holy angels...for I have no good deed
to balance the burden of my evil ones.

The idea has survived notwithstanding the changes of deity, Hades, Charon and God.

As in antiquity, the moment of dying was an *agón*, and for that reason came the call for silence in the funeral service:

You behold the great mystery; be silent in the dreadful hour,
that the soul may depart in peace, for it is engaged in great
ordeal.   Pitra *AS* 1.246

A full account of the funeral of Makrina, sister of Basil of Caesarea, is contained in one of the homilies of Gregory of Nyssa (331–96), in which he describes how in deference to her explicit wish the sorrowful company present at her passing restrained their anguish until the end.[9] It appears that the early Byzantine Church tried consciously to extend and develop the moral aspects of various popular beliefs current since antiquity concerning the last moments of life. In doing so, it was merely adapting elements of ancient superstition to a more acceptable Christian form.

The wake

As Gregory observes in his account of Makrina's death, the spontaneous lamentation which broke out once the struggle of the soul was over was all the more passionate for having been controlled for so long. As soon as the first violence of grief had passed, the ritual preparation of the body began. It had changed little since antiquity. First came the closing of eyes and mouth, still known by the ancient term καλύπτειν.[10] Sometimes a coin was placed on the mouth.[11] Then came the washing and anointing with wine and scents and the scattering of herbs. Clement's suggestion that this was to stop the souls from smelling in the Underworld may not be entirely frivolous, even if it was a rationalisation of popular belief, since it finds some support in one of Herakleitos' obscurer fragments.[12] The body was then dressed in a white winding-sheet (σάβανον), corresponding to the Homeric φᾶρος,[13] and in unworn clothes, sometimes rich gold and purple,[14] sometimes in full wedding attire, as in the case of Makrina.[15] Thus prepared, it was placed on a bier and strewn with the same evergreens and herbs as in antiquity – olive, laurel, palm, myrtle, cypress and celery. All was then ready for the formal wake, which took place at sunrise just inside the door of the house, with the bier facing towards the east.[16] Finally came the ritual breaking of clay vessels, believed to chase away the evil spirits hovering around to snatch away the souls by force to Hell.[17]

At the wake it was customary for the mourners to cover the body with their shorn hair. Digenis Akritas, legendary hero of the eastern frontiers of the Byzantine Empire, asks for this last tribute from his wife as he lies on his deathbed, according to the version of the epic preserved in the manuscript from Andros (sixteenth century):

Καὶ δάκρυά σου στάλαξον καὶ τὰ μαλλιά σου κόψον
ἀπάνω εἰς τὸ λείψανον Ἀκρίτου τοῦ ἀνδρείου.   *DA* 4481–2 (A)

Shed your tears, and cut your hair
upon the body of the brave Akritas.

All the evidence suggests that this was the scene of violent grief, in spite of the disapproval of the Church. In his homily *de Mortuis*, Gregory of Nyssa attempts to persuade people to be more moderate in their grief, arguing, like Lucian, that the dead cannot appreciate any of the attention lavished upon them.[18] The usual behaviour is described and roundly condemned by Basil of Caesarea (330–79), in his homily *de Gratiarum Actione*:

> Therefore neither men nor women should be permitted too much lamentation and mourning. They should show moderate distress in their affliction, with only a few tears, shed quietly and without moaning, wailing, tearing of clothes and grovelling in the dust, or committing any other indecency commonly practised by the ungodly.   Migne 31.229C

Violent lamentation was unseemly, even at the funeral of an Empress.[19] Most vehement of all is John Chrysostom, who denounces dirges as 'blasphemies'.[20] It is significant that he objects not only to the more violent practices, such as laceration of the cheeks, tearing of the hair, and rending of garments, roundly condemning a widow bereaved of her only son for her wild desire to bury herself alive with him in the tomb, but also to the very essence of the dirge, which he describes as self-centred and self-indulgent. Particularly offensive was the use of hired mourners, usually specified as Greeks. Chrysostom refers to them in no less than eight homilies and commentaries, complaining that 'this disease of females still persists'.[21] He is especially horrified at the pagan character of the scene, which with the incessant display of wailing and beating of the breast amounts to no less than a dance.[22]

The frequency and vehemence of these condemnations in the early Byzantine period are proof of the persistence of ritual lamentation. It was regarded as harmful not only because of its insidious effects on others, but also because, as Chrysostom understood, in the initial stages before Christianity was firmly established, such pagan customs were 'fatal to the Church'.[23] The Church fathers tried only to moderate the manner of lamentation, not to stamp it out completely. Restrained grief was a necessary release to the feelings, a pleasure (ἡδονή) sanctified by the Scriptures.[24] If the popular lament was condemned as pagan and effeminate, what was the Christian ideal?

Gregory's account of Makrina's funeral gives an interesting answer. All night long the body was laid out, lamented by holy sisters singing psalms. When day broke, and the crowds began to collect, the calm beauty of the psalms was threatened by noisy lamentation. But Gregory ensured that order was maintained by separating the men from the women, whom he wisely placed next to the holy sisters:

> I took care that the chants should be sung with due rhythm
> and harmony, by arranging the two groups of singers on
> opposite sides, as in the liturgy, so that the chanting was
> properly blended with the sound of all the people joining in.
>
> Migne 46.993A

This antiphonal lament, not unlike that sung by the Muses for Achilles in its arrangement, is reminiscent of the ideal prototype suggested by Plato for his Examiners in the *Laws*.[25] It is doubtful how often it was realised. True, as time went on the Church fathers objected less frequently and less vehemently to the evils of lamentation, but this was hardly because they had been eradicated, rather that the ritual had been accepted and gradually absorbed into Christianity.

The funeral procession

The funeral procession was an important occasion, more directly controlled by the Church than the wake, and fully exploited as a spectacle likely to impress the people. At important funerals, large numbers of men and women were hired by the Church, whose work was to give physical manifestation of their grief, to sing psalms and funeral hymns, and to tend the graves, as their official names suggest.[26]

The Church seems to have succeeded in gaining control, at least in the more important funeral processions. Their use of hired mourners and breast-beaters makes the denunciations of Chrysostom and Gregory appear somewhat hypocritical. What they objected to was not the custom itself but its pagan associations. Chrysostom, in a moment of anger, reveals the true cause of his indignation:

> What are you doing, woman? Tell me, would you shamelessly
> strip yourself naked in the middle of the market-place, you,
> who are a part of Christ, in the presence of men and in the very
> market-place? And would you tear your hair, rend your garments
> and wail loudly, dancing and preserving the image of Bacchic
> women, without regard for your offence to God?   Migne 59.346

His anger is directed against the 'rabble', which was accustomed to lead the funeral procession with loud noise, bright torches and women's dancing, by the busiest streets of the city and then to stop in the market-place for a longer and more organised performance.[27] This was just the kind of public display which the ancient legislation had been intended to combat.

At the funerals of holy men or of members of the imperial family, large crowds were encouraged. Makrina's funeral procession took a whole day to reach the tomb, only seven or eight stades away.[28] Gregory Nazianzen (329–89) describes in one of his homilies the sincere grief expressed by the people at the funeral of Basil of Caesarea, but his narrative makes it plain that while crowds were welcomed, there was more than a hint of conflict between the official psalm singing of the Church and the spontaneous lamentation of the people:

> There were crowds of people everywhere, in the market-places, arcades and buildings two and three storeys high, all attending his funeral and walking behind, in front and along-side, trampling on one another. Thousands of people of every race and age, not known before, psalms giving way to lamen-tations, and philosophy overcome by passion. It was a struggle between our followers and the outsiders – Greeks, Jews and immigrants...and the body itself only just escaped their clutches.
>
> Migne 36.601

In addition to the trained choirs singing religious music, the procession was given extra splendour by the torches and wax candles carried by the people. Gregory of Nyssa describes the mystical beauty of the psalms and torches at the funeral of Makrina:

> First came a large number of deacons and ministers, all advancing in order and with wax candles in their hands. It was rather like a mystic procession, with the sound of the chanting ringing forth in one voice from one end to the other.
>
> Migne 46.993B

The use of the lighted torch is explained by Chrysostom as an expression of the soul's journey towards the 'true light'. It was decorative, and also warming and cheering to the dead.[29] Its older, apotropaic properties, referred to by Athenaios, survive in Byzantine folklore, in a delightful story of how five monks carrying torches jumped into a disused country well to drive away the evil spirits lurking there, which tormented the nearby villagers. The combined strength of the smell of the candles and the sound of the psalms sung by the monks vanquished them, and they disappeared into the nooks and crannies at the bottom of the well never to re-emerge.[30]

Once the procession reached the tomb and the psalms were over, there was a fresh outbreak of uncontrolled grief as the *teleutaîos aspasmós* (last greeting) was given. Like the last tear and the stretching out of the right hand over the bier in the ancient *ekphorá*, it was essential for the peace of mind of the dead as well as of the next of kin.[31] The custom must have been Christianised at an early stage, because it is found in two early Byzantine funeral services.[32]

When the religious music was over and the earth was shovelled into the grave, once more the spontaneous lamentation of the people conflicted with the more formal *aspasmós* of Church tradition, as is evident again at this point in Makrina's funeral:

> That prayer caused the people to break out into fresh lamen-
> tation. The chants had died down . . . then one of the holy sisters
> cried out in disorderly fashion that never again from that hour
> should we set eyes on this divine face, whereupon the other
> sisters cried out likewise, and disorder and confusion spoiled
> that orderly and sacred chanting, with everyone breaking down
> at the lament of the holy sisters.   Migne 46.993D

Burial and after

After burial came the *enkómion* or *epitáphios lógos*. The early Church attached great importance to it, strictly adhering to its cold, rhetorical formality, perhaps to counteract the effects of what was considered the uncontrolled grief of the people. Whereas *enkómia* have survived in great number, there is no example of a popular lament, quoted in full from an actual funeral, which has come down to us. All we have are the accounts of the Church fathers, frequently exaggerated or distorted. But the ancient ritual custom of passionate invocation at the tomb is known to have persisted, alongside the literary convention of epigrams in dialogue form.[33]

On the evening of the funeral the household in mourning usually held a banquet, still known by its ancient name of *perídeipnon*, or *sýndeipnon*, which was attended by relatives, close friends and repre-
sentatives of the Church.[34]

Chrysostom directs some of his sharpest attacks against the practice, common among rich and poor alike, of offering food, clothing and lighted candles at the tomb. These offerings were made on the third, ninth and fortieth days after death. Chrysostom argues that the dead no longer have need of such material things, which the poor can ill afford. For the rich, on the other hand, is it not far better and far holier to ensure against such abuses by leaving property and money to the poor, or to the Church? His advice was followed by some, whose piety the Church rewarded with especially grand memorial services.[35] But the old practices still went on, with little change in the nature of the offerings since antiquity: wine, water, crops and *kóllyva*.[36] Gregory Nazianzen refers three times to *choaí* and *apárgmata* (libations and first-fruits) as ancient ritual offerings which he cannot approve of, still observed in his own day.[37] They were common enough to give rise to the medieval proverb ἀλλοτρίαις χοαῖς τοῖς γονεῦσιν αὐτοῦ ἐναγίζει (he honours his parents with other people's libations).[38]

A closer look at the evidence reveals once more that it was not the ritual itself so much as certain pagan associations which were considered harmful. Apostolic law recognised *tríta*, *énata* and *eniaúsia* (offerings on the third and ninth days and after one year), retaining the ancient terms but taking care to give an acceptable theological explanation, that Christ had risen on the third day, that the soul reaches Heaven on the ninth, and that the dead should be commemorated on the anniversary of their death.[39] The ancient *triakóstia* (offerings on the thirtieth day) were replaced by a memorial on the fortieth day, since that is how Moses was lamented by his people. Instead of dirges and invocations there were to be psalms, hymns and prayers.[40] But the ritual remained the same, and the priest himself had the sacred duty of sacrificing doves to the dead as a special tribute.[41] The strictest possible adherence to the rules for tending the tomb is laid down in Symeon's *de Ordine Sepulturae*, where it is implied that neglect could have serious consequences.[42] Saint Martha is said to have stricken with illness the steward at the monastery where she lay buried, appearing to him in a vision as he lay dying and upbraiding him for failing to see that her candle was kept alight.[43]

Mourning, in due moderation, was sanctified by the Church. For a year at least black clothes were worn, hair was allowed to grow long, and personal appearance generally neglected.[44] One mother, whose son has been martyred, is warmly commended by Gregory Nazianzen for refusing to observe the usual trappings of mourning, which she enumerates in a curious kind of negative lament:

I will not tear my hair, nor will I rend my cloak, nor will I scratch my flesh with my nails, nor will I start up the dirge, nor will I call up the mourning women, nor will I shut myself in darkness that the air might lament with me, nor will I await the comforters, nor will I prepare the funeral bread. For such things belong to vulgar mothers, who are mothers only in the flesh.   Migne 35.928A–B

Some people even went to the extreme of leaving their homes in the city, living for a whole year at the graves of their dead.[45]

The ancient idea that flesh, being earth, must return to earth after death, has survived unchanged in the early liturgy and in epigrams, prayers and hymns of all kinds. Here is an example from the funeral service:[46]

Οἱ βροτοὶ ἐκ γῆς διεπλάσθημεν / καὶ εἰς γῆν τὴν αὐτὴν
πορευσόμεθα / καθὼς ἐκέλευσας ὁ πλάσας με, / καὶ εἰπών
μοι· Γῆ εἶ, καὶ εἰς γῆν πορεύσῃ.   Pitra *AS* 1.242.2

We mortals have been fashioned from earth, and to this same
earth we shall depart, as my Creator bade, saying, 'Earth thou
art and to earth thou shalt depart.'

The evidence examined in this chapter is unfortunately too incomplete to provide an objective picture of the relation between lament and ritual in the Byzantine period, and of the extent to which ancient practices survived. Certainly, funeral ritual and lamentation were condemned by the early Christian fathers. But it is not known how general this attitude was and how far it reflected the official policy of the State. All that can be said is that these condemnations indicate the insidious pagan influence which such practices were believed to have on the minds of the people. As in antiquity, they could be regarded as constituting a social threat.

Towards the ritual at least there seems to have been a gradual change in the Church's attitude. Once sure of its control, it did not try to diminish the importance that funeral ritual had held in antiquity, but on the contrary it incorporated many elements it had formerly condemned into official ceremony, reinforcing them where possible with Old Testament tradition. Judging by the number of ritual practices in the Orthodox Church which can be traced back to antiquity, this process must have gone on at an unconscious as well as a conscious level.

The Church, then, tried to detach the ritual, which it found necessary and politic to conserve and possible to Christianise by means of new theological explanations, from the more violent forms and expressions of lamentation which it deemed incompatible with Christianity, such as self-mutilation, and the man-centred, pagan outlook of the ancient lament. It tried to replace their prominence at the wake, funeral procession and burial with its own highly organised performance of psalms, hymns and prayers. It is impossible to measure accurately the degree of its success. In learned and religious circles the unity of poetry and ritual characteristic of the lament in the classical period was broken down, so far as it is possible for us to judge from the literary laments which have survived. On its own evidence it is doubtful whether it was so successful among the people. It must be remembered that the popular laments are referred to by the Church fathers only to be condemned. The stereotyped language and recurrent, formalised *topoi* which characterise the examples they give us suggest a conventionalised distortion, designed to create an impression of uncontrolled, self-centred paganism; they are therefore not to be treated as a faithful recording of popular laments.[47]

For the early Byzantine period there is no independent witness by which to test the objectivity of the Church's attitude. A different picture emerges, however, from Buondelmonti's eyewitness account of a funeral in Crete, written in 1420:

> After the man had left this life, singers went to his house and, standing before the corpse among the womenfolk, they burst out into lamentations. Then everyone fell silent until each had praised the dead man in song. All the women took turns, sometimes cursing the Fates. Finally they gave a last farewell, and allowed themselves to be taken weary to their homes. Then at last came that long night which they voluntarily live, a year or more, without light, like animals on the ground. There on the earth they eat, and late and early they never cease calling in shrill lament upon the man who has now descended to the shades. For three or four years they shun the church, and choose to be in darkness and in solitude.[48]

The details are not essentially different from those referred to elsewhere, but the exacting ritual pattern laid down by tradition for the wake and after burial, and the orderly praise of the dead man, are seen in a more sympathetic light. And the mourner's long self-banishment from church not only explains official hostility, but also indicates the independence and strength of the popular customs.

It would seem that the popular lament, unlike its literary counterpart, which had been divorced from its ritual associations, might have preserved something of the ancient unity of poetry and ritual. For a fuller understanding of its character we must turn to the folk tradition of today.

3
Modern survivals

In a country with a large rural population like Greece, where geographical conditions and backward communications have led to the growth of isolated and self-contained communities, each preserving distinct its local dialect and traditions, it is natural to find many pre-Christian survivals, especially in connection with something so fundamental as death. The mere existence of ritual beliefs and practices in Greece today does not prove continuity of development from antiquity, since similar survivals can be found in most of the Balkan countries. I shall therefore attempt in this chapter not to enumerate details of ritual for their own sake, but to point out the thread of continuity and change, and above all to define the relation between poetry and ritual in the popular lament, since this was obscured in our sources for the Byzantine period.

A modern proverb, which calls to mind Elpenor's warning to Odysseus, illustrates that lamentation and funeral rites are as inseparable today as they were in antiquity:[1]

"Άκλαυτος κι ἀμνημόνευτος στὸν "Αδη τί γυρεύει;

What is he seeking in Hades unwept, and without memorial?

It was a misfortune for the living as well as for the dying. In the *Iliad*, Andromache reproaches Hector at his wake for dying before he could give her a last word of greeting. John Chrysostom, too, refers to the dying man's last words of farewell as a kind of blessing on the company of relatives and close friends. Similarly, many modern laments open with the dying man's farewell to life and to his closest kin.[2]

The fight with Death

Great importance is still attached to the manner in which a man's soul leaves the body. A good man dies easily, his soul leaving the body 'like a lamb'.[3] A protracted and agonised death, on the other hand, known as ψυχομάχημα (fight of the soul) or χαροπάλεμα (struggle with Charos), is thought to spring from one of several causes. First, the dying man may have committed some wrong which is unconfessed and unforgiven. In such a case as soon as the first signs of approaching death appear, an urgent summons is sent to the priest and also to any man known to have had a quarrel or dispute with the dying man. Sometimes it is not his own fault, and he may be paying for the sins of a parent or a grandparent.[4]

Second, his family may be under a curse which has not been revoked, or he may wish to revoke a curse which he has made himself. Sometimes there may be a vow or a curse which has not been fulfilled, as with Sokrates. In the famous ballad *The Song of the Dead Brother*, Konstantinos persuades his mother to consent to the marriage of Arete, his only sister, in foreign parts, and he gives a solemn vow that in case of sickness or death he will bring Arete back to his mother. But Konstantinos and his eight brothers are stricken with the plague, leaving their mother to lament at their graves and to curse Konstantinos for his arrogant vow. Until he rises from the dead and fulfils his promise, his mother's soul cannot be released.[5]

Third, the absence of a loved one can cause long agony and delay in the departure of the soul. In the same ballad, as soon as Arete steps over the threshold of her home and calls out to her mother that she has returned, the mother's soul, which has been lingering on since the death of her nine sons for this moment, is released at once. Similar non-literary instances have been recorded from the Pontos, where an article of clothing or some personal possession was substituted if the presence of the desired person was impossible.[6]

In the case of a young person, a protracted death need not have any moral implications, but may simply reflect a natural reluctance to leave the pleasures and responsibilities of life. The fight with death is then understood literally: the dying man may call out that he can see Charos approach, sword in hand, often dressed in black, or winged, like ancient Hades.[7] A girl from Thrace who died at the age of twenty-two in the influenza epidemic of 1917 was heard to shout out, an hour before she died, 'There he is! A young man is coming with a spear to cut me up! Bring me the long knife. He is going to slaughter me.' She then engaged in an imaginary but fierce fight.[8] In the ballads of the Underworld which describe a wrestling-match between Death and the young man, it is regarded as a mark of heroism and not as a sign of a sinful life for the young man to face Death with a challenge:

– Λεβέντη μ', μ' ἔστειλε ὁ Θεός, νὰ πάρω τὴν ψυχή σου.
– Χωρὶς ἀνάγκη κι ἀρρωστιὰ ψυχὴ δὲν παραδίνω,
μόν' ἔβγα νὰ παλέψουμε σὲ μαρμαρένιο ἁλώνι,
κι ἂ μὲ νικήσης, Χάροντα, νὰ πάρης τὴν ψυχή μου,
κι ἂ σὲ νικήσω πάλι ἐγὼ πήγαινε στὸ καλό σου.   Politis 214.11–15

– Young man, God has sent me to take your soul.
– Without force or sickness, I will not give up my soul.
Come, and let us wrestle on the marble threshing floor.
And if you win, Charondas, you can take my soul,
and if it is I who win, you must go and leave me.

This reluctance to yield to death without a struggle expresses a feeling closer to the story of Herakles' fight with Thanatos in Euripides' *Alkestis* than anything to have survived from Byzantine tradition, which emphasised the moral aspect. Something of the infinite variety of modern peasant beliefs, at once imaginative and concrete, is reflected in the abundance of expressions for the last struggle of the soul: ψυχομαχῶ, ψυχορραγῶ (my soul is fighting, struggling), τρεμοσβήνω (I tremble and go out), χαροπαλεύω (I wrestle with Charos), ἀγγελοσκιάζουμαι, ἀγγελομαχῶ (I tremble at, fight with, the angel).[9]

It is still important to maintain silence at this time. Weeping and wailing, above all lamentation, remind the dying of the grief he is causing, and so prevent the soul from leaving the body.[10] Before he died, my husband's maternal grandfather, from the village of Sklithron in Thessaly, instructed his relatives not to lament until he was properly dressed and laid out. Soon after, when he appeared to be dead, the women began keening, but with great effort he raised himself and told them to stop. Another danger of premature lamentation was that it scared away the angels and spirits which had come to accompany the soul, leaving it to the mercies of Charos. This is known as ἀγγελόκομμα (angel-cutting), a belief not unlike those described by the Church fathers, except that it is Charos, not the Devil, who now seizes the soul.

Washing, dressing and lamentation

Except for the closest relations, all young people leave the house, and the body is tended by old women. It is preferable for the eyes and mouth to be closed by the child, or next of kin, who has been supporting the head or clasping the hand of the dying man.[11] This detail, similar to many scenes on ancient vase-paintings, was not mentioned in the Byzantine sources. The coin which is still placed on the forehead or on the mouth is believed to serve as a charm against evil spirits, although one folk song has it that it is the fee for Charos to ferry the soul across the river of death.[12]

The body is then washed, either with wine or with water brought from outside the house, another point which ancient practice insisted upon. This divergence may indicate a fusion between the originally distinct practices of washing and anointing.[13] The dressing of the corpse has undergone little change. New clothes, especially new shoes, are essential, and wedding attire is still customary for the young or newly married.[14]

The decking of the body with flowers, herbs and evergreen leaves and branches is important. Those chosen vary in different parts of Greece, but basil and celery are usually included. Their purpose is not purely perfunctory. The use of evergreens, which are neither sweet-smelling nor decorative, suggests the survival of an older, regenerative function. And the idea is frequently expressed in the laments themselves that the flowers and ornaments help the dead on his journey to Hades and facilitate contact with the world of the dead, as is admirably illustrated by the following lines from a long lament improvised by an 88-year-old peasant woman from Kalamata at the funeral of Grigoris Lambrakis, the Greek Member of Parliament who was murdered in 1963:[15]

Γρηγόρη, σὲ φορτώσανε, βαρειὰ εἶσαι φορτωμένος,
Γρηγόρη μου, τὶς μυρουδιὲς νὰ μὴ τὶς ἐσκορπίσης,
νὰ τὶς βαστᾶς στὴν κάτω Γῆς στοὺς νιοὺς νὰ τὶς δωρίσης,
νὰ βάλουνε στὰ πέτα τους νὰ βγοῦνε στὸ σεργιάνι.

Grigoris, heavy is your burden, heavy your load of flowers.
Grigoris, do not allow their fragrance to scatter.
Keep them, and give them to the young ones in the
    Underworld,
and they'll wear them in their jackets when they go for a
    stroll.

Usually the body is placed with the head towards the east, but in the case of a violent or premature death it is laid in the porch of the house, or even outside, as in the archaic period of antiquity.[16]

The early Christian fathers had described popular lamentation at this stage of the ritual as something disorderly, only organised when the Church exercised some control. But among the people today, although the arrangement of the mourners varies in different parts, it is not random. Strange mourners must be present, and they are usually separated from the kinswomen. The procedure is strict and formal: one of the kinswomen usually leads off, helped by the rest who wail in chorus, and then, when the chief mourner from the other side wishes to 'take up' the dirge, she stretches her hand over the body and grasps the hand of the mourner on the left. By this silent stretching of the hand, the dirge is passed over from one group to the other all day long.[17] This scene of antiphonal lamentation forms a striking parallel to Hector's wake and to the scene on many vase-paintings of antiquity, as well as to Buondelmonti's account of a funeral in fifteenth-century Crete.

The rules about the kind of lament suitable at this stage are no less strict. Far from being an impromptu outburst of wailing, as the Church fathers had implied, the dirges at the wake concentrate on formalised praise of the virtues of the dead, often in partly traditional and partly improvised couplets.[18] In Mani the constant passing to and fro of the dirge takes the form of a contest, and afterwards the woman generally agreed to be the best mourner is congratulated by the next of kin with the words 'May you be rewarded with joy!'[19]

The use of strange mourners is considered a mark of respect and affection towards the dead. They are sometimes, but not always paid, and payment is in kind, with corn or pulse. A Cretan mourner expressed her dissatisfaction with the proffered payment by opening with these words:[20]

Πολλὰ μακρὺς μοῦ φαίνεται
καὶ τὰ κουκιά 'ναι λίγα!

The corpse seems too long, and the beans are too few!

And a Maniot mourner is promised by the dead man's next of kin:[21]

κλάψετε τόνε μου καλά – κούμουλα θά 'ναι τὰ κουκιά!

Sing me a fine lament for him, and you shall have a pile of beans.

Being less directly and personally involved, they are equipped to give a more accomplished and professional expression to their grief. This does not mean that they suffer less; on the contrary, because they are required to fulfil an obligation to the dead, their grief may be more acute.[22] Nor are they insincere, since, like the Trojan captives who mourned with Briseis for Patroklos, they may, with the permission of the kinswomen, lament their own troubles and their own dead, sending a message through the dead man to their own kinsmen in the Underworld:

Μιὰ φρόνιμη νοικοκυρά, μιὰ ταχτικὴ γυναίκα,
βουλήθηκε, ἀποφάσισε νὰ κατεβῆ στὸν Ἅδη.
Ὅπου ἔχει λόγια, ἆς τῆς τὰ εἰπῆ, παραγγολὲς κι ἆς στείλη,
κι ὅπου ἔχει γιὸ ξαρμάτωτον, ἆς στείλη τ' ἄρματά του.

Pasayanis 44

A wise housewife, an orderly woman,
has made up her mind and decided to go down to Hades.
If you have messages to send, give them to her to take,
and if you have a son unarmed, send him weapons too.

Sophia Lala, aged 66, from Samarina in western Macedonia, has explained to me that since the death of both her husband and her son in her youth, she has sung nothing but laments. When invited to lament at other funerals she would never refuse, because in this way she could sing for her own dead, 'I weep for my own, not for theirs.'

The result of such an antiphonal exchange between kinswomen and strangers was a gradual crescendo of emotion, of rising intensity but not without its traditional, ritual pattern. Moreover, lamentation in some areas was considered such a professional art that it was consciously cultivated among certain families, and the skill was handed down from mother to daughter. This was the case until recently in Mani and in the island of Imbros, where the fame of Samothracian mourners was such that it gave rise to a proverb, 'You need Samothracian women to lament you' (Loukatos 64).

The ritual character of the scene at the wake is further emphasised by the rhythmical movements of the women, who beat their breasts, tear their cheeks and pull at their loosened hair or at a black scarf, in time to the singing. Until recently in Crete, women would cut their hair to cover the face of the dead.[23] This is no longer customary, but the following description I recorded in 1963 from Stavroula Sarimvei, of Larisa, is reminiscent of scenes on many fifth-century Attic vases: 'In a village called Elateia, near Larisa, a mother died. Her two daughters let down their long hair and spread it upon their mother's face. They wept and lamented, first wetting her face with their tears, then drying it with their hair.' Women from the same part of Thessaly have described to me the equally ancient gesture of the raising of the right hand during lamentation. This formed the same combination of movement and gesture as in antiquity, and the same dance-like character.[24]

In Mani and elsewhere, dirges may continue unabated all day and all night. But in general, dirges must stop at sunset, for fear of disturbing the dead man's peace by reminding him of the life he has been robbed of.[25] Everywhere the body must be guarded during the night, usually by old women, who may comment on the futility and vanity of life, 'Mankind adds up to nothing. A life of strife, and only evil at the end!' (Loukatos 55). In the Pontos, there survived the habit of laughing strangely and saying 'There's never a funeral without joy, nor a wedding without a tear.' Then, on the morning of the second day, when the body is to be buried, came the climax of the whole wake, the 'great lament', sung for a particularly loved person by the whole village, and accompanied by wild displays of grief from the women.[26]

There are no longer any restrictions on the number of women permitted to lament. In Mani, the whole family of all who can trace a common ancestor several generations back must be present.[27]

From house to tomb

On the morning of the second day the slow tolling of the church bell summons the priest and the whole village to the house of the dead to accompany him on his last journey to the tomb. As soon as the bell is sounded, all over the village any water that has been standing in vessels is thrown away, and fresh water is fetched. Sometimes, the vessel too is broken.[28] This is apparently an extension of ancient custom, from the immediate family to the whole village.

The body is taken up by four men, who in Thrace must be neither close kin nor newly married, and laid in the coffin.[29] Mourning women throw on offerings of fruit and nuts – apples, quinces, walnuts and almonds – as a greeting to their own dead below. This ritual detail throws light on the opening phrase of so many dirges, giving it a meaning beyond its mere lyricism:

Τί νὰ σοῦ στείλω, μάτια μου, αὐτοῦ στὸν κάτω κόσμο;
νὰ στείλω μῆλο – σήπεται, κυδώνι – μαραγκιάζει,

σταφύλι – ξερογίζεται, τριαντάφυλλο – μαδιέται.
Στέλνω κι ἐγὼ τὰ δάκρυα μου, δεμένα στὸ μαντήλι.

Giankas 911.1–4

What shall I send you, my dear one, there in the Underworld?
If I send an apple, it will rot, if a quince, it will shrivel;
if I send grapes, they will fall away, if a rose, it will droop.
So let me send my tears, bound in my handkerchief.

As the priest enters with his censer, the lamentation reaches a climax, inspired less by the strange mourners than by the bereaved mother, wife or sister, who calls out a final reproach, just as they did for Hector, 'They are taking you away, my child! Who will look after your mother, my son?' 'Who are you leaving me to, husband? You are ruining your household, dear husband. Who are you leaving your children to? O, my support is gone!' (*Laog* (1934) 400).

In Epiros, the last greeting between dead and living before the final separation may take the form of an imaginary dialogue, in which the nearest kin is required to hold his hand over the body of the dead man, like Orestes, while the other mourners sing on his behalf:

῾Απλῶστε τὸ χεράκι σας καὶ πιάστε τὸ δικό μου,
κρατῆστε με νὰ σᾶς κρατῶ, νὰ μὴ ξεχωριστοῦμε,
γιατὶ ἂν ξεχωρίσουμε, δὲν θέλ᾽ ἀνταμωθοῦμε.

Laog (1960) 346.26, 5–7

Stretch out your hand, and take my hand in yours.
Clasp me, as I clasp you, so as not to part,
for once we part we'll never meet again.

The procession is led by non-relatives, who carry ritual objects and offerings. Then come the cantor and the priest, followed by the bier, again carried by non-relatives, and behind it the kinsmen, first men and last of all women.[30] Perhaps the less prominent part played by the next of kin at the procession is a relic of the primitive practice examined in chapter 1 of hiring men outside the clan to attend to this part of the ritual. Some superstitious relatives today actually refuse to follow the body to the grave, especially if it is the first death in the family, or the death of a son. In some villages of Chios, kinswomen take no part whatever in the procession.[31]

In Mani, the procession is swift, accompanied by wild cries and beating of the breast. In Epiros, there is no formal lamentation, just weeping and wailing. In the Pontos, the procession did not make straight for the church, but was taken round the main streets and to the market-place, a practice which survived in spite of legislation and Church disapproval.[32]

In the church, the priest reads the short and formal funeral service. But in some parts of Chios and in Mani the women have never reconciled themselves to their secondary position in church, and do not enter at all, preferring to wait outside.[33] Occasionally, when the dead man is thought worthy of a more public tribute, or when there has been no formal laying-out, the women transform the character of the church service, as in the following story I recorded in 1963 from Sophia Lala of Samarina:

> In 1947, during the brother-killing war, four young lads were killed in one battle, somewhere near Samarina. They were taken to the church. Fifty women gathered round and they all began keening. The burial was held up for hours, waiting for the dirge to come to an end. And the policeman, who at first gave orders for the bodies to be buried at once, when he heard the women he began to weep himself, and let them go on with their lament for as long as they liked.

The true purpose of ritual lamentation, a collective tribute to the dead from the whole community, is still sufficiently strong among the people, when occasion demands, not only to win over the Church, but even to withstand official opposition in a time of such bitter divisions as the late Civil War.

Burial and after

As in the Byzantine period, the priest presides over the actual burial, laying on the dead a piece of tile or pottery bearing the inscription ΙΣ ΧΣ ΝΙΚΑ (Jesus Christ Conquers) to ward off evil spirits, and sprinkling him three times with oil and wine taken from the central lamp of the church.[34] Then he throws on to the coffin a clod of earth, repeating the formula 'Earth thou art, and to earth thou shalt depart.' In Crete it is not the priest, but an experienced person, usually a woman, who officiates, touching the earth with her two forefingers and whispering softly to the dead, 'Τοῦτ' ἡ γῆς ποὺ σ' ἔθρεψε, τούτη θὰ σὲ φάη' (This earth which fed you shall also eat you), a phrase which has hardly changed since antiquity.[35] Similarly, the formula of many ancient epigrams finds an echo in the line 'I owe my body to the earth, my soul to the angel' (Theros 750). While the mourners throw into the grave their last

offerings of fruit and flowers, laments are sung, either in the form of
a dialogue between the dead and the living, or as a series of instructions
given to 'those long dead' and to Earth to take care of the
newcomer:

> Ἄι, πεθαμένοι συγγενεῖς,
> δόστε του ροῦχα, νὰ ντυθῆ,
> πυρῶστε το καὶ στὴ φωτιά,
> μὴ μοῦ κρυώση τὸ παιδί!   Theros 776.19–22

> Ái, dead kinsmen, give him clothes to wear,
> warm him by the fire. Don't let my child catch cold!

> Πλάκα χρυσή, πλάκα ἀργυρή, πλάκα μαλαματένια,
> τοῦτον τὸν νιό, ποὺ στέλνουμε, νὰ τὸν καλοπεράσης,
> φτιάσε του γιόμα νὰ γευτῆ, καὶ δεῖπνο νὰ δειπνήση,
> καὶ στρῶσ' τὸ στρῶμα του παχιό, νὰ πέση νὰ πλαγιάση.

> Golden tombstone, silver tombstone, tombstone all of gold,
> see that this boy we send you has a pleasant time there.
> Give him food to eat, and let him dine,
> and make his bed thick, that he may lie and rest.

But in this Maniot lament, unlike the ancient epigrams, the Earth has
an answer, and it is not a pleasant one:

> Τίγαρις εἶμαι ἡ μάνα του, νὰ τὸν καλοπεράσω;
> Μένα μὲ λένε Μαύρη Γῆ, μὲ λένε μαύρη πλάκα,
> κάνω μανοῦλες δίχως γιούς, γυναῖκες δίχως ἄντρες,
> κάνω τὶς μαῦρες ἀδερφὲς δίχως τοὺς ἀδερφούς τους.   Pasayanis 35

> Do you think I'm his mother, to give him a pleasant time?
> My name is Black Earth, my name is Black Tombstone,
> and I make mothers part from sons and wives from husbands,
> I make poor sisters part from their brothers.

Immediately after burial, water is passed round for all to wash their
hands, after which the *kóllyva*, wine, and bread with honey are tasted.
Sometimes the wine vessel, tray and basket are broken, or sometimes
they are placed outside the inner door of the house, with a bowl of
water, until evening falls.[36]
    All then gather in the house of the dead man's family to share in the
funeral feast, to which each must bring a contribution as a mark of

respect, including the priest. It is now known as *paregoriá* or *makaría*, not by its ancient and medieval name of *perídeipnon*, although the concept of consolation implicit in the modern terms appears to go back at least to the time of Lucian.[37] Instead of laments, short wishes and prayers are called out by each in turn as the food and wine are handed round, such as 'May God forgive him! Long life to your husband! Long life to yourself!'

After several days have passed, the house is thoroughly cleansed and purified with water and whitewash, and all clothing, including what was worn by the mourners at the funeral, must be washed in spring water, much as had been stipulated in the ancient legislation from Keos.[38]

On the third, ninth and fortieth days after death, and after one year, wine and water are placed on the tomb and in the house for the thirsty soul to return and drink. Dirges, mostly passionate invocations imploring the dead to return, are improvised by kinswomen at the tomb; sometimes they contain thinly veiled threats, arising, perhaps, out of considerations of inheritance and property. In the following Maniot lament for a girl who died childless, soon after marriage, her relations and relations-in-law take turns to improvise a couplet, ending with a threat, probably uttered by her mother-in-law, that her dowry will be returned to her mother's house:[39]

> – Καημένη, νὰ συλλογιστῆς,
> λυπήσου τὴ μητέρα σου.
> – "Αν δὲν ἐρθῆς, κι ἂν δὲν φανῆς,
> θενὰ σοῦ κάμουν προσβολή,
> θὰ πᾶν νὰ πάρουν τὰ προικιὰ
> ν' ἀπὸ τὸ σπίτι τοῦ ἄντρα σου,
> γιατὶ δὲν ἄφησες παιδί.   Pasayanis 107.14–20

> – Wretched girl, think again! Have pity on your mother.
> – If you do not return, if you do not appear,
> they will insult you, and go and take the dowry
> from your husband's house, because you left no child!

These harsh words perhaps indicate something of the violence of feeling which gave rise to the exaggerated displays of grief so hateful to Chrysostom, and to the ecstatic attitudes depicted on the fifth-century vases. The real function of invocation at the tomb has remained unaltered: the living, by their offerings and passionate invocations, can enter into communion with the dead.

In some parts of Greece the memorial days are referred to not by their Christian and more official term, *mnemósyna*, but as στὶς τρεῖς, ἐννιά, σαράντα, στὸ χρόνο (on the third, ninth, fortieth day, after a year), or even as *tríta*, *niámera*, *saránta*, terms which are structurally very similar to the ancient *tríta*, *énata* and *triakóstia*. They are not only occasions for personal offerings and invocations, but often for a more general feast at the tombs. Nuts, fruit, sweets and pies are shared round among all present, and each must sing a lament in turn for the dead. This feast, pagan in origin and at one time forbidden by the Church, is now presided over by the priest, who brings it to an end by scattering incense and giving to all a lighted candle to place on the graves.[40]

Some days in the Church calendar call for an even more lavish banquet, among them the first Friday of Lent and the Friday of Pentecost (known also as στοῦ Ρουσαλιοῦ, a popularised form of the ancient Roman *Rosalia*). The latter is referred to by the people as 'the day of the pies', because it is the day of the most extensive offering of ψυχόπιττες (pies for the soul), when the whole village – strangers, clerks, shepherds and herds-men together with their sheep, goats, cows and oxen – makes its way to the tombs. It is the last day of freedom for the souls, which have been freed since the Sunday before Lent by the blood of hens slaughtered over their graves. The ceremony may be a relic of the ritual blood sacrifice believed in antiquity to release the souls of the dead for a limited period.[41] The central part of this ritual is the *gonátisma* (kneeling), which takes place after the first part of the service has been sung inside the church. Everyone, young and old, walks in procession to the church-yard (*perívolos*), led by the women, who carry baskets of offerings covered with fine scarves, usually white. The women stay at the tombs to guard the offerings, kneeling with heads bent towards the earth, while the priest takes the men back to the church to continue the service, also kneeling. During this silent kneeling the souls are believed to rise to eat and drink. Afterwards the men come out of the church and sit round the tombs in a large circle, while the women hand round food and drink.

The separation of men and women during the vital moments of this ritual illustrates the importance of women in matters so intimately concerned with the dead. The formal service is led by the priest in the church, where men take first place; but it is the women who prepare and make the offerings, addressing not prayers to God but invocations to the dead, calling upon them by name.[42]

The custom of exhuming the dead after one, three or seven years is well known in all parts of Greece. The purpose is to examine the remains to see that there are no inauspicious signs for the dead man's relatives. If the body has dissolved, leaving the bones clean and white, all is well, and they are washed in wine and reinterred. But if the body is black and putrid, the chances are that the dead man has become a βρυκόλακας (*revenant*). According to the official explanation, he is in Hell, or, more picturesquely, in popular speech καίγεται στά Τάρταρα (he is burning in Tartara) (*Laog* (1911) 476–7). In a lament from Epiros, the macabre instructions are spelt out in full, as if by the dead:

– Κάμε τά χέρια σου τσαπιά, τήν πλάκα παραμέρα,
καί τράβα τό μαντήλι μου ἀπό τό πρόσωπό μου,
κι ἄν μ᾽ εὕρης ἀσπροκόκκινον, σκύψε κι ἀγκάλιασέ με,
κι ἄν μ᾽ εὕρης μαῦρον κι ἀραχνόν, τράβα καί σκέπασέ με.
Στίς τρεῖς πῆρα κι ἀράχνιασα, εἰς τίς ἐννιά μυρίζω,
κι ἀπ᾽ τίς σαράντα κι ὕστερα ἁρμούς ἁρμούς χωρίζω.

Giankas 885.4–9

– Make your arms into pickaxes, heave aside the tombstone,
and draw the kerchief from my face.
If you find me pink and white, bend down and embrace me,
and if you find me mouldering black, cover me once more.
On the third day I began to moulder, on the ninth I smell,
and from the fortieth my limbs fall one by one.

The Church has learnt to accept and supervise this pagan custom. In Mani the priest takes charge, and if he finds something amiss, as he usually does, he is paid for a special liturgy for the dead man's soul. Sometimes more drastic measures are required, such as cremation. This is what a seer advised an anxious assembly to do in the second century B.C. with the body of Philinnion, who had become a *revenant* after an untimely death.[43]

The whole village community is responsible for the care of the bones of their ancestors, on which their good fortune is thought to depend, as in antiquity.[44] In the case of sudden evacuation of a village, the bones are carefully dug up, put in special sacks, and taken with them to help found a new settlement. If there is no time for this, then the bones are burnt, to prevent the possibility of desecration by the enemy. When Parga, sold by the British to Ali Pasha in 1817, was ceded to the Turks in 1819, its inhabitants burnt the bones of their ancestors before they left, as is recorded in the historical lament:

Βλέπεις ἐκείνη τή φωτιά, μαῦρο καπνό πού βγάνει;
᾽Εκεῖ καίγονται κόκκαλα, κόκκαλα ἀντρειωμένων,

ποὺ τὴν Τουρκιὰ τρομάξανε καὶ τὸ βεζίρη κάψαν.
Ἐκεῖ 'ναι κόκκαλα γονιοῦ, ποὺ τὸ παιδὶ τὰ καίει,
νὰ μὴν τὰ βροῦνε οἱ Λιάπηδες, Τοῦρκοι μὴν τὰ πατήσουν. *Ibid.* 44

Do you see yonder fire, and the black smoke which it makes?
Bones are being burned there, bones of brave men,
who caused the Turks to be afraid, and burnt the vezir.
There a parent's bones are burned by his own child,
lest the Turkish infidels should find them and trample on them.

As for mourning, the duration and customs vary considerably, but everywhere the widow is required to observe the most exacting terms.[45]

This summary of ritual lamentation as it has been recorded from different parts of Greece for the past hundred years or so, while far from exhaustive, may perhaps indicate some important features in the continuity of Greek tradition. First, the general pattern of the ritual, and the distinctive types of lament characteristic of its three stages – at the wake, at the funeral procession and at the tomb – have remained fundamentally the same. Second, in spite of the changes, there are some striking similarities of detail, in the ritual practices themselves, in the explanations given for them by the people, and above all in the terminology. Further, relating the modern ritual to the ancient and Byzantine material already examined, we find that on the one hand there are some practices in modern folk tradition which can be paralleled in ancient ritual, but which are not recorded in Byzantine tradition, and on the other hand a certain discrepancy between the official attitude of the Church as expressed by the early fathers and as practised by the village priests today, who are by no means reluctant to preside over, or profit from, certain practices of demonstrably pagan origin.

This discrepancy reflects a subjective rather than an objective change. Now that paganism is no longer regarded as a powerful force among the people and the Church has no need to take a hostile attitude, the two are thoroughly integrated. There is no conflict because there is no real distinction. On the one hand the Church has learnt to tolerate what it had once discouraged or condemned; on the other hand, popular ritual has associated itself more or less directly with Christianity. The ancient figure of Hades has disappeared, but his popular successor is not God or Saint Michael but Charos, who is responsible for accompanying the dead to the Underworld, still known as Hades, and much more similar to its ancient counterpart than to the Christian concept of Hell. Along with Charos in Hades are to be found the Virgin, the saints and apostles, while Charos occasionally finds his way to Paradise, usurping Saint Peter as keeper of the gate. He has survived because there is no doubt in the minds of those who believe in him that he is the servant of God, and so it is to him that mourners address their prayers to release the dead from their graves on the Christian festivals. The assimilation has been complete, yet unconscious, as in the following folk song recorded from the Peloponnese:[46]

– Στὸν Ἅδη θὰ κατέβω καὶ στὸν Παράδεισο,
τὸν Χάρο νὰ τὸν εὕρω δυὸ λόγια νὰ τοῦ πῶ.

I will go down to Hades and to Paradise,
to find Charos and say a few words to him.

Perhaps one factor in this process of assimilation has been the change in the position of the Orthodox Church. During the long centuries of Turkish occupation, when it was no longer in a dominant position, through the lower village priests at least it played an important role in the struggle for national liberation and so became more closely united and identified with the people. Under these circumstances, since old divergences and disputes tended to be forgotten, some aspects of pagan ritual probably received official recognition.

Of course, ritual lamentation has not survived equally in all parts of Greece. There has been considerable attenuation in urban regions, where it is regarded as a personal matter to be decided and arranged by the family concerned. But in most of the villages, lamentation remains a social duty for the whole community, to be performed for all alike. The bereaved family is not asked if it wishes the dead to be lamented; the women simply come to the house and weep, first for whoever has just died, then for their own dead. It is an integral part of a complex ritual which by its very nature is dependent upon the collective participation of the whole community.[47]

This relation between lament and ritual affords a clue to continuity. The ancient lament, even in its most highly developed literary form, never entirely lost sight of its ritual connections. When this dynamic interplay of poetry and life was obscured in Byzantine learned tradition, the result tended towards a cold and formal literary excercise, divorced from popular language and culture. What is characteristic of the modern Greek folk lament – although by no means unique to Greek tradition – is that it has retained its ritual significance without any diminution of its poetic quality.

At present survival is threatened neither by legislation nor by the Church, but by a more insidious and gradual corrosion of the social conditions on which it depends. Will it inevitably disappear when its old functional value has gone, together with the practices and superstitions of which it is a part? It is too soon to answer such a question yet, but perhaps the vital unity of poetry and ritual, characteristic of Greek tradition and essential to the continuity of many features of the lament since antiquity in spite of the historical and religious changes, will ensure its survival in a different form in the future, perhaps in popular poetry of a new kind, which is neither exclusively folkloric, nor exclusively literary. Folk tradition, when deep-rooted in the consciousness of a people as it is in Greece, is extremely tenacious and at the same time adaptable.

PART II
GODS, CITIES AND MEN

4
The ritual lament for gods and heroes

The close connection between ritual and lamentation analysed in Part I suggests that the traditional lament for the dead fulfils a dual function: objectively, it is designed to honour and appease the dead, while subjectively, it gives expression to a wide range of conflicting emotions. But the lament for the dead should not be viewed in isolation from two other important and ancient types of lament, the lament for the death of gods and heroes, and the historical lament for disasters affecting a city or a people. By examining their growth in more detail, I hope in Part II to indicate how these three types of lament, for gods, cities and men, became fused in such a way as to provide material for a rich and varied poetic response, in both literary and vernacular laments.

Adonis, Linos and Hyakinthos

The earliest reference to the lament for Adonis in Greek literature comes from a fragment generally attributed to Sappho. It was probably part of a lament performed antiphonally as a dialogue between Aphrodite and the Nymphs:[1]

– Κατθναίσκει, Κυθέρη', ἄβρος Ἄδωνις· τί κε θεῖμεν;
– Καττύπτεσθε, κόραι, καὶ κατερείκεσθε κίθωνας.   140a L–P

– Tender Adonis is dying, Kythereia. What are we to do?
– Beat your breasts, maidens, and rend your tunics.

After Sappho, there is no further literary reference to Adonis until the comic poets of the mid-fifth century B.C. It seems that the *Adonia* was an essentially popular festival, at no time incorporated into official Athenian cults, and that it belonged exclusively to the women. In the *Lysistrata*, we are told how the women would make a wooden image of Adonis and lay it out on the rooftops for lamentation and interment, weeping and beating their breasts (387–98). Fragments from other comic poets confirm the popular character of the festival, and suggest that it was an occasion for ritual joy and ecstatic dancing as well as for lamentation.[2]

Nearly two centuries later, Theokritos describes the same popular festival as it was celebrated in Alexandria (*Idyll* 15). It is a penetrating sketch of two Syracusan ladies residing in Alexandria, who exchange gossip on children, servants, difficult husbands and the latest fashions as they prepare to attend the first day of the ritual for Adonis, organised by Queen Arsinoe within the precincts of the royal palace. After fighting their way through the crowded streets to the palace, they admire the intricacy of the tapestries, which realistically depict the dying Adonis, and listen to the hymn sung by a professional singer who had won a prize the previous year for her singing of dirges. The singer praises Adonis, and describes in detail the ritual cakes and the 'gardens of Adonis', or quick-growing seed plants in silver pots which will be taken, together with the image of Adonis, by the women on the next day to be thrown into the sea and lamented. She concludes with a farewell to Adonis until the following year, leaving the lady Gorgo to ponder, not on the importance of the ritual, but on returning home to prepare a meal for her irritable husband.

The *Epitáphios for Adonis*, attributed to Theokritos' contemporary Bion, is different in that it was probably intended for actual performance on the second day of the *Adónia*.[3] It has the quality of a love song as well as that of a lament: the poet tells us how the rivers, trees, springs and mountains join his dirge for the fair Adonis, killed by a boar while hunting, and the cry to Adonis is echoed in refrain throughout the poem by the Loves. Kythereia herself utters a passionate farewell, varying the ritual custom of the mourner's last greeting to the dead by asking Adonis for a final kiss before his lips are cold (42–50). At the end of the poem it is said that Hymenaios has quenched every marriage torch on the doorposts and has torn the bridal crown to shreds, changing his usual song to Hymen into a lament for Adonis (87–90).

Throughout antiquity the belief persisted that the cult of Adonis was associated with the ripening and harvesting of the fruit and flowers. The death of Adonis symbolised the cutting of the fruit and crops, his sojourn in Acheron their ripening underground.[4] If Adonis originated in some kind of vegetation cult, it is likely that the laments sung for his death in the countryside were very different in character from the sophisticated and literary laments which have come down to us. Even so, his connection with flowers and young plants was remembered not only in the words of the lament, where it has an obvious poetic value, but in the details of the ritual: he was laid out on a bed strewn with flowers of every hue, and the 'gardens of Adonis' which accompanied his departure were seen as a symbol of his ephemeral life on earth.[5]

The cult can be traced back to eastern origins of extreme antiquity, and it survived at least until the fourth century A.D. After the advent of Christianity there was a tendency for Adonis' seasonal return to earth to be regarded as a mystic death and resurrection. The resulting confusion in popular imagination between Adonis and Christ may not have been discouraged by the Church fathers during the first centuries of our era.[6] But whatever changes the cult may have undergone, the fundamental and constant element of the lament was the refrain, ὦ τὸν Ἄδωνιν, which survived as long as the memory of Adonis himself. This refrain, in Greek tradition personified into a young man who died a violent death and yet returned to earth, is thought to be Semitic in origin, meaning simply 'Ah, lord!'[7]

The history of Linos is not unlike that of Adonis, although it is rather more obscure and confused. Homer mentions the existence of a folk song called Linos, although it sounds more like a dance than a lament, and Herodotos identifies the Linos song with a song common in Cyprus, Phoenicia and Egypt, where it was known from earliest times, being the only song the Egyptians ever sang and going under the name not of Linos but of Maneros, the first Egyptian king, who invented agriculture but died young and was mourned by his people ever afterwards. In fact, Maneros may also be a mistaken personification of the refrain 'Maa-ne-hra!', or 'Come to the house!'[8] The Linos song is mentioned by Sappho and Pindar, and seems to have been developed as an art form in the sixth century, at the same time as the *thrênos*.[9]

Alongside the personified, mythical Linos and his cult song, there existed also the popular refrain αἴλινον, αἴλινον!, associated in tragedy both with the Oriental, barbaric cry of grief first uttered over the dead, and with the cry of victory. This divergence may reflect the dual nature of the cult and its ritual, death and return, lamentation and joy; if so, then the contradictory nature of the sources, some calling the *aílinos* a lament and others a folk song, would be explained.[10]

Related to Linos is the figure of Hymenaios. Known in Homer and

Hesiod as the nuptial hymn sung during the wedding procession, and in Sappho as a kind of bridal refrain, he is personified in a fragment of Pindar as the son of a Muse, brother of Linos and Ialemos, who was, like them, killed prematurely.[11] His nuptial hymn was, in one sense, the exact antithesis of the funeral songs associated with his brothers Linos and Ialemos; and yet the close connection between marriage and death, which has a long history in Greek tradition, is further borne out by Hymenaios' tragic intervention in so many funeral scenes in art and literature, where he quenches or reverses the marriage torches, and turns the wedding celebrations into funeral lamentation.[12]

Finally, according to the historian Polykrates, cited by Athenaios, in Laconia there was an annual festival to Hyakinthos and Apollo which lasted for three days. The first part was a period of mourning, devoted exclusively to Hyakinthos, who was killed by Apollo, probably accidentally. No garlands, bread or wine were brought to the banquets, and contrary to usual practice, the paean was not sung. But when the festivities to Apollo began on the second day, young boys played the lyre, sang to the accompaniment of the *aulós*, and danced in quick, anapaestic rhythm to express their praise of Apollo, while yet others performed, singing local songs to the accompaniment of dancers. The whole city, including the slaves, joined in the music, dancing, contests, procession and feasting (Ath. 139d–f). It was an annual festival which began with fasting and ritual lamentation, and ended in joyous feasting and ecstatic celebrations.

Lityerses, Bormos and Mariandynos

While mythology and literature have given to Adonis and Linos a separate lineage, identity and personality, Bormos and Lityerses appear to have existed mainly in local cults, frequently confused in ancient sources. The song for Lityerses was, according to one tradition, a comic version of the lament sung by the Black Sea people, the Mariandynoi, for Bormos, who is described by Athenaios as the son of a famous and wealthy man. In the prime of beauty and youth he disappeared while going to fetch water for the thirsty reapers, and has been invoked and lamented ever since by the Mariandynoi at harvest time. Another tradition has it that Tityos had two children, Priola and Mariandynos, and that Mariandynos was killed while hunting.[13]

None of these figures has attracted much attention from the poets, but the annual lament sung by the Mariandynoi made a deep and lasting impression. Aeschylus, in the *Persians*, refers to the Mariandynian mourner as particularly wild and ecstatic, and this is explained in two scholia with a quotation from the historian Kallistratos of the first century B.C., affirming that the popular lament of the Mariandynian *aulós*-players still continued in his own day (A. *Pers.* 935–40, cf. 937 Sch. (A), 938 Sch. (M) = *FHG* 4.353). Its survival is independently confirmed by Nymphis (third century B.C.), cited by Athenaios (619–20). Traditions about the Mariandynoi are also found in various Byzantine sources, and the memory of their lament survived in the proverb Μαρυανδηνῶν μέμνησο θρηνητηρίων (Remember the Mariandynian mourners!), frequently quoted without reference to its Aeschylean context until at least the thirteenth century.[14]

Although the details vary, and there is considerable confusion in the ancient sources, there are certain significant features common to all these ritual laments. First, all appear to have originated in some kind of vegetation cult, in which the reaping of the corn or the harvesting of the vine, fruit and flowers was lamented. Gradually, this ancient tradition of eastern origins was transformed and diversified in Greek mythology and literature into a fully personified story, sometimes involving violent death during hunting. This alternative tradition, in which the young god or man was the victim of a wild boar, may be no less ancient, and perhaps reflects the destructive effects of hunting on a predominantly field economy. Nor was the theme a creative source for mythology only in the archaic and classical periods. Besides many variations on old themes, the Hellenistic poets were constantly elaborating new ones, such as the story of Hylas in Theokritos' thirteenth Idyll, which is almost a replica of the story of Mariandynos. Although they became a pastoral convention, it is likely that many of the details of these stories were drawn not from imagination, but from the great diversity of local traditions. This is confirmed by the continued emphasis on the harvest associations of the ritual as it is known to have been practised by the people throughout antiquity. And one element of the primitive lament which was never forgotten or ignored, even in the most sophisticated literary compositions, was the refrain calling the dying man or god by name. This invocation was frequently expressed by the verb ἀνακαλεῖσθαι (to call upon, invoke).[15]

Second, there appears to be a connection between the development from primitive to ordered music with the adaptation and refinement of an early Oriental type of lament. According to one tradition, Linos, son of Ourania, was credited with the invention of the hexameter, and so was mourned by all the poets and lyre players.[16] In another, from Argos, he was the son of Apollo and a king's daughter, lamented antiphonally by mother and son. In Thebes, he was a musician killed by Apollo for exciting his jealousy by his musical skill; while according to Pindar he was celebrated in song by his mother, a goddess or a Muse.[17] Adonis, though not a musician himself, was mourned by Aphrodite and the Loves in an antiphonal lament. Of Mariandynos it is expressly stated 'that he developed particularly the singing to the *aulós* in lamentation, and that he taught this art to Hyagnis, father of Marsyas. There are in fact Mariandynian *auloí* specially suited to dirges, hence the current saying, "he plays on Mariandynian reeds", when playing in the Ionian style' (A. *Pers.* 937 Sch. (A), ed. Dindorf 498–9). This tradition helps to explain why the memory of the Mariandynian lament lasted for so long. Further, although little is known of the kind of music associated with lamentation in antiquity, in all these types of lament the evidence is consistent in saying that it was performed to the shrill, high-pitched tone of the *aulós* (Ath. 174f–175b).

Third, both ritual and myth centre on the death and return, the *káthodos* and *ánodos* (descent and ascent) of the god. Leaving aside the controversial question of origins, its significance here is that the lament for death is inseparable from the rejoicing for return, frequently enacted by women weeping over images and associated with fertility and the return of spring. It is possible that the connection between this lament and nature, which is imbedded in the ritual, explains the poetic convention of calling upon all nature to join in lamentation. Originally it belonged to the lament for the dying god, for whom nature mourned because without him it could not survive, but later it was extended to the lament for man as well.

Finally, although these laments appear to be of eastern origin, the personification into a fair youth killed prematurely is a characteristically Greek element. In myth and poetry alike great stress is laid on the youth and beauty of the god, and on the wounds which only enhance his looks, even in death:

καὶ νέκυς ὢν καλός ἐστι, καλὸς νέκυς, οἷα καθεύδων.   Bion 1.71

He is beautiful even in death, in death he is beautiful, as one who sleeps.

Lamentation in the hero cults and mysteries

In Herodotos' account of the hero cult for Adrastos, as reformed by Kleisthenes of Sikyon, there is no explicit reference to a lament, but the ritual character of the tragic dances for Adrastos' *páthea* (sufferings) is emphasised (Hdt. 5.67). Elsewhere, annual laments as part of heroes' festivals were common: the Thebans lamented Leukothea, but were warned by Lykourgos that if she were a goddess, it was not right to mourn her as mortal; and if mortal, it was not right to pay her divine honours. Achilles was mourned with beating of the breast and lamentation by the women of Kroton, Elis and Thessaly; and at Corinth there was an annual festival, known as 'the festival of mourning' for Medea's children, which included the same 'ritual and divine lament' as for Melikertes. Similarly the daughter of Klytias, king of Megara, who married Bakchos of the royal clan of the Bakchiadai of Corinth, died at an early age, and so the Megarians were made to send their young men and girls to Corinth in order to mourn her. The *thrênos* was probably sung antiphonally, with one choir of boys and one of girls.[18]

Besides the hero cults, many of which continued throughout antiquity, lamentation is known to have played a part in the Dionysiac and Orphic tradition and in the Eleusinian and later mysteries. As early as the sixth century B.C. the tragic dances for Adrastos were transferred to Dionysos, and we are also told that Orpheus attached to the worship of Dionysos the singing of *thrênoi*. Not much is known about the nature of these laments in the classical period, but later Christian writers are more explicit. Clement, at the end of the second century A.D., describes the mystic drama at Eleusis about Demeter and Kore as it was performed in his own day, mentioning mourning as an important and integral part of it. Eusebios of Caesarea (fourth century A.D.) may have exaggerated some of the activities that went on during the mysteries in his account, but his mention of *thrênoi*, supported as it is by other evidence, cannot be dismissed.[19] But it is Firmicus Maternus, a converted Roman senator, whose vigorous attack on Oriental and other mystery cults, written in about A.D. 345, affords the most complete account of the mystic lamentation:

Nocte quadam simulacrum in lectica supinum ponitur et per numeros digestis fletibus plangitur; deinde cum se ficta lamentatione satiaverint, lumen infertur: tunc a sacerdote omnium qui flebant fauces unguentur, quibus perunctis sacerdos hoc lento murmure susurrat:

Θαρρεῖτε μύσται τοῦ θεοῦ σεσωσμένου·
ἔσται γὰρ ἡμῖν ἐκ πόνων σωτηρία.

Take courage, initiates, for the god is saved,
and there shall be for us deliverance from sufferings!

de errore prof. relig. 22

This account may not be significant for our knowledge of lamentation in the mystery cults of antiquity, but it shows that in the fourth century A.D., at the dawn of the Byzantine period, there still survived a mystic, ritual lamentation over the image of a god, followed by the lighting of lamps and the joyful cry of salvation and deliverance from suffering.

The lament was therefore as important in religious and mystic ritual as it was in poetry and myth. Further, in the mysteries its associations with crop fertility became fused with the belief that it was a means of salvation and deliverance. The secret *páthea* made the mortal initiate into a god, as is affirmed in the following Orphic text inscribed on a gold tablet for burial with the dead (from Thurii in S. Italy, fourth to third centuries B.C.):

Χαῖρε, παθὼν τὸ πάθημα· τὸ δ' οὔπω πρόσθε ἐπεπόνθεις,
θεὸς ἐγένου ἐξ ἀνθρώπου.   Kern *OF* 32f. 3–4.

Hail, you who have suffered the suffering, which you had not yet
    suffered before.
From man you have become god.

The descent of god or hero to the Underworld no longer symbolised only the burial of the crops underground, but a journey deliberately undertaken to combat Hades and save mankind from death. Finally, the grief of Demeter for Persephone, of mother for child, was a dominant element of the Eleusinian mysteries until the end of antiquity, ritually enacted at the women's festivals.

The Virgin's lament

The story of the Crucifixion as told in the Gospels ignores the lament of the Virgin. Only in the Gospel of Saint John are there to be found two not very explicit statements on which later laments appear to have been partly based.[20] Greek tradition goes to the other extreme, sometimes focusing attention on the figure of the weeping Mother to the exclusion of Christ. The earliest example in Greek which can be dated with certainty is Romanos' *kontákion*, *Mary at the Cross* (early sixth century), in the form of a dramatic dialogue between Mary and Christ. Mary reacts to her son's theological arguments not as a woman who is divinely inspired, but as an ordinary woman of the people; and this characterisation is neither extraneous nor irrelevant, since it is through her gradual and painful realisation of the necessity of the Crucifixion that the dramatic tension is created and sustained.

What was Romanos' source? One of the hymns of Synesios of Cyrene (*c.* A.D. 370–414) had treated the theme of Christ's descent to the Underworld, but without reference to Mary (*Hymns* IX = Cantarella 34). The Church fathers had used the grief of Mary, as that of Sarah and Rachel, to illustrate an exemplary fortitude which the people would do well to emulate. On the other hand there seems to have been some precedent to Romanos' treatment in Syriac liturgy, and more especially in the work of Ephraem (A.D. 306–73), one of whose homilies refers to Mary as 'leaning her head against the Cross, and murmuring in Hebrew words of lamentation and sorrow'.[21] The boldness of Romanos' conception lies in his dramatic setting and in his use of dialogue: his Mary does not mourn her dead son at the foot of the Cross, but laments and challenges his fate on the way to Calvary.

If Romanos' *kontákion* was inspired partly by Syriac tradition, it certainly exercised a profound influence on later Greek liturgy. Some later *tropária* of the ninth century, attributed to the Emperor Leo VI, and known as *Stavrotheotókia* because their theme is the lament of the Mother of God at the Cross, share many similarities of detail with Romanos, although they are shorter and less dramatic in form.[22] Further, detaching the words from the music, a considerable number of verses fall easily into *politikòs stíchos*, the fifteen-syllable accentual verse of Greek folk poetry.[23] This suggests that from the ninth century at least there was some reciprocal influence between the liturgy and hymns for Good Friday and Holy Saturday, and the emerging songs of Byzantine popular tradition.

Five or six centuries later, after a modified form of the vernacular and the use of *politikòs stíchos* had become an established medium for poetry, we find probably the first extant example of the Virgin's lament in the vernacular. Its author is unknown, but the number of manuscripts in which it has survived suggests a wide popularity and diffusion. The similarity of many motifs and phrases with the earlier *Stavrotheotókia* and with Romanos' *kontákion*, together with the archaising tendency of the language, has led many scholars to believe that it is a literary composition, put together from the hymns and the liturgy.[24] No doubt there was some degree of literary redaction, but on the other hand it is unlikely to be altogether dependent on literary sources, since several features of its style, notably the use of incremental repetition in groups of three, and traces of a refrain at key points in the line, would seem to owe something to the techniques of oral poetry (*Thrênos Theotókou* 29–33, 65–6, 71–2). Further, the similarities could point to a common oral tradition rather than to literary interdependence; in either case, they indicate a gradual popularisation of the *kontákion*, in which striking and memorable features lived on in a new form and in more popular language.

Meanwhile the figure of the weeping Virgin had not been ignored by Byzantine learned tradition. The question of the date and authorship of the Christian tragedy *Christòs Páschon* is still unsolved. Since the attribution of the manuscripts and the Suda to Gregory Nazianzen was first doubted in the sixteenth and seventeenth centuries, most scholars have tended to support the view that it was written, not in the fourth to fifth centuries, but in the eleventh to twelfth. The most recent discussion of the problem is by Tuilier, who argues convincingly in favour of its traditional attribution to Gregory.[25]

More important for the present study is the question of sources. Out of a total of 2,600 lines, 1,304 are taken from ancient tragedies known to us, mostly from seven plays of Euripides, but also from Aeschylus and Lykophron. Other sources include the Old and New Testaments and the apocryphal gospels and acts. It is easy to deride the play as a ridiculous hotchpotch of unsuitable tags, with Medea's words lamenting the children she is about to kill put into the mouth of Mary weeping for Christ. But for all the slavish imitation of Euripides, and the deliberate attempt to compare Mary with Hekabe, there are signs of an influence of a different kind. First, there are several parallels to Romanos' *kontákion* and to the *Stavrotheotókia*, including one passage so similar to Romanos' opening strophe that they must be either interdependent, or taken from a common source.[26] Second, although Romanos' treatment of Mary is more convincing and more profound, several features in the *Christòs Páschon* are undoubtedly more popular. These include Mary's plea to Christ to manifest his divinity by rising from the dead, not in order to save mankind, as in Romanos, but to silence current slanders against her honour – slanders which are only hinted at in the Gospels, but which recur throughout the apocryphal gospels and acts.[27]

Then there is the theme of Mary's despair and wish for suicide, and her complaint that if her son deserts her, she will be alone in the world, without kin and without friends, a detail which is found in Symeon Metaphrastes' *Planctus*, written in learned prose during the tenth century, and also in the vernacular *Thrênos Theotókou*.[28] Perhaps it is hardly surprising that the suicide wish was not developed in the *kontákia*, which tended to reflect more official Orthodox doctrine; but it has remained an important motif in many of the modern folk ballads, where it provokes the reply from Christ that if his Mother gives way to suicide and despair, there can be no salvation for the rest of the world – a point which Romanos and later hymn writers do not omit to elaborate at some length (Romanos 19.6–9, *MMB* 5.180.11).

Finally there is the Virgin's curse. In the *Christòs Páschon* it lasts for eighty-one lines, containing, in addition to the Euripidean echoes, a hesitation formula comparable to one used to introduce a curse in folk poetry today.[29] Mary makes no curses in Romanos' *kontákion*, or in the other Byzantine laments; but in the modern ballads, on hearing the news, she hurries to the site of the Crucifixion, not omitting to call on the way at the house of the gipsy nail-maker, who made the nails to pierce Christ's body, and utters a curse that he should never make good, and never have a house and hearth (*DIEE* (1892) 722γ). In other versions she curses Judas and the whole race of Jews as well (*Laog* (1934) 252.90–1, cf. 255.72–6). Outside the *Christòs Páschon*, this theme is developed only in popular tradition.

One of the finest examples of the Virgin's lament in Byzantine homiletic tradition is Symeon Metaphrastes' *Planctus* of the tenth century, already referred to. It is too rigidly structured in the rhetorical style to move us as deeply as Romanos' *kontákion*; yet it contains much rich and evocative imagery, emphasising above all the physical beauty and youth of Christ (Migne 114.209–18). This theme, ignored in the *kontákia* and *Stavrotheotókia* but frequent in the *Christòs Páschon* and in the modern ballads, suggests that it would be a mistake to draw too fine a distinction between the learned and popular traditions.

Little is known about the date and authorship of the *Epitáphios Thrênos*, part of the liturgy still performed on Good Friday and Holy Saturday, except that it was in existence by the fourteenth century. Much of its content can be paralleled in Symeon Metaphrastes' *Planctus* and in the *Stavrotheotókia*.[30] It is punctuated throughout with references to the weeping Mother, so that although only parts of the lament are spoken by her, she, rather than Christ, is the central figure. Above all, it is pervaded with imagery more striking than any to be found in earlier laments. It is extravagant, but not lacking in structure, since it is concentrated on specific themes, such as the antithesis of life and death, god and man, man and nature. It also elaborates richly the Christian symbolism of sun and moon. Christ, the sun and prime source of light, life and righteousness, has descended to Hades, shedding his light beneath the earth, and depriving the earth and the moon, his mother, of light:[31]

> Δύνεις ὑπὸ γῆν, Σῶτερ, ἥλιε τῆς δικαιοσύνης· ὅθεν ἡ τεκοῦσα
> σελήνη σε ταῖς λύπαις ἐκλείπει, σῆς θέας στερουμένη.   Stasis 2.25

> You set beneath the earth, Saviour, sun of righteousness,
> whence the moon which gave you birth fades away in sorrow,
> deprived of the sight of you.

> Ὑπὸ γῆν ἐκρύβης, ὥσπερ ἥλιος, νῦν καὶ νυκτὶ τῇ τοῦ θανάτου
> κεκάλυψαι, ἀλλ' ἀνάτειλον φαιδρότερον, Σωτήρ.   Stasis 1.30

> Beneath the earth you have set, like the sun. Now you are
> veiled even by the night of death; yet rise more brightly,
> Saviour.

> Νέκρωσιν τὴν σήν, ἡ πανάφθορος, Χριστέ, σοῦ μήτηρ,
> βλέπουσα, πικρῶς σοι ἐφθέγγετο· Μή βραδύνῃς, ἡ ζωή, ἐν
> τοῖς νεκροῖς.   Stasis 2.54

> Beholding your death, Christ, your incorruptible mother
> cried out bitterly to you, 'Do not linger, life, among the dead.'

This Christian imagery of light and darkness is remarkably close to the imagery of the modern folk laments, where light has connotations not only of the divine wisdom and knowledge of God, but also of the vigorous health and beauty of life, as in the following tersely expressive couplet on the death of an only son:

> Ἥλιε μου, πῶς ἐβιάστηκες νὰ πᾶς νὰ βασιλέψῃς,
> ν' ἀφήσῃς τὸ σπιτάκι σου κι ἀλλοῦ νὰ πᾶς νὰ φέξῃς;   Politis 194

> My sun, how is it that you hastened to go and set,
> to leave your home and shed your light elsewhere?

In the *Epitáphios*, the associations of this theme are elaborated in verses which dwell, almost erotically, on Christ's youth and beauty even in death. Just as Aphrodite and the Loves had mourned for Adonis in Bion's *Epitáphios*, so here Mary and the 'chorus' sing, adapting the words of Psalm 46.3:

Ὁ ὡραῖος κάλλει παρὰ πάντας βροτοὺς ὡς ἀνείδεος νεκρὸς
καταφαίνεται, ὁ τὴν φύσιν ὡραΐσας τοῦ παντός.   Stasis 1.8

He who is fair in beauty beyond all mortals looks like a corpse
without form, he who gave beauty to the nature of the Universe.

And Joseph asks:

Ὄμμα τὸ γλυκὺ καὶ τὰ χείλη σου πῶς μύσω, Λόγε;   Stasis 2.23

How shall I close your sweet eye and your lips, Word?

Romanos' Ewe mourning the Lamb of God as he is led to the slaughter
(1.1–2) has here become the more classical, and yet at the same time
more popular, heifer lamenting her lost calf, her wild cry emphasised
by the use of ἠλάλαξεν:[32]

Ἡ δάμαλις τὸν μόσχον, ἐν ξύλῳ κρεμασθέντα,
ἠλάλαξεν ὁρῶσα.   Stasis 3.27

The heifer, seeing her calf which had been hanged on the Cross,
wailed in grief.

Again, just as Aphrodite had called on the mountains, valleys and streams
to join her lament for Adonis, so here Mary says:

Ὦ βουνοὶ καὶ νάπαι καὶ ἀνθρώπων πληθύς, κλαύσατε
καὶ πάντα θρηνήσατε σὺν ἐμοὶ τῇ τοῦ Θεοῦ ἡμῶν Μητρί.
    Stasis 1.68

O you mountains and valleys and host of men, weep,
all things lament with me, the Mother of our God!

Then comes the thrilling climax during the final section of praises, the
Áxion Estí:

Ὕπτιον ὁρῶσα, ἡ πάναγνός σε, Λόγε, μητροπρεπῶς ἐθρήνει·
Ὦ γλυκύ μου ἔαρ, γλυκύτατόν τέκνον, ποῦ ἔδυ σου
τὸ κάλλος;   Stasis 3.16

Beholding you stretched out, Word, the all-holy one lamented
as befits a mother, 'O my sweet spring, my sweetest child, where
has your beauty set?'

These lines reflect a feeling closer in tone than anything else so far examined in Byzantine tradition to the ancient belief that nature, too, participated in the lament for the dying god: in both, the god and the lost spring are identified.

What, then, are the sources and inspiration of the *Epitáphios*? Although some of its features can be paralleled in the earlier hymns, stylistically it is closer to Symeon Metaphrastes' *Planctus* than to Romanos' *kontákion* or to the *Christòs Páschon*. At the same time, in its obsessive concern with the weeping mother and the beauty of the dying son, its closest affinities are with the ancient laments for Adonis. Deliberate imitation may, of course, be excluded. The popular style and tone of the *Epitáphios* suggest that many simple but fundamental associations of the ancient ritual lament for the dying god had not been forgotten, and had re-emerged to influence the liturgy and become incorporated into the Good Friday service.

Confirmation of the popular character of the Virgin's lament in late Byzantine tradition comes from the second recension of the apocryphal gospel of Nikodemos, known as the *Acta Pilati*, and surviving in three manuscripts, none earlier than the fifteenth century.[33] All three manuscripts of this recension contain the lament – though with considerable variation and interpolation – which refers explicitly to its ritual character, 'And saying these words she scratched her face with her nails and beat her breast' (Tischendorf 283). The apocryphal lament constitutes a remarkable link between some of the earlier Byzantine material and modern folk tradition. It has some stylistic affinities with the *Epitáphios* and the vernacular *Thrênos Theotókou*;[34] but in the sequence and detail of the narrative, it is closest of all to the modern ballads. The most probable explanation is that the *Epitáphios*, the apocryphal lament and the modern ballads were drawing on a common tradition, the *Epitáphios* elaborating the lyrical elements and the ballads concentrating on the narrative. It is not possible to date this common tradition precisely, but it must have been well established and widely known by the time the second recension of the *Acta Pilati* was written down. The absence of the lament from the Latin versions of the *Acta Pilati*, which were probably based on the earlier recension of the fifth century, is indicative of the traditional character of the Virgin's lament in Greek. It is also essentially different from the *Stabat Mater* of medieval Latin tradition, where great emphasis is given to the Virgin's patience and fortitude.[35] No such lesson can be drawn from the Greek Virgin, whose grief is so violent that she has to be pushed aside:

And when she revived and arose, running like a lioness from a field and rending her garments, she looked askance at the Jews...saying 'Give me a path, men, for me to walk and embrace the neck of my lamb; give way to me, men, that I may weep for my dearest son, the lamb of my soul; give way to me, men, that I may reach him who was fed on the milk of my breasts (?); give way to me, that I may behold and lament my sweetest son.' And beating her breast she cried out, saying 'Alas, alas, sweetest son, light of my eyes, king of all things. Alas, alas, how can I bear to behold you hanging on the Cross?...' (MS C, Tischendorf 282–3.) 'Where have they gone', said she, 'the good deeds which you did in Judea? What evil have you done to the Jews?' So then the Jews who saw her lamenting and crying out came and drove her out of the way. But she could not be persuaded to leave, and remained there, saying 'Slay me first, lawless Jews.' (MSS A, B, C, Tischendorf 283.)

If the Virgin's lament had always existed in Greek tradition, and if it is true that it had absorbed certain features of the ancient laments for gods and heroes, then we should expect the modern ballads to bear some trace of their long oral history. It is notoriously difficult to date elements in oral poetry, because old themes and old stories are subject to constant variation and remoulding. But there are, as I hope to show, a sufficient number of indisputably ancient features, some of which are not found elsewhere, to establish that the modern ballads have a long history of their own. At the same time, the features which they share with the Byzantine laments indicate that, ultimately, they belong to the same tradition.

What, then, are the common features, and what are the main differences between the modern ballads and the earlier laments? The term *ballad*, as opposed to *lament*, is more appropriate to the modern songs in that they tell a story, which contains lamentation, but they are not addressed to the dead Christ in their entirety. They belong to the epic and dramatic rather than to the lyrical or functional songs.

These ballads have survived in fundamentally the same form, though with considerable local variation, from all parts of the Greek-speaking world – from Calabria in South Italy, from the Pontos, Asia Minor, Cyprus, Crete, the Dodecanese, the Ionian Isles, and from most regions of mainland Greece.[36]

First, the common features. The Cypriot *Song for Good Friday*, related to an Asia Minor version probably dating from the fifteenth century, opens with a demand for universal lamentation in sympathy with Mary, who has lost her only son, just as in the opening lines of Romanos' *kontákion* and the *Stavrotheotókia* (Sakellarios 2.84, 28, 1–3). As in the *Christòs Páschon*, Mary then calls on all the women to lament with her (*ibid.* 7–8, cf. *CP* 686–7). In modern tradition, this has an important ritual meaning, since until recently it was customary for all the women of the village to take part in the dressing and decoration of the Epitáphios, and to keep constant vigil over it throughout the night. Mrs Stamatopoulou, aged 86, from Sklithron informed me in 1962 that in her youth all the women, young and old, took part in the vigil, whereas now only a few do so. Mary then recalls the Annunciation, and thinks in anger of the betrayal of Judas. Christ interrupts her outburst with an appeal to her not to give way to excessive grief.[37] Next come Mary's despair and wish for death, found in the *Christòs Páschon*, the homilies and the apocryphal lament; and, in close association, the theme of her recurrent swooning (three times in one ballad).[38] Outside oral tradition, the swoon is found in Greek only in the apocryphal lament, thereby establishing a strong link between them. The significance of the despair, suicide wish and swoon in the ballads can be measured by the fact that in spite of local variations, these three motifs are never omitted. In answer to the rebuke from Christ which they provoke, she replies, as in the *Christòs Páschon*, Symeon Metaphrastes' *Planctus*, and the Byzantine vernacular *Thrênos Theotókou*, that her lament is justified by her deprivation of her only son. She then praises her son's beauty, in a line similar to the liturgy, and expresses a desire to kiss him, another motif found only in the *Christòs Páschon* and the apocryphal lament:[39]

Γιόκα μου, ποῦ εἶν' τὰ κάλλη σου, ποῦ εἶν' ἡ ὀμορφιά σου;
Γιὰ σκύψε, σκύψε, γιόκα μου, γλυκὰ νὰ σὲ φιλήσω,
νὰ βγάλω τὴν μπροστέλλα μου, τὸ αἷμα σ' νὰ σφογγίσω.

Laog (1934) 252.111–13

My son, where are your fine looks, where is your beauty?
Bend down, my son, bend down, that I may kiss you sweetly,
and with my apron wipe away your blood.

Finally, all nature joins in sympathy to mourn the death of Christ. Most ballads open with the line, reminiscent of Romanos' *kontákion On the Passion* (Maas–Trypanis 20):

Σήμερα μαῦρος οὐρανός, σήμερα μαύρη μέρα...

Baud-Bovy 2.248, 1

Today the sky is black, today the day is black...

In a version from Selybria in Thrace, Mary rises from her prayers on the fatal morning to see portentous signs in the heavens:[40]

Βλέπει τὸν οὐρανὸ θαμπὸ καὶ τ' ἄστρα φουρκωμένα
καὶ τὸ φεγγάρι τὸ λαμπρὸ στὸ αἷμα βουτημένο.
– Τί ἔχεις, ἥλιε, κι εἶσαι θαμπός; ἀστρί μου, φουρκωμένο;
καὶ σύ, φεγγάρι μου λαμπρό, στὸ αἷμα βουτημένο;

Laog (1934) 251.57–60

She sees the sky overcast and the stars dimmed by cloud,
she sees the bright moon drenched in blood.
– What is it, sun, that you are overcast? My star, why are you dim?
And you, my bright moon, why are you drenched in blood?

One idea, fundamental to the Virgin's lament, is interpreted so differently in Byzantine and modern tradition as to be quite distinct. In Greek tradition, both iconographic and literary, the purpose of the Crucifixion was Christ's descent to the Underworld and his victory over Hades. In Romanos' *kontákion*, as in other Byzantine laments, Christ explains at length to his Mother that he must die in order to save mankind from the curse of Adam, who sinned willingly. She cannot understand why man's salvation should require his death, and he replies, with a note of impatience, that it is not physical but spiritual salvation that must be won (19.9, 1–6). This essential point of theology is forgotten in the modern ballads, where Christ replies to her threat that she will throw herself over a cliff or hang herself, that if she despairs and kills herself, the whole world will follow suit. Instead, she is to return home, prepare the wine and rusk for the *paregoriá* (funeral feast), so that the whole world may partake of it, thereby uniting mother and child, brother and sister, husband and wife (*Laog* (1934) 252.120–8, cf. 256–7.98–115 and n. 5). Many of the women who sang these lines expressed the opinion that the custom of preparing *paregoriá* for their own dead originated here, but of course the truth is just the opposite: the ritual feast is an independent, pagan survival, which has become assimilated into Christianity. In the folk tradition the significance of the Resurrection lies not so much in the redemption of Adam's sins, but in the liberation of the dead from their miseries in Hades. This is often understood quite

71

literally, not as a symbolic reference to Judgement Day, since it is believed that on Holy Thursday the souls of the dead are freed, and return to celebrate the Resurrection with their families.[41] In popular tradition, Christ's descent to the Underworld still fulfils the same function as the descent of Herakles, Orpheus or Apollo in antiquity.

Yet other features in the ballads, which are not present in the earlier laments, are believed to have originated in the Gospels, short extracts of which are read out in church services during Holy Week. Christ's last words to Mary in the Gospel of Saint John, 'Woman, behold thy son!', meaning that John will become her spiritual son and she his spiritual mother (John 19.26–7), are interpreted more concretely in the ballads: before dying, Christ instructs John (sometimes confused with John the Baptist) to take the news to his mother, who arrives at the scene in a state of bewilderment, and fails to recognise her son:

Κι ἡ Παναγία μπρόβαλεν στὴν ἀμπατὴν τῆς πόρτας·
θωρᾶ λαὸν ἀμέτρητον, θωρᾶ πολὺν ἀσκέρι
καὶ δὲν ἐγνώρισεν κανεὶ μόνον τὸν ἄι Γιάννη.
– Ἁγιέ μου Γιάννη ἀφέντη μου καὶ βαφτιστὴ τοῦ γιοῦ μου,
δείξε με τὸν ἐγέννησα καὶ δὲν τὸν ἐγνωρίζω.
– Θωρᾶς ἐκεῖνον τὸν χλωμὸν καὶ τὸν πολλοδαρμένον;
ὁποὺ κρατεῖ στὸ χέριν του μαντήλιν ματωμένο;
ὁποὺ κρατεῖ καὶ στ' ἄλλο του μαλλιὰ τῆς κεφαλῆς του;
Ἐκεῖνος εἴν' ὁ γιόκας σου κι ἐμέν' ὁ δάσκαλός μου.

DIEE (1892) 722γ

And our Lady came out and stood in the doorway.
She sees countless people, she sees a great throng,
and she knew no one except for Saint John.
– Saint John, my master and baptist of my son,
show me the son I bore, for I do not recognise him.
– You see that pale and much-beaten man,
who carries in one hand a blood-stained handkerchief,
who carries in the other hair from his head?
That man is your son and my teacher.

This dramatic treatment of events is thought by Romaios to be based on a misinterpretation of the Gospels.[42] If so, the misinterpretation has a long history, since precisely the same sequence is found in the *Acta Pilati*, where Mary's question and John's reply are later balanced by Christ's address to his Mother, as in the Gospel:

So when they reached the throng of people, the Mother of God said to John, 'Where is my son?' John said 'Do you see him who wears the crown of thorns, and has his hands bound?' When the Mother of God heard this and saw him, she fell into a faint, falling backwards to the ground, and lay there for some time. (Tischendorf 282.) Then the Mother of God, as she stood and saw, cried out in a loud voice, saying 'My son, my son.' And Jesus turned to her, and seeing John beside her, weeping with the rest of the women, he said 'Behold, thy son.' Then he said also to John 'Behold, thy mother.' (*Ibid.* 284–5.)

John's message, the Virgin's swoon, the company of women, the bewildering crowd of people, her anxious question and the second swoon – all are found in the ballads from many parts of Greece. It is not a misinterpretation of the Gospel, but a characteristic example of the way in which oral tradition rehandles the same episodes and motifs in a more leisurely, yet inherently more dramatic manner. It is the same with the nails which are made for Christ's body: the Gospel mentions three, and a spear; but the gipsy nail-maker of the ballads says he is going to make five (John 19.33–4, cf. *DIEE* (1892) 722γ).

Let us turn now to those features of the ballads which are not to be found in Byzantine tradition, or in the biblical sources, and which point to a long period of oral transmission. First, there is the strange metamorphosis of Christ after Judas' betrayal, when the Jews arrive to seize him. In one of the versions from Thrace, Judas, true to his promise, takes the Jews to where Christ is sitting in the Garden of Gethsemane. Seeing them approach, Christ invites them to eat and drink with him, in a formula which has sinister echoes of Digenis' invitation to Charos in the Akritic ballads. Like Charos, the Jews reply:

– Ἐμεῖς ἐδῶ δὲν ἤλθαμε νὰ φᾶμε καὶ νὰ πιοῦμε,
μόνον σᾶς ἀγαπούσαμε κι ἤλθαμε νὰ σᾶς δοῦμε...
– Αὐτὸς εἶναι καὶ πιάστε τον, γλήγορα μὴ σᾶς φύγη.
Ὁ Χριστὸς σὰν τ' ἄκουσε, πολὺ βαρὺ τὸν ἦλθε·
πέντε λογιοῦ ἐγένηκε νὰ μὴν τὸν ἐγνωρίσουν.
Ἄλλοι τὸν βλέπουν σὰν μωρὸ καὶ ἄλλ' τὸν βλέπουν γέρο,
καὶ πάλι τὸν ἐγνώρισαν.
Ἀπ' τὰ μαλλιὰ τὸν πιάσανε, στὰ μάρμαρα τὸν κροῦσαν.

Laog (1934) 250.37–8, 41–6

(Jews) – We have not come here to eat and drink,
we only came to see you because we loved you...
(Judas) – That is the man, seize him quickly before he escapes you.
When Christ heard these words he was vexed and grieved.
He became five different shapes so that they should not know him.
Some saw him as a baby, others as an old man,
and again they recognised him.
They seized him by the hair, and threw him on the marble.

Its antiquity in local tradition is confirmed by a folk story with yet
another variation: when the Jews chased Christ on Maundy Thursday, he
turned into a small child and hid in the basket of a passing Arab girl,
who refused to give him away when asked if she had seen 'the son of
Mary, the magician'; in return for her kindness, Christ turned the hay
in her basket into rare herbs, and however much she carried, her head
never ached again. The story may have developed from a detail in the
apocryphal *Acta Pilati*, where one of the accusations brought against
Christ was that he was a magician (*Laog* (1934) 250 n. 3, cf. Tischendorf
270).

Second, there is the theme of the Virgin's bath. Mary Magdalene,
who brings the news of the Crucifixion, finds Mary in her bath, and
calls out accusingly:

– You, our Lady, are washing in a silver bath,
you, our Lady, are combing your hair with an ivory comb,
while Christ has been seized and is being tortured by the Jews.

Laog (1934) 255.48–50

It has been suggested that this motif has crept in from a common theme
in the Akritic cycle, as an extension of the swoon motif, after which
the women revive Mary with somewhat excessive quantities of water
(varying in different versions from one to sixty-two jars!), with the
detail of the combing added later. If so, it should be stressed that the
versions which portray her as bathing are no less 'authentic' than those
which portray her praying when the news is brought.[43] Again, it is the
inevitable process of oral variation, in which themes, old and new, are
introduced from other songs, not irrelevantly, but with deliberate effect,
as in the Thracian version of the conversation between the Jews and
Christ quoted above, which contains undertones of the grim dialogue
between Charos and Digenis Akritas.

The third and most curious motif of all is that of 'Saint Kalé'. She does not appear in all versions, and her identity is rarely the same: sometimes she is a saint, sometimes an ordinary woman, and sometimes even Mary's cousin.[44] Her behaviour in the following ballad from Asia Minor is hardly characteristic of a saint, any more than is Mary's answering curse:

'Η 'Αγιὰ Καλὴ ἡπέρασε ἀπ' ὄξω καὶ τσῆ λέγει:
– Ποιὸς εἶδε γιὸ εἰς τὸ σταυρὸ καὶ μάνα στὸ τραπέζι;
'Η Δέσποινα σὰν τ' ἄκουσε πέφτει, λιγοθυμάει.
Σταμιὰ νερὸ τὴν περιχοῦ καὶ πέντε βάζοι μόσχοι
κι ἀπόντας ἡσεφέρισε αὐτὸ τὸ λόγο λέγει:
– "Αντε κι ἐσύ, 'Αγιὰ Καλή, καὶ δόξα νὰ μὴν ἔχης,
ἄντε ποὺ νὰ σὲ χτίσουνε ἀνάμεσα πελάους,
οὔτε παπὰς νὰ λειτουργᾶ, διάκος νὰ μὴ σὲ ψέλνη,
οὔτε κερὶ καὶ λίβανο μὴν κάνη ἐμπροστά σου.
Νὰ γίνης μάντρα τῶν ἀρνιῶν καὶ μάντρα τῶν προβάτων,
κι ἀπάνω στὰ καμπαναριὰ κοράκοι νὰ κοιτάζουν.

MCh (1948) 217.93–102

Saint Kalé passed by outside and called to her,
– Who ever saw a son at the Cross, and his mother at the table?
When our Lady heard this, she fell into a faint.
They pour on her a jug of water, and five jars of musk,
and when she had recovered, she spoke these words:
– Away with you, Saint Kalé, and may you have no glory.
Away, and may they build for you a church out in the oceans,
that neither priest may chant a liturgy nor deacon sing a
      psalm for you,
that neither candle nor incense be brought before you.
Instead, may you become a pen for lambs, a pen for sheep,
and may the crows on the bell towers look down upon you!

Who is Saint Kalé? None other than *Kyrà Kalé* (the lady Kalé), a survival of the cult title of *Ártemis Kallíste*, whose many transformations may be traced through all the byways of ancient traditions and modern folklore – from Ino or Leukothea, referred to in the *Odyssey* as *Kalé* (5.346–7, 459–62), to Kalé, the leader of the Nereids, associated with the Virgin and Saint John in the healing of sheep (Politis *Paradóseis* 683), to Kalé, the daughter or sister of Alexander the Great, who drank by mistake the water of life intended for him and so leapt into the sea to become a Nereid (a story preserved in folklore and in a later manuscript of Recension B of the *Life of Alexander*, ed. Bergson 2.41, cf. Politis *Paradóseis* 651–2), and finally to Καλὴ τῶν 'Ορεῶν (Kalé of the Mountains) of Byzantine and modern tradition, transformed in Cyprus to Καλὴ τῶν 'Οβκῶν (Kalé of the Jews), mistress of magic and of evil spirits. This last may not be just a 'mistake', but a parallel survival of ancient Kallíste, who was Hekate herself as well as a nymph.[45]

Kalé, then, is an ancient figure of pagan origin who has survived in diverse forms, always magic and not infrequently evil, and hence grafted on to the concept of the wickedness of the Jews and their responsibility for the Crucifixion. Her presence in the ballads, where all the old pagan associations are implicit, is proof both of the independence and of the antiquity of their oral transmission. It only remains to explain how she came to be connected with the Virgin.

First, the Virgin's biblical associations are frequently overlaid in Greek folklore by the more familiar background of Nereids and mountain creatures. In one tradition from Alikokkos, an old suburb of Athens, she was known as *Panagía Trístratos* (Our Lady of the Crossways), like ancient Hekate, and her ghost could sometimes be seen coming out of her church to sit and weep at the crossways, as a sign that one of her parishioners was about to die (Politis *Paradóseis* 512).

Further, a recurrent theme in the folk stories and the folk songs is that of weeping maidens, mothers and Nereids. Besides Kalé and the Nereids who wept for Alexander the Great, there were the three columns of the Temple of Olympian Zeus, who disturbed the sleeping city at night by weeping for their lost sister, hacked down by a Turk in 1759 for a new mosque (*Paradóseis* 135); there were the five marble Daughters of the Fortress, as the Karyatids of the Erechtheion were known, who wept so bitterly for their sister snatched away by 'my Lord' that they frightened away the Turk, who returned at night to steal them as well (*ibid.* 136); finally, there was the old woman in a lonely house who, when awakened at midnight by the Nereids as they brought in a dead man and began a ritual lament for him, did not hesitate to join their lamentation, and was rewarded in the morning by finding the table where the dead man was laid out covered in silver (*ibid.* 803). These, and many similar stories, prove that until the last century there survived in Greek folklore a rich and creative use of an old theme.[46] They also help to explain why the figure of the weeping Virgin made such a deep and lasting impression in Greek tradition.

Besides Mary weeping for Christ, there is the tradition of a lament for Isaac, spoken by Abraham or Sarah before the sacrifice, which can be traced back to the homilies of the Church fathers and to Romanos.[47] The seventeenth-century Cretan play, *The Sacrifice of Abraham*, differs from its Italian model, Groto's *Lo Isach*, in its treatment of Sarah, whose many laments for Isaac are at times so close to folk poetry that many formulae, themes and couplets can be paralleled in the Cretan laments today.[48] To argue which came first, the drama or the folk laments, is to miss the essential point of close reciprocity between literary and folk poetry, which has determined also the development of the Virgin's lament. The immediacy of the Virgin's lament to the mourner of today is illustrated by a fine couplet from Nisyros, in which a bereaved mother begs the Virgin to give her fortitude:

Δός μου καὶ μέναν, Παναγιά, (ν)ἀφ' τὴν ὑπομονή σου,
ὁποὺ τὴν ἔκαμες καὶ σὺ (ν)εἰς τὸ Μονογενῆ σου.   Baud-Bovy 2.165

Grant to me, our Lady, of the endurance
which you showed for your only son.

Finally, the antiquity of the Virgin's lament is confirmed by some of the details of the ritual of which it is still an integral part. On the morning of Good Friday, women and girls gather in the church to decorate the Epitáphios, in which is laid a gold-embroidered likeness of the dead Christ. They weave garlands of spring flowers – violets, lilies, roses and lemon blossom – singing the Virgin's lament. All day long the villagers come to the church to kneel beside the Epitáphios; and when evening falls, it is taken in slow procession around the streets by the people, each carrying a lighted candle, to the accompaniment of the tolling of the bells. During the procession, women place outside the windows of their homes icons, lighted candles; and in Thrace, shallow dishes of quick-growing seeds are prepared, not unlike the 'gardens of Adonis' placed round the *eídolon* of Adonis in antiquity.[49] The lamentation and vigil over the Epitáphios are kept up until midnight on Holy Saturday, the lament being sung usually by women, but in Thrace performed antiphonally by twelve girls on one side and twelve boys on the other. The Resurrection on the third day is welcomed in the church with joyful shouts of 'Christ is risen!' and with a sudden blaze of light, as the candles of the congregation are lighted one by one.

Details of the ritual which can be paralleled in antiquity include the prominence of the women, who decorate and then lament over an image, the use of spring flowers and quick-growing seeds, the torchlight procession, and the final scene of joy and light on the third day. To the peasant, the Resurrection still signals the liberation of both dead and living from their miseries and the return of spring – and it is sometimes believed to ensure the safety of the year's crops.[50]

Leidinos and Zafeiris

The association with nature in the Virgin's lament for Christ is implicit in much of the poetic imagery and in some of the details of the Easter ritual. But in the seasonal festivals ritually enacted in many parts of Greece for the death and return of a youth, it is both explicit and important. The name of the youth, the time of year of the celebration, and the details of the lament and ritual, vary considerably; but in all, the function of the ritual is similar.

In the village of Chalasméni in Aigina, on 14 September (the Feast of the Cross), an image of a young man called Leidinos is made out of cloth, straw and chaff. It is laid out and decorated with flowers, among which the most prominent is the Leidinos-flower, said to have first flowered on the grave of the dead Leidinos. It is then mourned and taken round the village streets in solemn procession, and laid down in the market-place. 'Incense', in the form of animal dung, is burnt over it, and *kóllyva* are handed round to all present as for the dead. The ritual used to be exclusive to the women; now it is prepared by the women and enacted by the children.[51]

Leidinos is a personified, dialect form of *deilinós*, which means *supper*. According to one local tradition, he was the youngest of three sons born to Hunger – Kolatsó (Snack), Yéma (Lunch) and Leidinós (Supper). When he was only three days old he was so puny that the Fates condemned him to live and support mankind for only half the year, the working half, and for the remaining half to hibernate underground. His festival coincides exactly with the end of the summer season, when labour contracts expire, and with them the summer habits of an afternoon rest and an evening meal, both known in Aigina as *leidinós*.[52]

Whether this neat, aetiological explanation is in fact the oldest one is to be doubted when we consider the words of the lament sung for him:

> Λειδινέ μου, Λειδινέ μου,
> τσαὶ κλησαρωμένε μου,
> ὅπου σὲ κλησαρώσανε μὲ τὴ ψηλὴ κλησάρα
> τσαὶ ὅπου σὲ περνούσανε ἀφ' τὴν ἁγιὰ Βαρβάρα.
> Λειδινέ μου, Λειδινέ μου.

Φεύγεις, πάεις, Λειδινέ μου,
τσ' ἐμᾶς ἀφήνεις κρύους,
πεινασμένους, διψασμένους
τσ' ὄχι λίγο μαραμένους.
Λειδινέ μου, Λειδινέ μου.

Πάλι θἄρθης, Λειδινέ μου,
μὲ τοῦ Μάρτη τὶς δροσές,
μὲ τ' 'Απρίλη τὰ λουλούδια
τσαὶ τοῦ Μάη τὶς δουλειές.
Λειδινέ μου, Λειδινέ μου.

'Ηρθ' ἡ ὥρα νὰ μᾶς φύγης,
πάαινε εἰς τὸ καλό,
τσαὶ μὲ τὸ καλὸ νὰ ἔρθης
τσ' ὅλους νὰ μᾶς βρῆς γερούς.
Λειδινέ μου, Λειδινέ μου
τσαὶ κλησαρωμένε μου.   Kyriakidis *EL* 36–7

My Leidinos, my Leidinos,
you who have been well sifted,
sifted by the finest sieve,
you who have been taken round by Saint Barbara,
My Leidinos, my Leidinos.

You are going, you are leaving, my Leidinos,
and you leave us cold,
hungry, thirsty,
and not a little shrivelled.
My Leidinos, my Leidinos.

You will return, my Leidinos,
with the dews of March,
with the flowers of April,
and with the labours of May.
My Leidinos, my Leidinos.

The time has come for you to leave us,
go with our blessing,
and may you return again
to find us in good health.
My Leidinos, my Leidinos,
you who have been well sifted.

Leidinos is here revealed as the spirit of vegetation, who withers and dies at the approach of winter and is invoked in the refrain to return in the spring. The tradition referred to above shows the same tendency to personify and rationalise the event as was apparent in the ancient cults. And whatever his origins, as he is now celebrated in Aigina he is in the process of merging with the Christian festival of the Cross. In other parts of Greece the lamented figure has disappeared, but the ritual has survived in the custom of sowing seeds in the ground on the Feast of the Cross, in order to ensure the return of spring and fertility.[53]

A festival from the village of Zagori in Epiros celebrates Zafeiris, who symbolises the death and return of spring. In early May, the women and children go to the fields. One of the boys lies down on the grass as if dead, while the girls strew him with flowers and mourn him with an ecstatic lament, known not as *moirológi*, but as *kommós*. Its passionate, lyrical character contrasts sharply with the sceptic tone of the song for Leidinos:

Γιὰ ἰδέστε νιὸν ποὺ ξάπλωσα
– φίδια ποὺ μ' ἔφαγαν –
γιὰ ἰδέστε κυπαρίσσι,
– ἰώ, ἵ!
	See the young man I have laid
	    out
	  – snakes that have eaten me –
	see the cypress tree,
	– ió, í!

δὲ σειέται, δὲ λυΐζεται
– κόσμε μ', σκοτῶστε με –
δὲ σέρν' τὴ λεβεντιὰ του.
– ἰώ, ἵ!
	he does not move, he does not
	    sway,
	  – kill me, my people –
	he does not step forth with
	    gallant youth.
	– ió, í!

Ποιὸς σὄκοψε τὶς ρίζες σου
– ἄχου, ψυχούλα μου –
καὶ στέγνωσ' ἡ κορφή σου;
– ἰώ, ἵ!
	Who has cut your roots
	  – áchou, my soul –
	and dried your topmost
	    branches?
	– ió, í!

Τί μὄκανες, λεβέντη μου,
– φίδια ποὺ μ' ἔφαγαν –
τί μὄκανες, ψυχή μου!
– ἰώ, ἵ!
	What have you done to me, my
	    brave one,
	  – snakes that have eaten me –
	what have you done, my soul!
	– ió, í!

Μήνα 'ναι καὶ χινόπωρος
– ἀλήθεια λέω 'γώ –
μήνα 'ναι καὶ χειμώνας;
– ἰώ, ἴ!

Τώρα ν ἔρθεν ἡ ἄνοιξη
– ἄχου, παιδάκι μου –
ν ἔρθεν τὸ καλοκαίρι,
– ἰώ, ἴ!

παίρνουν κι ἀνθίζουν τὰ κλαδιὰ
– κούσε, παιδάκι μου –
κι οἱ κάμποι λουλουδίζουν,
– ἰώ, ἴ!

ἔρθαν πουλιὰ τῆς ἄνοιξης
– ἄχου μούρ μάτια μου –
ἔρθαν τὰ χελιδόνια,
– ἰώ, ἴ!

γιὰ κι ἡ Μεγάλη Πασκαλιὰ
– φίδια ποὺ μ' ἔφαγαν –
μὲ τὸ Χριστὸν ἀνέστη,
– ἰώ, ἴ!

ποὺ ντυοῦνται νιοὶ στὰ κόκκινα
– ἄχου, λεβέντη μου –
γερόντοι στὰ μουρέλια,
– ἰώ, ἴ!

κι ἐσύ, μωρὲ λεβέντη μου,
– ἄχου, λεβέντη μου –
μέσα στὴ γῆ τὴ μαύρη,
– ἰώ, ἴ!

ποῦ νὰ σειστῆς, νὰ λυϊστῆς
– φίδια ποὺ μ' ἔφαγαν –
νὰ σύρς τὴ λεβεντιά σου;
– ἰώ, ἴ!

Ξεσφάλισε τὰ μάτια σου!

Do you think it is autumn
– it is the truth I am telling –
do you think it is winter?
– ió, í!

Now the spring has come
– áchou, my child –
now the summer has come,
– ió, í!

the branches are bursting into
   flower
– listen, my child –
and the plains are blossoming,
– ió, í!

the birds of spring have come
– áchou, my eyes –
the swallows have come,
– ió, í!

see, Eastertide is here
– snakes that have eaten me –
and Christ is risen,
– ió, í!

when young men dress in red
– áchou, my brave one –
and old men in dark colours
– ió, í!

while you, my brave one
– áchou, my brave one –
in the black earth,
– ió, í!

how can you move, how can you
   sway
– snakes that have eaten me –
how can you step forth with
   gallant youth?
– ió, í!

Unseal your eyes!
Kyriakidis *EL* 37–8

Then everyone shouts 'Arise, Zafeiris, arise!', Zafeiris gets up and all run to the fields, singing. According to information recently collected, until the last war the ritual of Zafeiris was celebrated on four successive Sundays in May, not with a child impersonating the dead spirit, but with a wooden image of Zafeiris made in the shape of a cross, which was taken into the church for a liturgy to be sung for it. It was then taken to the fields and dressed with pieces of cloth to resemble a young man, and afterwards returned to the church until the next Sunday. When the ritual was over and Zafeiris had truly risen, the image was destroyed and the wood thrown away.[54] These details, and the explicit injunction in the *kommós* that as now Christ has risen, and the swallow has returned, so must Zafeiris, illustrate how hard it still is in Greece to draw the line between Christian and pagan belief.

Leidinos and Zafeiris are just two examples, out of several which have survived, of seasonal cults for the death and return of a spirit of nature. They show how alongside the Virgin's lament there has persisted the same kind of cyclical, seasonal ritual as in antiquity, preserving in the case of Leidinos a similar mythical treatment, and in the case of Zafeiris a similar poetic use of invocation and nature imagery.

5

The historical lament for the fall or destruction of cities

Laments for cities are inspired initially by historical events. They do not belong essentially to the same group of ritual, functional songs as the laments for the dead or for gods which have been discussed so far. It would therefore be outside the scope of the present book to make an exhaustive study of all the available material, especially of the numerous literary *thrênoi* written in the vernacular language during the two centuries following the fall of Constantinople in 1453, and of the vast wealth of folk songs lamenting historical events which have been recorded from many parts of Greece since the last century. Nor can I attempt to discuss in detail the diverse and complex problems which they raise, such as the historical accuracy of the modern folk songs referring to events as distant as the fall of Constantinople. What I hope to do in this chapter is to indicate that there has been an unbroken tradition of such historical laments in Greek, both learned and vernacular; and also to demonstrate something of their poetic technique and their significance and relevance within the tradition of lamentation as a whole.

The ancient lament for cities

In Aeschylus' *Persians*, the news of the defeat of the Persian army is brought by the Messenger during the first episode. Four lines of lamentation spell out the extent of the disaster:

ὦ γῆς ἁπάσης Ἀσιάδος πολίσματα,
ὦ Περσὶς αἶα καὶ πολὺς πλούτου λιμήν,
ὡς ἐν μιᾷ πληγῇ κατέφθαρται πολὺς
ὄλβος, τὸ Περσῶν δ' ἄνθος οἴχεται πεσόν.   A. *Pers.* 249–52

O cities of the entire Asian land,
O Persian earth, and great haven of wealth,
how in one stroke is your great happiness
shattered, the flower of the Persians fallen and perished!

There follows a *kommós* in which the lyrical lament of the chorus is interrupted by the Messenger's bald statement of facts in two lines of iambic trimeter (268–73). The theme is taken up in lyrical form in the first stasimon (532–97), in narrative form by the spirit of Dareios (759–86), by the chorus again (852–906), until the climax is reached in the closing *kommós*, where the chorus' persistent questions about the fate of Persia's heroes are answered by Xerxes (955–77). At the end of the play Persia's glory is mourned as gone for ever – a fact which is emphasised by the recurrent use of the perfect tense:

Ξε. βεβᾶσι γὰρ τοίπερ ἀγρέται στρατοῦ.
Χο. βεβᾶσιν, οἵ, νώνυμοι.   1002–3

Xe.: Gone, then, are the army's leaders. *Cho.*: Gone, alas, unnamed!

Ξε. πεπλήγμεθ' οἵᾳ δι' αἰῶνος τύχᾳ·
Χο. πεπλήγμεθ'· εὔδηλα γάρ.   1008–9

Xe.: We are stricken with misfortune through the ages.
Cho.: We are stricken – it is too clear.

The chorus in Euripides' *Trojan Women* invoke the Muse to sing 'a funeral song of new hymns' for the fall of Troy (511–14). Later, Andromache and Hekabe weep together for their city's destruction, reiterating the perfect tense as did the chorus at the end of the Persians, βέβακ' ὄλβος, βέβακε Τροία (happiness has gone, Troy has gone!).[1]

Did this type of lament have any basis outside tragedy? Euripides wrote an *epikédeion* for the defeat of the Athenians at Syracuse, and another is said to have been written for the loss of some Spartans.[2] An anonymous tragic fragment lamenting the fall of Persia, and probably written not long after the event, contains the same formulaic structure of repeated questions with *where?*, and answered by the statement of the last line, as was used in Aeschylus' *Persians*:[3]

Ποῦ γὰρ τὰ σεμνὰ κεῖνα; ποῦ δὲ Λυδίας
μέγας δυνάστης Κροῖσος ἢ Ξέρξης βαθὺν
ζεύξας θαλάσσης αὐχέν' Ἑλλησποντίας;
ἅπαντ' ἐς Ἅιδην ἦλθε καὶ Λήθης δόμους.   Nauck 909.372

Where are those majestic things? Where is Kroisos,
great lord of Lydia, or Xerxes, who yoked
the deep neck of the sea of Hellespont?
All are gone to Hades and to Lethe's halls.

This structure appears to have been traditional to the lament for cities.
It occurs again in an epigram by Antipater of Sidon (second century
B.C.) for the sack of Corinth by L. Mummius in 146 B.C.:[4]

Ποῦ τὸ περίβλεπτον κάλλος σέο, Δωρὶ Κόρινθε;
   ποῦ στεφάναι πύργων, ποῦ τὰ πάλαι κτέανα;
ποῦ νηοὶ μακάρων; ποῦ δώματα; ποῦ δὲ δάμαρτες
   Σισύφιαι λαῶν θ' αἵ ποτε μυριάδες;
οὐδὲ γὰρ οὐδ' ἴχνος, πολυκάμμορε, σεῖο λέλειπται,
   πάντα δὲ συμμάρψας ἐξέφαγεν πόλεμος.   *AP* 9.151

Where is your much-admired beauty, Dorian Corinth?
   where is your crown of towers, where are your possessions
   of old?
where are the temples of the immortals, the houses, the wives
   of Sisyphian Corinth, and the myriads of people?
Not even a trace has been left of you, ill-fated town,
   but all has been seized and devoured by war.

By the end of antiquity, the historical lament was familiar also in
prose, in the form of the rhetorical *monodía*. When Smyrna was destroyed
by an earthquake early in the second century A.D., Aelian Aristeides
wrote a famous monody, said to have moved even the Emperor to tears.
Among its stylistic features may be noted once more the same structure
of question and answer with *where?* as in the verse laments.[5] The ancient
evidence is, unfortunately, unsubstantial and fragmentary in character.
Nevertheless, the fact that this type of lament is known to have existed
in several different literary forms, with some degree of similarity in
formulaic structure, suggests that it may have had some kind of common
basis.

Byzantine tradition and the laments for the fall of Constantinople

Historical events during the Byzantine period ensured the survival and
extension of the tradition of laments for cities. The histories and chronicles
tell of one disaster after another, many explicitly said to have been
lamented. According to Malalas (sixth century), when Antioch was

destroyed by the sixth successive disaster in A.D. 443, it was lamented everywhere, as was the final catastrophe which struck the city in 526. No details of these laments are given, but the disasters are usually attributed to man's sinfulness in the form of lingering pagan influences, curable only by the public display of holy relics.[6] This sombre, moralising tone probably derived in part from Hebrew models, such as the Book of Job and Lamentations. Together with the continued tradition of rhetorical monodies, it tended to establish a formalistic pattern, so that certain learned *topoi* were incorporated into accounts of disasters whether they purported to be eye-witness accounts or not.[7]

With the gradual collapse of the Byzantine Empire, cities were threatened and lost with increasing frequency. According to the historian Niketas Choniates (*c.* 1150–*c.* 1210), the defeat of the Byzantine army by the Bulgarians in 1189 caused widespread lamentation in the cities and countryside alike.[8] The same author wrote an elaborate and rhetorical lament for the sack of Constantinople by the Franks during the Fourth Crusade of 1204, in which he draws freely on the Book of Jeremiah and the Psalms.[9] The same year saw the conquest of Athens by the Franks, which forced Michael Choniates, brother of Niketas and Metropolitan of the city, to flee. Among his extant works is an archaising, rather florid poem lamenting the fall to the barbarians of a city so ancient and glorious.[10] The siege and sack of Thessaloniki in 1430 are described in detail by the contemporary historian John Anagnostes, who uses many of the accepted clichés and *topoi*; these events are also lamented in contemporary verse.[11]

But perhaps for no other single event in history were so many laments composed in Greek as for the fall of Constantinople in 1453. Among the literary texts relating to the fall published by Lambros in 1908, six are monodies. Even here, where a predominantly rhetorical style and archaising influence might be expected, a considerable variety is apparent. The author of one is the scholar and philosopher Andronikos Kallistos, who later taught at Bologna and Rome. In style, his monody is learned and rhetorical, its ideas and imagery more dependent upon classical sources than on Hebrew and Christian models. It is the tragic loss of the Greek cultural heritage, and not the defeat of Christianity by Islam or the moral responsibility of the people, which he emphasises and mourns, in classical style: Ὦ Ῥώμη νέα, . . . ποῦ σου νῦν τὰ καλά; (O new Rome, where now are your fine things?).[12] The other prose monodies draw more on biblical tradition: one, written by a *nomophýlax*, is modelled on the Book of Job and Lamentations; another, which is anonymous, opens with a quotation from the Psalms lamenting Jerusalem, but continues to relate the last hours of the Emperor in thoroughly popular style and vernacular language, not unlike the modern *paradóseis* in tone and manner.[13]

Even among the prose laments, then, there is evidence of a diversity of influences. The same is true of the *thrênoi* written in verse, which may be divided according to language and style into two main groups: those written in archaising, even pseudo-Homeric verse, and those written in some form of the vernacular and in *politikòs stíchos*.[14] The former are exclusively and overtly classical in tone, but among the latter there is once more a wide range of religious and popular influences at work. Their authors are sometimes known to have been monks, of no great learning, but most are anonymous.

The chief problem connected with the vernacular *thrênoi* is that of their composition and sources. In the absence of any reliable external evidence for authorship and dates, some scholars have attempted to argue the derivation of one poem from another by comparing the language, content and style.[15] Discussion has centred in particular on the Ἅλωσις τῆς Κωνσταντινουπόλεως (*Capture of Constantinople*), a poem of 2,000 lines once wrongly attributed to Emmanuel Georgillas of Rhodes, and on the shorter Ἀνακάλημα τῆς Κωνσταντινόπολης (*Lament for Constantinople*), generally assumed Cretan until Kriaras put forward his case for its Cypriot authorship. The problem lies in the lack of firm criteria for establishing these hypotheses: the language of these poems, which might have been a useful indicator, is a standardised form of the vernacular with a number of archaisms but without sufficient use of dialect words to prove beyond doubt their provenance from either Cyprus or Crete.[16] More crucial perhaps is the question of the interdependence of the two poems. Eight passages have been claimed to occur in similar form in both the *Álosis* and the *Anakálema*, which, taken separately, might each be described as traditional phrases, but taken together have been argued to point to the knowledge, at least, of the one poem by the author of the other. If the *Álosis* was written not long after May 1453, as is generally supposed, then the author of the *Anakálema* could have known and used it. Another possibility has been suggested: that both poems are based on a third 'archetypal' lament which has not survived.[17]

None of these theories can be proved or disproved. But all rest on the by no means certain assumption that the authors were working from a number of widely distributed literary texts. In fact, it can be demonstrated that of the eight parallel passages, one is not a true parallel, while the rest are made up of whole-line or half-line formulaic expressions and stock epithets which would have been part of the repertoire of every popular poet of the time, and therefore invalid proof of inter-dependence.[18]

What, then, is the relationship between these vernacular verse laments? On the one hand the general uncertainty of authorship and dates suggests a degree of anonymity and perhaps a period of oral transmission before they were written down; and this is supported by the common fund of motifs and stylistic features. On the other hand, none of them is, in the strictest sense of the term, a folk poem. In the case of the *Álosis*, the author chooses to remain anonymous, but gives clear proof of his individuality by referring to two moles on his hands, and also by his aspiration to touch the hearts and so alter the minds of the politicians of east and west.[19] The author of the *Anakálema* on the contrary is concerned fundamentally neither with morals nor with politics, but with the presentation of events in the most dramatic manner. It is possible to divide these vernacular *thrênoi*, as Knös has done, into two kinds: those which are generally close to folk tradition, and those which show influences of a more literary kind. The former, he argues, are lively, dramatic and short, with traces of popular legend, and tragic rather than moralising in tone. The latter are more diffuse and didactic, emphasising, with fatalistic acceptance, that man has been punished for his sinfulness, and having more in common with the religious alphabets on the sinfulness of man than with genuine folk tradition.[20]

Such a distinction should not be too sharply drawn, however. The *Anakálema*, perhaps the liveliest of the surviving poems of its type, opens and closes with the usual tag, couched in uncompromisingly archaising language:

Θρῆνος, κλαυμὸς καὶ ὀδυρμὸς καὶ στεναγμὸς καὶ λύπη,
θλῖψις ἀπαραμύθητος ἔπεσεν τοῖς Ρωμαίοις.   *Anakálema* 1–2

Lamentation, weeping and wailing, tears and grief,
inconsolable sorrow has befallen the Romaioi.

Nor is the *Álosis* consistently learned. Demotic words and formulaic expressions common in folk poetry frequently break through, giving the classical allusions a lively and popular colour.[21] In the following passage, Aphrodite weeps for the slaughter of the Christians:

Ἄρης ἐπερνοδιάβαινε τὴν Τρίτην βουρκωμένος
ἀπὸ τὸν ἅγιον Ρωμανόν, ὅλως αἱματωμένος,

στὸ αἷμα τῶν Χριστιανῶν αἱματοκυλισμένος.
Ἡ Ἀφροδίτης ἔστεκε τὰ δάκρυα γεμισμένη,
νὰ κλαίη νέους εὔμορφους, κοράσια ὡραιωμένα.
Καὶ ὁ Ἑρμῆς τάχα θρηνῶν, παρηγορῶν ἐκείνην:
– τί ἔχεις, Ἀφροδίτη μου, καὶ εἶσαι χολιασμένη;
Καὶ ἡ Σελήνη ἀπὸ μακρεὰ στέκει καὶ οὐδὲν σιμώνει,
καὶ βλέπει καὶ θαυμάζεται, καὶ τρέμει ἀφ' τὸν φόβον·
καὶ τὰ στοιχεῖα τ' οὐρανοῦ κλαίουν, θρηνοῦν τὴν Πόλιν.

Álosis 420–9

Ares came along with glowering looks on Tuesday
by the Church of St Romanos, all covered in blood,
bathed in the blood of Christians.
Aphrodite stood, her eyes filled with tears,
weeping for the fine young men, for the beautiful girls.
And Hermes, as if lamenting and comforting her, said:
– What is it, my Aphrodite, why are you sulking?
And the Moon keeps her distance and does not come near,
she sees and marvels, and she trembles from fear.
And the elements of Heaven weep and mourn for the City.

Similarly, the Θρῆνος τῶν Τεσσάρων Πατριαρχείων (*Thrênos of the Four Patriarchates*), which takes the form of an imagined discussion between Constantinople, Jerusalem, Alexandria and Antioch, draws on the literary tradition of the past for much of the content, but on popular poetry for its language and style.[22]

The reason for the apparent 'confusion' lies both in the general characteristics of vernacular poetry in the fifteenth century, and in the specific factors which contributed to the evolution and composition of these *thrênoi*. While a modified form of the vernacular was an accepted medium for verse of this type, the use of dialect was still only incidental, not yet part of a conscious attempt to create a new and consistent poetic language such as begins later in Cyprus and finds its culmination in Crete. Hence any poet, whatever inspiration he drew from folk songs which were familiar to him, would modify to a greater or lesser extent. This explains the mixture of archaisms and demoticisms which is found in all our texts. Further, as we have seen, laments on other historical themes in learned prose as well as in popular poetry were already part of a well-established tradition by the time of the fall.[23] Some ideas, such as the tendency to view adversity as punishment from God for man's own iniquity, run through all the laments of this type, learned and popular alike. Finally, with the disruption of established cultural patterns subsequent to the fall, poets were in a favourable position to exploit and be influenced by popular tradition to a hitherto unprecedented extent. This would explain why many well-defined features of folk style, such as swiftly-interchanging dialogue, catechistic questions and incremental repetition, make their sustained appearance for the first time at this period.[24] But it is not until over a hundred years later, when Cyprus was lamented after its fall to the Turks in 1570, that we find more concrete evidence of the writing-down of oral laments in the form of an appeal from the poet of the *Thrênos* himself:[25]

Ὅστις ἠξεύρει γράμματα καὶ γράφει μὲ κονδύλιν,
κοντά μ' ἂς ἔλθη νὰ σταθῆ γιὰ νὰ τοῦ παραγγείλω
νὰ γράψη μοιρολογικὰ ὅλοι νὰ λυπηθῆτε.   595–7

Whoever knows letters and can write with a pen,
let him come and stand by me, and I will recite
for him to write laments, so that you will all grieve.

Modern historical laments

During the two hundred and sixteen years between the fall of Constantinople in 1453 and the fall of Crete in 1669, the historical lament continued to flourish and expand. Laments have survived not only for important historical events, such as the fall of Athens (1456), the siege of Malta (1565), the fall of Cyprus (1570), and the fall of Crete (1669),[26] but also for disasters which affected the lives of large numbers of people, such as Emmanuel Georgillas' poem Θανατικὸν τῆς Ρόδου on the plague which swept the island of Rhodes in 1498–9, and Manolis Sklavos' Συμφορὰ τῆς Κρήτης on the earthquake which shook Crete on 30 May 1508.[27] The extreme archaising style and the direct imitation of classical models had not died out; but increasingly they gave way to a richer and more consistent form of the vernacular, and to the use of rhyming couplets in *politikòs stíchos*. In addition to a greater popularisation of form, we may also detect a new awareness on the part of some of these poets of the value of the distinctive folk traditions of their people. Georgillas, for example, does not mourn the ravages of the plague only in general platitudes, but describes in detail the beauty of the village girls, with their costumes, embroideries and handicrafts, and sketches vividly the festive atmosphere of families strolling together on feast days and holidays (120–81).

Two historical works of particular interest to the present study are concerned with the Cretan Wars of 1645–69, one in 1,400 rhymed verses by Anthimos Diakrousis of Kephallonia, and the other in 12,000 rhymed verses by Marinos Tzanes Bounialis, of a noble Cretan family from Rethymnon.[28] Although they are chronicles of the war, not *thrênoi*, both poems are pervaded with the theme of lamentation, sometimes in the form of short, lyrical *thrênoi* – which, especially in Diakrousis' poem, tend to be more conventional and archaising in language and style than the rest of the work – but more frequently and more forcefully in the form of comment upon the events which both writers witnessed at first hand. The traditional idea of man's responsibility for the disaster is still there, but it is presented through a lively dialogue with God. Sometimes, Crete herself begs for mercy, asking what she has done to deserve such cruelty.[29] As the population of Rethymnon prepares to evacuate in November 1646, before the final battle, Rethymnon herself mourns, tearing her cheeks and pulling her hair:

– Στράφου, Θεέ, καὶ κοίταξε σήμερον τὰ παιδιά μου
πῶς ἔχουν νὰ μ' ἀπαρνηθοῦ ὀγιὰ τὰ κρίματά μου.
– Μὴν κλαίης, μηδὲ θρήνεσαι, μηδὲ μοιρολογᾶσαι
κι ὅλοι θὲ νὰ μισεύσουσι καὶ μὴ παραπονᾶσαι.
Ἐκτύπησε τὰ στήθια της καὶ βαρυαναστενάζει
καὶ ἄρχισεν ὅλους νὰ φιλῆ νὰ τσὶ σφικταγκαλιάζη
καὶ ὅλους νὰ τσὶ παρακαλῆ, γιὰ νὰ μὴ τὴν ἀφήσου
μ' ἂς πᾶσιν ὅλοι στὰ χωριά, ὀγιὰ νὰ κατοικήσου.

Bounialis 220.10–17

– Turn, Lord, and behold today my children,
how they have to abandon me for my sins.
– Do not weep, do not lament, do not sing dirges,
for they will all leave you, so do not complain.
She beat her breast and sighed heavily,
and began to kiss them all and to embrace them,
and to beg them all not to leave her,
but to go to the villages, that they might dwell there.

The horror of war is felt through the concrete detail of everyday life – the hunger of the women and children, the desecration of the churches and monasteries – and there are moments of real passion, as when Bounialis takes leave of his native Rethymnon after its fall:

– Πατρίδα μου, μισεύγω σου, ψυχή μου καὶ καρδιά μου,
καὶ τ' ὄνομά σου μοναχὰς θ' ἀκούεται στ' αὐτιά μου,

γιατὶ δὲν στέκω νὰ θωρῶ, πατρίδα, τὸν καημόν σου,
καὶ ποιὰ καρδιὰ νὰ μὴ ραγῆ τὸν ἀποχωρισμόν σου; *Ibid.* 229.13–16

– My home town, I am leaving you, my soul and my heart,
my ears will hear only the sound of your name,
for I cannot bear to behold, my home, your grief,
– and what heart would not break at parting from you?

At the end of Bounialis' poem, the devastation and desolation caused by
the war and by emigration of so many Christians are lamented by
Kastro (modern Iraklion) in a series of questions with *where?*[30]

῎Οφου! ποῦν' τόσος μου λαός; ποῦ τόσοι πλοῦσοι ἀνθρῶποι;
ποῦν' οἱ δασκάλοι κι οἱ σοφοί; δάρσου, καημένη Εὐρώπη!
῎Επεσαν οἱ ὀλπίδες σας στὸ μαυρισμένον ἄδη...   *Ibid.* 555.23–5

Ófou! where are all my people? where are all my rich men?
where are the teachers and men of wisdom? Beat your breast,
    wretched Europe!
All your hopes have fallen, gone to blackened Hades...

The *thrênoi* we have discussed so far are all literary compositions or
redactions, however closely they may approximate in some respects to
folk tradition. Actual folk songs lamenting historical events were first
recorded in the last century, and the tradition continues to this day.
How do they compare with the more literary laments of the past? The
songs are of two kinds, those which appear to refer to events of the
distant past, and those which belong to the more immediate past or to
the present.

It is the first group which raises the most complex problems. The
authenticity of some of these songs has been questioned, and the collectors
of the last century have sometimes been accused of 'stitching together'
versions which were never actually sung in the form in which they are
published, or even of inventing the songs altogether. But the case for
complete fabrication can rarely be proved, and there is a sufficient
number of songs of indisputable authenticity to establish beyond
reasonable doubt the memory of events as distant as the fall of Constantinople in modern oral tradition. This does not mean, of course,
that collectors have not been guilty of the kind of minor editing of
texts to which Politis admits in the introduction to his collection of
1914.[31] As to the historical accuracy of these folk laments, it can be
stated at the outset that their value to the historian is almost negligible,

since they do not document events, but reflect what has remained in popular consciousness. History is seen not as it was, but as through a prism of the intervening centuries, so that the details of one disaster become fused with another, more recent, or only a dim sense of tragedy remains, as in the *Song for Adrianople*, which refers, according to Politis, not to the capture of the city by the Russians in 1829, but to its fall to the Turks in 1362:[32]

Τ' ἀηδόνια τῆς 'Ανατολῆς καὶ τὰ πουλιὰ τῆς Δύσης
κλαίγουν ἀργά, κλαίγουν ταχιά, κλαίγουν τὸ μεσημέρι,
κλαίγουν τὴν 'Αντριανόπολη τὴν πολυκουρσεμένη,
ὁπού τήνε κουρσέψανε τὶς τρεῖς γιορτὲς τοῦ χρόνου·
τοῦ Χριστουγέννου γιὰ κηρί, καὶ τοῦ Βαγιοῦ γιὰ βάγια,
καὶ τῆς Λαμπρῆς τὴν Κυριακὴ γιὰ τὸ Χριστὸς 'Ανέστη.   Politis 1

The nightingales of the East and the birds of the West
weep late, weep early, weep at mid-day,
they weep for Adrianople, sacked so many times,
sacked upon the three festivals of the year:
at Christmas with the candle, on Palm Sunday with the palm,
and on Easter Sunday at the cry of 'Christ is risen!'

A further cause of confusion in identifying the events referred to is the recurrence of a large number of formulaic expressions and phrases in songs of differing date and theme. It has been argued, with some plausibility, that of the songs stated by Passow to refer to the fall of Constantinople, two were in fact composed for the capture of Thessaloniki by the Turks in 1430:[33]

Πῆραν τὴν πόλη, πῆραν την, πῆραν τὴ Σαλονίκη.
πῆραν καὶ τὴν ἁγιὰ Σοφιά, τὸ μέγα μοναστῆρι,
πού 'χε τριακόσια σήμαντρα κι ἑξήντα δυὸ καμπάνες·
κάθε καμπάνα καὶ παπάς, κάθε παπὰς καὶ διάκος.
Φωνὴ τοὺς ἦρτ' ἐξ οὐρανοῦ ἀγγέλων ἀπ' τὸ στόμα:
– 'Αφῆτ' αὐτὴ τὴν ψαλμωδιά, νὰ χαμηλώσουν τ' ἅγια·
καὶ στεῖλτε λόγο στὴν Φραγκιά, νὰ 'ρτουνε νὰ τὰ πιάσουν,
νὰ πάρουν τὸν χρυσὸ σταυρὸ καὶ τ' ἅγιο τὸ βαγγέλιο,
καὶ τὴν ἁγία τράπεζα, νὰ μὴ τὴν ἀμολύνουν.
Σὰν τ' ἄκουσεν ἡ δέσποινα, δακρύζουν οἱ εἰκόνες.
– Σώπασε, κυρὰ δέσποινα, μὴν κλαίγης, μὴ δακρύζης·
πάλε μὲ χρόνους, μὲ καιρούς, πάλε δικά σας εἶναι.   Passow 194

They have taken the city, taken it, they have taken Saloniki.
And they have taken Saint Sophia, the great monastery,
with its three hundred clappers and sixty-two bells,
for every bell a priest, for every priest a deacon.
A voice came to them from heaven, from the mouth of angels:
– Cease this chanting, and let them lower the sacred things,
and send word to the West to come and fetch them,
to take the golden cross and the holy Gospel,
and the sacred altar, lest it be defiled.
When our Lady heard it, the icons wept.
– Be quiet, our Lady, do not weep, do not mourn,
with the years, with time, they shall be yours again.

Apart from the specific reference to Thessaloniki, there is little to distinguish this lament from its better known counterpart for Constantinople. The note of optimism at the end of these laments, which stands in striking contrast to the fatalistic acceptance of the fifteenth-century *thrênoi*, should not in my opinion be taken as an expression of Greek expansionism, as a popular form of the 'Great Idea', but rather as an example of simple, deeply-felt faith that one day, Saint Sophia would be returned to the Christians.

A particularly good illustration of the poetic technique of these historical laments is a ballad from the Pontos preserved by Periklis Triandafyllidis in 1870.[34] Its form is lyrical, not narrative, and there is considerable confusion in the presentation of events. According to Megas, its subject is the fall of Trebizond in 1461, but there is nothing in the text to exclude the possibility that this, like other Pontic ballads of the same type, refers to the fall of Constantinople.[35] The last six lines are obscure and confused, and may have been incorporated from another ballad; this in no way diminishes the interest of the song, rather it indicates that transmission over a long period of time is dependent upon such a process of accretion, in which themes from one ballad are fused unconsciously with those of another. What is important is not the sequence of events, but the sense of tragedy imparted by the sympathetic reaction of nature, and the tension of the dialogue, which is maintained not, as in the literary *thrênoi*, by sententious appeals, but by the concentrated ellipse of every superfluous fact:

’Ακεῖ ’ς σὸ πέραν τὸ λιβάδ’ μέγαν φωνὴν ἐξέβεν·
‘‘Σκοτῶθαν οἱ δράκ’ ″Ελλενοι καὶ μύριοι μυριάδες.’’
Οἱ μαῦροι ἐχλιμίτιзαν ’ς σὰ γαίματα βραχμένοι.

"Ποῦ πᾶς; ποῦ πᾶς; ἀιλὶ ποῦ πᾶς; ποῦ φέρεις καὶ τοὺς μαύρους; "
– Ἀιλὶ ἐμᾶς καὶ βάι ἐμᾶς, ᾽πάρθεν ἡ ἀφεντία!

– Ντ᾽ ἐποίκαμέ σε, νὲ Θεέ, ᾽ς σὰ γαίματα βραχμένοι;

Ντὸ ἔπαθες, τρυγόνα μου, ᾽κι πίν᾽ς ἆς τὸ νερόν μας;
– Ἐγὼ φαγὶν πᾶς κ᾽ ἔφαγα, νὰ πίν᾽ ἆς τὸ νερόν σας;
Ἐμὲν κορώνα ᾽κ εἶπανε νὰ πίνω νερὸν κ᾽ αἷμαν,
ἐμὲν κορώνα ᾽κ εἶπανε νὰ τρώγω στούδ᾽ καὶ κρέας.
Ἐμὲν τρυγόνα λέγ᾽νε με στὰ ᾽ψηλὰ τὰ κλαδόπα·
τὰ γαίματα μ᾽ ἐτύφλωσαν τῶν δράκων τῶν Ἑλλένων.

Κάτ᾽ ᾽κι τερεῖς τὸν ποταμὸν πῶς πάγνε τὰ κιφάλια;
ἐκεῖ κιφάλια μοναχά, ὠτία καὶ μυτία.
– Γιὰ δεῖξ᾽τε με καὶ τὸ σπαθίν, ντ᾽ ἐντῶκεν καὶ τὸν γιοῦκα μ᾽.
– Μέρος πάγει ὁ ποταμὸς καὶ μέρος τὸ σπαθίν ἀτ᾽.
Οἱ Τοῦρκ᾽ ἄτον ἐκύκλωσαν ἀφκὰ στὴν φτεριδέαν.
Χίλιους ἐκόψεν τὸ πουρνόν, μύριους τὸ μεσημέριν·
κ᾽ ἡ μάννα τ᾽ ἡ χιλιάκλερος στὰ δάκρυα εἶν᾽ βαμμένη.
– " Ἀιλὶ ἐμᾶς καὶ βάι ἐμᾶς, ἐλλάεν ἀφεντία! "

Laog (1957) 379–80

There in yonder meadow a great voice was heard:
'The brave Greeks are slain, in tens upon tens of thousands!'
The horses whinnied, soaked in blood.
'Where are you going? Where, alas? Where are you taking
  the horses?'
– Alas for us! Woe upon us! The empire has been taken!

– What have we done to you, Lord, that we are bathed in blood?

What is the matter, turtle-dove, that you do not drink our water?
– Do you think I have eaten food, that I should drink your
  water?
I am no crow that I should drink water and blood,
I am no crow that I should eat bones and flesh.
I am called the turtle-dove and I dwell in lofty branches,
and the blood of the brave Greeks has blinded me.

Why can't you see how the river carries along the heads?
Only the heads are there, and ears and noses.
– Show me the spear that struck my child.
– On the one side flows the river, on the other side is his spear.
The Turks ringed him round down where the ferns are
  growing.

He slew thousands in the morning, at mid-day tens of
    thousands,
and his mother, forlorn, is bathed in tears.
– 'Alas for us! Woe upon us! The empire has changed!'

To turn now to the folk songs which refer to events of the more
immediate past, some indication of their popularity is afforded by the
number and variety of those collected from Epiros alone between 1786
and 1881.[36] Almost every year, there was something to lament: sometimes
an intensive campaign, fought and lost, as in Souli from 1792 to 1803,
and sometimes a particularly traitorous agreement, such as the sale of
Parga by the British to the Turks in 1817–19. The ballad, already
discussed in chapter 3, makes it clear that it was not so much the loss of
Parga which aroused popular indignation, as the means by which it
had been accomplished – the people had not been defeated in battle, nor
had the city been razed by fire, but they had been sold like cattle and
driven from their homes (Giankas 44.5–8). The universal, collective
character of their lamentation is also emphasised:

Τραβοῦν γυναῖκες τὰ μαλλιά, δέρνουν τ' ἄσπρα τους στήθια,
μοιρολογοῦν οἱ γέροντες μὲ μαῦρα μοιρολόγια,
παπάδες μὲ τὰ δάκρυα γδύνουν τὶς ἐκκλησιές τους.

Giankas 44.10–12

Women pull their hair and beat their white breasts,
and old men lament with black dirges.
Priests strip their churches with tears in their eyes.

Similarly, the treaty of Berlin signed in 1881 by 'eight royal powers'
was regarded by the people of Epiros as a betrayal, because it separated
Epiros north of Arta from the rest of Greece and kept it in subjugation
to the Turks. The note of anger is sustained by the formulaic reiteration
of the past tense at the same point of a line or half-line:

Σ' ὅλον τὸν κόσμο ξαστεριά, σ' ὅλον τὸν κόσμον ἥλιος
καὶ στὰ καημένα Γιάννενα μαῦρο, παχὺ σκοτάδι·
τὶ φέτο ἐκάμαν τὴ βουλὴ ὀχτὼ βασίλεια ἀνθρῶποι
κι ἐβάλανε τὰ σύνορα στῆς Ἄρτας τὸ ποτάμι.
Κι ἀφήκανε τὰ Γιάννενα καὶ πῆρανε τὴν Πούντα,
κι ἀφήκανε τὰ Γιάννενα καὶ πῆρανε τὴν Ἄρτα,
κι ἀφήκανε τὸ Μέτσοβο μὲ τὰ χωριά του γύρα.

Ibid. 66

Clear skies and sun are upon the whole world,
and in wretched Iannina there is darkness, black and thick.
For eight royal powers have held council this year,
and they set the frontiers at the river of Arta.
They have left Iannina and taken Pounta,
they have left Iannina and taken Arta,
and they have left Metsovo with its villages around.

Like the folk songs for the fall of Constantinople, many of these ballads open with the theme of weeping birds – nightingales, swallows and cuckoos – which, as sole survivors of the disaster, bring the news to others and are called upon to join in the general lamentation:[37]

Μαῦρο πουλὶν ἐκάθονταν στοῦ Μπερατιοῦ τὸ κάστρο
μοιρολογοῦσε θλιβερὰ κι ἀνθρώπινα λαλοῦσε...   *Ibid.* 37.1–2

A black bird was sitting on the fortress of Berati,
it sang sad dirges and spoke with human voice...

Sometimes, the birds are instructed not to sing at all.[38]

'Αηδόνια, μὴ λαλήσετε, κοῦκοι νὰ βουβαθῆτε,
καὶ σεῖς, καημένη 'Αρβανιτιά, στὰ μαῦρα νὰ ντυθῆτε,
μὲ τὸ κακὸ ποὺ κάμεταν τοῦτο τὸ καλοκαίρι.   *Ibid.* 58.1–3

Nightingales, do not sing; cuckoos, be silent;
and you, wretched Albanians, dress in black,
because of the evil which was done this summer.

The formula is essentially the same as the one found in the *thrênoi* for Constantinople, and in the folk song for Adrianople;[39] and the idea may be compared with one in the ancient epigram, where only the Nereids remain to tell of the fall of Corinth, σῶν ἀχέων μίμνομεν ἀλκυόνες (we remain as halcyons of your griefs) (*AP* 9.151.8).

Other recurrent formulaic structures include the repetition of specific verbs, such as κλαῖνε (they weep) and πῆραν (they have taken) at the beginning of a line or phrase. This last device is common in all the folk laments, for more distant as well as for more recent disasters.[40] In one of the shorter laments for the fall of Souli, the news is conveyed by means of stichomythic dialogue, as in the *Anakálema*:

"Ενα πουλάκι ξέβγαινε ἀπὸ τὸ κακοσούλι.
Παργιῶτες τὸ ρωτήσανε, Παργιῶτες τὸ ρωτοῦνε:
– Πουλάκι, ποῦθεν ἔρχεσαι; πουλί μου, ποῦ πηγαίνεις;
– 'Απὸ τὸ Σοῦλι ἔρχομαι, καὶ στὴν Φραγκιὰν πηγαίνω.

– Πουλάκι, πές μας τίποτε, κάνα καλὸ μαντάτο;
– ῍Αχ, τί μαντάτα νὰ σᾶς πῶ; τί νὰ σᾶς μολογήσω;
Πῆραν τὸ Σοῦλι, πήρανε, κι αὐτὸν τὸν ᾽Αβαρίκον,
πῆραν τὴν Κιάφαν τὴν κακήν, ἐπῆραν καὶ τὸ Κούγκι,
κι ἔκαψαν τὸν καλόγερον μὲ τέσσερες νομάτους.   Giankas 32

A bird was coming out from wretched Souli.
Men from Parga asked it, men from Parga ask it:
– Bird, where do you come from? My bird, where are you
        going?
– I come from Souli, and I am going to the West.
– Bird, tell us something, some good tidings!
– Ach, what tidings can I bring you? What can I tell you?
They have taken Souli, they have taken it, and Avarikos as well,
they have taken wretched Kiafa, they have taken Koungi too,
and they have burnt the monk together with four men.

Καράβιν ἐκατέβαινε στὰ μέρη τῆς Τενέδου
καὶ κάτεργον τὸ ὑπάντησε, στέκει κι ἀναρωτᾶ το:
– Καράβιν, πόθεν ἔρκεσαι καὶ πόθεν κατεβαίνεις;
– ῍Ερκομαι ἀκ τ᾽ ἀνάθεμα κι ἐκ τὸ βαρὺν τὸ σκότος,
ἀκ τὴν ἀστραποχάλαζην, ἀκ τὴν ἀνεμοζάλην·
ἀπὲ τὴν Πόλην ἔρχομαι τὴν ἀστραποκαμένην.
᾽Εγὼ γομάριν δὲ βαστῶ, ἀμμὲ μαντάτα φέρνω
κακὰ διὰ τοὺς χριστιανούς, πικρὰ καὶ δολωμένα:
Οἱ Τοῦρκοι ὅτε ἤρθασιν, ἐπήρασιν τὴν Πόλην,
ἀπώλεσαν τοὺς χριστιανοὺς ἐκεῖ καὶ πανταχόθεν.   *Anakálema* 6–15

A boat was coming down to the regions of Tenedos
and a galley met it, and it stops to ask it:
– Boat, where do you come from and where have you come
        down from?
– I come from the accursed and from the heavy darkness,
from lightning and hail, from storm and whirlwind,
I come from the City which is stricken with lightning.
I carry no cargo, but I bear tidings
evil for Christians, bitter and grievous:
When the Turks came, they took the City,
they annihilated the Christians there and everywhere!

Finally, Roumeli's lament for John Kapodistrias, the President of Greece
who was assassinated in 1831, uses the same formula in a dialogue

between a Greek and Roumeli as occurred in the dialogue between Hermes and Aphrodite in the *Alosis*:

– Τί ἔχεις, καημένη Ρούμελη, καὶ βαρυαναστενάζεις;
– Ἕλληνα, σὰν μ᾿ ἐρώτησες, θὰ σοῦ τὸ μολογήσω.   Giankas 55.2–3

– What is it, wretched Roumeli, that you groan so heavily?
– Greek, since you have asked me, I will tell you why.

This is only a limited selection of traditional formulae taken from the historical laments of one region over a period of a hundred years. A more exhaustive and extensive study would bring others to light, and demonstrate how deeply rooted such expressions are in similar songs from all parts of Greece.[41] But perhaps these examples are sufficient to indicate first, the unbroken tradition of laments for cities, both learned and popular, and second, something of their technique, thanks to which the same ideas, formulaic structures and phrases are re-used and adapted to suit the occasion, so that in the event of sudden calamity, the popular poet has to hand a ready-made stock of material. Further, that these historical laments grew up by a gradual process of accretion and refinement dependent upon a long period of oral transmission, is confirmed by the topical and political character of many of the more modern examples. They are historical distichs, embryonic laments, as in the following couplet taken from the diary of a Cretan soldier mobilised during the First World War:

᾿Ανάθεμά σας, Γερμανοί, δέκα φορὲς στὴν ὥρα!
Γιατί μας ἐτραβήξατε στὴν ἐδική σας χώρα;   *Laog* (1921) 410

A curse upon you, Germans, ten times an hour!
Why did you drag us into your country?

This tradition has not died out, even today. A folk song from the village of Paramythia in Epiros laments the slaughter of forty-nine youths by the Germans during the last war in dialogue form:

– ᾿Ωρέ, Παραμυθιά, γιατί φορεῖς τὰ μαῦρα;
– Οἱ Γερμανοὶ μοῦ σκότωσαν σαράντα-ἐννιὰ καμάρια,
ὠρέ, τοὺς πῆραν ἀπὸ τὰ σπίτια τους
χωρὶς νὰ ποῦν οὔτε μιὰ καλὴ νύχτα.

– Oré, Paramythia, why are you dressed in black?
– The Germans have killed forty-nine of my bravest men,

oré, they took them from their homes,
they could not even bid goodnight.

In 1963, I recorded a group of such laments – some in Greek, some in
Vlachic – from the village of Rhodia in Thessaly. The people who sang
them to me claimed to know a sufficient number, all composed by themselves during the last war, to last for several days and nights. The first,
in Vlachic, is called *Lament for 1940*, and stresses the importance of
a united Balkan resistance to the Germans:

> 1940 was a very bad year. Lelé, lelé!
> First came the Italians, then the Germans. Lelé, lelé!
> Five aeroplanes came down and hid the sun. Lelé lelé!
> Stand up, Balkan people, and do not submit! Lelé, lelé!
> Arise, Balkan people, and resist the enemy! Lelé, lelé!

Another, in Greek, refers to the Italian occupation of 1940, and to the
battles fought in western Macedonia near the Albanian border:

> 'Εσεῖς βουνὰ τῆς Κόνιτσας κι ἐσεῖς βουνὰ τοῦ Γράμμου,
> ποτὲς μὴν λουλουδίσετε, χορτάρι μὴ φυτρῶστε,
> μὲ τὸ κακὸ ποὺ ἔγινε τοῦτο τὸ καλοκαίρι,
> γέμισαν τὰ βουνὰ κορμιά, καὶ οἱ χαράδρες αἷμα.

> You mountains of Konitsa, and you mountains of Grammos,
> never burst into flower, do not grow grass,
> because of the evil which took place this summer.
> The mountains are filled with bodies, and the ravines with
>   blood.

The same lines, with very slight variation, are found in a lament for the
Asia Minor catastrophe of 1922, recorded soon after the event.[42]

These formulaic survivals reflect a continuity of consciousness as
well as of form. The villagers who sang the laments for the last war
also recorded for me several laments in Kleftic style for heroes of the
Greek struggle for independence from the Turks. The names of the
heroes and their feats were a matter of passionate concern to them,
because they saw them as part of their own history. One young boy of
fifteen, employed in a small workshop in Larisa, after listening to the
older historical songs and to the animated discussion which they aroused,
remarked spontaneously, 'When I hear such things, my eyes fill with
tears and my hair stands on end.' It is true that with the passage of time,

details are confused and forgotten, and that many longer ballads have become fragmented. But these laments are not unhistorical, because they are a poetic expression of a long chain of events throughout Greek history which have called for lamentation, the memory of recent events keeping alive and merging with the memory of older calamities. The tradition will die out only when it becomes historically and culturally irrelevant to the people in whose consciousness it is preserved.

6
The classification of ancient and modern laments and songs to the dead

The difficulties involved in making a satisfactory classification of ancient types of lament arise from the conflicting nature of the evidence. Classical and post-classical poetic usage tended to treat the various terms as synonymous, with few real distinctions. In an attempt to impose order, Alexandrian and later scholars neatly divided and defined, but with such variety of criteria that it is impossible to know what to accept as genuine archaic and classical usage, and what to reject as subjective theorising.[1] Confusion in the terminology is inherent in the classical literary tradition, but we should not therefore infer that there had never been any distinct types of ancient lament. The problem of poetic forms and their origins cannot be solved in isolation, without an investigation of their relation to ritual and official practice. For this reason, I shall attempt in this chapter to indicate only the more basic distinctions, and to trace which types of lament have survived in Greek tradition and how they were transmitted.

The ritual lament of the women: thrênos, góos, kommós

Both *thrênos* and *góos* are words of ancient Indo-European origin, meaning a shrill cry.[2] In their most primitive form, these laments probably consisted mainly of inarticulate wailing over the dead man. But etymology, though an invaluable indication of the origins and of the antiquity of words, cannot be pressed too far as a guide to their subsequent development. By the time *thrênos* and *góos* first appear in Greek literature, they had clearly emerged from this primitive stage.[3]

It was suggested in chapter 1 that Homeric and archaic usage may have distinguished *thrênos* and *góos* according to the ritual manner of their performance, using *thrênos* for the set dirge composed and performed by the professional mourners, and *góos* for the spontaneous weeping of the kinswomen. Further, early instances point to the *thrênos* as more ordered and polished, often associated with divine performers and a dominant musical element.[4] This is reflected in the extant choral *thrênoi* of Pindar and Simonides, which are characterised by a calm restraint, gnomic and consolatory in tone rather than passionate and ecstatic; the *góos*, on the other hand, while less restrained, was from Homer onwards more highly individualised, and since it was spoken rather than sung, it tended to develop a narrative rather than a musical form.[5]

These are tentative distinctions, drawn from pre-classical and frag-mentary evidence only. In the classical period, the *thrênos* was still remembered as a distinct type of lyric poetry, but it was interchangeable with *góos*, especially in tragedy, and could be used to refer to any kind of lament, not necessarily for the dead.[6] The older distinctions are partially retained in the later scholarly definitions of *thrênos* as a lament for the dead which contains praise, sung before or after burial or on the various occasions for mourning at the tomb; the ritual element of the *góos* on the other hand is less frequently emphasised after tragedy, and in the Lexica it is glossed with *thrênos*.[7]

The *kommós* is first known as a specific type of tragic lament. The examples collected and analysed by Diehl suggest that it was accompanied by wild gestures and associated with Asiatic ecstasy, like the *iálemos*.[8] These eastern connections, which seem to be old, make it unlikely to have been a term exclusive to the tragedians, and it may have evolved as a dramatic form of the ritual antiphonal lament between the professional and predominantly choral mourners on the one hand, and the mainly solo and narrative improvisations of the kinswomen on the other. In tragedy, it retained its specific form and passionate character, but by the Alexandrian period it had become another poetic synonym.[9] Since it is ignored by later scholars, it may be assumed that it had no further literary development outside tragedy.

From the classical period onwards, then, there was a tendency to treat as synonymous the different terms for a poetic lament, which had originally denoted distinct aspects of the ritual lamentation of the women. The explanation may lie partly in the fact that the most usual forms of official lamentation were no longer primarily musical or poetic, but rhetorical. Their origins and development are quite distinct.

The men's part: praise of the dead

The ancients had no doubt about the mournful and funeral origins of the *élegos*, deriving it rather dubiously from ἒ ἒ λέγειν (to say *é é*) and εὖ λέγειν τοὺς κατοιχομένους (to speak well of the departed).[10] Although their etymology is suspect, it is hard to reject entirely their unanimous association of the word with lamentation. The problem is that the early extant elegies range from sympotic to political and military in content, but none is addressed to the dead or even remotely mournful in tone. How can this contradiction be explained?

Although no early mournful *élegoi* have survived, they are known to have existed. It is possible that Echembrotos, the Peloponnesian poet who was famous for his mournful *élegoi* accompanied by the *aulós*, was only one of a school of Dorian elegists, who used the form for a kind of lament; and it was this same Echembrotos whose music to the *aulós* was disqualified at the Delphic festival in 578 B.C. on the grounds that its mournful character was unsuitable to Apollo.[11] Was it under some kind of pressure from the religious reforms of the sixth century that the mournful *élegos* was discontinued by the lyric poets, surviving only as a literary term?

Features agreed to be common to the early extant *élegoi* are the use of alternating lines of hexameter and pentameter, and the concise, commemorative and proverbial style. How can these be reconciled with a hypothetical origin in some kind of lament? First, just as there is some connection between the Homeric *thrênos* and the *thrênoi* of Pindar and Simonides in their unemotional character, so the later *thrênos* and *élegos* share a reflective, gnomic and consolatory tone.[12] There is therefore no need to postulate a complete change in the development of the *élegos*, only an extension of theme. Further, there is some evidence to suggest that elegiac poetry evolved and developed its particular functions and characteristics within the archaic institution of the common meal, known as *syssition* or *andreîon*. Like the *skólion* (drinking song), the *élegos* was an after-supper song, but its purpose was to educate, exhort and inform, not merely to entertain, and hence the early extant *élegoi*, though not funereal, have a comparable seriousness of purpose.[13] Such an origin would explain both the peculiarity of the metre, which as a self-contained couplet was ideally suited to a song passed round the table from one improviser to another, and the sympotic, commemorative tone. If the ancients are right and the first *élegoi* were funereal, they may well have been improvised couplets commemorating a man, hero or event, and hence easily adapted to incorporate wider political and social themes. Finally, if they were originally performed at the common meal, they were restricted to the men, and praise was therefore more appropriate than lamentation, which was traditionally left to the women.[14]

This hypothesis receives some support from our knowledge that it was an ancient ritual custom to praise the dead at the funeral feast, a practice described by the phrase ἐπιδέξια λέγειν...ὡσπερεὶ τεθνηκότι (to speak cleverly, as of the dead), implying some kind of witty improvisation (Anaxandrides *fr.* 1, Edmonds *FAC* 2.44).[15] Secondly, there is the famous fifth-century Attic *skólion* addressed to Harmodios. It is not in elegiacs, though some *skólia* were; but it is an excellent illustration of how a song may be sympotic, with a political theme, and at the same time an address to the dead:

Φίλταθ᾽ Ἁρμόδι᾽, οὔ τί πω τέθνηκας,
νήσοις δ᾽ ἐν μακάρων σέ φασιν εἶναι,
ἵνα περ ποδώκης ᾽Αχιλεὺς
Τυδεΐδην τέ φασι τὸν ἐσθλὸν Διομήδεα.   Page *PMG* 894

Dearest Hermodios, you are not dead,
but gone, men say, to the Isles of the Blest,
where swift-footed Achilles,
and brave Diomedes, Tydeus' son, are said to be.

The epigram was a dedicatory inscription written on tombstones or on votive offerings. Since it presupposes literacy, it cannot have been widely current before the end of the seventh century, but similarities of style and metre point to its relation to the *élegos*. Elegiac inscriptions begin at the end of the seventh century and continue throughout antiquity. The tone of the archaic examples is detached and impersonal, almost serene, and in no sense like a lament. Their purpose was purely functional, to mark a grave, as is shown by the following inscription from Attica (sixth century):

σῆμα Φρασικλείας· | κόρε κεκλέσομαι | αἰεί,
ἀντὶ γάμο | παρὰ θεῶν τοῦτο | λαχοσ᾽ ὄνομα.   Peek 68

Phrasikleia's grave. I shall always be called maiden,
for the gods gave me this name instead of marriage.

With the development of the literary epigram which began with Simonides, a more personal note appears, although conciseness was still the rule. Gradually epigrams were written on themes other than the commemoration of the dead, and their composition became the elegant *parergon* of many fifth- and fourth-century writers. The same relaxation of restraint is perceptible in the non-literary funerary inscriptions of the late fifth century and after, perhaps as a result of the changes in ritual and lamentation already discussed at the end of chapter 1. The growing importance of the scene at the tomb, illustrated by its prominence on later fifth-century Attic vase-paintings, is also reflected in the elaboration and popularisation of the funerary inscription. The disintegration of archaic ritual forms like the *thrênos* and *góos* may have created a demand for the expression of a more intimate contact between mourner and dead than was possible in the formal and rhetorical *epitáphios lógos*. Dialogues, reproaches, sentiments of grief, begin to replace mere statements of death, as can be seen in the following inscriptions, the first from Halikarnassos (fourth century B.C.), the second an extract from a long inscription from Kotiaion (fourth century A.D.):

‒⏑⏑ ‒⏑⏑ ‒⏑⏑ ‒⏑⏑ ‒⏑⏑ ‒⏑

Θουριέας ξείνηι τῆιδε κέκευθα κόνει ·
Εὔκλειτον, τὸμ πρῶτ[ο]ν δὴ κατετύψατο μήτηρ
ὀκτωκαιδεχέτη παῖδα καταφθίμενον,
δωδεχέτη δὲ μετ᾽ αὐτὸν ἀνέκλαυσεν Θεόδωρον ·
αἰαῖ τοὺς ἀδίκως οἰχομένους ὑπὸ γῆν.   Peek 748

. . . .

I lie hidden in this foreign dust of Thouriea.
Eukleitos died first, a boy of eighteen years,
      and his mother beat her breast for him;
after him she wept for twelve-year-old Theodoros.
      Alas for those who are gone beneath the earth unjustly!

᾽Αμμία, θυγάτηρ πινυτή, πῶς θάνες ἤδη;
τί σπεύδουσα θάνες ἢ τίς (σ)ε κιχήσατο μοιρῶν;
πρίν σε νυνφικὸν ἰς (σ)τέφανον κοσμήσαμεν [ἐ]ν θαλάμοισιν,
πάτρην σε λιπῖν πενθαλέους δὲ τοκῆας ·
καὶ θρήνη]σε πατὴρ κ(αὶ) πᾶσα πατ[ρὶς] κ(αὶ) πότνια μήτηρ
τὴ[ν] σ[ὴν] ἀωροτ[ά]τ[η]ν κ(αὶ) ἀθαλάμευ[τον] ἡλικίην.

Kb. 372.26–31

Ammia, wise daughter, how is it you died so soon?
Why did you hasten to die, or which of the Fates overtook you?
Before we decked you for the bridal garland in the marriage
      chamber

you left your home and your grieving parents.
Your father, and all the country, and your mother lamented
for your most untimely and unwedded youth.

These inscriptions are an invaluable source of evidence for the present
study, since they are probably the closest reflection of popular language,
style and thought in antiquity that we possess, although we cannot be
sure of the exact manner of their composition. The vast majority are
anonymous, written for a wide range of people from differing social
classes from the whole of the Greek-speaking world. The large number
of common ideas and formulae, many derived from classical literature,
others found also in the epigrams of the Anthology, points to a degree
of standardisation. It has even been argued that the stone-cutters used
manuals of stock formulae from which the bereaved might choose their
themes, and that the inscriptions are therefore minimally creative.[16] But
in the absence of any specific evidence for the use of such manuals in
Greek, it would surely be a mistake to dismiss them as entirely derivative:
within the bounds of the convention, ideas, language and style vary
considerably according to the time and place of composition, and
according to the status of the deceased. The inscriptions afford us a
unique insight into a complete cross-section of society; and it is frequently
the more humble, semi-literate examples which offer the most valuable
evidence. Finally, the striking similarities of formulae and style in these
inscriptions and some of the modern *moirológia*, discussed in Part III,
may throw some light not only on the origins of the modern laments,
but also on the traditional nature of the inscriptions themselves.

Both the *epitáphios lógos* (funeral oration) and the *epikédeion* have their
origins in the literary rather than the popular tradition of the classical
period. The *epitáphios lógos* was the spoken oration delivered at the
funeral in praise and commemoration of the dead.[17] With the rise of
rhetoric, it tended to replace the earlier poetic forms, at least in the more
developed urban society of Athens. Both composition and delivery
belonged to the men. In the post-classical period, *epitáphios* was extended
to refer to a poetic lament. The *epikédeion* presents rather more problems.
In Homer, *kêdos* is used only for the practice of mourning, while Pindar
uses it for the actual lament (*Il.* 4.270, 5.156, Pi. *P.* 4.112). Its adjectival
form *epikédeios* is used with *odé* by Euripides for the Muse's lament for
Troy, and by Plato in the strictly ritual sense of the *funeral songs* of the
Carian women (E. *Tr.* 511, Pl. *Lg.* 800e).[18] The substantival form
epikédeion gained wide currency towards the end of antiquity, and is

defined somewhat tortuously by Alexandrian and Roman scholars as a kind of elegy, epigram and *thrênos*, containing a moderate expression of grief and considerable praise, not circumscribed in time or place, and public rather than private in character.[19] Its history indicates that it was a later literary development, not an archaic ritual lament, differing from the *epitáphios lógos* in that it was written in verse, not prose, from the *thrênos* in that it contained praise rather than lamentation, and from the *élegos* and epigram in that it was concerned with public events rather than with ordinary individuals.

The main distinctions between the two categories so far examined appear to be that while the *thrênos*, *góos* and *kommós* were based on a ritual act or cry of lamentation, performed by the women often to a musical accompaniment, the epigram, *élegos*, *epitáphios lógos* and *epikédeion* grew out of the social and literary activity of the men, developing the elements of commemoration and praise, which had been present in the archaic *thrênos*. This second group tended gradually to replace the first as a recognised form of honouring the dead; and at the same time the changing emphasis from lamentation at the wake to lamentation at the tomb weakened still further the older distinctions within the first group. The archaic terms ceased to correspond to ritual custom or to official practice. And since lyrical laments flourished chiefly in poetry, it was natural for later poets to exploit the rich inheritance of terms for poetic variety – a tendency which is incipient in tragedy and which reaches its peak in the Hellenistic period, thereby precipitating a total confusion of usage in the ancient terminology.

The growth of a new terminology

Since the old terms were dependent for survival on written tradition alone after the end of antiquity, when the literary composition of ancient forms was purely derivative and imitative, they were bound to disappear from the spoken language of the people. A few have lived on in modified and restricted form. Today, the *Epitáphios Thrênos* denotes the Holy Week lament for Christ, an important part of the ritual of the Orthodox Church. An exceptional survival of *thrênos* and *kommós* was found in the annual lament for Zafeiris, deeply rooted in seasonal ritual of pagan character. *Góos* has been forgotten, but its Homeric equivalents *stenagmós* and *odyrmós* are still common in the spoken language and in the folk laments, although they refer to the act of weeping rather than to the lament itself.

Did the disintegration of ancient terminology necessarily entail a disappearance of the old ritual forms of lament among the people? The question is impossible to answer without much more evidence for popular tradition in antiquity than we possess. But there are a number of modern Greek terms associated with lamentation of sufficient antiquity to indicate some interesting connections. One of these is the use in Cypriot dialect of the verb ἀνακαλιέμαι (to call upon). In ancient Greek, the verb ἀνακαλεῖσθαι is used of the persistent calling of the dead by name during the supplication at the tomb, usually accompanied by offerings and libations. Its function was to raise the spirit of the dead from the grave. It is used in this specific sense by Aeschylus for the invocation of Dareios' spirit in the *Persians*, by Euripides, and also in one of the later epigrams:[20]

Πολλάκι τῷδ' ὀλοφυδνὰ κόρας ἐπὶ σάματι Κλεινὼ
  μάτηρ ὠκύμορον παῖδ' ἐβόασε φίλαν,
ψυχὰν ἀγκαλέουσα Φιλαινίδος, ἃ πρὸ γάμοιο
  χλωρὸν ὑπὲρ ποταμοῦ χεῦμ' Ἀχέροντος ἔβα.   *AP* 7.486

Often at this girl's tomb has her mother Kleino
  in tears cried out for her dear short-lived child,
invoking the soul of Philainis to return, who, before wedlock,
  passed across the pallid stream of Acheron.

But it was not restricted to literature. The verb ἀνακαλεῖν, as we have seen in chapter 4, was commonly used for the refrain invoking the dying god by name to rise again, an indispensable element of the ancient lament for gods. Its importance may be judged by the use of the cognate forms ἀνακλήθρα and ἀνακληθρίς for the stone on which Demeter is said to have sat when she invoked Persephone. The ritual enactment of this *anáklesis* was continued by the women of Megara until Pausanias' day.[21] The verb form is also frequently found in the more popular Byzantine laments, where it is used for the Virgin's invocation to the dying Christ, and the noun form *anakálema* later denotes the lament for the fall of Constantinople.[22]

The proper function of the ancient term was to invoke the dead to rise again. As such it was rooted in popular ritual of a primitive kind. This ancient function is illustrated nowhere outside tragedy so clearly as in modern Cypriot popular usage, where besides the verb ἀνακαλιέμαι it has developed various new noun forms, all used of a particularly insistent type of dirge. As one woman put it, Ἐκείνη ἡ 'ρκὰ (γριὰ) ποὺ

Gods, cities and men

ἔθαψεν προχτὲς τὸν γιό της οὐλ᾽ ἡμέρα ἀνακαλιέται (That old woman
who buried her son the other day *invokes* all day long), Sakellarios
2.446. An even closer parallel is provided by the Cypriot version of the
folk ballad, *The Song of the Dead Brother*, where the deserted mother
raises her dead son Kostandis from the grave with her invocations,
weeping first for all her sons:[23]

οὔλους στὸ μνῆμαν ἔκλαιεν, οὔλους ἀνακαλιέτουν.

she wept for all at the tomb, all of them she invoked.

The use of ἀνακαλιέμαι is therefore a striking example of continuity
in a specific type of lament, the ritual invocation of the dead at the
tomb. It begins to appear in fifth-century literature, just when vase-
paintings and funeral inscriptions point to the growing importance of
lamentation at the tomb. Its popular character is further confirmed
by its survival today, not in the religious tradition, where its meaning
is less specific, and not at all in learned tradition, but in popular speech
and in folk song. It suggests that ancient terminology was preserved
most strongly when associated with ritual practice.

The song to Fate – origin of the modern moirológi?

A solution to the problems of the etymology of *moirológi*, the general
word today for the *lament for the dead*, would afford concrete information
about the origins of the modern popular lament, and at the same time
provide linguistic confirmation of the continuity already indicated by
so many survivals of ritual and ideas. Two points may be made at once:
first, both elements, *moiro-* and *-lógi*, are of ancient origin; second, the
word belongs to demotic. In the learned and religious language, *thrênos*
is used. The word is ancient, but popular.

Taking the first element of the word first, the problem is whether it is
derived from the noun *moîra* (fate), or from the verb *mýromai* (to
lament), or even from the adjectival prefix *myrio-* (ten-thousand-fold),
as it is pronounced in many regions today. The question is not new.
Nearly two hundred years ago, the philologist Adamantios Korais
(1748–1833), basing himself on a passage of Hesychios, argued in favour
of its derivation from *mýromai*, spelling the word *myrológi* (*Atakta* 2.225).
More recently, a detailed linguistic analysis by John Schmitt has demonstrated the correctness of its derivation from *moîra*.[24] His arguments,
entirely convincing from a formal point of view, may perhaps be supple-

mented by a study of general usage, particularly in the Hellenistic and Greco-Roman periods.

Confusion between the prefixes *moiro-*, *myrio-*, *mýro-* (from *mýron* = unguent, scent) and *mýromai* is common. It goes back to Firmicus and Hesychios in the learned tradition, and to one of the scholiasts on Homer.[25] In the popular inscriptions, where the spelling is less correct and hence a closer reflection of actual pronunciation, *oi* and *u* are confused earlier and more frequently. In an inscription from Ankyra, *Moira* is misspelt as *Myra* (*SEG* 6.46.4). The root of the problem lies in the confusion of homophones caused by the changes of pronunciation in the Greek language, particularly in the process known as iotacism, the fronting–raising–closing of the vowels. The diphthong *oi* was beginning to lose its original value and to become assimilated with *u* as early as the third century B.C.[26] Since confusion between the two began before the first known occurrence of our word, nothing conclusive can be argued from the spelling of the written evidence. The only sound basis for discussion is a linguistic analysis of compound word formation, sense and usage.

Korais' sole support for his derivation from *mýromai* is Hesychios' entry 1883: μυρᾳδεῖ· θρηνῳδεῖ which he connects with the separately entered μυρομένη· ὀδυρομένη. From this, he argues the existence of a verb μυρῳδεῖν (to lament). But there are several difficulties. First, μυρᾳδεῖ cannot stand. Nor is emendation to μυρῳδεῖ entirely convincing, because the *a* is protected by the word order of the Lexicon and hard to dismiss as a mere slip. Other attempts at emendation are even less acceptable (see 1883 *app. crit.*). Such a dubious text cannot be used to prove the existence of μυρῳδεῖν. But even if it were accepted, it does not take us far, since Hesychios enters μυρᾳδεῖ separately from μυρομένη, so that in view of the frequent confusion of spelling, from which the text of Hesychios is by no means immune, it would be impossible to determine whether the true form was μυρῳδεῖν or μοιρῳδεῖν.

Against Korais' interpretation, Schmitt has pointed out that the verb μυρῳδεῖν presupposes a noun μυρῳδία. There is no ancient evidence for such a word, and it is unlikely to have arisen in the Byzantine period for the simple reason that μυρωδία, from μυρώδης, was already current in the language with the meaning *anointing*, *fragrance*, or *smell*. Since Greek has shown throughout its history a tendency to avoid homophones, it is *a priori* improbable that a new word μυρῳδία or μοιρῳδία should have become current at a time when confusion had already set in.[27]

Schmitt demonstrated also that a compound form μυρῳδία or μυρολόγι could only be formed from a noun form *mȳron* = lament, not from the verb *mȳromai*, and that there is no certain evidence for such a noun in ancient or Byzantine sources. The case may be put more strongly: first, compounds ending in *-odía*, *-lógion*, *-logé*, *-logía* are all formed with substantival, adjectival or prepositional prefixes, never with verbal prefixes; second, throughout the history of the Greek language, *mȳromai* has produced no other compound form, whereas compounds with *mȳro-* (= smell), *myrio-* and *moiro-* have been common since antiquity, and are still being formed today.

Decisive evidence in favour of derivation from *moîra* comes from a passage in the *Life of Alexander*, attributed to Pseudo-Kallisthenes (*c.* 300 B.C.), although none of the versions which have come down to us is earlier than A.D. 300. Alexander taunts the astrologer-prophet Nektanebos for aspiring to interpret the stars when he does not even know how he will meet his death. Nektanebos replies that he already knows that he will be killed by his own son. Attempting to prove him wrong, Alexander strikes him to the ground, mortally wounding him. Nektanebos then reveals that he, and not Philip, is Alexander's true father, and that the fate which he had prophesied for himself is now fulfilled: Φοβερῶς εἴληφα τὸ πρᾶγμα· ἀλλ᾽ οὐκ ἔστιν οὐδένα θνητὸν νικῆσαι τὴν εἱμαρμένην...ὡς γὰρ ἐμοιρολόγησα ἐμαυτόν, ηὗρον εἱμαρμένον μοι ὑπὸ ἰδίου τέκνου ἀναιρεθῆναι· οὐκ ἐξέφυγον οὖν τὴν μοῖραν, ἀλλ᾽ ὑπὸ σοῦ ἀνηρέθην. *V.Alex.* 1.14 (ed. Kroll). The word *moirologô* means here, 'I prophesy my own fate, tell my own doom'. The prefix *moiro-* is protected not by the spelling, but by the meaning. Is there any evidence to suggest that the idea had any connection with lamentation?

In Aeschylus' *Agamemnon*, Cassandra, as a prophetess, knew the fate in store for her before she entered the fatal palace. As she waited to go in, she cried out against her ill-starred fortune, lamented her own *moîra*, then, calling on the sun to help avenge her death, she sang her own dirge, extended at the end into a general lament for the tragedy of human life:

ἀλλ᾽ εἶμι κἀν δόμοισι κωκύσουσ᾽ ἐμὴν
᾽Αγαμέμνονός τε μοῖραν. ἀρκείτω βίος.   A. *Ag.* 1313–14

ἅπαξ ἔτ᾽ εἰπεῖν ῥῆσιν, ἢ θρῆνον θέλω
ἐμὸν τὸν αὐτῆς. ἡλίου δ᾽ ἐπεύχομαι
πρὸς ὕστατον φῶς τοὺς ἐμοὺς τιμαόροις
ἐχθροὺς φανεῖσι δεσποτῶν τίνειν ἴσα

δούλης θανούσης, εὐμαροῦς χειρώματος.
  ἰὼ βρότεια πράγματ᾽· εὐτυχοῦντα μὲν
σκιά τις ἂν τέρψειεν· εἰ δὲ δυστυχοῖ,
βολαῖς ὑγρώσσων σπόγγος ὤλεσεν γραφήν.   *Ibid.* 1322–9

I will go now, and lament my fate and Agamemnon's
inside the house. Enough of life!

Yet one word more, my own dirge for myself.
I pray the Sun, on whom I now look my last,
that he may grant to my master's avengers
a fair price for the slave-girl slain at his side.
O sad mortality! when fortune smiles,
a painted image; and when trouble comes,
one touch of a wet sponge wipes it away.[28]

It is true that Cassandra's position was a peculiar one; but her protest against fate and farewell to life, both essential parts of her lament for herself, are themes which constantly recur in tragedy. Further, the lament of the tragic hero or heroine for his own fate or death accounts for a high proportion of the laments in Greek tragedy. Other tragic figures who sing their own dirges include the Suppliant Women in Aeschylus, Ajax, Jokasta, Oedipus, Antigone, Deianeira and Philoktetes in Sophokles, and Alkestis, Hekabe, Polyxena, Medea, Phaidra, Andromache and Iphigeneia in Euripides. Their laments contain a striking number of common formulae and themes; and in all, *moîra* and *týche* are of the utmost importance.[29] This suggests a basis in popular belief outside the confines of tragic drama.

   In Homer, *moîra* is frequently found in formulaic phrases as the agent of death or bringer of doom.[30] Equally common is the hero's protest to the gods at a reversal of fortune, and farewell to life when on the point of death.[31] In Homer, *moîra* is restricted in sense, but always personified in concrete form; while in tragedy, although *moîra* and *týche* are more frequently appealed to than in Homer, their personality and function are less clearly delineated. It is in the popular funerary inscriptions that *moîra* retains both her wide range of functions and her well-defined personality.[32] But the fundamental idea in all is the inescapability of a man's allotted fate. It is traditional to much of Greek poetry and thought, and has given rise to a common fund of formulae and formulaic phrases which can be traced in Homer, lyric poetry drama, verse and prose inscriptions.[33] It is also implicit in the passage from the *Life of Alexander*, where the verb *moirologô* first occurs.

The idea of the inevitability of man's fate finds particularly varied expression in the funerary inscriptions. A detailed investigation by Mayer has yielded no fewer than 230 different formulae used with *moîra*, selected from only the more striking examples. In the dedicatory and consolatory inscriptions, on the other hand, only six could be found. Of these formulae, forty are used of *moîra* in the impersonal sense of a man's allotted part, either in life or death, while the rest describe the goddess *Moîra*, usually as she brings death, as in Homer.[34] The formulae, stock epithets and verbs which are appropriate to this destructive *moîra* are sometimes Homeric; but this does not mean that they can be dismissed as literary borrowings, rather that the Homeric formulae continued to express popular feeling and belief.[35] These traditional attitudes explain why *Moîra* is directly addressed and reproached in so many of the inscriptions, as in an inscription from Ilion in the first to second centuries A.D., ὦ Μοίρης πικρὰ λογιζομένης... (O Moîra, who calculates bitter things!) (Peek 1350.16).[36] The mourner first reproached *Moîra* for having caused the death of a loved one, then lamented his own *moîra*, deserted and grieved. *Moirologô* would be exactly appropriate to such a practice. Even if the word is a *hapax legomenon* in ancient Greek, it is rooted in ancient traditional beliefs. Finally, the evidence of the funerary inscriptions suggests that the *protest to fate* or *lament for oneself*, elaborated in drama to the highest point of tragic art, continued to flourish in popular tradition.[37]

It is over a thousand years before our word reappears, this time in the noun form *moirológema*, but the main steps of its transmission are clear. In the Greek novels of love and adventure, where Fortune's cunning tricks and reverses lead to innumerable escapes and imagined deaths, ample opportunity is provided for heroes and heroines to indulge in lamentations and protests to Fate.[38] In *The Fall of Troy*, Quintus of Smyrna (fourth century A.D.) takes up the story of the Trojan War where Homer left off, and relates in each of the fourteen books the terrible fate which befell one hero after another. Much of the epic is composed of lamentation and accounts of funerals, and in every lament the idea of Fate in connection with death is emphasised.[39] Then, in the Byzantine prose and verse romances of the twelfth and thirteenth centuries, which constitute to some extent a learned revival of the earlier Greek novel, Fate has taken over many of the functions of the ancient Olympians, and plays a dominant role. Some of the phrases in which she is reproached incorporate formulaic expressions from the funerary inscriptions.[40] That the importance of Fate and Fortune was not merely a learned extension of earlier usage, but also owed much to the popular tradition of the Byzantine period, becomes clear with the emergence of the anonymous romances in *politikòs stíchos* and popular language in the fourteenth century and after. In *Kallimachos and Chrysorrhoe*, for example, *Týche* appears, just as she does in the modern folk tales, in the guise of a beggar woman dressed in black (1329–46). Besides the idea of the woven thread of Fate the Spinner, we find the decree of Fate, written down by *Moîra* herself at the birth of a child, and closely linked with the child's prospective marriage – a theme central to the stories of *Belthandros and Chrysantza* and *Lybistros and Rhodamne*, where it gives rise to many new epithets, verbs and compounds.⁴¹

It is in this wider literary context that the occurrence of the word *moirológema* in *Kallimachos and Chrysorrhoe* should be viewed. Chrysorrhoe, having been rescued from the Castle of the Drakos by Kallimachos, is snatched away from him to become wife of a king. While the king is away on campaigns, Kallimachos finds his way to the royal palace and takes on work as a gardener's boy in order to be near his loved one. As he toils and sweats, he curses Fate:⁴²

Στενάζει, βάλλει τὸ νερόν, ποτίζει καὶ τὸν κῆπον,
μοιρολογεῖ τραγώδημαν, τούτους τοὺς λόγους λέγει:
('Ιδοὺ τὸ μοιρολόγημαν τοῦ ξένου Καλλιμάχου
τοῦ μισθαργοῦ, τοῦ κηπουροῦ, τοῦ νεροκουβαλήτου.)
– Στῆσον ἀπάρτι, Τύχη μου, πλάνησιν τὴν τοσαύτην... 1669–73
Τύχη, καὶ τί τὸ σ' ἔπταισα, Τύχη μου, τί σ' ἐποῖκα
καὶ τί παράλογον πρὸς σὲ ποτέ μου ἐνεθυμήθην...; 1677–8

He groans, he fetches water, he waters the garden,
he sings a lament, and says these words:
(Behold the lament of Kallimachos, far from home,
the labourer, the gardener, the water-carrier.)
– Cease now, at last, my Fortune, such great deceit...
Fortune, how have I wronged you, my Fortune, what have
    I done,
and what unreasonable thought have I ever entertained against
    you?

The connection here between lamentation and Fate could not be more plain. Its popular character is further demonstrated by similar reproaches in the modern folk laments:⁴³

Gods, cities and men

Παρακαλῶ σε, Μοῖρα μου, νὰ μὴ μὲ ξενιτέψῃς,
κι ἂν λάχῃ καὶ ξενιτευθῶ, θάνατο μὴ μοῦ δώσῃς.   Passow 385

I beg you, my Fate, not to send me into foreign parts,
but if it is my lot to go, do not let me die there.

In modern folk tradition, *moirológi* is not the lament for oneself or protest to fate sung at any angry moment; it is specifically the ritual lament, sung usually at death, and avoided on other occasions as ill-omened. Far from being a recent development, the reason lies partly in the survival today of many of the oldest and most fundamental associations of *moîra*.[44] In the Byzantine romances, *Moîra*, together with *Éros*, recorded in a book at a man's birth the decree which was to decide his future love – a relatively late and literary conception. But in folk tradition, the three *Moîres* decide above all the time and manner of a man's death. Nor do they always record their decree in a book; their use of spindle, distaff and scissors is reflected in many proverbs, sayings and *paradóseis*, while the *grapsímata* are not letters written with pen and ink, but marks left by the *Moîres* on the face in infancy.[45] As recently as 1966, Mrs Photeine Papageorgiou, aged 77, from Berko in Naupaktos, recalled how she used to lay out the bones of the dead in the churchyard together with other women, as was the custom, and on examining the unusual ραφές (seams) on the forehead of the skull, they would murmur to each other, Νά, ἐδῶ τὰ ἔγραφε ἡ Μοῖρα του! ('Look, this is where Moira wrote his fate!'). This fusion of *writing* and *weaving* is used of the *Moîrai* as early as the Greco-Roman period, again, significantly, in the inscriptions: Μοῖραι...ἐκλώσαντο...γραψάμεναι...(The Fates, having written...wove) (Peek 1029.3–4).[46]

The linguistic and historical evidence, then, leaves no doubt that *moîra* and not *mýromai* is the correct origin of *moirológi*. The transmission of the role of Fate in lamentation has been traced from antiquity to the present through the inscriptions and the novel to the learned and popular Byzantine romance; and modern folk tradition also shows signs of independent ancient survivals. But perhaps the formal aspect should not be overemphasised. In words of popular origin and transmission, confusion by analogy is common; and once *mýromai* and *moîra*, closely associated in meaning, had become homophones, identification was natural. The most likely explanation is that the phrases *moîran légo*, or *moîran katalégo*, current in the language since Homer, acquired a new significance with the development of *Moîra* as a figure instrumental in bringing a man's death, and of the tragic song to fate or lament for oneself, hence forming a compound *moirológeo* just as *mythológeo* was formed from *mýthon légo*.[47] This coincided with the phonetic changes in the language, and the consequent confusion between *mýromai* and *moîra* may have affected the final transference of meaning from *song to fate* to *lament*.

It is difficult to date this process precisely. *Mýromai* is frequent in Homer in the sense of *weeping the dead*; it occurs once in Hesiod, though the form is possibly corrupt; then there is a gap until the Alexandrians, who use it again exclusively for *weeping the dead*, and the funerary inscriptions.[48] It appears to have been a dialect word, present in epic but not in Attic, and not used in poetry after Homer and Hesiod until the Hellenistic age. The suspicion that it ceased to be widely used after the introduction of the *koiné* is confirmed by the treatment of the Lexica, where it is always glossed with the commoner κλαίειν and θρηνεῖν but never used as a gloss itself.[49] This would place *mýromai*, if it is the cause of the confusion, somewhere in the early Hellenistic period, and hence the emergence of some form of *moirológó* in its present sense from the third to first centuries B.C.

One more problem remains. Attention has so far been directed only to *moiro-*; but the ending *-lógi* presents some difficulties. Is it a popular form of *-lógion*, and if so, can it bear the meaning of *song, word*, as is usually assumed? While compounds in *-logó*, *-logía*, *-lógos* and *-lógema* are all classical, the neuter form *-lógion* first appears in Hellenistic Greek. Its compounds, when formed with substantival prefixes, give the meaning *collection of* or *instrument for*. Further, most nouns in *-lógion* are technical or literary terms, not popular words.

The first known noun form for our word is *moirológema*. The ending *-lógi*, which is current from the fourteenth to fifteenth centuries, is inconsistent with other Hellenistic and Byzantine nouns of its type in the following respects: first, the word is exclusively demotic, while other nouns in *-lógion* are learned; second, on the analogy of other nouns it ought to mean *collection of fates*, or *instrument for fates*; third, other modern Greek compounds in *-logó* give noun forms in *-lógema* if the sense is concrete, in *-logía* if abstract, while nouns in *-lógi* rarely have verb forms at all. Some of these discrepancies may be explained on the analogy of *katalógi*, as it evolved in Byzantine and modern Greek.[50] In the popular language of the romances, it could mean *love song, message, enkómion*, as well as *story* or *song*; while in the dialect of Lesbos today, *katalóg'* signifies the *epitáphios thrênos*, and both *katalogiázo* and *katalogístra* are used interchangeably with *moirológó* and *moirologístria*.[51]

It is therefore probable that the Byzantine popular form *katalógi*, derived from ancient *katalogé* and not from *katalógion*, had some influence on the final form of *moirológi*, especially as one of its meanings was the same. Analogous to the development *katalégo* > *katalogé* >*katalógema* > *katalógi*, *moirológi* probably arose from *moirologó* > *moirológema*, and not from *moirológion* at all. It was a general tendency of medieval Greek for certain feminine nouns to become neuter, throwing into temporary confusion those of the neuter endings which were phonetically indistinguishable.[52] Since the ending *-lógi* in our word did not become stabilised until late Byzantine Greek, when neuter endings were in a transitional stage, the rules of noun formation which govern Hellenistic and learned Byzantine compounds in *-lógion* and their modern derivatives in *-lógi* are not applicable. Finally, related to *katalógi* is another modern word, *paralogé* (ballad), from ancient Greek *parakatalogé*, deriving, like *katalógi*, from the epic recitation peculiar to Ionian tradition.[53]

These considerations give some support to the historical and linguistic analysis of both elements of *moirológi* in pointing to the ultimate origins of the modern word in the Hellenistic age. *Moirológi* can, with some confidence, be added to the modern types of folk song analysed by Kyriakidis, which are rooted in the language and traditions of late antiquity.[54] Can this continuity be further supported by its form and content?

Moirológia *for departure from home, change of religion, and marriage*

Although *moirológi* is a general term, there are several recognised distinctions.[55] How far can they be related to the ancient types of laments and songs to the dead discussed at the beginning of this chapter? Not all *moirológia* are intended for the dead, although they have a strong ritual character. Among these are the laments for those who have left their country, for change of religion, and for marriage.

Classical literature appears to have developed only the lament for those who died away from home. But in Homer, there is evidence of another kind, spoken for or by a man leaving home or known to be in distant parts. Hearing of Telemachos' departure, Penelope sits on the threshold – a ritual position – and weeps, with all her maidservants around her.[56] Perhaps because these laments are not connected with any official ritual, they are rarely mentioned in historical or literary sources. Our next sample is a tender farewell to home written in iambic trimeters by the Byzantine poet Ioannes Euchaites (eleventh century), which contains certain formulae similar to those found both in antiquity and in modern folk tradition.[57] That there may have been a well established medieval popular basis for these laments is suggested both by their occurrence in the romances, and by the number found in medieval manuscripts, written probably by monks of limited learning in idle and nostalgic mood to fill up empty spaces. They are not fine poetry, but their popularity is evident from the use of common formulae, some of which can be related, like Euchaites' lament, to both ancient and modern laments.[58]

Today, laments for those who leave their country form an important and distinctive group, especially in Epiros, where emigration has been a part of the life of the people for many generations. They usually take the form of an address by the bereaved family to the absent person, or to *Xenitiá* (distant parts), who is personified. Occasionally there is a dialogue between them in which the washing of the travel-stained handkerchief is made into a striking poetic symbol of the bond with home.[59] Their mood is one of harsh complaint, their melody and style strident and undecorated, like the following example I recorded in 1963 from Alexandra Tsipi, an Epirot girl now living in Larisa:

>"Αχ, ξενετεμένα μου παιδιά, αὐτοῦ στὰ ξένα ποῦ εἶστε·
>ἄχ, ἡ ξενετιὰ σᾶς χαίρεται τὰ νιάτα τὰ γραμμένα·
>ὄχ, ἀνάθεμά σε, ξενετιά, ἐσὺ καὶ τὰ καλά σου,
>ἄχ, μᾶς πῆρες ὅλα τὰ παιδιὰ μέσα στὴν ἀγκαλιά σου!

>Ach, my children far from home, there where you are in
>   foreign lands.
>Ach, foreign lands enjoy your allotted youth.
>Och, a curse upon you, foreign lands, you and your good things!
>ach, you have taken all our children into your embrace!

One reason for the peculiar intensity of these laments is the fear of death in foreign lands, which is also known to have existed in antiquity:[60]

>Νὰ κλαῖτε τοὺς κακότυχους, τοὺς κακοπεθαμένους,
>ὁποὺ πεθαίν'ν στὴν ξενιτιὰ καὶ στὰ νοσοκομεῖα.   *Laog* (1960) 376

>Weep for those of evil fortune, for those whose death is bad,
>who die in foreign lands and who die in hospitals.

The laments for change of religion appear to have arisen in modern Greek tradition out of the custom of *paidomázoma*, common in the post-Byzantine period, according to which children were seized to be trained as janissaries in the Turkish army. Little recorded in contemporary sources, some elements of these laments have survived in oral tradition. Although related to the historical laments for cities, they are not exclusively historical: to the mother who saw her son taken from home and forced to turn Moslem, with no prospect of return except as an enemy soldier, the only course was to lament him as dead. The ritual element is again expressed by the use of formulae common to laments for the dead and for those who have left their country.[61] One may also compare the folk song about the Jewish girl who is wooed by a Christian and asked to change her religion, but is told by her mother that she would rather her daughter die than do such a thing (Passow 589).

Closest to the laments for the dead in structure and form are those sung for the bride as she leaves her father's house. The similarities are due not to lack of originality, but to the sustained parallel in the ritual of the two ceremonies of wedding and funeral: the solemn ablutions of bride and bridegroom, the anointing with nuptial oils and perfumes, the elaborate dressing, the wearing of the marriage garland and the use of torches – all can be matched remarkably closely in the ritual preparation of the dead as he was about to depart on his last journey.[62] Further, a deliberate fusion is indicated by the custom, ancient as well as modern, of dressing those who died young in wedding attire.[63] Popular belief viewed death and marriage as fundamentally similar occasions, signalling the transition from one stage in the cycle of human existence to another. The bride leaves home to start a new life, and as she steps over the threshold for the last time as a girl, her family take leave of her as they do for the dead, while she replies with complaints similar to those made by the dead in the laments. The structural and formulaic correspondences between the wedding and funeral laments may be illustrated by two examples, the first a funeral lament from Olympia, the second a wedding lament from Crete. In both, the sense of bereavement is intensified by an allusion in the first line to the lament of the Virgin:

Σήμερα μαῦρος οὐρανὸς κι ἀραγνιασμένη μέρα,
σήμερα ξεχωρίζουνε ἀιτὸς καὶ περιστέρα,
σήμερα ξεχωρίζουνε παιδάκια ὀχ τὸν πατέρα.
Τέσσεροι στύλοι τοῦ σπιτιοῦ, ἔχετε καλὴ νύχτα,
καὶ πέστε τῆς γυναίκας μου, δὲν ἔρχουμαι ἄλλη νύχτα.
Τέσσεροι στύλοι τοῦ σπιτιοῦ, ἔχετε καλὸ βράδι,
καὶ πέστε τοῦ πατέρα μου δὲν ἔρχουμ' ἄλλο βράδι.

Laog (1912–13) 183

Today the sky is black and the day is gloomy,
today the eagle and the dove take leave,
today children take leave of their father.
Four columns of the house, I bid you goodnight,
tell my wife I'll come at night no more;
four columns of the house, I bid you good evening,
tell my father I'll come at evening no more.

Σήμερο μαῦρος οὐρανός, σήμερο μαύρ' ἡμέρα,
σήμερ' ἀποχωρίζεται μάνα τὴ θυγατέρα.
Ἄνοιξαν οἱ ἑφτὰ οὐρανοὶ τὰ δώδεκα βαγγέλια,
κι ἐπῆραν τὸ παιδάκι μου ἀπὸ τὰ δυό μου χέρια.
Μισεύγεις, θυγατέρα μου, καὶ πλιὸ δὲ θὰ γελάσω,
σάββατο πλιὸ δὲ θὰ λουστῶ οὐδ' ἑορτὴ θ' ἀλλάξω.   Vlastos 74

Today the sky is black, today the day is black,
today a mother takes leave of her daughter.
The seven skies have opened the twelve gospels,[64]
and have taken my child from out of my arms.
You are leaving, daughter, and I shall never laugh again,
nor wash on Saturdays, nor change for a festival.

As the bride makes her ritual farewells, her mother breaks down,
calling out, as if at a funeral, 'You are leaving – my eyes have gone, my
comfort has gone, the keys of my breast and the pillar of my heart has
gone!' (Vlastos 51). When the priest arrives, it is the bride's turn to
lament and hang back. Sometimes she requires force:

– Σέρνε με κι ἂς κλαίω,
κι ἃ κλαίω ποιὸ πειράζω;
– Σέρνε με κι ἂς κλαίω κιόλας.   Vlastos 51

– Drag me away, though I am weeping.
If I weep, whom do I harm?
Drag me away, though I weep still.

Or at the last moment she begs her mother to hide her. This resistance,
suggesting, beneath the convention, her real fear of leaving girlhood,
brings her mother to her senses:

Ἄσπρη κατάσπρη βαμβακιὰ τὴν εἶχα στὴν αὐλή μου,
τὴ σκάλιζα, τὴν πότιζα, τὴν εἶχα γιὰ δική μου.
Μά 'ρθε ξένος κι ἀπόξενος, ἦρθε καὶ μοῦ τὴν πῆρε.

– Κρύψε με, μάνα, κρύψε με, νὰ μὴ μὲ πάρη ὁ ξένος.
– Τί νὰ σὲ κρύψω, μάτια μου, ποὺ σὺ τοῦ ξένου εἶσαι·
τοῦ ξένου φόρια φόρεσε, τοῦ ξένου δαχτυλίδια,
γιατὶ τοῦ ξένου εἶσαι καὶ σύ, κι ὁ ξένος θὰ σὲ πάρη. Politis *LS* 3.281

I had a pure white cotton plant growing in my courtyard;
I weeded it, I watered it, and it was all my own.
But a stranger, yes a stranger came and took it from me.
– Hide me, mother, hide me, so the stranger cannot take me.
– How can I hide you, dear one, now you belong to him:
wear the stranger's clothes, wear the stranger's rings,
for you belong to him, and he will take you.

Similarly, in a funeral lament from Tsakonia, the dying girl sees Charos
approach, and begs her mother to hide her in a cage, in a chest, among
the basil and balsam plants; but her mother replies sternly that she will
not, that she gives her over to Charos (*Laog* (1923) 40). The allusive
quality of these songs, where the imagery of the funeral laments, especially
for those who died young, is imbued with the imagery of the wedding
songs, may owe something to the antiquity in Greek tradition of the
theme of death as marriage, which can be richly illustrated from tragedy,
from the epigrams of the Anthology, from rhetorical and narrative
works, and, most abundantly, from the funerary inscriptions.[65]

All three types of lament, for departure from home, for change of
religion and for marriage, are deeply rooted in ritual beliefs. They are
interesting not only in themselves, but also for the range and depth of
poetic response which they have inspired in the whole tradition of
funeral lamentation.

Moirológia *for the dead*

Let us turn now to the different types of *moirológia* for the dead, since
it is here that the closest parallels to ancient forms are to be found. First,
there are the laments sung by the women at the laying-out and at the
tomb. At the laying-out, both kinswomen and strangers, but more
especially the latter, concentrate on praising the dead in a series of
formal and well-ordered verses in the third person, drawing from
a common fund of conventional *topoi*:[66]

'Εδῶ σὲ τοῦτ' τὴ γειτονιά, ἐδῶ σὲ τοῦτ' τὸ σπίτι
ἦταν βρυσούλα μὲ νερὸ καὶ δέντρος ἰσκιωμένος,
ποὺ κάθονταν στὸν ἴσκιο του ἀδέρφια καὶ ξαδέρφια,

κάθονταν καὶ ὁ ἄντρας της μαζὶ μὲ τὰ παιδιά της.
Τώρα ν ἡ βρύση στέρεψε κι ὁ δέντρος ξεριζώθη.

Laog (1960) 367.1

Here in this neighbourhood, here in this house,
there was a fountain with water and a shady tree,
where brothers and cousins would sit in its shade,
where her husband would sit and with him her children.
Now the fountain has dried up, and the tree is uprooted.

In Mani, the mourner may begin with a stereotyped, proverbial opening in fifteen-syllable verse, and continue with a direct address, improvised in eight-syllable rhyming couplets:

Ποιὰ μάνα Τούρκα τό 'λεγε τ' ἀδέρφια δὲν πονιοῦνται;
τ' ἀδέρφια σκίζουν τὰ βουνά, ὅσο ν' ἀνταμωθοῦνε.
  Ἔ, ἀδερφούλι μου χρυσό,
  γι' ἄνοιξε τὰ ματάκια σου . . .   Laog (1960) 385.7, 1–4

What Turkish mother said that brothers feel no mutual pity?
Brothers rend mountains asunder until they meet again.
  É, my golden brother,
  open your eyes now!

The improvisations at the laying-out are usually long, lyrical reproaches from the next of kin, which follow a traditional pattern according to the person addressed, whether a mother, father, husband, brother or child (*Laog* (1960) 366–74, 379). Sophia Lala of Samarina, well known as an expert mourner, complained to me in 1966 that today, many women do not bother to observe the correct distinctions in their laments, and sing the first thing that comes into their heads, whereas if she is invited to lament at a funeral, she always thinks carefully before she starts what type of lament is proper to the occasion. In Mani, where the custom of lamentation is particularly vigorous, the mourner introduces into her improvisation many specific details from the past: in a lament for a young girl who died of leukaemia after graduating in Greek literature, her aunt recounts to her in detail how many doctors were consulted, and how many friends came to give blood, in a vain attempt to save her life (*Laog* (1960) 396.3, 5–10).

When the body is raised for the funeral procession, the dialogue form again predominates, as one of the mourners sings the dead man's last farewell to his house and family. Sometimes a more macabre note is introduced, and he takes leave not only of the four walls of his house but also of his good looks, instructing in turn his hair, eyes, hands and feet to prepare themselves to enter the black earth (*Laog* (1929) 26.85, 1–2).[67] This, and the moment of burial, call for passionate lamentation from the next of kin, who weep and cry out on the dead not to leave them:

– Ἔ, Πότη μου, ἄκου νὰ σοῦ πῶ,	– E, my Potis, listen to me,
κλαίγοντας παρακαλετῶ,	weeping I beg you,
μὴ φύγης, μὴν ἀναχωρῆς,	do not go, do not depart,
μὴν πᾶς ἐσὺ γιὰ νὰ κλειστῆς	don't get yourself shut up
στὸν Ἄδη καὶ στὴν κάτω γῆ.	in Hades and the Underworld.

Laog (1960) 380.2, 5–9

But not all laments at the tomb are passionate reproaches and addresses to the dead by name, or long dialogues. In some of the Cypriot *anakalémata*, and above all in the couplets from Karpathos, terse and detached distichs are improvised, similar in style and content to the ancient inscriptions. Sometimes it is the dead man who speaks, informing the world of the manner of his death:

Ἐμένα μὲ σκοτώσασιν ὀμπρὸς στὸ μαγαντζίμ μου,
ἀπού λου(γ)άριαντζα νὰ ζῶ, νὰ θάψω τὸ παι(δ)ίμ μου.

Laog (1934) 185

I was killed in front of my shop,
where I hoped to live, to bury my child.

Young Stasia, three months buried, begs Charos to let her join her brothers, who have just come home from abroad, but Charos replies sternly that she will see them only when they come to light candles on her grave (*ibid.* 188.9). A Cypriot mother accuses Charos in a formula similar to that of the ancient inscriptions:[68]

Χάρε σκληρέ, σκληρότατα ἐπῆρες τὸ παιδίν μου,
ποὺ ἦταν τὸ καμάριν μου, ποὺ ἦταν ἡ ζωή μου.

Laog (1953) 444.13

Cruel Charos, most cruelly have you taken my child,
who was my pride, who was my life.

The function of the ritual lamentation of the women is the same as in antiquity. It soothed wrath in cases of cruel or untimely death; or, alternatively, like the *góos éndikos* (just lament) of Orestes and Elektra, it roused the spirit of revenge (A. *Ch.* 327–31). This is the purpose of the long, narrative *vendetta ballads* from Mani: in one, entitled *The Blood*, a mother relates how, one Easter morning, she prepares for the revenge of her husband's murder eighteen years before. Returning from church, she lays an extra place at the Easter meal, telling her five children that it is for their father, and instructing them to avenge his death by seeking out the enemy clan and making sure to kill the leader that very Easter Day, or else her black curse will pursue them everywhere. They ask her solemn blessing, which is given over the ritual tasting of the lamb, and then go out. Greeting their return at evening when the deed is done, she acclaims them as worthy at last, and gives thanks to Fortune (Pasayanis 146).

Such might be the motive. But there is a more subjective aspect: grief, finding expression, is relieved and lightened, hence the ritual lament is just as necessary for the mourner as it is for the dead. This idea was almost proverbial in antiquity; as the chorus of Trojan women say to Hekabe:[69]

ὡς ἡδὺ δάκρυα τοῖς κακῶς πεπραγόσι
θρήνων τ' ὀδυρμοὶ μοῦσά θ' ἢ λύπας ἔχει.   E. *Tr.* 608–9

How sweet are tears to those of evil fortune,
and the weeping of dirges, and the sorrowful Muse.

It is echoed in many laments today. A Maniot woman sings:

Καλὰ ποὺ εἶναι τὰ κλαήματα, γλυκὰ τὰ μοιρολόγια,
    κάλλιό 'χω νὰ μοιρολογῶ,
    παρὰ νὰ φάω καὶ νὰ πιῶ.   Pasayanis 88.5–7

How good are tears, how sweet are dirges,
    I would rather sing dirges
    than eat or drink.

The second group of *moirológia* belongs neither exclusively to the women nor to funeral ritual, but to the *epitrapézia tragoúdia* (songs of the table). The institution of the common meal restricted to male members of the community has long disappeared; but large gatherings of family and friends persist, especially at festive meals, and with them the practice of *after-supper songs*. The range of theme is wide, and the length varies from improvised and competitive couplets to longer narrative ballads.[70] Some are concerned with or addressed to the dead, but they are not laments. A large number of the so-called *moirológia of the Underworld and Charos* betray connections with songs of the Akritic cycle, especially with the theme of the death of Digenis and his struggle with Charos; others appear to be fragments of longer ballads, ending before the story is complete. One may observe here a tendency for the longer, narrative poems to break up into shorter and more lyrical pieces, and for parts to become absorbed into the women's ritual laments.[71]

Another important type in this group is predominantly historical. Like their ancient counterparts, these songs were concerned less with lamentation for the dead than with praise of a hero. Their function was not ritual, but educative, to inspire the present generation to the same heroic feats as the last. Many of the historical and Kleftic songs fall into this category, some being specifically addressed by the old men to the young, bequeathing to them their skill and experience in battle, others recounting exploits and heroic deaths 'while we eat and drink'.[72] Once more, some distinctive songs for heroes come from Mani. During the Balkan Wars of 1912–13, news reached Pachianika near Mount Tainaron that the soldier Dimitrios Livanas had been killed in battle. It was Christmas Day, and all gathered in his family's house to honour his memory. First to speak was a woman from a neighbouring village whose son had also been killed in battle: beginning with the Balkan Entente, and Venizelos' decision to fight the Turks, she recalls how, when their sons were called up, all the women sent them off with exhortations 'to slay the Turk, and if they do not defeat him, not to come home again'. She asserts that it is an insult to the dead to weep, commenting that the ancient Spartans likewise refused to lament those slain in battle. In conclusion, she tells Livanas' relatives not to make cowards of their son by singing dirges, but to pray instead to the Virgin to keep a watchful eye on Venizelos, now in London, lest he be deceived by 'the strong and...unjust powers'. She is answered by the dead man's nurse, who claims that neither the Spartans nor the Mavromichalaioi were ashamed to lament, but agrees that it is not fitting at present: 'You men, who have weapons, leave for Iannina! Help our children to defeat the Turk!' (*Laog* (1912–13) 3–11).[73] This is not a lament, but a passionate discussion on patriotic themes, interspersed with political commentary on current affairs. At the same time, it is a solemn tribute to the dead.

Finally, there are the *gnomikà moirológia* (gnomic laments), comparable to the ballads of the Underworld and to the songs for heroes in that they are not necessarily mournful, but different in both form and content. They are mostly distichs, and express with the utmost conciseness some consolatory and proverbial wisdom about life and death, as though the imposition of order on irrational feelings can effect some control over the disturbing and incomprehensible process of death. Most depend on the intricate elaboration of imagery by antithetical similes, which compare and contrast the world of nature with the world of man – a technique which permits the highest degree of explicit and implicit comment without referring to the actual fact of death. The following examples are taken from Karpathos and Aigina:[74]

Ἐμίσεψε τὸ γιασεμὶ τσ' ἐπῆρε τσαὶ τὴ ρίζα,
ποὺ πλώναμε τὰ ροῦχα μας ἀπάνω τσαὶ μυρίζα. *Laog* (1934) 184.8

The jasmine has gone and has taken the root
where we hung our clothes to take its scent.

Σφαῖρα 'ναι τοῦτος ὁ ντουνιὰς κι ὅλο στριφογυρίζει,
ἄλλους τοὺς ἀνταμώνει ὁ Θιὸς κι ἄλλους τοὺς ξεχωρίζει.
Laog (1921) 544.107

This world is a ball, and it keeps on turning;
some God brings together, others he sunders.

The exact circumstances in which these gnomic laments are performed are hard to define; but they are appropriate to the all-night vigil over the dead during the wake, and to the funeral feast. Many of the more formal ritual laments of the women sung at the wake also open proverbially:

Ἂ δὲ φουσκώση ἡ θάλασσα, ὁ βράχος δὲν ἀφρίζει,
κι ἂν δὲ σὲ κλάψη ἡ μάνα σου, ὁ κόσμος δὲ δακρύζει.   Politis 198

If the sea does not swell, the rock does not foam,
and if your mother does not weep for you, the world sheds
    no tears.

Finally, one of the laments I recorded in 1963 from the village of Rhodia in Thessaly, sung by a group of men in chorus to the slow, monotonous and mournful tune characteristic of the Thessalian plain, approaches the spirit of some of the ancient elegiacs.[75] As the words indicate, it is appropriate to a gathering of men:

Ὡρὲ χαριτωμένη συντροφιά, χαρεῖτε νὰ χαροῦμε
ὡρὲ τοῦτον τὸν χρόνον τὸν καλόν, τὸν ἄλλον ποιὸς τὸν ξέρει;
ὡρὲ γιὰ ζοῦμε γιὰ πεθαίνουμε γιὰ σ' ἄλλον κόσμον πᾶμε.

Joyful company, rejoice that we may enjoy
this good year, who knows what the next will bring?
whether we live or die or go to the other world.

This brief classification of modern *moirológia* suggests that while the ancient terms have disappeared, a high proportion of similar features have survived in each type. Among the women's ritual laments, the gnomic, consolatory and laudatory tone balances the passionate, informal addresses at the laying-out; while at the tomb, terse distichs are performed as well as long and sometimes inflammatory dialogues. At the same time, to praise and commemorate the dead there exists the tradition of men's heroic songs and ballads sung after meals to educate and inspire the younger generation. Belonging to the whole community are the gnomic distichs, similar to riddles and proverbs in form and content, which serve the vital social function of helping the bereaved adjust themselves to the world of the living. Finally, that this modern popular tradition of laments for men and songs to the dead has its roots in antiquity is supported by the history of its terminology.

1 Black-figure *loutrophóros* amphora by the Sappho painter, *c.* 500 B.C. *Próthesis:* the dead man is laid out on a bier, his head resting on a pillow. A child is standing at the head. To the left are six mourning women in varying attitudes of lamentation, the first with her right hand on the dead man's head, the others with their left hands to their heads and their right arms outstretched.

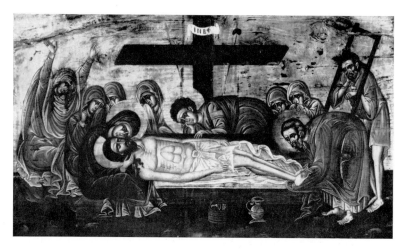

2a   Panel-painting by an unknown Cretan artist, early seventeenth century. *Thrênos:* Christ has been taken down from the cross. The Virgin holds Christ's head with both hands. John is in the centre, and probably Joseph of Arimathaea at the feet; behind stands Nikodemos, holding the ladder. Behind are six unidentified mourning women. The black triangles beneath the eyes of all figures except for Christ, indicating grief, are a typically Cretan detail. Beneath Christ is a bag with the nails and an ointment vessel.

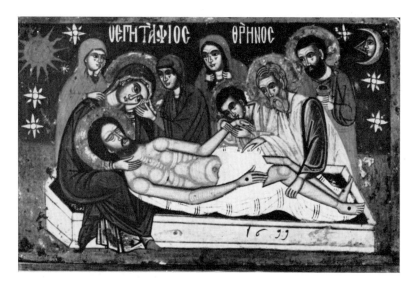

2b   Panel-painting, dated 1699. *Thrênos:* Christ has been taken down from the cross. The Virgin holds his head and weeps, comforted by two women, while a third pulls her hair with both hands. There is no cross in the background, but the presence of the moon, stars and dimmed sun is probably an intrusion from the Crucifixion scene.

3a Elderly women at the tomb lament antiphonally for a child, probably at a memorial after the funeral, since the cross has been erected. On the grave are placed fruit and food, which are shared out among the women after the lament is finished.

3b Three women lament at the tomb, which is covered with fresh flowers, after the burial. The bereaved widow is at the head of the tomb, and two relatives on the left.

4a Women at the cemetery lament during the memorial held on the fortieth day after the death of a young man, killed by lightning. The whole village took part in the memorial, but only the women entered the cemetery for the lament, which lasted for over an hour.

4b Same occasion as 4a. A woman hands round wine, fish, meat and sweetmeats to the mourners after the lament is finished.

PART III
THE COMMON TRADITION

7
Antiphonal structure and antithetical thought

So far we have considered the lament for the dead both in relation to the funeral ritual of which it is still an integral part, and in relation to other kinds of ritual laments and songs to the dead. The similarities between the ancient and modern material may be explained partly in terms of the common cultural basis of all such ritual beliefs and customs in all parts of the world, irrespective of geographical and national boundaries, but partly also in terms of the cultural and linguistic continuity of the Greek people from antiquity to the present day. By examining in more depth the parallels in structure and thought, poetic conventions and imagery, which are to be found in the ancient and modern laments, I hope to define more precisely in this final section first, the nature and extent of this continuity as reflected in our material, and second, the interaction of traditional forms and poetic originality, which enabled the poets to draw on a living vernacular tradition, itself continually enriched by what it had absorbed from a long literary past.

Form and structure

In ancient literature, the lament is presented in a variety of forms: with a soloist, accompanied by chorus only in the refrain; with a chorus alone; with one or more soloists and a chorus, singing antiphonally; and finally, in the form of an imagined dialogue between living and dead. What was the relation between these different forms, and how was each developed in ancient tradition?

The words used in Homer for beginning the dirge are ἐξάρχειν (to lead off) or ἄρχειν (to begin).[1] Their significance is most fully illustrated in the laments for Hector at the end of the *Iliad*, where each of the women leads off in turn, keeping her improvisation to a similar length and structure, and is followed by a refrain wailed by the whole company of women in unison. This gives the simple strophic pattern *Ax Ax Ax*.[2] Although discarded by the lyric poets in favour of the monodic and triadic forms, its traditional character is indicated by its survival in popular hymns, such as the Hymn of the Kouretes and the Elian Hymn to Dionysos.[3]

Of the *thrênoi* of Pindar and Simonides, too little has survived to understand more of their structure and form than that they were choral, with an important musical element.[4] It is in tragedy that the greatest diversity is to be found. In addition to the solo lament, which is always answered by a refrain of cries from the chorus,[5] and the antistrophic choral lament, there is the *kommós*, sung antiphonally by one or more actors and chorus, giving the more complex pattern *AA BB CC DD* etc.[6]

Although the most flexible, mature and dramatic, and the last to emerge as an art form, this antistrophic, antiphonal lament of tragedy may be shown to contain elements more ancient than either the solo lament with refrain, or the purely choral lament. Traces of antiphony have already been analysed in the Homeric laments for Hector and Achilles, and are perhaps indicated in the laments of Briseis and Achilles for Patroklos.[7] If the antiphonal lament was not an entirely new development in tragedy, but the formal expression of the ritual exchange between two groups of mourners, as I have suggested in chapter 1, then the predominance of the solo laments with refrain and the choral laments in the earlier period could be explained by the tendency of epic to develop the narrative element at the expense of antiphony and refrain, and of lyric to concentrate on the choral and musical elements. The tragedians revived antiphony because of its inherently dramatic potentiality, but all three had grown out of a common tradition.

It is of course impossible to retrace this process in detail. But an analysis of the actual use of these forms in the ancient laments will serve to confirm their common origins, and at the same time to indicate how the subsequent growth of each contributed to the shaping of the basic forms of lamentation in Greek tradition. Taking the solo lament first, an analysis of the three laments for Hector at the end of the *Iliad* reveals that they not only conform to a similar length and type, but that each is built up on the same three-part form:

Andromache (24.725–45)

A 725–30: Direct address and reproach to Hector for having died so young, ἄνερ, ἀπ' αἰῶνος νέος ὤλεο . . .

B 731–9: Narrative, in which her own and her son's future is imagined.

A 740–5: Renewed address and reproach to Hector for having left her such grief, ἄρρητον . . . γόον καὶ πένθος ἔθηκας, | Ἕκτορ.

Hekabe (748–59)

A 748–50: Direct address to Hector as the dearest of all her sons, Ἕκτορ, ἐμῷ θυμῷ πάντων πολὺ φίλτατε παίδων.

B 751–6: Narrative, how Hector and her other sons were killed.

A 757–9: Renewed address and lament for Hector, now lying dead, νῦν δέ μοι . . . | κεῖσαι.

Helen (762–75)

A 762–4: Direct address to Hector as the dearest of her husband's brothers, Ἕκτορ, ἐμῷ θυμῷ δαέρων πολὺ φίλτατε πάντων.

B 765–70: Narrative, her own past and Hector's kindness to her.

A 771–5: Renewed address for Hector and for herself, τῶ σέ θ' ἅμα κλαίω καὶ ἔμ' ἄμμορον ἀχνυμένη κῆρ.

The mourner begins with a preliminary address to the dead, then remembers the past or imagines the future in a predominantly narrative section, and finally renews her opening address and lament. This is ternary form, *ABA*, in which the opening section, an address or appeal, is reinforced and modified by the intervening narrative of the second section. While by no means every lament conforms to this pattern, there is a sufficient number of examples, early and late, to establish its traditional basis beyond doubt.[8]

This three-part form was not exclusive to the *thrênos*, but was shared also by the *hýmnos*, *enkómion* and *epitáphios*. The Homeric Hymns open and close with an address or reference to the name of the god who is to be praised, while the central section contains an account of the god's genealogy and accomplishments. Sappho's *Ode to Aphrodite* begins with an appeal to the goddess, then she reminds her of how her prayers have always been answered in the past, and actually sees her coming in her imagination, and finally she repeats her prayer with renewed force and confidence.[9] The same basic pattern was later formalised in the rhetorical *epitáphios*. The origins of this ternary form, in which the prayer is first stated, then enacted as though fulfilled, and finally repeated, are to be sought in primitive ritual. The form was developed in all kinds of ritual poetry.

In contrast to the *hýmnos*, *enkómion* and *epitáphios*, the development of the three-part form did not in the *thrênos* lead to the total disappearance of the refrain. The lament was always in some sense collective, and never an exclusively solo performance. There is no example in Greek antiquity of a lament which has lost all traces of refrain. Is there any evidence about the nature of its contents which might help to determine its function and significance? First, the word *epodé* means not simply *after-song*, but a song sung over someone, a *désmios hýmnos* (binding song) or magic incantation, designed in the dirge to bring the dead man back to life. That is perhaps why it disappeared in many of the hymns and odes, but not in the dirge. Its magical function was never quite forgotten.

This is confirmed by the use of both *epodoí* and *ephýmnia* in the choral odes of tragedy. The *epodós* usually comes at the end of the ode (*AA BB CC x*), while the *ephýmnion* may be placed either between the antistrophic pairs (*AAx BBx CCx*) or between strophe and anti-strophe (*Ax Ax Bx Bx Cx Cx*). Both are formal refrains, metrically distinct from the rest of the ode. One of the most striking features of their use is that they occur most frequently in odes which are laments or invocations, at the moment when the dramatic tension within the ode has reached its highest pitch. The three *ephýmnia* in the *párodos* of Aeschylus' *Suppliant Women* all follow an invocation to Zeus and culminate in an incantation cursing their enemies (117–19, 128–32, 141–3, 151–3, 162–7, 175a–f). In the *Persians*, the chorus conclude both their invocation to Dareios and their final ecstatic lament with *epodoí* (672–80, 1066–77). In the *Seven Against Thebes* the antiphonal lament of Antigone and Ismene is interspersed with choral *ephýmnia* and concluded with an *epodós* (975–1004). The *kommós* at the end of the *Agamemnon* is an angry exchange between the chorus and Clytemnestra, in which the chorus interrupt the first and third strophes and the second strophic pair with four *ephýmnia*, crying out on the fate of their murdered king in lamentation (1455–61, 1489–96, 1513–20, 1537–50). In the *Eumenides*, the Furies leap and dance round the sleeping Orestes chanting an *ephýmnion* after the first strophe and antistrophe which bear all the characteristics of a magic incantation (328–33, 341–6). These and other examples suggest the conscious use of the formal refrain to heighten the impact of an invocation or lament.[10] What were its contents? The commonest Homeric formula to follow a lament is ἐπὶ δὲ στενάχοντο γυναῖκες (and the women wailed in answer).[11] It implies the reiteration of wails and cries. The cry is no less essential to the *epodoí* and *ephýmnia* referred to above, sometimes forming the basis of its entire contents, as in the *epodós* which concludes the *Persians*:

Ξε. βόα νυν ἀντίδουπά μοι.	*Xerxes.* Cry aloud, echo my cries.
Χο. οἰοῖ οἰοῖ.	*Chorus.* Oioî, oioî!
– αἰακτὸς ἐς δόμους κίε.	– Go, wailing, to your homes.
– ἰὼ ἰὼ [Περσὶς αἶα δύσβατος].	– Ió, ió!
– ἰωὰ δὴ κατ᾽ ἄστυ.	– Ioá, thoughout the city!
– ἰωὰ δῆτα, ναὶ ναί.	– Ioá, yes indeed!
Χο. γοᾶσθ᾽ ἁβροβάται.	*Ch.* Sing dirges as you walk on
Ξε. ἰὼ ἰώ, Περσὶς αἶα δύσβατος.	gently.
– ἠὴ ἠή, τρισκάλμοισιν,	*Xe.* Ió, ió, Persian land, grievous
ἠὴ ἠή, βάρισιν ὀλόμενοι.	to tread.
– πέμψω τοί σε δυσθρόοις γόοις.	– Alas for those who died,
	alas for the three-tiered ships.
	– I will send you forth to the
	dismal sound of dirges.
	A. *Pers.* 1066–77

Besides the metrical refrain of the choral odes, traces of refrain structure may also be found in the repetition of certain lines throughout a lament, whether choral or solo in form. The third strophe and antistrophe of the invocation to Dareios both end with the same command: βάσκε πάτερ ἄκακε Δαριάν, οἴ (Come, guileless father Dareios, oí!) 663, 671. Similarly, the chorus of Euripides' *Elektra* open both strophe and antistrophe of their lament with the call: σύντειν᾽ – ὥρα – ποδὸς ὁρμάν· ὤ|ἔμβα, ἔμβα κατακλαίουσα·|ἰώ μοί μοι. (Press on – it is time! – with speed of foot. O go onward, onward, weeping bitterly! Alas for me!) (112–14, 127–9). And in Bion's *Epitáphios*, the lines αἰάζω τὸν "Αδωνιν· ἀπώλετο καλὸς "Αδωνις· | ὤλετο καλὸς "Αδωνις, ἐπαιάζουσιν "Ερωτες (Alas for Adonis, I cry, the fair Adonis is dead! The fair Adonis is dead. Alas! cry the Loves in answer) are repeated eight times with slight variation at regular intervals throughout. Finally, in Moschos' *Epitáphios*, the appeal "Αρχετε

Σικελικαί, τῷ πένθεος ἄρχετε Μοῖσαι (Begin, Sicilian Muses, begin the dirge!) is repeated at short and regular intervals. All these refrains contain a cry of lamentation.

In addition to repeated lines and phrases, there is also the reiteration of cries. In the *kommós* at the end of Sophokles' *Antigone*, every cry in the strophe is answered by a similar cry in the antistrophe (1261–76, 1284–1300). This balancing of cries is found in many other choral laments, and points to its calculated use at regular intervals, as a kind of refrain.[12] Another technique was to build up the emotional tension gradually to a climax by increasing the frequency of cries, as in the long *kommós* at Agamemnon's tomb in the *Choephoroi*.[13] Reiterated cries also established contact with the dead. While Elektra pours her libation to Agamemnon, the chorus of the *Choephoroi* cry out to him to hear their prayer:

κλύε δέ μοι, σέβας,
κλύ᾽, ὦ δέσποτ᾽, ἐξ ἀμαυρᾶς φρενός.
ὀτοτοτοτοτοῖ.　　　　　　　　　　　　　156–9

 ...Listen to me, august one,
 listen, o lord, from your shadowy sense.
 Otototototoî!

Both here and in the invocation to Dareios, the cry accompanies a command. In the latter, it also contains an appeal to the dead by name, which appears to have a special significance, since it was frequently avoided, even in a direct address to the dead.[14] It has been preserved in that part of the lament where the ritual function was strongest.

One more traditional feature of the refrain was the reiterated statement of death. The refrain in Bion's lament for Adonis contains the phrase 'the fair Adonis is dead', and a similar line is repeated in Moschos' lament for Bion (7, 12, 18). In the *Persians* the words βασιλεία γὰρ διόλωλεν ἰσχύς (the royal might has perished) close the third strophe of the first stasimon, which laments the destruction of the Persian army (589–90); while the choral *ephýmnia* lamenting Agamemnon repeat the phrase κεῖσαι δ᾽ ἀράχνης ἐν ὑφάσματι τῷδ᾽ | ἀσεβεῖ θανάτῳ βίον ἐκπνέων (You lie in that spider's web, expiring by a wicked death!).[15]

The main contents of the refrain, as it has survived in tragedy and in later poetic laments, would therefore seem to include the reiteration of cries, statements of death and appeals by name. Its function was to rouse the spirit of the dead and establish contact, and therefore in keeping with the essential meaning of the word *epodé*. Further, as we have seen in chapter 6, the etymology of both *thrênos* and *góos* suggests that this refrain of cries – which, far from being meaningless, was a kind of incantation – may once have formed the basis of the lament. It was only after the role of *éxarchos* had been developed, with the separation of leader from chorus, that the refrain became subordinate. Even so, its function was not forgotten, and has left important traces both in the choral laments of tragedy, where it was deliberately exploited for dramatic effect, and in Alexandrian poetry, where there are signs that it was beginning to form structural divisions of a new, almost stanzaic type.

If it is correct that the simple solo and refrain grew out of an originally antiphonal tradition, then antiphony may be expected to have left some impact on later development. Some evidence for this is suggested by the use of stichomythic dialogue, which finds its most concentrated and highly developed expression in tragedy, where it is frequently used as prelude or interlude to the laments to heighten tension. In Sophokles' *Trachiniai*, the news of Deianeira's death is not told as a simple statement of fact, but revealed gradually, point by point, in a prolonged series of statement and counter-statement, question and answer:

> Τρ. βέβηκε Δηάνειρα τὴν πανυστάτην
> ὁδῶν ἁπασῶν ἐξ ἀκινήτου ποδός.
> Χο. οὐ δή ποθ' ὡς θανοῦσα; – πάντ' ἀκήκοας.
> – τέθνηκεν ἡ τάλαινα; – δεύτερον κλύεις.
> – τάλαιν', ὀλεθρία· τίνι τρόπῳ θανεῖν σφε φῄς;
> – σχετλίῳ τὰ πρός γε πρᾶξιν. – εἰπὲ τῷ μόρῳ,
> γύναι, ξυντρέχει.   874–80 (cf. 881–95)

Nurse. Deianeira has gone on the last
   of all roads, without stirring a step.
Chorus. You mean she is dead? – You have heard all.
   – Is poor Deianeira dead? – That is the second time you
      hear it.
   – Poor ruined soul! How did she die?
   – It was a dreadful deed. – Tell us, woman,
      how she met her death.

This technique of catechistic questions is an integral part of the structure of many tragic laments.[16] In the *Persians*, the ghost of Dareios appears in answer to the chorus' invocation, and questions them, in a tense passage of stichomythia in trochaic tetrameters, point by point about past and present; then, after his intervening lament for Persia's fate, they question him in turn about the future (702–38, 787–800). Sticho-mythia is here the medium of expression for the dialogue between living and dead.

Had it any basis in Greek tradition outside tragedy? In epigrams and funerary inscriptions from the fifth century on, the use of dialogue is extremely common, usually in the form of a swift exchange of question and answer, through which the interlocutor learns step by step of the dead man's family, his life and manner of death, as in the following terse couplet of Simonides:[17]

– Εἰπόν, τίς, τίνος ἐσσί, τίνος πατρίδος, τί δ' ἐνίκης;
– Κασμύλος, Εὐαγόρου, Πύθια πύξ, 'Ρόδιος.   *ALG* 2.115.149

– Say, who are you, who is your father, what is your country,
   where were you victorious?
– Kasmylos, son of Euagoras, Pythian boxer, from Rhodes.

It is true that developed stichomythic form is not found in non-literary inscriptions before tragedy, and literary influence cannot therefore be excluded; but the imagined dialogue between living and dead, on which its use in the lament was based, can be traced much further back. The statement to the passing traveller by the dead man or his tomb is found in some of the earliest extant inscriptions from the seventh century, and became increasingly common during the sixth century.[18] Sometimes the address is reversed, and it is the traveller who speaks to the dead man, as in the following inscription for a doctor from Phokis (sixth to fifth centuries):

χαῖρε, Χάρōν· | οὐδὶς τὺ κακōς | λέγει οὐδὲ θα|νόντα,
πολὸς | ἀνθρόπōν λυ|σάμενος | καμάτο.   Peek 1384

Hail, Charon. No one speaks ill of you even in death,
for you freed many men from pain.

The use of the formulaic greeting χαῖρε (hail) and of the vocative[19] indicate that these two modes of address were in fact complementary aspects of an imagined dialogue, in which the dead man or his tomb informed the passer-by of who he was and of his death, and the traveller in turn gave an assurance of his pity and concern. After the relaxation of the austere brevity of the archaic style, both addresses are found together in the same inscription, and the interlocutor is no longer an impersonal passer-by but a relative or friend.[20]

Further, the formulaic greeting which is found in the funerary inscriptions occurs for the first time in Greek literature in a highly significant ritual context. In the *Iliad*, Achilles leads off the lament for Patroklos with a solemn oath that he will avenge his friend's death:

χαῖρέ μοι, ὦ Πάτροκλε, καὶ εἰν ᾿Αΐδαο δόμοισι·
πάντα γὰρ ἤδη τοι τελέω τὰ πάροιθεν ὑπέστην...   23.19–20

Hail, Patroklos, even in Hades' halls.
I am fulfilling all the promises I made to you before.

Later, Achilles' oath is answered by a reproach from the soul of Patroklos that he has neglected his funeral rites (*ibid.* 69–70). That the formula 'Hail, though in Hades...' was traditional to the address to the dead, and not merely a literary borrowing, is indicated first by its frequency in inscriptions from all parts of the Greek-speaking world throughout antiquity, and secondly by the number of variations in which it is found.[21]

D. L. Page has said that the use of the voice of the dead man or his tomb in the funerary inscriptions is an indication of a later sophistication, asking 'whether in any case a *thrênos* can properly be uttered by the dead man or his tomb' and concluding, with characteristic logic, that it cannot.[22] Lattimore, more cautiously, comments that the convention is appropriate to the inscribed epitaph and nothing else, and presents a unique example of the influence of inscriptions on literature.[23] If, however, the convention arose out of the dialogue between living and dead, it belongs to one of the oldest and least sophisticated elements of the lament. It is generally accepted that belief in the intercourse between the world of the living and the world of the dead is extremely primitive. Some traces of this belief have survived in the form and structure of later laments, particularly in the more popular tradition of funerary inscriptions. And the dialogue between living and dead, performed by two antiphonal groups of mourners, is still a significant element in the modern *moirológia*, many of which are, precisely, laments 'uttered by the dead man or by his tomb'.

By the end of antiquity, the three-part form had been reduced by literary convention to mere formalism, satirised by Lucian in his *de Luctu* (second century A.D.) as follows:

The common tradition

            1   Τέκνον ἥδιστον
    A   οἴχῃ μοι   καὶ τέθνηκας
            καὶ πρὸ ὥρας   ἀνηρπάσθης
        ⎧ 2   μόνον ἐμὲ τὸν ἄθλιον καταλιπών,
    B   ⎪ 3   οὐ γαμήσας   οὐ παιδοποιησάμενος
        ⎨ 3   οὐ στρατευσάμενος   οὐ γεωργήσας
        ⎩ 2   οὐκ εἰς γῆρας ἐλθών·
    A   οὐ κωμάσῃ πάλιν   οὐδ᾽ ἐρασθήσῃ, τέκνον,
            1   οὐδὲ ἐν συμποσίοις μετὰ τῶν ἡλικιωτῶν μεθυσθήσῃ.

            Sweetest child
            you are gone from me   and you are dead
            and before your time   you have been snatched
                leaving me behind, wretched and alone,
            not having married   not having begotten children
            not having been a soldier   not having been a farmer
                not reaching old age;
            You will not revel again   nor will you fall in love,
                child,
            nor will you get drunk with your comrades at drinking
            parties.

This lament was intended as a parody. The symmetrical arrangement, first analysed by Reiner, with the opening and closing address neatly balanced with three finite verbs, and the corresponding pairs of participles in the central section forming a pattern with their endings *abc cba*, is rhetorical – one might almost say mathematical – rather than literary in character.[24] But although a caricature, the features of the formal lament have been distorted, not invented, as may be seen by comparing Lucian's parody with the highly stylised *planctus* from Achilles Tatius' romance *Leukippe and Kleitophon* (second century A.D.).[25]

In these circumstances it is natural to expect certain changes in the structure of the lament in Byzantine literature. The three-part form continued to play a dynamic part not in the archaising laments of secular poetry, but in the more popular pagan hymns, such as the magic incantations and Orphic Hymn to Physis of the fourth century.[26] In the archaising laments which have come down to us, divorced as they were from ritual or religion, it was first reduced to a perfunctory convention, and then discarded altogether. Was there any attempt to introduce new forms?

In the fifteenth book of Nonnos' *Dionysiaka* (fourth to fifth centuries), there are two short laments for the dead Hymnos. First the bulls, cows and heifers weep for their dead herdsman in a lament of eight lines, with the repetition of a refrain at the first and fifth lines, 'the fair herdsman has perished, slain by the fair girl' (15.399, 403). Then follows the lament of the wild animals – wolf, bear and lion – with a similar refrain at the first and sixth lines and half-line echoes at the third and eleventh. Nonnos, modelling himself perhaps on Bion's lament, is carrying the incipient stanza-refrain one stage further towards a regular pattern. By the eleventh century, Christophoros of Mytilene has completely regularised this structure in his *planctus* for his sister Anastasia, which although formal, is not without a touching sincerity:

Ῥοδοεικέλην γυναῖκα
θάνατος μέλας κατέσχεν,
ἐπὶ τῆς κλίνης δὲ κεῖται
ἀποτμηθὲν ἔρνος οἷα·
ἀρετῆς δ' ἄσυλον ὅρμον
περικειμένη καθεύδει
ἀνακειμένη δὲ λάμπει
νενεκρωμένη περ οὖσα.
Νεφέλαι ὀμβροτόκοι, δάκρυα χεῖτε,
ὅτι καλλίστη ἄφνω ἔσβετο κούρη.

Cantarella 156.6, 1–10

A woman fair as a rose has been snatched by black Death, and lies on her deathbed like a severed shoot. She sleeps, wreathed with a garland of virtue, inviolate; she shines forth, though she lies dead. You rain-bringing clouds, shed tears, for the fairest girl has suddenly been quenched.

The poem contains four eight-line 'stanzas', each followed by two longer lines of invocation, like a refrain. The metre is Anacreontic, one of the more popular of classical metres among Byzantine poets, perhaps because it permitted them to adhere to the rules of classical prosody while maintaining a regular number of eight or twelve syllables in each line, thereby combining quantity with stress. Some of the later Anacreontics are almost indistinguishable from the stressed eight- and twelve-syllable metres of modern folk song.[27] Christophoros' Anacreontic *planctus* therefore provides an important link with Byzantine popular and religious poetry.

On the whole, however, the Byzantine archaising lament shows a stagnation of form and a decline in the dynamic use of structure. The three-part form had fallen into disuse; while instances of stanza and refrain reflect, to a greater or lesser degree, some imitation of Alexandrian poetry, with little added beyond what had to be conceded to the changes in the language and the development of stress. The dialogue form of the ancient funerary inscriptions was imitated in the later epigrams,[28] but it had lost its vitality and immediacy, nor was it adapted to other kinds of lament.

In striking contrast, the religious laments of the early church show considerable experimentation with form. Many of the *kontákia, kanónes* and *tropária* begin and end with an invocation, although the three-part form is no longer basic to the structure as it was in the ancient hymns. Structurally and poetically among the most exciting compositions of this type is Romanos' *kontákion, Mary at the Cross,* whose strophic and melodic construction is a *koukoúlion* of four lines followed by seventeen *tropária* of the same elaborate metrical pattern, forming the acrostic ΤΟΥ ΤΑΠΕΙΝΟΥ ΡωΜΑΝΟΥ (by the humble Romanos). Each *tropárion* ends with a refrain. Without attempting to enter into the controversy about the origins of the *kontákion,* it is worth pointing out that not all these features were entirely new. There are several examples of both linear and strophic acrostic from the pre-Byzantine period, in pagan hymns and secular songs, thus suggesting that even if the immediate origins of the *kontákion* are to be sought in Syriac religious poetry, one of its most prominent features had already existed in Greek tradition before the advent of Christianity.[29] Similarly, the elaborate strophic construction finds a general parallel in the choral odes of tragedy, and coincides with some tendencies already noted in the archaising poetry, where eastern influence was negligible. Thus, even if the particular combination of forms in the *kontákion* was new, its immediate assimilation into Greek may be explained in terms of the history of Greek verse forms.

Further, a closer analysis of Romanos' *kontákion* reveals that there is more to its structure than the melodic or strophic pattern. Besides the invocation of the poem and final *tropárion,* with the intervening dramatic dialogue between Mary and Christ, both Mary's first lament and Christ's reply show traces of artistically balanced three-part form:

A Proem: Invocation to all to join in praising Mother of God

1–16: Dramatic dialogue between Mary and Christ

1–3 *Mary*: *A* Address and reproach, Ποῦ πορεύῃ, τέκνον; (Where are you going, child?)

B Frustration of past hopes, injustice of Christ's death and failure of his disciples to help, Οὐκ ἤλπιζον, τέκνον (I did not expect, my child...)

A Renewed address and lament, θνῄσκεις, τέκνον, μόνος...(You are dying, child, alone...)

4–6 *Christ*: *A* Address, Τί δακρύεις, μῆτηρ; (Why do you weep, mother?)

B   *B* Crucifixion is fulfilment of past prophecies

A Renewed address, μὴ οὖν κλαύσῃς, μῆτερ (Do not weep, mother)

7–8 *Mary*: Why die to save mankind?

9–10 *Christ*: For salvation of man's soul, not his body

11 *Mary*: Shall I see you again?

12–14 *Christ*: At the Resurrection, which will reveal the true meaning of the Crucifixion

15 *Mary*: Renewed lamentation

16 *Christ*: No cause to weep, μὴ κλαύσῃς, ὦ μῆτερ (Cease weeping, mother)

A 17: Praise of Christ, through sufferings of Mary

After Mary's opening lament and Christ's reply, both three strophes in length, the pace quickens, as in answer to his Mother's protests that Christ has no need to die to save mankind, having performed so many miracles in the past, Christ points to the past sins of Adam and Eve and their present misery as proof of the necessity of man's redemption through the Crucifixion (7–10). Then, in answer to Mary's single strophe of short, anxious questions, he assures her that she will see him again after he has risen from the dead, and describes the future joy and hope of the Resurrection (11–14). The dialogue ends with a short, dramatic exchange, in which Mary's grief is contrasted with Christ's hope in a series of parallel antitheses (15–16).

In a single *kontákion*, Romanos has exploited all available forms, strophe–refrain, dialogue and three-part form. Nor is his artistry ever static, developed for the sake of form alone. At every stage it reinforces the depth of insight with which Mary's gradual and painful realisation that her son must be crucified is described. As in the best of the ancient laments, the three-part form reflects a dynamic change: the final strophe is a reappraisal of Christ in the light of Mary's suffering, described in the central section. The refrain at the end of each strophe, ὁ υἱός καὶ θεός μου (my son and God), itself a terse expression of Mary's conflicting emotions for Christ, who is at the same time her son and God, is used in a variety of ways – questions, statements, appeals – and with a wide range of feelings – affection, despair, triumph. It is never purely perfunctory. But it is above all the dialogue which sustains the dramatic tension, swiftly moving as it does from the personal to the universal, from despair at Christ's death to hope in the future life of mankind. And it is through his use of dialogue that Romanos achieves the interweaving of corresponding planes of time and place – past, present, future, Hades, earth, Paradise – which both widens and deepens our whole conception of the theme. This close integration of form and content, typical of the best of Romanos, is not an abstract convention, but a poetic response to the diversity of forms actually current in Greek liturgical singing of the time.[30]

In a similar context, we find elements of refrain, possibly deriving from Romanos, both in the ninth-century *Stavrotheotókia* and in the later and more popular *Thrênos Theotókou*, where there are also traces of three-part form.[31] In the latter, besides the repetition of the familiar line 'Where are your fine looks, my son, where is your beauty?' (40, 67), the cry of refrain occurs fifteen times in all, six times in the form ὁ υἱός μου καὶ θεός μου (my son and my God), and nine times in the form υἱέ μου (my son). Its position in the line is of some metrical interest, since it is always found in the second half of the *politikòs stíchos*, the full form on syllables 9–15 (8, 41, 61, 65, 85, 106), and the shorter form usually on the last three syllables (13, 22, 37, 49, 102, 108), but also on 9–11 (18, 27) and once on 11–13 (74). This kind of usage suggests the irregular but indispensable refrain of oral tradition.

Turning now to the laments for the fall of Constantinople, we find, in addition to the predominantly narrative ballads which open and close with a direct address, rather in the self-conscious manner of a Broadside ballad, an important development in the use of dialogue. In the more popular *Anakálema*, the news of the city's capture is told in stichomythic dialogue between a ship coming from Constantinople and a galley which it meets near the island of Tenedos. Although the dialogue conforms to a formulaic pattern common in Greek folk song, there is evidence that the meeting of the ships was a historical event: it was at Tenedos that the Venetian galleys on their way to Constantinople had planned to meet an escort from the Greek fleet on 20 May 1453; but while anchored at Chios awaiting a favourable wind, Genoese ships from Pera arrived and told them that the city had already fallen.[32] Another lament takes the form of a dramatic dialogue between the fallen Constantinople and the still prospering city of Venice;[33] while in the *Thrênos of the Four Patriarchates*, Constantinople, Jerusalem, Alexandria and Antioch each laments in turn the passing of her glory, a device which finds some parallels in ancient epigrams.[34]

The Virgin's lament and the *thrênoi* for the fall of Constantinople provide a useful link between Byzantine and modern popular tradition; but they are not folk songs, and it might therefore be argued that the signs of formal structure we have noted are due to literary influence. In order to determine whether the old forms had survived independently, and what their function was, we must look at the modern *moirológia*. There are two types of lament which show traces of three-part form. First, in a historical ballad from Karpathos about the earthquake which ravaged the island on 26 June 1924, the poet begins with an appeal to his mind and heart to prove equal to the task of telling the terrible story – which he proceeds to relate in detail – and concludes with a brief prayer to Christ and the Virgin to avert such catastrophe in the future and a strengthened appeal to his own mind and heart (Michaelidis-Nouaros 317A). Although presented in a more lively manner, this technique is not essentially different from that of numerous Byzantine historical and religious laments. Among the ritual laments, however, there are several which show a more dynamic use of this form. A Maniot woman opens her lament by addressing the dead directly, 'Yiannaki, tell me, what shall I do with my love for you?', then goes on to elaborate in the central, narrative section the theme of her grief for her dead son, returning at the end to a direct address, more passionate than the first, 'Yiannaki, water of life, my royal ship...!' (Theros 686). This structure is not fortuitous, since it can be paralleled elsewhere, and the divisions are further emphasised by a change in metre from the fifteen-syllable *politikòs stíchos* to rhyming couplets in eight-syllable verse.[35]

More universal and fundamental than the three-part form is the refrain. Like the ancient *epodé*, it frequently contains reiterated cries, commands, appeals by name, and statements of death.[36] In a passionate lament from Karpathos, a young girl implores her lover to awake and embrace her, repeating the cry 'awake!' with a crescendo of emotion:

Ξύπνα, καλέ μου, ξύπνα,
ξύπνα, σφιχταγκάλιασε κορμὶ τσυπαρισένο,

ξύπνα, γλυκοφίλησε δγκυὸ χείλη μερзανένια.[37]
Ξύπνα, ξύπνα, μίλησε στὴκ κόρην ἀπού ἀγάπας. *DAr* (1956) 285

Awake, my fair one, awake,
awake, tightly embrace my body like a cypress tree,
awake, sweetly kiss two coral lips.
Awake, awake, speak to the girl you loved.

A mourner from Crete repeats the fact of her daughter's death over and over to herself, with mesmerising effect, ἐπόθανες, ἐπόθανες, μηλιά μου . . . (you are dead, you are dead, my apple-tree . . . !) (Lioudaki 420).

Unfortunately, a complete analysis of the refrain in the modern *moirológia* is at present precluded by the usual practice of editors, which is to print texts without music and to omit all cries and repeated syllables and phrases which are *extra metrum*. When sung, each fifteen-syllable line of these laments may be followed by a refrain of eight or five syllables. Usually the number of syllables in the refrain is constant throughout, while the actual phrase may be varied, as in the following verse from a narrative lament from the island of Astypalaia in the Dodecanese, recorded by Baud-Bovy – one of the few collectors of Greek folk songs to have published the music as well as the texts in full:

'Εχτὲς βραδὺν ἐμπρόβαλα ἀπὸ τὸ παναθύρι
(ὄχου τὸ μαῦρο Χάροντα) –
θωρῶ τὸν κάμπο πράσινο, καὶ τὰ βουνὰ σπαρμένα
(ὄχου πράμα ποὺ τὸ πάθαμε) –   Baud-Bovy 2.102

Yesterday evening I looked out from the window
(Óchou, black Charondas) –
I see the green plain, and the sown mountains
(Óchou, what we have suffered!) –

Frequently, short cries and appeals by name are inserted within the line, sometimes dividing words, or one or more syllables of the same word may be repeated. This kind of flexible melismatic decoration is still indispensable to certain types of lament, where variety is achieved not through the melody (which to the unaccustomed ear at first resembles a monotonous drone), but through the skilful manipulation of ornamentation and refrain.

But the most significant and characteristic feature in the structure of the modern folk laments is the use of dialogue and antiphony. Often, the lament takes the form of an imagined dialogue, in which the mourner asks the dead when he will return, and the dead replies that he cannot, begging the mourner not to weep excessively but to accept his departure, as in the ancient funerary inscriptions.[38] Rarely, he may promise to return in the spring, as in this lament from the Peloponnese:

Σώπα, μανούλα, καὶ μὴν κλαῖς καὶ μὴν παραπονιέσαι,
κι ἐγὼ τὸ Μάη θὲ νὰ 'ρθῶ μὲ τὰ χελιδονάκια. . .
νὰ ἰδῶ ποιὸς μὲ χλίβεται καὶ ποιὸς κλαίει γιὰ μένα.　　Tarsouli 210

Be quiet, mother, do not weep and do not complain,
for I will come back in May with the swallows. . .
to see who grieves for me, who weeps for me.

Sometimes the mourner may address the tomb or the black earth, instructing them to care tenderly for the dead, or telling them in which order to rot his limbs and features.[39] Or it may be a more general appeal to the whole company of dead in Hades, and especially to kinsmen, to look after the newcomer.[40] Nor do the dead speak only in reply to persistent questions and lamentation; sometimes they and their tombs address the casual passer-by, and reproach him for trampling upon him.[41] It may even be the dead man's weapons which tell the passer-by the story of his bravery:

– Καλὴ μέρα σας, ἄρματα. – Καλῶς τους, τοὺς διαβάτες.
– Ἄρματα, ποῦ 'ν' ὁ ἀφέντης σας καὶ ποῦ 'ναι ὁ καλός σας;
– Ὁ Χάρος τὸν ἐγύρεψε παιδὶ γιὰ νὰ τὸν κάνη.

Laog (1909) 264.57

– Good day to you, weapons. – Welcome to you, passers-by.
– Weapons, where is your master and where is your fine one?
– Charos sought him out to make him his child.

Sometimes a macabre scene takes place within the tomb itself, as the dead man pleads with the two-headed snake which threatens to eat away his flesh.[42]

　　The variety is infinite, showing how vital the belief still remains in the intercourse between the world of the dead and the world of the living. But the dialogue is not restricted to this type of dirge. It may involve two mourners, like the following version of a well-known Epirot lament which I recorded from Alexandra Tsipi in 1963, in which a mother urges her daughter, five days a bride and then widowed, to stop weeping and marry again, and receives an angry refusal in reply. The concise antitheses give expression to a situation so commonly found in the ancient inscriptions:

Πέντε μέρες παντρεμένη, χήρα πάει στὴ μάνα της.
Μὲ τὰ τέλεια στὴν ποδιά της, ἔκλαιγε τὸν ἄντρα της.
– Σώπα, κόρη, καὶ μὴ κλαῖς, μὴ παραπονεύεσαι.
Εἶσαι νέα καὶ ὡραία, καὶ ξαναπαντρεύεσαι.
– Τί μοῦ λές, μωρ' μαύρη μάνα, πῶς νὰ ξαναπαντρευτῶ;
Ἔχασα τὸν πρῶτο μ' ἄντρα, σὰν τὰ μάτια μου τὰ δυό.

Five days married, she goes, a widow, to her mother.
With the ritual garlands in her apron, she wept for her husband.
– Be quiet, daughter, do not weep and do not complain.
You are young and fair, and you can wed again.
– What are you saying, wretched mother, how can I wed again?
I have lost my first husband, dear as my own two eyes.

A common means of expression in these dialogue laments is sticho-mythia. It may also be used to vary the narrative of a long ballad, or to increase the dramatic tension. In the ballad *The Young Girl and Charos*, Kostandis, riding home to his betrothed from the wars, sees a crowd gathering as if in funeral procession outside her house, and suspects bad news. Passing the churchyard, he sees the grave-digger, and asks whose grave he is preparing. The news that it is Evgenoula's has to be extracted point by point, first in riddling phrases, and finally in grim reality:[43]

– Νὰ ζήσης, πρωτομάστορη, τίνος εἶν' τὸ κιβούρι;
– Εἶναι τἀνέμου, τοῦ καπνοῦ καὶ τῆς ἀνεμοζάλης.
– Γιὰ πέ μου, πρωτομάστορη, καθόλου μὴ μοῦ κρύψης.
– Ποιὸς ἔχει γλώσσα νὰ στὸ πῆ, στόμα νὰ σοῦ μιλήση,
τοῦτ' ἡ φωτιὰ ποὺ σ' ἄναψε, ποιὸς θὲ νὰ σοῦ τὴ σβήση;
Ἡ Εὐγενούλα ἀπέθανε νὴ πολυαγαπημένη... Politis 217.32–7

– Long life to you, master craftsman. Whose is the coffin?
– It belongs to the wind, to the smoke and to the whirlwind.
– O tell me, master craftsman, do not conceal it from me.
– Who has the tongue to tell you, lips to utter it?
Who will quench for you this fire which has engulfed you?
Evgenoula, your dearly beloved one, has died...

Sometimes, stichomythia takes the form of catechistic questions, which may be asked and answered by the mourners themselves. It is a popular technique, serving the same ritual function of counting the dead and assessing the loss as was found in Aeschylus' *Persians*:[44]

– Γιὰ κάτσετε, σιγήσετε, νὰ ἰδοῦμε ποιὸς μᾶς λείπει;
– Μᾶς λείπει ὁ κάλλιος τοῦ σπιτιοῦ κι ὁ πρωτονοικοκύρης.

Politis 186.8–9

– Sit down, be silent, and let us see who is missing.
– It is the pride of the house, the first man, who is missing.

Finally, in a Tsakonian lament already referred to in chapter 6, of penetrating quality and power, we find a rare combination of antiphony and choral refrain. One woman takes the part of the girl, another the part of the mother, while the rest form the chorus; they enact a kind of drama at the girl's wake. Each line is followed by a refrain of cries, wailed by the whole company in unison:

Κόρη. Κρϛοῦψέ μι, μάτη, κρϛοῦψέ μι, νὰ μή με ἄρϛη ὁ
        Χάροοο!
Χορός. Ὀνώβω σι! ὀνώβω σι!
   –   Φκιάσε κουϊδὶ τϛαὶ βάλε μι!
   –   Ἐναίβαι σι! ἐναίβαι σι!
   –   Σεντοῦτϛι τϛαὶ κλείδουσέ μι!
   –   Οὐνούβου σι! οὐνούβου σι!
   –   Βάλε μι τ'οὐ βασιλικοῦ!
   –   Ὀνώβω σι! ὀνώβω σι!
   –   Βάλε μι τ'οὐ βαρσάμου!
   –   Ἐναίβαι σι! ἐναίβαι σι!
   –   Βάλε μι, μάτη, κρϛοῦψέ μι!
   –   Οὐνούβου σι! οὐνούβου σι!
Μητέρα. Ὤνι βάνα ντι, τοῦ Χάρου ντ' ἔν συνοϊδάϛα!
Χορός. Ἐναίβαι σι! οἰμαὶ ἀ κακομοίρα! οὔ! οὔ!   *Laog* (1923) 40

Daughter: Hide me, mother, hide me, so that Charos cannot
           take me!
Chorus: Woe to you, woe to you!
   –   Make a cage and put me in!
   –   Woe to you, woe to you!
   –   Make a chest and shut me in!
   –   Woe to you, woe to you!
   –   Put me among the basil!
   –   Woe to you, woe to you!
   –   Put me among the balsam!
   –   Woe to you, woe to you!

149

–	Take me, mother, hide me!
–	Woe to you, woe to you!
Mother:	I will not hide you, I give you to Charos as company!
Chorus:	Woe to you! Alas, what an evil fate! Ού, ού, ού!

Antiphony, dialogue and refrain, among the oldest structural features of the Greek lament, are still vital and dynamic elements of the modern *moirológia*. They have survived, not because they have been consciously preserved – in the archaising laments of Byzantine learned poetry they were almost extinct – but because antiphony is still imbedded in the ritual performance, with more than one group of mourners, sometimes representing the living and the dead and singing in response to each other. The collective rather than individual performance also explains the continued importance of the refrain; and why the three-part form, as belonging primarily to the soloist, is the least universal today. Continuity has been strongest and most spontaneous in popular tradition.

Antithetical style and antithetical thought

Antithetical style is a fundamental and integral part of the structure and thought of the lament, though by no means exclusive to it. A study of its use and function will provide an opportunity to trace developments through a cross-section of archaising, religious and popular laments both in poetry and prose, and thereby to determine to what extent it became a literary affectation, and to what extent it remained rooted in the vernacular language and popular tradition.

In an antiphonal lament at the end of the *Seven against Thebes*, Antigone and Ismene together weep for the fate of their brothers, Eteokles and Polyneikes, each slain by the other. While the following lines illustrate all the most characteristic qualities of Greek antithetical style, antithesis is not a mere stylistic affectation, but is determined both by the antiphonal structure and by the underlying thought:

Αν. παιθεὶς ἔπαισας.		Ισ. σὺ δ' ἔθανες κατακτανών.	
–	δορὶ δ' ἔκανες.	–	δορὶ δ' ἔθανες.
–	μελεοπόνος	–	μελεοπαθής
(–	ἴτω γόος,	–	ἴτω δάκρυ,)
–	πρόκεισαι,	–	κατακτάς.

A. Th. 961–5

Antigone: Stricken, you struck.	*Ismene*: Killing, you were killed.
– With the spear you slew.	– With the spear you were slain.
– Wretched in your deed.	– Wretched in your suffering.
(– Let forth the dirge,	– Let forth tears,)
– You lie prostrate,	– you, who killed.

Such contrast of thought, sometimes expressed antiphonally, is extremely frequent in the tragic laments.[45] In a highly inflected language like Greek, the result is inevitably alliteration, assonance and homoioteleuton. Far from being avoided, these devices are exploited to the full, and the rhythm is further intensified by the use of parallelism and asyndeton, as in the chorus' opening lines from the *kommós* in the *Persians*, ἄνι᾽ ἄνια κακὰ νεόκοτα | καὶ δάι᾽. αἰαῖ, διαίνεσθε, Πέρ-|σαι, τόδ᾽ ἄχος κλύοντες (Grievous, grievous disaster, distressful and destructive! Alas, Persians, weep at the news of this calamity!) (A. *Pers.* 256–8).[46] A similar effect is achieved by the repetition of an emotive word in different cases, as in the *kommós* sung after the suicide of Ajax, where the chorus sing πόνος πόνῳ πόνον φέρει (toil upon toil and trouble upon trouble) (S. *Aj.* 866). In Aristophanes' *Frogs*, Aeschylus is made to ridicule Euripides for abusing this device; but the point is hardly a fair one, since it is extremely common in the laments of tragedy, not excluding Aeschylus' own.[47] Another favourite technique is the allusive play on the tragic associations of proper names.[48] Further, antithesis may coincide with metrical diaeresis, dividing the line into two contrasting and balancing *kôla*.[49] Their cumulative impact, when reinforced with incremental repetition, may best be illustrated from the lines which open the first strophe and antistrophe of the first stasimon from the *Persians*: Ξέρξης μὲν ἄγαγεν, ποποῖ, | Ξέρξης δ᾽ ἀπώλεσεν, τοτοῖ, | Ξέρξης δὲ πάντ᾽ ἐπέσπε δυσφρόνως | βαρίδεσσι ποντίαις... (Xerxes led forth, alas!, Xerxes laid low, alas!, Xerxes managed all things rashly with his sea-faring ships), νᾶες μὲν ἄγαγον, ποποῖ, | νᾶες δ᾽ ἀπώλεσαν, τοτοῖ, | νᾶες πανωλέθροισιν ἐμβολαῖς... (the ships...led forth, alas!, the ships laid low, alas!, the ships, under the fatal attack) 550–3, 560–3.[50]

All these stylistic features find more formalised expression in the rhetorical funeral oration and in the later prose laments. A fragment from a funeral oration by Gorgias of Leontinoi (fifth century B.C.), who is regarded as the founder of Greek rhetoric, is almost entirely composed of antithetical clauses, which, although elaborated for the sake of form rather than content, give the piece a distinctive rhythm and shape. Even more flamboyant are the stylised *planctus* in Achilles Tatius' prose romance *Leukippe and Kleitophon* (second century A.D.). Charikles' father is mourning his son's death in a riding accident, developing and repeating the antitheses of love and death, marriage and funeral rites:

Οἷος ἀπ' ἐμοῦ προελθών, οἷος ἐπανέρχῃ μοι, τέκνον·
ὦ πονηρῶν ἱππασμάτων, οὐδὲ κοινῷ μοι θανάτῳ τέθνηκας·
  οὐδὲ εὐσχήμων φαίνῃ νεκρός...
  ...ἡ μὲν γὰρ ψυχή σου πέφευγεν·
οὐχ εὑρίσκω δέ σε οὐδὲ ἐν τῷ σώματι.
πότε μοι, τέκνον, γαμεῖς;
πότε σου θύσω τοὺς γάμους, ἱππεῦ καὶ νυμφίε;
νυμφίε μὲν ἀτελές, ἱππεῦ δὲ δυστυχές.
τάφος μέν σοι, τέκνον, ὁ θάλαμος,
γάμος δὲ ὁ θάνατος, θρῆνος δὲ ὁ ὑμέναιος,
ὁ δὲ κωκυτὸς οὗτος τῶν γάμων ᾠδαί.
ἄλλο σοι, τέκνον, προσεδόκων πῦρ ἀνάψαι·
ἀλλὰ τοῦτο μὲν ἔσβεσεν ἡ φθονερὰ τύχη μετὰ σοῦ·
ἀνάπτει δέ σοι δᾷδας κακῶν.
ὦ πονηρᾶς ταύτης δᾳδουχίας·
ἡ νυμφική σοι δᾳδουχία ταφὴ γίνεται.   I.13, ed. Vilborg

How different you were when you left me, and how different you are now you have come back, child! Ah, wretched sport of riding horses! You did not even die an ordinary death. Nor has death preserved your fine looks... Your soul has departed, and I cannot find you in this corpse. When, my child, will your wedding be? When shall I arrange your wedding, horseman and bridegroom? Bridegroom without a wedding, horseman without fortune. Your bridal chamber, child, is the grave, your wedding hymn the funeral dirge, your nuptial songs these wailings. I hoped to kindle a different fire from this, my child, but envious Fortune has extinguished it and you together, lighting instead for you torches of evil. Ah, what a cruel torch-bearing is this! Your marriage torches have become a funeral.

This kind of rhetorical display, characteristic of Greek prose style in late antiquity, has led E. A. Norden to conclude that the principal distinction between antithetical style in Greek and Hebrew is that in Greek, the form is the most important factor, and that clarity of thought is frequently sacrificed for the desired stylistic effect, whereas in Hebrew, there is a real contrast of ideas – *Gedankenparallelismus* rather than *Satzparallelismus*.[51] While it is true that the antithetical style of the New

Testament, which influenced the style of the liturgy and of Byzantine religious poetry, conforms more to Hebrew than to Greek type, it should be pointed out that earlier, in the writings of Herakleitos, antithetical style is inseparable from the essence of his thought: the unity of opposites and the opposition of unities find perfect expression in antithetical clauses, where words and phrases opposite in meaning but similar in sound are juxtaposed.[52] The same is true of the laments from tragedy, where the conflicting emotions of the mourner are expressed and developed by means of a series of antitheses.

If we turn now to the prose style of the early Paschal homilies, of the Byzantine funeral oration, and of the liturgy, we shall see that it owes much to the rhetorical style of the classical and late antique periods. Gregory of Nyssa has preserved for us a lament for the death of Makrina, performed by the holy sisters at her wake, where the sense of bereavement is conveyed by antitheses which are sharpened by the use of parallelism and asyndeton:[53]

> Ἐσβέσθη... τῶν ὀφθαλμῶν ἡμῶν ὁ λύχνος· ἀπήρθη τὸ φῶς τῆς τῶν ψυχῶν ὁδηγίας· διελύθη τῆς ζωῆς ἡμῶν ἡ ἀσφάλεια· ἤρθη ἡ σφραγὶς τῆς ἀφθαρσίας· διεσπάσθη ὁ σύνδεσμος τῆς σωφροσύνης· συνετρίβη τὸ στήριγμα τῶν ἀτονούντων, ἀφηρέθη ἡ θεραπεία τῶν ἀσθενούντων· ἐπὶ σοῦ ἡμῖν καὶ ἡ νὺξ ἀντὶ ἡμέρας ἦν, ἐν καθαρᾷ ζωῇ φωτιζομένη· νῦν δὲ καὶ ἡ ἡμέρα πρὸς ζόφον μεταστραφήσεται.   Migne 46.988A

The lamp of our eyes has been quenched. The light of our souls' guidance has gone. Our life's assurance from danger has been sundered. The seal of incorruptibility has been broken. The bond of moderation has been torn apart. The support of the weary has been shattered, the treatment of the sick taken away. When you were with us, even night was as good as day, under the spiritual light of pure life. But now, day itself will be turned into darkness and gloom.

In the Paschal homilies and in the liturgy, Christ's victory over Hades and the triumph of life over death are acclaimed with antitheses hardly less striking than Herakleitos' own:[54]

> Θάνατος ἐξ ἀνθρώπων ἐλαύνεται, καὶ ᾅδης τὴν πολυετῆ δυναστείαν ἀποτίθεται...Ἡ γὰρ τοῦ βίου παρουσία τοῦ θανάτου τὴν βίαν ἐνίκησεν.

> S. Athanasii *Sermo in sanctum Pascha*, Migne 135.1025C

Death is being driven out from among men, and Hades is laying aside his age-old dynasty... The presence of life has vanquished the force of death.

Κύριε Θεέ μου, ἐξόδιον ὕμνον καὶ ἐπιτάφιον ᾠδήν σοι ᾄσομαι, τῷ τῇ ταφῇ σου ζωῆς μοι τὰς εἰσόδους διανοίξαντι, καὶ θανάτῳ θάνατον καὶ ῞Αδην θανατώσαντι.   *IS* 424

O Lord my God, I will sing to you a funeral hymn and a burial song, for by your burial you have opened to me the gateway of life, and by your death you have put Death to death.

᾿Αθάνατοι θνητοί, θνητοὶ ἀθάνατοι, ζῶντες τὸν ἐκείνων θάνατον, τὸν δ' ἐκείνων βίον τεθνεῶτες.   Hklt. 62

Immortals are mortal, mortals are immortal, living their death and dying their life.

Of the early Christian hymns, Wellesz has remarked that 'it is the frequent use of antitheses, characteristic of Semitic poetry, which adds a new element to that of Greek thought'.[55] But, as we have seen, there seems little evidence to support his suggestion that Greek thought was not expressed by means of antitheses before the influence of Semitic. The most sustained and perhaps the finest example of antithetical style in Byzantine hymns is to be found in the *Akáthistos Hýmnos*, of uncertain date and authorship but tentatively attributed by Wellesz to Romanos, where it is a perfect expression of the profound contradictions inherent in the mystery of Christ's birth, and complementary to the complex structure of the hymn as a whole.[56] In the context of the Virgin's lament, it is again by means of antitheses that Christ's greatness through the sufferings of the Virgin is expressed:

Υἱὲ τῆς παρθένου,   Θεὲ τῆς παρθένου,
    καὶ τοῦ κόσμου ποιητά,   σὸν τὸ πάθος, σὸν τὸ βάθος
        τῆς σοφίας·
    σὺ ἐπίστασαι ὃ ἦς   καὶ ὃ ἐγένου·
    σὺ παθεῖν θελήσας   κατηξίωσας ἐλθεῖν   ἀνθρώπους σῶσαι·
    σὺ τὰς ἁμαρτίας   ἡμῶν ἦρας ὡς ἀμνός,
    σὺ ταύτας νεκρώσας   τῇ σφαγῇ σου, ὁ σωτήρ, ἔσωσας
        πάντας·
    σὺ εἶ ἐν τῷ πάσχειν   καὶ ἐν τῷ μὴ πάσχειν,
        σὺ εἶ θνήσκων, σῴζων,   σὺ παρέσχες τῇ σεμνῇ
        παρρησίαν κράζειν σοι·   "ὁ υἱὸς καὶ Θεός μου." Romanos 19.17

Son of the Virgin, God of the Virgin,
and creator of the world, yours is the suffering, yours the
depth of wisdom.
You know what you were and what you have become.
You accepted suffering, and you deigned to come to save
mankind.
You have borne for us our sins, like a lamb;
you, by putting them to death by your sacrifice, Saviour, have
saved all mankind.
You exist, both in suffering and in the absence of suffering;
you exist, by dying and by saving; you granted to the Holy
Lady
the freedom to cry out to you, 'My son and my God!'

It is true that parallels to this style can be found in the poetic homilies
of Ephraem (A.D. 306–73), and in Melito's *Homily on the Passion* (second
century), which is thought to have been written originally in Syriac and
then translated into Greek.[57] At the same time, antithetical style is no
less important a feature of some pagan hymns as well as those of
Apollinarios and Gregory Nazianzen, both of whom were writing
before the significant influence of Syriac on Byzantine hymnography.[58]
It would therefore be more cautious to conclude that the style of Byzantine
hymns in the period of their maturity (sixth to seventh centuries) is
neither exclusively Semitic nor exclusively Greek in origin. The contribution of Hebrew and Syriac was to restore the seriousness of thought
and content which was in danger of becoming obscured in some of the
learned and rhetorical Greek writers; that is why the style is at its best
in the religious and not in the archaising poets. But its poetic treatment
is essentially Greek, as is shown by the untranslatable quality of the
closing strophe of Romanos' *Mary at the Cross*.

The independent survival of antithetical thought and antithetical style
in a different context, associated with a more popular tradition of lamentation, is attested by the funerary inscriptions. Contrasts are expressed
antithetically: especially common are the *topoi* 'instead of the wedding
chamber, the tomb' and 'not marriage, but death...'.[59] In a late
inscription from Teos, the fate of a girl who died in childbed is emphasised
by a series of balancing, antithetical *kôla*, further heightened in the final
couplet by the use of the same formula to introduce contrasting ideas:[60]

Ἐννέα καὶ δέκ' ἐτῶν ἤμην ἔτι παρθένος, εἶτ' ἐγάμησα·
εἴκοσι δ' ἐκτελέσασα χρόνους ἔγκυος οὖσ' ἔθανον·

κεῖμαι δ' ἐν τύμβοις ἔνβρεφος οὖσα, ἄλαλος,
ἡ τὸ πάλαι σεμνὴ Πρόσοδος, μείνασα χρόνον.
Ἦλθε δὲ Κύπρεις καὶ ζεῦξεν Ζωσίμῳ ἐς εὐνήν·
ἦλθε δὲ Μοῖρα καὶ λῦσεν τὴν ἀτελῆ Πρόσοδον.   Le Bas–Wadd. 116

At nineteen years I was still a virgin, then I married.
When I completed my twentieth year, I was with child, then
    I died.
I lie in the tomb, speechless, my child within me,
the once revered Prosodos, having awaited my time.
Love came and joined me to Zosimos' bed.
Fate came and released the unfulfilled Prosodos.

Sometimes, an emotive word is repeated, with cumulative impact, either within the line or at the beginning of successive lines, as in the following inscription from Rome (second to third century A.D.):[61]

Κλαίει μέν σε τέκνον, κλαίει δ' Ἀγαθάνγελος ὠνήρ,
    μυρόμενος φιλίην τερπνοτάτην ἀλόχου·
μύρονται δ' ἀδελφοὶ Μηνᾶς καὶ Δάψιλος ἄμφω
    ἠδ' ὅσσοι σ' ἐφίλουν κἠπόθεον δι' ὅλου.   Peek 1981.1–4

Your child is weeping for you, your husband Agathangelos is
    weeping for you,
    lamenting the joyful affection of his wife.
Your brothers, too, Menas and Dapsilos, are both lamenting,
    and all those who loved you and longed for you always.

Finally, the use of assonance, alliteration and word-play is no less prominent a feature of this style in the inscriptions than in the laments of tragedy.[62]

In Byzantine secular literature, some of the most remarkable laments are to be found in Eustathios Makrembolites' prose romance *Hysmine and Hysminias*, written in the second half of the twelfth century. Although closely dependent on the love novels of late antiquity in structure, theme and tone, it stands out among the Greek romances, ancient as well as Byzantine, both for its bold eroticism – which, conveyed largely through the dream sequences of the narrator, Hysminias, has the effect of over-shadowing the conventional intricacies of plot – and for its extravagant imagery, which has flashes of brilliance not unlike the imagery of the folk songs. In particular the dual antitheses of death as marriage and marriage as death are interwoven in the dreams and in the laments throughout the romance, matched by powerful and rhythmic, if rhetorical, use of antithetical style. Hearing of the marriage planned for Hysmine by her parents, Hysminias vows that he will kill himself and wed in Hades. He embraces her, then laments his fate:[63]

> ...Καὶ σὺ μὲν εἰς Αὐλικώμιδα, πατρίδα τὴν σήν,
> ἐπὶ λαμπρῷ νυμφίῳ παλινοστήσεις νύμφη λαμπρά·
> καὶ σοὶ τὸν ὑμεναῖον βασιλικῶς κατεπᾴσονται,
> ἐγὼ δ᾽ ἐς Ἅιδου φοιτήσω, καὶ ὅλον χορὸν Ἐριννύων συναγαγών,
> ὅλον κατατραγῳδήσω μου τὸ δυστύχημα·
> καὶ σοὶ μὲν ὁ καλὸς Σωσθένης ἐπιθαλάμιον ᾄσει,
> ἐμοὶ δ᾽ ὁ πατὴρ ἐπιτύμβιον·
> ὁ μὲν σὸς πατὴρ ἐπὶ σοί, γλυκεῖα νύμφη, καὶ γλυκὺ μελῳδήσει μελῴδημα,
> ὁ δ᾽ ἐμὸς ἐλεεινὸς Θεμιστεὺς ἐπὶ νεκρῷ παιδὶ γοερὸν ἀνακρούσεται·
> ὁ μὲν ᾄσμα χορεύσει γαμήλιον, ὁ δ᾽ ἐμὸς ἀθλιώτατος πάντων
> πατὴρ ἐλεεινὸν μονῳδήσει καὶ πικρὸν ἐξιτήριον.   6.556.7

You will return to Aulikomis, your homeland, a splendid bride for a splendid bridegroom. Royally the marriage hymn will sound forth for you. But I shall make my way to Hades; leading the Furies' dance, I shall sing out against my whole misfortune. Your good father, Sosthenes, will chant the nuptial lay, mine the burial song. Yes, while your father sings you a sweet melody, sweet bride, my father, wretched Themisteus, will strike up the dirge for his dead son. Your father will dance the wedding song, while mine, unhappiest of all fathers, will sing alone the bitter, plaintive funeral hymn.

The same style, although less rhetorical and effusive, is evident in some of the later vernacular laments in *politikòs stíchos*, as in the following lament for absence from home preserved in a manuscript of the seventeenth century, where each line divides into two balancing or contrasting parts. Here, as in the funerary inscriptions, the effect is frequently achieved by the repetition of emotive words at key points in the line:[64]

> [Θ]λίβει με τοῦτος ὁ καιρός,   λυπεῖ με ὁ χρόνος τοῦτος.
> Οἱ μῆνες ὅλες πταίγουν με   κι ὅλες οἱ ἑβδομάδες.
> Τί νὰ γέν᾽ ὁ ταπεινός,   καὶ τί νὰ ποῖσ᾽ ὁ ξένος;
> Γυρεύω φίλον γκαρδιακὸν   νὰ μὲ παρηγορήση,

καὶ δὲν εὑρίσκω 'δὲ τινάν,   καὶ τί νὰ γέν' ὁ ξένος;
'Επῆρα στράτα τῆς αὐ[γ]ῆς   καὶ ⟨ἡ⟩ στράτα ὁδηγεῖ [με]...

Bouvier 1, p. 10

This season gives me grief, and this year gives me sorrow.
All the months vex me, and all the weeks.
What is to become of poor me, and what am I, the stranger,
    to do?
I seek a friend close to my heart to give me comfort,
but I find no one, and what is to become of me, the stranger?
I took the path of dawn, and the path leads me...

In a modern lament from Epiros, the conflicts and tensions of a mother's attempt to measure her grief for her son's death in terms of nature's universal lamentation, and his reply that it is only her grief which concerns him, are lyrically sustained by the repetition of a traditional formula, similar to the one found in the third-century inscription from Rome:[65]

– 'Ακριβέ μ', σὲ κλαίγ' ἡ ἄνοιξη, σὲ κλαίει τὸ καλοκαίρι,
    σὲ κλαῖν καὶ τἄμορφα πουλιὰ κι οἱ δροσερὲς βρυσούλες.
– Γιατί μὲ κλαίγ' ἡ ἄνοιξη, γιατί τὸ καλοκαίρι,
    γιατί μὲ κλαῖν καὶ τὰ πουλιὰ κι οἱ δροσερὲς βρυσούλες;
    Μένα μὲ κλαῖν ἡ μάνα μου κι ἡ δόλια μου ἡ γυναίκα
    μὲ πόνο, μὲ παράπονο καὶ μὲ καημὸν μεγάλο.   Giankas 896.1–6

– My dear one, spring is weeping for you, summer is weeping
        for you,
    and the fine birds and cool springs are weeping for you too.
– Why is spring weeping for me, why is summer weeping?
    Why are the birds and cool springs weeping for me too?
    It is my mother who is weeping for me, and my wretched
        wife,
    with pain, with complaint, and with bitter grief.

Another common technique of the modern laments which was also found in the inscriptions is emphasis by contrast, as in the following Kleftic lament, where the harsh freedom afforded by the mountains is contrasted with the easy, but subject, life of the plains:[66]

Κλαῖνε τὰ μαῦρα τὰ βουνά, παρηγοριὰ δὲν ἔχουν.
Δὲν κλαῖνε γιὰ τὸ ψήλωμα, δὲν κλαῖνε γιὰ τὰ χιόνια·

ἡ κλεφτουριὰ τἀρνήθηκε καὶ ροβολάει στοὺς κάμπους.

Politis 57.1–3

The black mountains are weeping, they cannot be comforted.
They are not weeping for their height, they are not weeping
  for the snow;
the Klefts have deserted them and are stalking the plains.

In a lament from Athens mourning the death of a husband, the effect is sharpened by simple contrasts rather than by prolonged repetition:[67]

Ὅλα τὰ δέντρα ἀνθίσανε, κι ἕνα δεντρὶ ξεράθη,
ὅλα τὰ ταίρια σμίξανε, καὶ τὸ δικό μου χάθη. Theros 726

All the trees have blossomed, and one tree has withered,
all creatures have mated, and my own mate has died.

A Maniot mother laments the death of her only daughter in terse antitheses, with little external connection or sentence construction, heightened by internal assonance and alliteration as well as by the rhyme:

Σαραντα πέντε λεμονιὲς στὸν ἄμμο φυτρωμένες,
δίχως νερό, δίχως δροσιά, καὶ πάλι δροσισμένες.
Καὶ μιὰ δική μου λεμονιὰ
καὶ μὲ νερὸ καὶ μὲ δροσιά,
καὶ πὸ'λι μαραμένη.
Ἄκου το, ἄκαρπο δεντρί,
μέλισσα δίχως μέλι . . . Pasayanis 82.1–6

Forty-five lemon trees planted in the sand,
without water, without coolness, yet they are cool and fresh.
And a single lemon tree of mine,
with both water and coolness,
is parched and withered.
Listen, tree without fruit,
bee without honey . . .

These few examples, while far from exhaustive, serve to illustrate that antithetical style remains a dynamic feature of the folk laments; as in the best of the ancient and Byzantine literary laments, it is not external to, but dependent upon, the structure and thought. At the same time, the close stylistic affinities of the folk songs with the funerary inscriptions suggest the possibility that the inscriptions were drawing on a living vernacular tradition as well as on an established literary technique. Certainly, the long history of artistically developed antithetical style in Greek, together with the interdependence of literary and popular tradition (which can be attested in some detail from the late Byzantine period), has ensured not merely its survival, but its poetic quality.

8
Conventions, themes and formulae

We have seen in the last chapter that the structure of the ancient *thrênos* had much in common with the structure of the *hýmnos*, *enkómion* and *epitáphios*. The same is true of many of the ideas.[1] The similarities between these ancient forms arise from their common ritual basis: since the dead were not infrequently men who had become heroes and were entitled to be worshipped as gods, the distinctions between songs to the dead and hymns to the gods cannot be too sharply drawn, as is reflected in the use of these terms in tragedy.[2] In this chapter, I shall examine in detail the importance of these common elements in the lament, and the extent of their survival today.

Initial hesitation and questions

It was traditional to the ancient *thrênos*, *hýmnos*, *enkómion* and *epitáphios* for the speaker to begin by expressing anxiety lest he should fail to find words adequate for the occasion.[3] This initial hesitation is most frequently expressed by means of questions.[4] The chorus begin their lament for Agamemnon with the words:[5]

– ἰὼ ἰὼ βασιλεῦ βασιλεῦ,
   πῶς σε δακρύσω;
   φρενὸς ἐκ φιλίας τί ποτ᾽ εἴπω;   A. *Ag.* 1489–91

– Ió, ió, my king, my king,
   how shall I weep for you?
   what can I say to express my affection?

In the lament, the opening question may not only imply caution, but may also be used to emphasise the plight of the mourner. When Hector is killed and his body mangled by Achilles, Hekabe leads the lament of the Trojan women with the words, 'Ah child! I am wretched – why should I live on in misery and suffering now that you are dead?' (*Il.* 22.431–2).[6] Or, as well as beginning a lament with a series of questions, the mourner might break off a train of thought, as if in sudden realisation of loss, with quick, short questions, which emphasise the transition from the central narrative section to the final lament and address. In Sophokles' *Ajax*, Teukros begins his lament for the fallen hero with a series of questions, poignantly emphasising the extent of his sorrow, then thinks of the distress and anger he will cause their father Telamon at home with the news of Ajax' suicide. Suddenly he turns from his own anguish, present and future, to the body which lies before him, and cries out, 'Alas, what can I do? How can I free you from this bitter, glittering sword, the murderous agent of your death? You see how Hector, in the course of time, although he now lies dead, was destined to be the cause of your destruction?' (S. *Aj.* 1024–7).[7]

By the end of antiquity, the convention was well established in poetic and prose laments of all kinds, including the funeral oration and the funerary inscriptions.[8] It survived in the Byzantine funeral oration and in the archaising poetic laments, where it was a more or less direct imitation of classical models rather than a creative renewal.[9] But in the laments of Byzantine religious literature there is considerably greater variety and spontaneity. Mary begins her lament for Christ in Romanos' *kontákion* with an address framed as a question: 'Where are you going, child? For whose sake are you completing this swift course?' (Romanos 19.1, 5). The 'Great Kanon' of Andreas of Crete (*c.* 660–740), a penitential hymn for Mid-Lent week, begins the lamentations with the *tropárion*:[10]

Πῶς ἄρξομαι θρηνεῖν   τὰς τοῦ ἀθλίου μου βίου πράξεις;
  Ποίαν ἀπαρχὴν   ἐπιθήσω, Χριστέ,
τῇ νῦν θρηνῳδίᾳ;   Cantarella 100

How shall I begin to lament the actions of my wretched life?
What beginning shall I preface, O Christ,
to my present lamentation?

Outside the context of religious poetry and prose, the convention of initial hesitation expressed by means of questions was well established in the laments of the anonymous verse romances of the fourteenth to fifteenth centuries, in the epic poem *Digenis Akritas*, and in the *Thrênoi* for the fall of Constantinople.[11] That it was not merely a literary convention, but continued to exist in the ritual laments of the people, is perhaps suggested by its frequency in the laments recorded in the *Lives of the Saints*, uttered by the grief-stricken fathers and mothers for the martyrdom of their children. Some of the examples cited by Symeon Metaphrastes are worth quoting in full, because they illustrate the traditional nature of certain motifs which recur in association with the convention. In the *Life of Saint Euphrosyne*, Paphnoutios, overcome with grief, plucks the hair of his beard and tears his cheeks with his nails, crying out:

> Ποῖ πεπόρευσαι, τέκνον; . . .τί με τὸν σὸν πενθεῖν καὶ σκυθρω-
> πάζειν γεννήτορα καταλέλοιπας; οὐκ ἐπὶ τοιαύταις ἐλπίσιν
> ἀνέτρεφον, ἀλλ᾽ ὥστε βακτηρίαν τοῦ γήρως ἔχειν, καὶ τῆς
> ἀσθενείας παράκλησιν. Οἴ μοι! τέκνον ἐμόν, πῶς τὴν σὴν οἴσω
> στέρησιν; πῶς ἐνέγκω τὴν μόνωσιν;   Migne 114.316A

> Where have you gone, my child? . . .Why have you deserted me, your father, to grieve for you in sadness? It was not with expectations such as these that I reared you, but to have a staff of support in my old age, and some consolation in my weakness. Alas! my child, how can I bear your loss? How can I endure the loneliness?

In the *Life of Saint Xenophon*, the news of the death by drowning of a man's sons is greeted with the words, Οἴ μοι!. . .τί τὰ γεγονότα ταῦτα; . . .ποία γλῶττα τῷ ὑμετέρῳ πατρὶ τὸ ὑμῶν οἴκτιστον ἀπαγγελεῖ θάνατον; (Alas!. . .What events are these? What tongue will tell to your father the news of your pitiful death?) *ibid.* 1029. The same thought is expressed in another lament spoken by a mother for the death of her child:[12]

> Φεῦ, ὅτι τὸ σὸν ἐγὼ τέλος ὁρῶ, ἥτις ὑπὸ σοὶ μᾶλλον καὶ ταῖς
> σαῖς ἐλπίσι γηροτροφηθήσεσθαι ἤλπιζον, τοιαῦτά μοι νῦν
> ἐκτίνεις, ὁ φίλτατος, τὰ τροφεῖα; Τοιούτους ἡ δειλαία τῶν
> ἐλπίδων ἐγὼ δρέπομαι τοὺς καρπούς; Ποίῳ στόματι, ποίᾳ
> γλώσσῃ τὰ σὰ φθέγξομαι, ποίοις ὄμμασιν ἀνακλαύσομαι;
>   Migne 115.1156B–C

> Alas that I should see your end, I who hoped to be nursed in my old age by you, and by your hopes! Are these the wages

that you pay me for my care of you, dearest one? Are these the fruits I reap from my hopes, wretched that I am? With what mouth, with what tongue shall I utter your misfortunes, with what eyes shall I weep?

Despite the archaising language, and the inclusion of certain stereotyped motifs which emphasise the self-centred concern of the parent, it is possible to glimpse here something of the traditional contents of these laments, most of which are explicitly stated to have been accompanied by ritual gestures of lamentation.

That the convention continued to exist in the laments of popular tradition is shown by the diversity of form in which it survives today. A mourner from Karpathos stops to think before she can find the appropriate manner of lamentation:[13]

Πῶς νὰ σὲ κλάψω σήμερο στέκω καὶ συλλοοῦμαι...
Michaelidis-Nouaros 316.
I stop and think how I can mourn for you today...

Another, from Mani, opens with questions expressing her concern to find the right words:[14]

Τίνος τὸ ξέρει ἡ γλώσσα του, τίνος τὸ βγάνει ὁ νοῦς του,
νὰ τοῦ τὸ βρῆ, νὰ τοῦ τὸ εἰπῆ τ' ὅμοιο του μοιρολόι;
Pasayanis 18.1–2
Whose tongue can know it, whose mind can conceive it,
to find for him and say for him the dirge he deserves?

In the ballad *The Young Girl and Charos*, the grave-digger cannot find words to tell Kostandis of the death of his beloved. The formula he uses is strikingly similar to that in the *Lives of the Saints* cited above:

Ποιὸς ἔχει γλώσσα νὰ στὸ πῆ, στόμα νὰ σοῦ μιλήση,
τούτ' ἡ φωτιὰ ποὺ σ' ἄναψε, ποιὸς θὲ νὰ σοῦ τὴ σβήση;
Politis 217.35–6
Who has the tongue to tell you, lips to utter it?
Who will quench for you this fire which has set you alight?

Another common device is to follow the introductory question with a series of hypotheses, which are then contrasted with the reality, as in another of the so-called ballads of the Underworld:[15]

Γιατί εἶναι μαῦρα τὰ βουνὰ καὶ στέκουν βουρκωμένα;
Μὴν ἄνεμος τὰ πολεμᾶ, μήνα βροχὴ τὰ δέρνει;

Κι οὐδ' ἄνεμος τὰ πολεμᾶ, κι οὐδὲ βροχὴ τὰ δέρνει,
μόνε διαβαίνει ὁ Χάροντας μὲ τοὺς ἀποθαμένους.   Politis 218.1–4

Why are the mountains black, why are they shrouded in cloud?
Does the wind torment them, or does the rain lash them?
The wind does not torment them, and the rain does not lash
     them,
it is Charondas who passes by with his company of dead.

These modern examples, while far from exhaustive, are perhaps sufficient to indicate that beneath the survival of a poetic convention there has persisted the same ritual belief as in antiquity that insufficient or unsatisfactory lamentation of the dead man may provoke his anger and revenge.[16]

The contrast: past and present

A common method of prayer or appeal in the ancient hymn and ode was to remind the god addressed of past services the speaker had rendered him, or of previous occasions when similar prayers had been answered. Its traditional formula, 'if ever before, so now...' rested on the contrast between past and present.[17] Similarly in the lament, the mourner frequently reinforced an appeal by contrasting past and present, her own fate with that of the dead. After the introductory address, which frequently contained questions, the mourner turned to reflect on what the dead was in his lifetime, and what he has come to now; the hopes cherished then, the despair he has now caused; the journey he is now making to Hades, and the desolation of those left behind. Seeing Patroklos dead, Briseis throws herself on his body and tears her cheeks, neck and breast, crying out:

Πάτροκλ' ἐμοὶ δειλῇ πλεῖστον κεχαρισμένε θυμῷ,
ζωὸν μέν σε ἔλειπον ἐγὼ κλισίηθεν ἰοῦσα,
νῦν δέ σε τεθνηῶτα κιχάνομαι, ὄρχαμε λαῶν,
ἂψ ἀνιοῦσ'· ὥς μοι δέχεται κακὸν ἐκ κακοῦ αἰεί.   *Il.* 19.287–90

Patroklos, my soul's delight! Woe is me!
I left you alive when I went out of the tent,
and now I come back to find you dead,
leader of people. My life has brought one grief after another.

This type of contrast was traditional, and is found in some form in nearly all kinds of lament throughout antiquity, including the epigrams and the funerary inscriptions.[18] In the choral odes of tragedy it is extended from the essentially self-centred expression of grief for one person's death into a tragic assessment of the futility of human life in general. What man had seemed so favoured by the gods and so fortunate as Oedipus? ask the chorus of Sophokles' *Oedipus Tyrannus*, and reply, 'But now, whose story is more bitter to tell?', thus giving a new perspective to their opening lament for mankind, that all the generations of mortal man add up to nothing (*OT* 1186–1212).[19]

In the ancient lament, the commonest formula for this convention was to contrast one clause, introduced by *before* or *then*, with a second clause, introduced by *now*.[20] Frequently it marked the transition from the opening address to the central narrative section, or from the central section to the final address, thus forming part of the structure.[21] How was it affected by the disintegration of the three-part form, on which it was to some extent dependent, towards the end of antiquity? As early as in Alexandrian poetry, the contrast between past and present in its Homeric and classical form appears to give way to the reiteration of *now*, usually introducing an invocation to nature to join in the lamentation, as in Moschos' *Epitáphios for Bion*:

Νῦν φυτά μοι μύρεσθε καὶ ἄλσεα νῦν γοάοισθε,
ἄνθεα νῦν στυγνοῖσιν ἀποπνείοιτε κορύμβοις·
νῦν ῥόδα φοινίσσεσθε τὰ πένθιμα, νῦν ἀνεμῶναι,
νῦν ὑάκινθε λάλει τὰ σὰ γράμματα...   Moschos 3.3–6

Now mourn, plants, now sing dirges, groves,
flowers, now expire with gloomy clusters.
Now roses, now anemones, put on mourning crimson,
now, hyacinth, speak out your letters...

This device was further elaborated in the rhetorical structure of the prose laments of late antiquity. In Aelian Aristeides' *Monody on Smyrna*, written when that city was destroyed by earthquake in the early second century A.D., the frequent repetition of *now* is balanced in every case by the past tense of a finite verb, thus preserving the classical form of the contrast with slight variation (18.5, 8, 9 ed. Keil). The same style is evident in the Byzantine funeral oration and epigram;[22] while in the archaising laments of Quintus and Psellos, the Homeric and Hellenistic forms are preserved without any further development.[23]

In the religious laments, however, the contrast is found in a great variety of forms, some of them new. In the *Testament of Job* (c. first century B.C.), there is a remarkable lyrical *planctus* for Job's wife – who was forced by poverty to sell her hair to Satan in order to buy bread – where a long series of contrasts between past and present becomes the basis for a highly stylised piece of rhythmic prose:[24]

Τίς οὐκ ἐξεπλάγη ὅτι αὕτη ἐστιν Σίτιδος ἡ γυνὴ τοῦ 'Ιώβ,
ἥτις εἶχεν σκεπάζοντα αὐτῆς τὸ καθεστήριον βῆλα δεκατέσσαρα,
καὶ θύραν ἔνδοθεν θυρῶν ἕως ἂν ὅλως καταξιωθῇ τις εἰσαχθῆναι
    πρὸς αὐτήν,
νυνὶ δὲ καταλλάσσει τὴν τρίχα αὐτῆς ἀντὶ ἄρτων;
Ἧς αἱ κάμηλοι γεγομωμέναι ἀγαθῶν ἀπέφερον εἰς τὰς χώρας
    τοῖς πτωχοῖς,
ὅτι νῦν ἀντιδίδωσιν τὴν τρίχα αὐτῆς ἀντὶ ἄρτων.
Ἴδε ἡ ἔχουσα ἑπτὰ τραπέζας ἀκινήτους ἐπὶ οἰκίας
    εἰς ἃς ἤσθιον οἱ πτωχοὶ καὶ πᾶς ξένος
    ὅτι νῦν καταπιπράσκει τὴν τρίχαν ἀντὶ ἄρτων.
Βλέπε τίς εἶχε τὸν νιπτῆρα τῶν ποδῶν αὐτῆς χρυσοῦ καὶ
    ἀργύρου,
    νυνὶ δὲ ποσὶ βαδίζει ἐπὶ ἐδάφους,
    ἀλλὰ καὶ τὴν τρίχα ἀντικαταλλάσσει ἀντὶ ἄρτων.
Ἴδε ὅτι αὕτη ἐστιν ἥτις εἶχεν τὴν ἔνδυσιν ἐκ βύσσου
    ὑφασμένην σὺν χρυσῷ
    νῦν δὲ φορεῖ ῥακκώδη
    καὶ ἀντικαταλλάσσει τὴν τρίχαν ἀντὶ ἄρτων.
Βλέπε τὴν τοὺς κραββάτους χρυσέους καὶ ἀργυρέους ἔχουσαν,
νυνὶ δὲ πιπράσκουσαν τὴν τρίχα ἀντὶ ἄρτων.

Testament of Job 25, ed. James *TS* 5.1 (1897) 118

Who has not been struck with amazement that this is Sitidos, Job's wife, who had her chamber hung with fourteen curtains, and doors within doors until one was judged quite worthy to be admitted to her, and now she exchanges her hair for bread. She whose camels laden with goods would take them to the poor in the villages, now she gives her hair in exchange for bread! Behold, she who had in her home seven tables permanently fixed at which the poor and every stranger would eat, now she sells her hair for bread! See, she whose foot-basin was of gold and silver, now she walks barefoot on the ground, yes now she exchanges her hair for bread! Behold, it is she whose dress was of fine yellow flax with golden threads, yet now she wears rags and exchanges her hair for bread! See,

she whose beds were made of gold and silver, now she sells
her hair for bread!

Similarly, in all forms of the Virgin's lament throughout Greek tradition,
the contrast has remained an important and vital element. In Romanos'
kontákion, Mary begins the narrative section of her first lament with the
words, 'I did not expect to see you, child, in these straits, nor did I ever
believe that the lawless ones would reach such a state of fury, and that
they would lay hands on you unjustly...And now, for what reason
has a worse deed been accomplished?' (19.2, 1–3, 7).[25]

The use of the invocational *now* is rather more restrained in the religious
than in the learned laments, reserved on the whole for the emphasis of
important feast days, especially Easter.[26] In close association with this
is the reiteration of σήμερον (today), which is used specifically to announce
the day of Crucifixion or of Resurrection, and hence common in the
Virgin's lament.[27] Like the invocational *now* in ancient tradition, it
commands or emphasises the sympathy of nature, but the sound of the
word imparts a heavier, more solemn rhythm, as in the splendid opening
lines of Romanos' *kontákion On the Passion*, which set the scene for the
Crucifixion:

Σήμερον ἐταράττετο   τῆς γῆς τὰ θεμέλια
ὁ ἥλιος ἠλλοιοῦτο   μὴ στέγων θεωρῆσαι.
ἐν σταυρῷ γὰρ περιέκειτο   ὁ πάντων 3ωοδότης.

Romanos 20.1, 1–3

Today the foundations of the earth were confounded,
the sun changed its course, unable to endure the sight;
for he who gave life to all things was laid on the cross.

Lines similar to these are still an almost invariable opening to the Virgin's
lament in modern folk tradition; and the formula also introduces several
dramatic themes in the Akritic poems.[28] In a modern ritual lament from
Mani, the same formula is used to describe the cataclysmic forces of
nature in sympathy with the mourner's grief:

Σήμερα ἐγίνη ἀλαλαγμός,
ὁ ἥλιος ἐσκοτείνιασε
στὸν κάμπο τοῦ Σολοτεριοῦ...
Σήμερα ἐγίνηκε σεισμός...
Σκοτάδι χειμωνιάτικο
κι ἡμέρα νύχτα ἔγινε.

Pasayanis 169.1–3, 7, 18–19

Today there has been a great cry,
the sun has darkened
on the plain of Soloteri...
Today there has been an earthquake...
There is winter blackness,
and day has turned into night.

Here we have an extension of a formula which originated in religious literature, preserved in popular tradition to the present day with a fine sense of dramatic economy for only the most solemn declaration of tragic events.

As for vernacular poetry of the post-Byzantine period, in the laments for the fall of Constantinople the contrast was further elaborated in the form of a reiterated finite verb in the past tense – usually *you were* or *you had* – which is contrasted with a finite verb in the present tense and *now*. This is how Constantinople is addressed and lamented in the *Thrênos for Constantinople*:

Ἤσουν φωστῆρας τοῦ οὐρανοῦ, ἄστρον τῆς Ἀφροδίτης,
αὐγερινὸς λαμπρότατος, ὁπού 'φεγγες τὸν κόσμον,
ὁπού 'φεγγες κι ἐδρόσιζες ὅλην τὴν οἰκουμένην...
Μὰ τώρα ἐσκλαβώθηκες, οἴμοι, ἐγίνης δούλη.

Zoras 201.23–5, 31, cf. 36–45

You were the illuminator of the sky, the star of Aphrodite, the brightest morning star, who shed your light on the world, who shed your light and coolness on the whole universe...But now you have been enslaved, alas, you have become a bondmaid.

In the seventeenth-century Cretan play, *The Sacrifice of Abraham*, Sarah laments Isaac's imminent death in similar, but less stylised terms:

Ἐννιὰ μῆνες σ' ἐβάσταξα, τέκνο μου, κανακάρη,
'ς τοῦτο τὸ κακορίζικο καὶ σκοτεινὸ κουφάρι.
Τρεῖς χρόνους, γιέ μου, σοῦ 'διδα τὸ γάλα τῶ βυζῶ μου
κι ἐσύ 'σουνε τὰ μάτια μου κι ἐσύ 'σουνε τὸ φῶς μου.
Ἐθώρουν κι ἐμεγάλωνες ὡσὰ δεντροῦ κλωνάρι
κι ἐπλήθενες στὴν ἀρετή, στὴ γνώση καὶ στὴ χάρη·
καὶ τώρα, πέ μου, ποιὰ χαρὰ βούλεσαι νὰ μοῦ δώσῃς;   375–81

For nine months I carried you, my child, my darling one, in this miserable and dark body of mine.

For three years, my son, I gave you milk from my breasts,
and you were my eyes and you were my light.
I watched you grow up like a shoot from a tree,
and with you grew your virtue, your sense and your charm.
And now, tell me, what joy do you think you will give me?

Exactly the same formulaic structure is used lyrically in the modern folk laments to introduce elaborate imagery in praise of the dead, as in the following example from Kynouria:[29]

Ἐγώ, μάτια μ᾿, καλὰ σ᾿ ἀγάπαγα, ἐγὼ καλὰ σὲ εἶχα·
σὲ εἶχα μόσκο στὸ κουτὶ καὶ σύρμα στὸ καλάμι,
σὲ εἶχα κι ἀσημοκάντηλο κι ἐφώταγες τὸ σπίτι.
Τώρα τὸ σύρμα σκούργιασε, ὁ μόσκος δὲ μυρίζει,
τώρα τ᾿ ἀσημοκάντηλο ἔπεσε κι ἐτσακίστη.   *Laog* (1911) 489–90

My love, I loved you well, I kept you well.
I kept you as musk in the box and wire in the reed, (?)
I kept you as a silver lamp which lit up the home.
Now the wire has rusted, the musk has lost its fragrance,
now the silver lamp has fallen and shattered.

Occasionally, τώρα (now) is reiterated, like the ancient νῦν, to command the sympathy of nature:[30]

Τώρα, οὐρανέ μου, βρόντησε, τώρα, οὐρανέ μου, βρέξε,
ρίξε στοὺς κάμπους τὴ βροχὴ καὶ στὰ βουνὰ τὸ χιόνι,
στοῦ πικραμένου τὴν αὐλὴ τρία γυαλιὰ φαρμάκι.   Politis 173.1–3

Now, my sky, thunder, now, my sky, rain!
Send rain to the plains, snow to the mountains,
and three phials of poison to the courtyard of the embittered
    one.

Finally, just as in the ancient hymn the speaker strengthened his prayer by reminding the god of past services, so in the following lament from Mani a mother reproaches Saint Dimitrios for failing to save her son – who has the same name – from drowning, in spite of their careful attentions to his chapel and his icon:

– Ἁηδημήτρη ἀφέντη μου,	– Saint Dimitris, my Lord,
δὲ σὲ δοξάσαμε ποτές;	did we never glorify you?
Δὲ σὲ φωτολοήσαμε;	Did we not keep your lamp burning?

Δὲ σ' ἤφερε ὁ Δημήτρης μου   Did my Dimitris not bring you
τρία ἀσημοκάντηλα   three silver oil lamps
καὶ μανουάλια τέσσερα;   and four candelabra?
Τὶς πόρτες σου μὲ τὶς μπογιὲς   Painted doors for you
καὶ μιὰν εἰκόνα ὁλόχρυση;...   and an icon of gold?
Πῶς δὲν ἐβοήθησες καὶ σὺ   How then did you not help
μὲς στοῦ Τσιρίγου τὸ νησί,   at the island of Tsirigo
ποὺ ἀναθεώθη ἡ θάλασσα...   when the sea was confounded...
κι ἐπνίγηκε ἡ μπουμπάρδα μας;   and our boat was sunk?

                                  Pasayanis 218

Similarly, in a vendetta ballad also from Mani, a mourner incites the wife of the murdered man to vengeance by reminding her of the past, of how her husband was suddenly attacked by three men and shot dead. This narrative of the past, introduced by the words, 'Do you remember?', is used to strengthen the final appeal, which calls on the dead man to think of the future of his children and ensure that justice is done (Pasayanis 155).

Thus, although on the whole the same themes of contrast between past and present and the same forms of expression recur in the lament throughout Greek tradition, there are some distinctions: in the Byzantine learned lament, both in poetry and prose, the main emphasis is on the rhetorical form, whereas in both the religious and the popular laments the actual content of the contrast is more important, and old forms are adapted or new ones introduced. But perhaps the closest parallels to the contrast in the ancient lament are to be found in the modern folk laments, which because they are intended for ritual performance and are not literary compositions, have preserved something of the ancient function of the convention as well as its variety of form and content.

The contrast: mourner and dead

Inseparable from the contrast between past and present in the ancient lament was the contrast between mourner and dead, so that parallel to clauses introduced by *before* and *now* was the formulaic structure *I* and *you*.[31]

In ancient Greek, the use of the second person pronoun, in all cases, with verbs, relatives and participles, was a universal mode of ritual address in praise of god, hero or man, to be found in the *hýmnos*, *enkómion*, *epitáphios* and *thrênos* alike. But whereas in the lament, the dead man's fate, introduced by the pronoun σύ (you), was contrasted with the mourner's present or future condition, introduced by ἐγώ (I), in the other three forms it was more usual to emphasise exclusively the power and virtue of the god or hero. Since this convention was so deeply rooted in ancient tradition, it is worth examining its subsequent development in the lament in some detail. In an exhaustive study of modes of address in ancient Greek, Hebrew and Christian religious literature, E. A. Norden has shown that the similarities between them are sufficient to indicate a common origin in the ancient near Eastern tradition of Egypt and Babylonia. He does, however, draw certain distinctions between the Greek and Oriental formulae, both of which he believes to have influenced the Christian liturgy: first, whereas in ancient Greek, the first and third person pronouns are most frequently found with finite verbs of action, with participles and with relative clauses, by far the commonest Oriental formula is with the verb *to be* (*you are* and *he is*); second, absent from Greek but predominant in the east is the corresponding *I am* formula, expressing the power and nature of the god. These differences, Norden argues, reflect a distinct attitude to religion – the Oriental static, absolute and god-centred, the Greek more dynamic and man-centred. If, as the evidence suggests, it was not until the period of Hellenistic expansion that these two formulae came into Greek from the east, then mere correspondence between ancient and later modes of address in Greek does not prove continuity of a single tradition, but rather that the Christian liturgy was influenced in this respect mainly by Oriental tradition and only indirectly by ancient Greek.[32]

It is a plausible argument, and if correct, not without an important bearing on the question of continuity. But before we accept all the implications of Norden's conclusions, the ancient Greek evidence needs closer examination. First, the use of the copula, particularly of εἶναι, was not highly developed in ancient Greek. Further, in main clauses the concept *I am, you are*, was expressed either by the verb or by the pronoun, but only by both together where particular emphasis was required. Finally, it was only in Greek of the Hellenistic period that εἶναι became established as the commonest form of the copula.[33] The apparent absence of the so-called 'Oriental' modes of address in ancient Greek may therefore be due to linguistic rather than to religious factors.

Modes of address in the second person, most commonly with the verb *to be* (ἐσσί), are frequent in the ancient hymns as part of a ritual formula which marks the culmination of a prayer after an address with the reiteration of the pronoun σύ.[34] In the lament, this formula is found frequently in the past tense in the contrast between mourner and dead, emphasising the virtues of the dead man. Lamenting Hector, Hekabe tells him how he was greeted by every Trojan as a god:[35]

> ...ἦ γὰρ καί σφι μάλα μέγα κῦδος ἔησθα
> ζωὸς ἐών· νῦν αὖ θάνατος καὶ μοῖρα κιχάνει.   *Il.* 22.435–6

> ...for you were their greatest glory
> while you were alive. But now, Death and Fate have come
> upon you.

With the address in the third person, the verb *to be* is found in the past tense in hymns and laments alike as part of the ritual account of past deeds, sometimes following a series of participles and relatives;[36] occasionally, the verb is subject to ellipse, and we have a praise formula much like one found in the modern folk laments.[37] As for Norden's Oriental *I am* formula, granted its predominance in Oriental tradition and the rarity of both pronoun and verb together in Greek, ἐγώ and εἰμί are used separately with exactly the same force, and are associated in the ancient hymns with gods and heroes.[38] Related to this formula of divine or prophetic proclamation in the hymns is the opening of many funerary inscriptions and epigrams, early and late:[39]

> Χαλκέη παρθένος εἰμί, Μίδεω δ' ἐπὶ σήματι κεῖμαι.   Hom. *Ep.* 3.1

> I am a maiden of bronze, set upon the tomb of Midas.

In an interesting inscription on a stele from Mesembria (second century A.D.), the dead woman is deified, and clearly identified with Hekate:

> Ἐνθάδε ἐγὼ κεῖμε Ἑκάτη θεός, ὡς εἰσορᾷς·
> ἤμην τὸ πάλαι βροτός, νῦν δὲ ἀθάνατος καὶ ἀγήρως,
> Ἰουλία Νεικίου θυγάτηρ, μεγαλήτορος ἀνδρός.   Peek 438a

> I lie here, the goddess Hekate, as you see.
> Once I was mortal, but now I am immortal and ageless.
> Julia, daughter of Nikias, a great-hearted man.

An inscription from Aptera in Crete (third to fourth centuries A.D.), written by Nikon for his wife, concludes:

> εἰμὶ δ' ἐγὼ (ὁ) γράψας Νεῖκων ὁ ἀνὴρ αὐτῆς γεγονώς γε, νῦν
> δ' οὐκέτι.   Guarducci *RF* (1929) 378–82

I am Nikon, who wrote this; I was once her husband, but now
I am no longer.

Contrary to Norden's view, there would therefore appear to be no
consistent avoidance in Greek of the association of the concept of
essence or being with divinity.[40] It is possible that the original forms,
common to the hymn and the lament, may have been composed of
a series of contrasts between man and god, mourner and dead, in the
past and the present. In the hymn, addressed by man to god or hero, it
is the immediate appeal which is emphasised, and so the address in the
second person predominates, except where the god's reply and prophecy
are quoted. The lament, developing as it does the double contrast
between past and present, mourner and dead, contains both kinds of
address, in the second and first person. Their preservation is perhaps
strongest in the funerary inscription, often in dialogue form or uttered
as if by the dead. It is not that both modes of address did not exist in
Greek; but owing to the greater literary development in Greece than
elsewhere of the hymn and the lament as art forms, they tended to lose
their exclusively ritual significance, and separate from each other much
earlier.

All the basic features of these ancient formulae have survived in later
Greek tradition, not without certain modifications and developments.
First, almost exclusive to the lament, as in ancient Greek, is the contrast
between *you* and *I*. It has survived in religious as well as archaising
laments, and is particularly evident in Symeon Metaphrastes' *planctus*
where Mary complains to Christ:

Ἀλλὰ σὺ μὲν ἄπνους ἐν νεκροῖς καὶ ᾅδου ταμεῖα φοιτᾷς τὰ
ἐνδότερα· ἐγὼ δὲ τὸν ἀέρα πνέω καὶ μετὰ ζώντων περίειμι...

But you are lifeless among the dead, and you journey to the
inner chambers of Hades, while I breathe the air, and walk
about among the living.   Migne 114.209A

In a late-eighth-century Life of Saints David, Symeon and Georgios, the
formulae are reversed, as the dying David addresses Symeon with the
words:

Ἐγὼ μὲν... τὸν δρόμον τετελεκὼς τελευτᾶν ἐπείγομαι, καὶ
ἰδοὺ μετὰ τρίτην ἡμέραν ἀπαίρω τῶν ἐντεῦθεν, καθ᾽ ἃ πάντες
οἱ ἐπὶ γῆς· σὺ σὲ ἀπόδος τὸν χοῦν τῷ χοῖ καὶ σπουδαίως τὴν
ἡμῶν πατρίδα ἐπανάκαμψον...

I, having completed the course, am in haste to be gone; and
behold, after the third day I shall depart from hence, as do
all men on earth. But you, having rendered libation upon
libation, must return again to our homeland . . .

On receiving these instructions to make the libations due to the dead,
the holy Symeon groans loudly, beats his breast with his fists, and
replies, weeping bitterly:

Σὺ μέν, πάτερ, ὡς φῂς, γλυκύτατε, τὸν ἀνθρώπινον ὑπεξέρχῃ
βίον, ἐμὲ δὲ τίνι ἐᾷς πάντοθεν ἀπορφανισθέντα καὶ ἀπορούμενον;
AB 18.219.10–20

You, father, as you say, my sweetest one, are withdrawing from
human life. But to whom are you leaving me, orphaned on
every side, and without means?

The second person address introducing praise, commands and prayers
was just as important in the Byzantine hymns and liturgy as it had been
in the ancient hymns, occurring frequently in the so-called Oriental
form *you are* (σὺ εἶ).[41] But in the vernacular laments of the fourteenth and
fifteenth centuries there is a gradual tendency to replace this formula
either with the reiteration of the pronoun *you* and a relative clause or
a finite verb of action, or with the rhythmic repetition of the verb *to be*
in present or past tense, without the pronoun.[42] It is a reversion to the
ancient type of address, and it is also the commonest form of address
in the modern folk laments. In the following lament from Epiros, a
mother addresses her daughter in a series of elaborate images:

– Μήνα εἶσαι, κόρη μου, μικρὴ νά 'χεις καὶ μικρὸν πόνο;
Ἤσουν καλὴ ἀπ' τὶς καλὲς κι ἀπὸ τὶς διαλεγμένες,
ἤσουνε στὸ σπιτάκι σου στύλος μαλαματένιος . . .
ἤσουνε στὰ παιδάκια σου Μάης μὲ τὰ λουλούδια,
ἤσουν καὶ στὴ μανούλα σου κασσέλα κλειδωμένη,
ἤσουν τιμὴ τῆς γειτονιᾶς καὶ τοῦ χωριοῦ καμάρι.   Giankas 891

– Are you a small child, my daughter, to cause small
      grief?
You were good, of the best and of the chosen ones,
you were a pillar of gold to your house . . .
you were May with flowers to your children,
and you were a locked chest to your mother,
you were the honour of the neighbourhood and the pride of
      the village.

Sometimes the contrast is implicit, and not emphasised by repetition of the pronoun. Like Andromache lamenting Hector at the end of the *Iliad*, a widow from the Pontos laments her husband by reproaching him for deserting his family, ending with the theme of her own grief:[43]

"Ηλε μ', π' ἐχπάστες καὶ θὰ πάς, καὶ ποῦ θ' ἀφίντς τὴ χόρα σ';
καὶ ποῦ θ' ἀφίντς τὴ μάννα σου γραῖαν μὲ τ'ἡμ'σὸν ψἤν-ι;
καὶ ποῦ θ' ἀφίντς τὰ ὀρφανά σ' μικρὰ καὶ μουτζιρούμ'κα;
καὶ ποῦ θ' ἀφίντς τ' ἀδέλφα σου; ἀτὰ ξαί 'κι λυπᾶσαι; . . .
ἐφέκες με παντέρημον, ποῖον στράταν νὰ παίρω;
καὶ κάτ' ἂν πάω, ἕν κρεμός, καὶ ἄν' ἂν πάω, φούρκα.
Θὰ πάω 'γὼ σὸ Μαναστήρ' καὶ θὰ φορῶ τὰ μαῦρα,
θ' ἀφίνω τὰ πουλλόπα σου, τὴ μάννα σου τὴ γραῖαν.

ArP (1951) 189–90

My sun, where have you set off to, and where will you leave
    your widow?
and where will you leave your mother, an old woman with
    half a soul?
and where will you leave your orphans, young and weak as
    they are?
and where will you leave your brothers? Have you no pity
    for them?
You have left me desolate, what path am I to take?
If I turn downwards, there is a precipice, if upwards, a storm.
I will go to the monastery, I will put on black,
I will leave your children, I will leave your old mother.

Owing to changes in the language, the third person forms have undergone a different development. In Byzantine archaising and religious laments, the relative and participial address is the most usual;[44] but after the disappearance of the ancient relative pronoun and the participle in the spoken language, the commonest forms in later Byzantine and modern laments are the demonstrative pronoun and the repetition of the verb *to be* in present and past tense (εἶναι and ἦν or ἦταν). In the twelfth-century romance *Hysmine and Hysminias*, Panthia laments her daughter Hysmine's inauspicious departure with the words:[45]

Ζεῦ πάτερ, φεῖσαι πολιᾶς ταύτης ἐμῆς . . . φεῖσαι νεότητος
θυγατρός· αὕτη μοι παραμύθιον, αὕτη μοι παραψυχή, αὕτη
μοι τοῦ γένους ἐλπίς.

7.12.213

Father Zeus, spare these grey hairs of mine, spare the youth
of my daughter! She is my comfort, she is my consolation, she
is the hope of our stock.

In the modern laments, this type of address is also found with the
relative, as in the following Nisyrot lament, sung by a mother for her
only son:

Γειτόνισσες τοῦ Ποταμοῦ κι ἀπ' τὰ ὀπίσθιά του,
πητέ μου ποῦ 'ν' ὁ ἀετὸς ποὺ κτύπαν τὰ πτερά του.
Ποὺ 'τον ἡ χρυσοπέρδικα δεξιὰ κι ἀριστερά του,
ὁποὺ τὸν ἀγαπούσανε μὲ τὰ φρονήματά του.
Δὲν μ' ἐλυπήθης, Χάροντα, κι ἐπῆρες τὸν ὑγιόν μου,
ὁποὺ 'τον στύλος τῆς καρδιᾶς καὶ φῶς τῶν ὀμματιῶν μου.

Sakellaridis 187–8, 11, 12, 21

My neighbours from Potamos and from the regions behind,
tell me, where is the eagle whose wings beat in flight,
at whose left and right side was the golden partridge,
who was loved because of his good sense.
You had no pity for me, Charondas, you took my son,
who was the pillar of my heart and the light of my eyes.

Throughout its history, the contrast between mourner and dead in
the Greek lament is inseparable from the contrast between past and
present, so that in spite of the changes in form the function has remained
the same. Taking into account the changes in the Greek language, the
same modes of address have persisted to a remarkable degree. The
reiteration of the second person pronoun, a fundamental part of the
ancient hymn and lament, was taken over into the Christian hymn and
reinforced with the Hebrew form, *you are*, independent but ultimately
of the same common origin. On the other hand, the reiteration of the
verb *to be* without the pronoun, frequent in the ancient lament from
Homer onwards to introduce elaborate praise images, seems to have
survived independently, reinvigorated in the popular laments by new
ideas and intricate imagery. The ancient relative and participle, so
convenient in the account of past deeds and virtues, continued to
characterise much of Byzantine religious and archaising lamentation;
but it was the pronoun and verb, traceable to rhetoric and the funerary
inscriptions, which found their way into the vernacular tradition.

Wish and curse

Another element traditional to the ancient lament was the expression of an unfulfilled wish. It took one of the following forms: first, that the mourner had died instead of the dead, or that they had died together, or that neither had ever been born; second, that the death had occurred at a different time or place, or in a different manner; and third, that the enemy of the dead might suffer the same fate. The last wish is in fact a curse.

The first type is found in Homer, where both Helen and Andromache wish that they had never been born, so great is their grief at Hector's death; and it is also extremely common in the laments of tragedy.[46] As with the contrast, this traditional idea arising out of the mourner's desire to impress on the dead the extremity of her grief has been extended in the choral ode of Sophokles' *Oedipus at Kolonos* to express the common despair of all mankind in the face of adversity and death, that the greatest good is not to be born at all, but having been born, the next best is to pass through life as quickly as possible (1224–8).

Underlying the second type of wish is the mourner's concern to avert the wrath of the dead, should his death have been untimely or unfortunate. Hekabe, mourning Astyanax' cruel death before marriage and before succession to his birthright, wishes it had been different:

> ὦ φίλταθ', ὡς σοι θάνατος ἦλθε δυστυχής·
> εἰ μὲν γὰρ ἔθανες πρὸ πόλεως, ἥβης τυχὼν
> γάμων τε καὶ τῆς ἰσοθέου τυραννίδος,
> μακάριος ἦσθ' ἄν, εἴ τι τῶνδε μακάριον·
> νῦν δ' αὔτ' ἰδὼν μὲν γνούς τε σῇ ψυχῇ, τέκνον,
> οὐκ οἶσθ', ἐχρήσω δ' οὐδὲν ἐν δόμοις ἔχων.   E. *Tr.* 1167–72

O dearest child, how wretched was your death!
If only you had died for your city, knowing youth,
marriage, and royal power like a god's,
you would have been happy, if there is any happiness here.
But as it is, your soul could only see and perceive, child,
you had no knowledge, no advantage of your home.

In the long *kommós* at Agamemnon's tomb in the *Choephoroi*, this leads to the third type, the curse: Orestes opens his appeal to his father's spirit by wishing that he had died on the battlefield at Troy, because then he would have been buried in glory;[47] the chorus continue the same idea, saying that if he had died at Troy, he would now be king of justice in the Underworld; finally, Elektra breaks in – it is not Agamemnon who should be dead, but his murderers. The remote wish has become a curse, and this emphasises more sharply the need for revenge.[48] There is no decline in the frequency of this convention in the Hellenistic period. It is found in Alexandrian poetry; while in the prose laments and funerary inscriptions, where the tradition was less rigidly archaising, new forms were emerging all the time, possibly because of the decline in the use of the optative mood in the spoken language.[49] In the inscriptions, the curse is especially prominent, warning off plunderers and cursing enemies if there had been a violent death. It might take the form of a direct imprecation, or of an invocation to some divine power, especially the sun.[50] The invocation to the sun in an appeal for revenge, first found in Homer, is also common in the modern folk laments, and constitutes an interesting survival of a primitive idea in association with an ancient poetic convention.[51]

A variation of the wish which became increasingly frequent in the post-classical period was the introductory formula ἔδει, χρῆν or ἔπρεπε (it was right). Its Greek origin has been disputed;[52] and the epigraphic evidence is not sufficiently conclusive to prove that the formula was taken over into Latin, where it was extremely common (*debuit..., fas erat...*) from Greek. On the other hand, cases of such decisive Latin influence on Greek epigraphic formulae are rare, and until earlier literature of all kinds has been exhaustively studied, no firm conclusions can be drawn. Even if it was new as a regular formula in the lament, it expressed exactly the same thought as the traditional wish that the death had occurred differently, only rather more forcefully, as in the following inscription from Rome (fourth century A.D.), addressed to a mother who died leaving three small children:[53]

νηλὴς ὦ θάνατος, πολὺ δὴ μέγ᾽ ἀκαίριος ἥκεις·
χρῆν γὰρ ἐπ᾽ ὠδείνεσσιν ἔχειν χέρα καὶ τότ᾽ ὀλέσσαι.

Peek 1571.11–12

O pitiless death, you have come at the wrong time!
You should have laid hand upon her when she gave birth, so
that she died then!

The same formula occurs in Aelian Aristeides' *Monody on Smyrna*,[54] and also in Euripides' *Herakles*, when Herakles is discovered in a deep sleep after he has murdered his children in a fit of madness. The chorus address him:

τότε θανεῖν σ᾽ ἐχρῆν, ὅτε δάμαρτι σᾷ
φόνον ὁμοσπόρων ἔμολες ἐκπράξας
Ταφίων περίκλυστον ἄστυ πέρσας.　　　　　　E. *HF* 1077–80

You ought to have died then, when you went out
to avenge the blood of your wife's kin on the Taphians,
and to sack their sea-washed city.

The subsequent history of this formula can be traced, not in the Byzantine archaising laments, where classical forms are more rigidly adhered to, but in the funeral oration and *enkómion* of rhetorical prose, and in vernacular poetry.[55] In a short lament for the sinfulness of man, ῾Αμαρτωλοῦ Παράκλησις, (twelfth or thirteenth century), the same formula appears in vernacular Greek, combined with incremental repetition:

᾽Εμέν᾽ οὐ πρέπει νὰ λαλῶ, οὐδὲ νὰ συντυχαίνω,
οὐ πρέπει ἐμὲν νὰ βλέπωμαι, οὐδὲ πάλιν νὰ βλέπω,
οὐδὲ νὰ τρέφωμαι τροφὴν τὴν πρέπουσαν ἀνθρώποις.
᾽Εμένα πρέπει νὰ θρηνῶ, ἡμέραν ἐξ ἡμέρας.
　　　　　　　　　　　　　　　　Legrand *BGV* 1.17 = Zoras 72.6, 1–4

I ought not to speak, nor to converse,
I ought not to be seen, nor yet to see,
nor to eat food that is fitting to men.
I ought only to lament, day after day.

It is possible that the writer was adapting a folk song which he knew; certainly the structure and context, as well as the formula, are the same as those of the modern ritual laments:[56]

Δὲν πρέπει ἐγὼ νὰ χαίρωμαι, οὐδὲ κρασὶ νὰ πίνω·
μόν᾽ πρέπ᾽ ἐγὼ νᾶμ᾽ σ᾽ ἐρημιὰ σ᾽ ἕνα μαρμαροβούνι,
νὰ κείτωμαι τὰ πίστομα, νὰ χύνω μαῦρα δάκρυα,
νὰ γίνω λίμνη καὶ γυαλί, νὰ γίνω κρύα βρύση.　　　　Passow 347

I ought not to be happy, nor to drink wine,
I ought only to be on a desolate marble mountain,
to crouch down head forwards, to weep black tears,
to become a lake, a piece of glass, to become a cool spring.

The wish occurs in the modern laments in a wide variety of forms. Like Andromache in the *Iliad* mourning for Hector, a Maniot woman wishes she might never have lived rather than learn of the death of the man she is lamenting (Petrounias A 4).[57] Often, the hyperbole of the wish is designed to impress upon the dead the extremity of the mourner's grief. Taken one step further, this type of wish might become a cry for vengeance, as in another lament from Mani where the mourner wishes she could send a bird with a letter for her brother, that he might come at once and pursue their enemies (*ibid.* 8. 15b). Frequently, the wish is a fanciful flight into the realm of the unreal and impossible: a Nisyrot mother wishes that Charos had two children, that she might take one of them and so grieve him as he has grieved her;[58] or the dead may be asked to do the impossible, and return to the land of the living, as in the following Epirot lament:

Μήτρο, γιὰ γένει σύγνεφο, γένει κομμάτ' ἀντάρα
καὶ ἔλα μὲ τὸν ἄνεμο κι ἔλα μὲ τὸν ἀέρα,
ἔλα τὸ γληγορώτερο στὸ σπίτι τὸ δικό σου.   Giankas 901.1–3

Mitro, become a cloud, become a piece of mist,
and come with the wind, and come with the breeze,
come back as soon as you can to your own home!

But such a wish can never be fulfilled, and the dead may reply with a series of *adynata*, that come what may, he can never return:[59]

– Πές μου, πές μου, πότε θάρθῆς, καὶ πότε θὰ γυρίσης,
νὰ ρίξω μόσκο στὰ κλαριὰ καὶ μυρουδιὰ στὴ στράτα,
νὰ μαρμαρώσω τὴν αὐλή, νὰ βγῆς νὰ γκιζερίζης.
– Φόντας θὰ κάνη ἡ ἐλιὰ κρασὶ καὶ τὸ σταφύλι λάδι,
καὶ θὰ στερέψη ἡ θάλασσα νὰ τὴ σπείρουν σιτάρι,
τότες, μάνα μ', κι ἐγὼ θὰρθῶ νἀπὸ τὸ μαῦρο 'Ανάδη.
                                                        Spandonidi 215

– Tell me, tell me when you will come, and when you will
          return,
    that I may strew musk on the branches and scent on the path,
    that I may lay marble on the courtyard, for you to take a stroll.
– When the olive makes wine and when the grape makes oil,
    and when the sea runs dry and is sown with wheat,
    then, my mother, shall I return from black Hades.

This expression of the irrevocable finality of death performs a vital function: by asking for the impossible, the mourner gains an assurance that the dead has accepted his lot and will never return, either to help or harm the living.

The common tradition

Praise and reproach

Just as the unfulfilled wish might, in certain contexts, be turned into a curse, so too the praise of the dead was often reversed: instead of seeking his goodwill by praise, as was usual,[60] you provoked him by reproaching, blaming or abusing him. Agamemnon, in the *kommós* of Aeschylus' *Choephoroi*, receives his full due of praise; but afterwards, Orestes and Elektra make sure of his attention to their pleas for help in executing vengeance by means of a series of short, sharp reminders:

– μέμνησο λουτρῶν οἷς ἐνοσφίσθης, πάτερ.
– μέμνησο δ' ἀμφίβληστρον ὡς ἐκαίνισαν –
– ἆρ' ἐξεγείρῃ τοῖσδ' ὀνείδεσιν, πάτερ;
– ἆρ' ὀρθὸν αἴρεις φίλτατον τὸ σὸν κάρα;   491–2, 495–6

– Remember the bath in which you were slain, father!
– Remember the net which they devised for you!...
– Are you not stirred by these reproaches, father?
– Will you not raise up your dear head?

An even stronger kind of accusation is made in an interesting but poorly spelt inscription from Seldjouk-ghazi near Prusa:[61]

Ὦ πάτερ, μεμφόμεθα σ' ἀν|φότεροι ὃς προθανὼν ἡμῶν | ὀλίγον
χρώνον μητρὸς ἀφήρπασες | ἀνφοτέρους μήδ' ἐλεῶν μη|τέρα
τὴν ἀτυχῆς, μηδὲν εἰδοῦσα | ἐξ ὑμῶν ἀγαθόν.
                              Mendel *BCH* (1909) 312–14

O father, we both blame you because you died a short time
before us and then snatched us both from our mother, feeling
no pity for her wretchedness, even though she saw nothing
good from us.

A comparable sentiment is expressed in a modern Epirot lament, where the dead girl is accused by her mother:[62]

Δικό σ' εἶναι τὸ φταίξιμο, δικό σ' εἶναι τὸ σιούκι,
σὰν ἀπὸ τί, καὶ ἀπὸ ποιὸ νὰ πέσῃς νὰ πεθάνῃς;   Giankas 904.1–2

You are to blame, it is your fault!
What reason, what cause was there for you to die?

Even where the idea of blame is less forcefully expressed, the mourner may address the dead with a reproach, as if to remind him of his forgotten

182

duties. Andromache, like Hekabe and Helen, praises Hector in her lament at his wake; but unlike them, she opens and closes with a faint note of reproach:

ἄνερ, ἀπ᾽ αἰῶνος νέος ὤλεο, καδ᾽ δέ με χήρην
λείπεις ἐν μεγάροισι.   *Il.* 24.725–6

οὐ γάρ μοι θνῄσκων λεχέων ἐκ χεῖρας ὄρεξας,
οὐδέ τί μοι εἶπες πυκινὸν ἔπος, οὗ τέ κεν αἰεὶ
μεμνήμην νύκτάς τε καὶ ἤματα δάκρυ χέουσα.   *Ibid.* 743–5

Husband, you were too young to die, and you leave me
a widow in the palace!

When you died you did not stretch out your hands to me
from your bed,
you did not even say a kind word to me, that I might always
have remembered, as I shed tears by day and by night.

The reproach implied in the verb *you leave* (λείπεις), signalling the grief left behind by the dead to his relatives and friends, was traditional, and is especially common in the funerary inscriptions.[63] It is no less frequent in the ritual laments today, expressed by the modern verb ἀφήνεις. A mother from Crete reproaches her daughter for dying too soon and deserting her small children:[64]

Παιδί μου, καὶ ποῦ τά ᾽φηκες, τ᾽ ἀνήλικα παιδιά σου!
Δὲν τὰ λυπᾶσαι τ᾽ ἀρφανά, νὰ πηαίνης νὰ τ᾽ ἀφήσης,
Στοὶ πέντε δρόμους τ᾽ ἄφηκες, παιδί μου, τὰ παιδιά σου.
                                                          Lioudaki 408

My child, where have you left your children so young!
Have you no pity for the orphans, that you should go and
leave them?
You have left your children on the streets, my child!

Similarly, just as Andromache reproaches Hector for dying before he could address a parting word of comfort to her, the heroine of the Cretan tragedy *Erofile* (c. 1600) weeps over the dismembered body of her husband Panaretos, and asks:

Γιάντα σωπᾶς στὸν πόνο μου; γιάντα στὰ κλάηματά μου
δὲ συντυχαίνεις δυὸ μικρὰ λόγια παρηγοριά μου;   5.463–4

Why are you silent at my grief? Why do you not speak
two small words of comfort to me in my weeping?

The same thought is echoed in another line of the modern Cretan
lament just quoted:[65]

Ἄχι καὶ γιὰ δὲ μοῦ μιλεῖς, νὰ μὲ παρηγορήσης;   Lioudaki 408

Áhi, why don't you speak to me, to give me comfort?

It was this kind of reproach that Lucian caricatured in his *de Luctu*,
and it is a stock element of the laments referred to by the Church
fathers to demonstrate the pagan, un-Christian character of lamentation.[66]
Certainly, it reflects an essentially self-centred outlook, and this is
perhaps why it has survived more strongly in the modern ritual laments
than in the Byzantine archaising or religious laments. But it should be
seen within the context of the lament as a whole, where it is complementary to and inseparable from its opposite, elaborate praise of the
dead man's virtues.

It is precisely this kind of balance of opposites which forms the basis
for the development of thought in the lament throughout Greek tradition.
The mourner begins with a hesitant address, questioning her ability to
give proper due to the dead. She then continues with elaborate praise,
which may turn into reproach or even blame. She recalls the past and
imagines the future, perhaps with a wish that things had been different,
perhaps with a curse on the dead man's enemies. These past or hypothetical events are then contrasted with the present reality, her fate
with that of the dead, thus strengthening the force of her final address
and lament.

These themes and conventions are both ancient and traditional. That
their survival in the Greek folk laments of today marks essentially the
development of a single tradition is indicated not only by the nature
of the ideas – many of which are found in folk laments from other parts
of the world – but by the similarity of the formulae through which they
are expressed.

9
The allusive method

Part of the artistic economy in the language of folk tradition is the allusive method, by which a fact or an idea is expressed indirectly but concretely, through symbols.[1] In the lament, it has a further ritual significance, since the mourner may deliberately avoid explicit reference to death, addressing the dead in a series of striking images and elaborating her theme through metaphors and similes. Since this is a universal characteristic of the ritual lament, and not peculiar to Greek, continuity must be sought in specific terms of form and content rather than in the general survival of the practice.

Form

The simplest form of allusion is the series of unconnected epithets which may introduce the address in the ancient hymn and *enkómion*. This form passed into the late pagan and early Christian hymns without affecting the more secular lament.[2] Closely related and equally ancient is the series of nouns or noun groups, often introduced by a verb. It differs in that it is not merely a descriptive address, but implies a transferred identification. In Euripides' *Andromache*, Hermione greets the arrival of Orestes with the words, 'O harbour appearing to sailors in a storm, son of Agamemnon!' (891).[3] Capable of greater and more subtle elaboration, this mode of address is found in popular tradition in similar form, as is illustrated by the following examples, the first a vernacular prose lament of the sixteenth century, and the second a modern lament:[4]

Χελιδόνι ἡ γλώσσα του, ἀηδόνι ἡ φωνή του, παγώνι
ἡ μορφή του.   Valetas 1.88–9

His tongue a swallow, his voice a nightingale, his form a
  peacock...

Ἀφέντη μου, στοὺς ἀπεζοὺς φαίνεσαι καβαλάρης,
καὶ μέσα στοὺς καβαλαρούς πύργος θεμελιωμένος.   Fauriel 2.62.7

My lord, to those on foot you seem like a horseman,
and among horsemen, like a well-founded tower.

Another method was to describe through symbols. This might take
the form of a simile, both simple and developed. The simile is associated
with the lament in Homer and in the funerary inscriptions, but not in
tragedy; nor is it prominent in the hymn and *enkómion*.[5] In the Byzantine
period, too, the simile was more characteristic of the laments than of the
hymns; and, while it is found in all types of lament, the developed simile,
in which the point of comparison is elaborated for its own sake on both
sides, is found only in the more popular tradition.[6] A Cretan mourner
of today uses a developed simile which is remarkably close to Homer's
simile for Achilles lamenting the death of Patroklos:[7]

Ὡς κλαίει ἡ μάνα τὸ παιδί, ὄντινα τοῆ πεθάνη,
κλαίω κι ἐγὼ γιὰ λόγο σου, μὰ ὁ νοῦς σου δὲν τὸ βάνει.
                                                    Lioudaki *LK* 121

As a mother weeps for her child who dies,
so I weep for you, but you cannot perceive it.

ὡς δὲ πατὴρ οὗ παιδὸς ὀδύρεται ὀστέα καίων,
νυμφίου, ὅς τε θανὼν δειλοὺς ἀκάχησε τοκῆας,
ὡς Ἀχιλεὺς ἑτάροιο ὀδύρετο ὀστέα καίων.   *Il.* 23.222–4

As a father weeps for his son, when he burns his bones,
a bridegroom, who caused grief to his wretched parents by
  his death,
so Achilles wept for his comrade as he burnt his bones.

Even commoner than the simile in the modern laments, which compares
a real event with an imagined one, is the more flexible expression of
reality entirely through symbols. In a couplet from Mani, the tragic
circumstances of death are conveyed through imagery alone: because
of a feud, two leading families were extinct in the male line except for
one orphaned boy, who was carefully tended by female relations in
order to take revenge until at the age of eight he fell ill and died:

Ἡ ἄμπαρη ξεθύμανε κι ἔσπασε τ' ἀλαβάστρο.
Μικρὸ κανόνι κρέπαρε, μὰ ξαρματώθη κάστρο. Theros 771

The hold has burst and the alabaster has shattered,
a small gun has exploded into pieces, but a fortress is disarmed.

Light

Among the most ancient features of light symbolism in Greek tradition
is the identification of light as the sacred source of life, warmth, joy
and knowledge, the means of scattering the darkness of death and
ignorance.[8] To see the light was equated with life and understanding;
hence light and sight were used synonymously from Homer onwards.[9]
Conversely, darkness veiling the eyes meant death;[10] and it was usual
for the dying to take formal leave of the light of day, like Ajax, Antigone
and Iphigeneia.[11] This symbolism is implicit in the light imagery of
some of the earliest address formulae, where the warmth and comfort
afforded by the presence of a valued person were identified with the
light of dawn or the sun of summer scattering the darkness of night or
the cold of winter. Eumaios greets Telemachos in the *Odyssey* with the
words, 'You have come, Telemachos, sweet light' (16.23).[12] Clytemnestra hails Agamemnon's return to his hearth and home as a warm
spell in the winter's cold (A. *Ag.* 968-9).

In the lament, such an address was evocative of all the subtle mystical and
eschatological associations of light. Andromache says she would rather die
herself than lose Astyanax, her only remaining eye of life now that Hector
is dead (E. *Andr.* 406).[13] In an epigram, Plato addresses his friend Aster:

Ἀστὴρ πρὶν μὲν ἔλαμπες ἐνὶ ζωοῖσιν Ἑῷος,
νῦν δὲ θανὼν λάμπεις Ἕσπερος ἐν φθιμένοις. AP 7.670

Aster, once you shone like the morning star among the living.
Now you are dead, you shine like the evening star among
those departed.

This kind of imagery is further extended in the funerary inscriptions.
A divine power may be reproached for quenching the torch of
light too soon, envious of another's victory (Peek 736.3). Sometimes
there may be associations with the mystic symbol of the torch in the
course of life:[14]

τὸν καλὸν ἐνθάδε κοῦρον ἔχει τέλος. Ὦ Φθόνε †νεικᾶς†
ἔσβεσες ἁπτομένην λαμπάδα καλλοσύνης. MAMA 1.88

The end holds this fine youth here. O Envy (?of his triumph),
you have put out the kindled torch of his beauty.

Light symbolism as it occurs in the Byzantine religious tradition
marks a further development, joining to Greek the Christian heritage
from Syriac and Hebrew.[15] But it retains many of its ancient features,
which permeate the imagery of the hymns, especially the *Akáthistos
Hýmnos*, where the Virgin is hailed as the light-giving lamp appearing
to those in darkness and kindling the immaterial light itself, and as
a ray of the intellectual sun, bringing the dawn of knowledge to the
world of darkness. This symbolism explains why light imagery, especially
of the sun and moon, played such an important role in the Virgin's
lament, as we saw in chapter 4. It may have been through the more
popular versions, such as the *Epitáphios Thrênos*, that light imagery
acquired its particular significance in the modern ritual laments. In a fine
Maniot lament, the murdered chief of the Kaloyeroyiannis family is
hailed as saint, archangel, source of light, at whose death the skies
darken in sympathy as at the Crucifixion (Pasayanis 169).

But there were other sources of transmission, outside the Christian
tradition. Quintus' Briseis mourns Achilles with an image in the classical
style, as 'the sacred day and light of the sun' (3.563–4). Other classical
motifs, such as the loss of sight, which is the light of life, the quenching
of a single lamp or candle in the midst of darkness, the setting of the
sun and the waning of the moon, can all be traced from learned poetry
and rhetoric to popular tradition through the romances.[16] Apart from
the archaising language, the dirge of Dianteia for her son Hysminias in
Eustathios' novel is strikingly similar to popular laments, in both the
form and the range of imagery, as can be seen by comparing it with
some of the modern laments.[17]

Ἥλιον εἶχον τὸν παῖδα, καὶ νῦν τοῦ παιδὸς κρυβέντος, ἀνήλιος
ἡ μήτηρ ἐγώ. Ἀστήρ μοι παῖς ἐκεῖνος περιφανής, ἀλλ'
ἀπεκρύβη, καὶ νὺξ ἀφεγγὴς τὴν μητέρα με κατέλιπε. Φῶς ἦν
μοι παῖς ἐκεῖνος, ἀλλ' ἀπεσβέσθη, καὶ νῦν ἐν σκότει πορεύομαι.

10.381–2

I had my child as the sun, and now that my child is obscured
I, his mother, am without sun. My child was a bright star, but
now he is hidden, and the gloom of night has enshrouded me,
his mother. My child was light to me, but he is quenched, and
now I walk in darkness.

Μοὺρ πῶς δὲ μὲ λελίζεσαι καὶ δὲ μ' ἐλεημονιέσαι,
ὁπόχασα τὰ μάτια μου, ὁπόχασα τὸ φῶς μου,
σὰν ἥλιος ἐβασίλεψα, σὰν τὸ φεγγάρι ἐσώθ'κα,
καὶ πάγωσαν τὰ χέρια μου ἀπανωθιὰ στὰ στήθια.

Giankas 879.4–7

O why don't you pity me, and why do you have no mercy?
For I have lost my eyes, I have lost my sight,
like the sun I have set, like the moon I have waned,
and my hands have frozen upon my breast.

In the Cretan *Sacrifice of Abraham*, Sarah mourns Isaac first as her eyes
(378), and later as her only candle, in a couplet which can be paralleled
almost exactly from Crete today:

κι ἂς τάξω, δὲν τὸ γέννησα, μηδ' εἶδα το ποτέ μου,
μά 'ναν κερὶν ἀφτούμενον ἐκράτουν κι ἤσβησέ μου.   *Thysia* 401–2

I must make myself think that I did not give him birth, that
      I never saw him,
but that I held a single lighted candle and it was put out.

Ἄς τάξω δὲ σ' ἐβύζασα, δὲ σέ 'δα 'γὼ ποτέ μου,
κι ἕναν κεράκι ἀφτούμενο ἐβάστουν κι ἤσβησέ μου.   Lioudaki 416.2

I must make myself think that I did not give you suck, that
      I never saw you,
but that I carried a single lighted candle and it was put out.

The themes in these laments belong to a common tradition. Besides
the more general concept of light, there is the sun, symbol of life,
warmth and justice; the dawn, contrasting light with darkness; the
moon and stars as cherished objects of brightness; the more homely
lamp and candle, put out before their time and leaving the mourner to
continue her way in gloom; and finally, the identification of light and
sight, without which man is blind. Although the symbolism is naturally
most explicit in the religious tradition, the images themselves are so
closely integrated into the Greek lament of all periods that much of their
allusive quality is lost without an understanding of their evolution and
history.

Journey

One of the most fundamental and universal beliefs about life after death
is that the dead must undertake a long and hazardous journey, a *passage*

from this world to the next. In ancient Greek, this idea is clearly expressed in the detailed instructions for the soul's journey to the Underworld inscribed on the so-called Orphic gold tablets which were buried with the dead (dating from the fourth century B.C.). In ancient mystical thought, this journey was regarded as a continuation of the journey of life.[18] These ideas are reflected in the imagery of many of the ancient laments, and some of them have survived today.

First, the idea of life and death as two stages of a single journey is imbedded in the language and formulae of many of the funerary inscriptions. Much of the evidence is late; but the importance of the theme in Greek tradition is attested by its comparative rarity in Latin, and by the number of variations in which it is found.[19] In one inscription the dead man tells the passer-by to go on his way, since the voyage to death is common to all (Peek 1833.9–10). Another talks of death as a sojourn at a wayside inn – an idea which can be traced back to the comic poet Antiphanes (fourth century B.C.).[20] Yet another man tells us that he has repaid the loan of life and is going on his way, where all is dust (*Stud. Pont.* (1910) 143).

Second, life is not only a journey by road but also a voyage by sea, which leads to a single harbour beneath the earth.[21] This theme finds frequent expression in the imagery of ancient tradition. In many of the praise formulae, the security afforded by a husband or son is identified with a harbour or calm weather appearing to a ship after a storm, with the mainstay of the ship or with the helmsman, on which the safety of all depends. Again, Clytemnestra salutes Agamemnon on his return as 'the stay that saves the ship' and as 'the shore despaired-of sighted far out at sea' (A. *Ag.* 897, 899).[22] Greeting Pylades, Orestes says that a faithful friend to a man in distress is 'better than the sight of calm to sailors' (E. *Or.* 728). When applied to the dead, these images acquire a new dimension, since they refer at the same time to the living, left to continue their voyage without help, and to the last voyage of the dead beneath the earth.

How were these themes of travel, both by road and by sea, so closely integrated in ancient Greek, developed in later tradition? Some aspects were incorporated into Christianity and elaborated in the Byzantine hymns: in the *Akáthistos Hýmnos*, Christ is ὁδηγὸν πλανωμένοις (a guide to those who stray), an idea which may owe something to the ancient mysteries;[23] and in Romanos' *kontákion* Mary opens her lament with the question, 'Where are you going, child? For whose sake are you completing the swift course?' (19.1.10–16). Christ as the haven of souls, the helmsman of sailors, the sea to drown all sinners, is familiar from the early liturgies; but apart from some striking variations in the *Akáthistos Hýmnos*, this imagery is rather stylised, and does not appear to have had a direct influence on the lament.[24] In Dianteia's dirge for Hysminias, on the other hand, from Eustathios' *Hysmine and Hysminias*, the classical praise formulae are perfectly appropriate to the occasion of lamentation:

Εὐάγκαλός μοι λιμὴν Ὑσμινίας ὁ παῖς, κἀγὼ δ' ὡς ναῦς ἐν
λιμένι νηνεμίαν ἦγον καὶ ἤμην ἀκύματος· νῦν δ' ὁ λιμὴν
οὐδαμοῦ, κἀγὼ δ' ἡ ναῦς ἐν πελάγει μέσῳ κατακλυδωνιζομένη
τοῖς κύμασιν.   10.381

My son Hysminias was a welcome harbour to me, and I, like
a ship in port, enjoyed calm, and was unruffled by the waves.
But now the harbour is nowhere to be seen, and I, the ship,
am driven out into the ocean and overwhelmed by the waves.

The same theme is recognisable in a *Monody for Constantinople* written by the Byzantine scholar Andronikos Kallistos: 'O haven once sweet and kind to ships, now unfortunate, indeed a very Skylla.' Were these just archaisms, or may they have owed something to contemporary vernacular poetry?

Certainly, allusion to travel is nowhere so complex and flexible in Byzantine laments as in the modern ritual laments. During his lifetime, the dead man was 'a well-equipped ship to his home' (Politis 197.6). Without his protection, his orphaned children are desolate:

σὰν τὸ καράβι στὸ γιαλὸ πού 'ναι χωρὶς τιμόνι,
φυσάει βορᾶς, μέσα τὸ πάει, κι ὁ μπάτης τὸ γυρίζει,
καὶ ὁ πουνέντης ὁ τρελλὸς στὴν ξέρα τ' ἀρμενίζει.
                                                    Laog (1911) 266.4, 2

... like the ship by the shore which has no rudder,
the north wind blows and drives it in and the sea breeze
    turns it back,
and the mad west wind dashes it on to the reef.

Nor is this all. When the dead is dressed for the wake before the funeral procession, he is thought of as a ship about to depart for the Underworld; and, since it is a maiden voyage, it has golden masts, silver stern and sails of silk. As if unknowing, the mourner asks its destination:

– Καράβι πρωτοτάξιδο κι ἀσημαρματωμένο,
   πὄχεις πανιὰ μεταξωτὰ κι ἔχεις κουπιὰ ἀσημένια,
   κι ἔχεις κι ἀντενοκάταρτα χρυσά, μαλαματένια,
   ποῦθε θὰ ρίξης σίδερο, θὰ δέσης παλαμάρι;
– Στὴν Κάτου Γῆς τὸ σίδερο, στὸν Ἅδη παλαμάρι,
   καὶ μέσ' στὸν Ἅι-Λιὰ μπροστὰ θ' ἀράξη τὸ καράβι.

Romaios KR 228

– Boat decked out in silver for your maiden voyage,
   you whose sails are of silk and whose oars of silver,
   and whose yardarm and masts are made of finest gold,
   where will you lay anchor, where will you moor your ropes?
– I will anchor in the Underworld, I will moor in Hades,
   and I will come to rest in front of Saint Elijah.

Sometimes the idea of a journey by road is interwoven with the idea of a voyage by sea. In a Pontic lament, a widow asks her dead husband, whom she always addresses as 'my sun', what road he is taking, and why he is going into exile. The black boat at the door, she warns him, is not going to foreign lands, but to the land of no return, to Hades. And if he sets out on this journey, what road remains for her? (*ArP* (1951) 187). The allusion here and elsewhere is developed by rapid transition to the black boat of death, with Charos as its helmsman, stopping like a pirate ship only to steal the souls of men. It is a common theme from laments in all parts of Greece.[25] The image of the ship is thus applied simultaneously to the living, left to continue without a helmsman, to the dead, both as he was in his lifetime and as he is now, and also to Death itself.

By the same complex allusive method, the dead was praised in his lifetime as 'horseman among those on foot' (Fauriel 2.62.7). Now that he is dead, they are saddling outside a horse with golden spurs and silver reins. It is the familiar preparation for any traveller's journey on horseback. Yet the lament continues inexorably:

Νὰ πάη στῆς Ἄρνας τὰ βουνά, στῆς Ἄρνησης τὰ μέρη,
π' ἀρνιέται ἡ μάνα τὸ παιδί, καὶ τὸ παιδὶ τὴ μάνα.

Romaios KR 231.5–6

he is to go to the mountains of Denial, to the regions of
   Denial,
where mother denies her child and child denies its mother.

Finally, just as the image of the dead as a ship is fused with that of the
ship of Charos, so here, parallel to the dead horseman about to set off
on his perilous journey, is the terrible figure of Charos the huntsman:

Μὰ νά τον καὶ κατέβαινε στοὺς κάμπους καβελάρης,
μαῦρος ἦταν, μαῦρα φορεῖ, μαῦρο καὶ τ᾽ ἄλογό του.

Politis 219.11–12

But see, there he was coming down the plains on horseback.
He was black, his clothes were black, and his horse was black.

    The themes of ship and horseman belong to a common tradition of
ideas arising out of the ancient belief that life and death are two stages
of a single journey. In both, the dual relevance of the allusion, to the
living and to the dead, is exploited to the full, not by a logical sequence
of mutually exclusive ideas, but by a process of accretion, in which one
association is fused with another. This complex but compressed allusive
method is dependent for its effect both on a long history of oral transmission, and also on the solemn sense of the occasion on which these
laments were sung, just as the dead was about to leave on his last journey
from house to grave. Some motifs, such as the emphasis on journey
by horseback rather than on foot, and the figure of Death the Hunter,
are probably medieval in origin;[26] but they have been fused with what
is demonstrably an ancient tradition. The importance of oral tradition
in the transmission of these themes is indicated by the relative lack
of variety and cohesion in their treatment in Byzantine archaising and
religious laments, and by their richness in the ritual laments of today.

Support

It was common in the ancient lament for the mother, sister or wife to
complain to the dead of the hope and comfort of which his death has
deprived her, and the wretched prospect of her old age without his
protection.[27] This is often expressed by identifying the dead man with
an object of support or defence. The idea is not exclusive to the lament:
Clytemnestra greets Agamemnon, with grim irony, as 'the sturdy pillar
of a lofty roof, a father's only child' (A. *Ag.* 897–8). The image is
traditional. In an anonymous tragic fragment, children are referred to as
στηρίγματ᾽ οἴκου (supports of the house);[28] and in Euripides' *Iphigeneia
in Tauris*, Iphigeneia relates her dream that the house of Argos has
been shaken to the ground from its foundations, leaving only one pillar

standing, over which she poured a libation as if to the dead. Her interpretation of the dream, that Orestes is dead, rests on the traditional identification of the son as pillar of the house; as she says, 'male children are the pillars of homes' (57, cf. 42–60).

In Byzantine laments, the theme was common only in its more general form of lost comfort and relief.[29] But today it is found in many variations developed again by complex allusion. In his lifetime, the dead man was praised as 'a sturdy tower' (Fauriel 2.62.8). Premature death might be likened to the falling of a tower, a simile common in Homer.[30] Sometimes, there is some suggestion of another related theme, that a man, by building a strong and lofty fortress for his home, was safe from Charos' incursions. The result was just the opposite, since in this way he attracted Charos' attention, tempting him to a trial of strength, as in the following Akritic ballad:[31]

Ἀκρίτης κάστρον ἔχτισε, Χάρος νὰ μὴν τὸν εὔρη,
διπλοῦν τριπλοῦν τὸ ἔχτισε σιδερογκαρφωμένο.
Ἐγύρισε κι ἐτράνησεν, Χάρος τὸν παραστέκνει.　　*Laog* (1903) 247

Akritis built a fortress, so that Charos should not find him.
he built it with double, treble walls and nailed it with iron.
He turned and looked – Charos was there beside him.

Even more significant is the wide diffusion in laments from all parts of Greece of the identification of a dead husband or son with the pillar of the house, found nowhere to my knowledge in Byzantine tradition. It is often introduced incidentally as one of the praise formulae: 'you were a pillar of gold to your house' (Giankas 891.3). But it is also developed in a more fundamental way. In Crete, the relatives sometimes call out to the dead man as he is carried over the threshold, 'We have lost the pillar of our house! Ófou! and when the pillar of the house falls, the beams will fall too!' (Lioudaki 407). In a Pontic lament, a mother warns her dead son 'and a house without a pillar soon falls to ruins' (*ArP* (1951) 187.15). This gains added significance when we remember the ritual custom of the mourner calling on the pillar of the house, as well as on the door and walls, to weep and take their leave of the dead as he is carried out.[32] The underlying implication, as in Iphigeneia's dream, is that with his departure the very structure of the house is threatened with ruin.

Ὀσπίτα μου, 'κι φλίνηστουν, στουλάρα μ', κάτι κλαίτε,
κ' ἐσύ, βασιλοστούλαρο μ', κατ' 'κὶ σταλάζεις αἵμαν;

The allusive method

Γουρπάν'ς, ὀσπιτοχάλαστε καὶ τζαχοζεμέντσα,
ἐχάλασες τὴν κερχανά σ' κ' ἐπόζεψες τὸν κέγρος,
τ' ὀσπίτα σ' ἐσκοτείνεψαν, αὐλή σ' ἐχοχολῶθεν.

ArP (1946) 108.44

My houses, do you not grieve, my pillars, why do you not
weep?
And you, chief pillar of the house, why do you not drip blood?
Woe is me! May house and hearth fall into ruins,
for you have destroyed your home and brought down your
fortress,
your houses have darkened, your courtyard is filled with rubble.

Spring and harvest

The juxtaposition of man and nature is an ancient and universal element
in folk poetry. An aspect of nature is compared or contrasted with
a human condition, throwing it into sharper relief. In its simplest form,
the comparison is expressed in a couplet, the first line describing nature, the
second pointing the parallel. In Greek tradition, the idea of life as a plant
or a flower is as old as the oldest of the lyric poets.[33] Particularly suitable
to lamentation was the comparison of early death with a flower withered
before its time, or cut off in full bloom, frequently extended to include
allusion to spring and harvest, blossoming and reaping, as in a fragment
of Euripides: βίον θερίζειν ὥστε κάρπιμον στάχυν (to reap life like fruitful
corn) E. *Hyps. fr.* 757 Nauck.[34] When combined with the untimely
snatching of Hades and applied to a young girl, it suggests the violent
marriage rite of death, in which the girl is ravished by Hades.[35] The
image has ancient mythical associations with the story of Demeter and
Kore, but in later poetry it was developed for its own sake. In one of
Meleager's epigrams (second to first centuries B.C.), it has become an
evocative but literary affectation:

αἰαῖ, ποῦ τὸ ποθεινὸν ἐμοὶ θάλος; ἅρπασεν "Αιδας,
ἅρπασεν· ἀκμαῖον δ' ἄνθος ἔφυρε κόνις.   AP 7.476.7-8

Alas, where is my lovely shoot? Seized by Hades,
seized! Dust has defiled the flower in full bloom.

In the funerary inscriptions, the idea finds frequent and varied expression
throughout antiquity, as in the following inscription from Larisa (second
to third centuries A.D.), where the imagery suggests imminent sexual
fulfilment suddenly denied by death:[36]

[παρ]θένος οὖσα τέθ[νη]κα Λε|[ο]ντὼ ὡς νέον ἄνθος |
ὥρης παντοθαλοῦς πρωτο|[φ]ανὴ⟨ς⟩ καλύκων
καὶ μέλλου|[σα] γάμῳ δεκαπενταετὴς | μείγνυσθαι
ἐν φθι|μένοις κεῖμαι, ὕπνον | ἔχουσα μακρόν.　　Peek 988

I, Leonto, died a maiden, like a young flower
　when it bursts its bud and first shows its petals,
– fifteen years old, just ready to be joined in wedlock,
　I have come to lie among the dead in a long sleep.

Variations on the same theme are extremely common in Byzantine literature, as in one of the epigrams of Gregory Nazianzen:

'Εμὲ γὰρ ῥάδαμνον ὥσπερ
νέον ἐξέκοψεν ᾅδης...
'Ακόρεστος εἷλε Πλούτων
ἐμὲ Παῦλον, ὥσπερ ἔρνος
ἀπαλὸν τεμὼν πρὸ ὥρας.
Θάνατος νέων τὸ κάλλος
ὅλον, ὡς χλοήν, θερίζει
δρεπάνη.

Hades has cut me down
like a young branch...
Insatiable Plouton has seized
me, Pavlos, plucking me like
a tender young plant, too soon.
Thanatos reaps the full beauty
of the young, like grass,
with his scythe.

Carmina Epitaphia, Migne 38.2, 80–1

Each of these details recurs throughout the learned poetry and prose, especially in the romances,[37] where there are also signs of a connection with popular tradition. A new image in Theodore Prodromos' novel *Rhodanthe and Dosikles* (twelfth century) is of the dead Rhodanthe as a withering apple: μαραίνεται τὸ μῆλον, ἡ ῥοιὰ φθίνει (the apple is withering, the pomegranate is fading 6.299, 258). It is a startling comparison, until we remember the love songs of modern folk poetry, where the fresh beauty of the girl to be won is likened, as in Sappho's fragment, to a ripening apple;[38] conversely, in the modern laments, the phrase 'like a withered apple' is a stock simile which dates back at least to the version of *Digenis Akritas* preserved in the Escorial manuscript (end of fifteenth century).[39] The nature of the simile is precise enough to suggest that Prodromos may have been drawing on popular tradition. It is interesting to note that in general, this theme is well developed in learned and popular poetry but comparatively rare in the hymns.[40]

In the modern laments, just as men were, on the whole, identified with the ship, horseman, tower and pillar, the imagery of spring and flowers belongs to mothers, wives, sisters and daughters. A mother from Kalymnos addresses her daughter:

Ρόδο τῆς πρώτης ἄνοιξης μὲ πέντε θεωρίες,
κεφάλιν ἤσουν, κόρη μου, μέσα στὶς κοπελλοῦ[δ]ες. Baud-Bovy 2.39

Rose of the first spring with five colours,
you were the chief, my daughter, among the young girls.

A child's death is frequently seen in relation to the seasons of the year; and, like Hades in the ancient inscriptions, it is usually Charos who is blamed for the premature plucking:[41]

Γιὰ ἰδὲς καιρὸ ποὺ διάλεξες, Χάρε μου, νὰ τὸν πάρης,
νὰ πάρης τ' ἄνθη ὀχ τὰ βουνά, λελούδια ἀπὸ τοὺς κάμπους.

                                                            Politis 192

See what a time you have chosen, my Charos, to take him,
to take blossoms from the mountains and flowers from the plains!

As in antiquity, death is seen as the reaping of the crop of life; once more, the prime reaper is Charos, as in the following Maniot lament:

Σταράκι μου καθαριστὸ κι ἀγουροθερισμένο,
ποὺ σ' ἀγουροθερίσανε τοῦ Χάρου οἱ θεριστάδες. Pasayanis 98.1–2

My corn that has been husked and reaped before its time,
reaped too soon by the reapers of Charos!

This leads us directly to the simile of the deserted mother in *The Song of the Dead Brother*, who is left, after the ravages of Charos, 'like stubble on the plain' (Politis 92.21). The allusion here is to the stubble left behind by the reapers after their work is done and then scorched, as is clear from a developed form of the same simile in a lament from Karpathos, where the girl accuses her dead lover:[42]

τσαὶ σοῦ μ' ἀπαλησμόνησες σὰκ καλαμιὰ στὸκ κάμπο,
ἀποὺ τὴ σπέρου τσ' ἀνεμμᾶ τσ' ὕστερα τὴθ θερίζου,
τσαὶ τῆς ἐπαίρου τὸκ καρπὸ τσ' ἡ καλαμιὰ πομένει,
βίου τῆς καλαμιᾶς φωδιὰ τσαὶ μένει στάχτη μόνο.

                                                        DAr (1948) 285.12–13

You have forgotten me like stubble on the plain,
which men sow and it grows, and then they reap,
and they take the crop and leave behind the stubble,
they set fire to the stubble and only ashes are left.

The tree

Closely associated with spring and harvest is the imagery of the tree, but it deserves separate consideration because there are some sufficiently precise details both in the associations of the theme and in its application to trace its evolution continuously through Greek tradition.

The parallel between man and tree can be traced at every stage of growth. Just as Thetis mourns Achilles, thinking of his childhood in terms of a carefully tended shoot, so too, in the seventeenth-century Cretan play, *The Sacrifice of Abraham*, Sarah tells how she watched Isaac grow like the shoot of a tree (*Il.* 18.55–7, *Thysia* 379). The same thought is implicit in the modern laments, in the formulaic praise of a young man's beauty 'tall as a rod, slim as a reed' and 'straight as a cypress tree' (Passow 347.16, 350.12), which can be traced back to the fifteenth-century Byzantine *Achilleid* (61–2).

Further, a good man might be compared with a full grown tree, whose foliage affords welcome shade from the heat of summer.[43] His loss is lamented in these terms in the modern laments: one Maniot mourner complains 'the plane tree has withered with its thick shade'; another, introducing a characteristic modernisation, addresses a young man as 'my silken umbrella where many took shelter' (Pasayanis 58.2, 116.8–9). But as old age approaches, the leaves fall. Old men are likened to bare posts or trunks whose leaves have been torn away by the wind.[44]

But it is the final stage in the parallel that is the most sustained. Twice in extended similes, Homer compares the falling of men in battle with a tree struck down from its roots:[45]

ὡς δ' ὅθ' ὑπὸ ῥιπῆς πατρὸς Διὸς ἐξερίπῃ δρῦς
πρόρριζος...
ὣς ἔπεσ' Ἕκτορος ὠκὺ χαμαὶ μένος ἐν κονίῃσι.   *Il.* 14.414–15, 418

As when an oak falls to the ground by a gust from father Zeus, uprooted...
so fell brave Hector suddenly to the dust.

The idea was traditional in antiquity, and is frequently found in association with the dead. Herodotos, compressing the simile into a single adjective πρόρριζος, applies it to the sudden downfall inflicted by a jealous fate on those who are tempted to greater wealth than the gods permit. Amasis, king of Egypt, warns the prosperous tyrant of Samos, Polykrates, that he has never yet heard of a man so fortunate throughout his life who did not come to a terrible end and 'die root and branch' (ἐτελεύτησε πρόρριζος 3.40). When his end finally comes, and his cruel death is announced to the people of Samos by Maiandros, it is commented that Polykrates 'fulfilled his own destiny' (ἐξέπλησε μοῖραν τὴν ἑωυτοῦ 3.142). Solon's famous warning to Kroisos on the dangers of excessive wealth contains the same allusion, that God may give wealth to many and then cause their downfall, root and branch (1.32–3); and the Spartans conclude the moral tale told to the Athenians about the perjuror Glaukos, pursued by an unseen avenger until his whole house was destroyed without a trace, with the words 'and he has been wiped out root and branch from Sparta' (ἐκτέτριπταί τε πρόρριζος ἐκ Σπάρτης 6.68). Herodotos has invested an old idea with a new significance: let the rich beware of tempting the gods too far, else his house will be uprooted for ever. The moral arose from the social conditions of the time, which saw the rise and fall of many a tyrant and aristocrat.

In Sophokles' *Elektra*, the idea is incorporated into the lament. The chorus conclude their prophecy of ultimate vengeance with a dirge for the House of Pelops, emphasising the fatal chariot race, in which Pelops fell headlong (πρόρριζος) to his doom and brought unending troubles upon the future generations of his House (S. *El.* 504–15). Then comes the fictitious story of Orestes' fall from his chariot and his death, and the chorus break out into lamentation. Their prophecy seems to have come true, and Díke has done her work, though not as they expected:[46]

– Φεῦ φεῦ· τὸ πᾶν δὴ δεσπόταισι τοῖς πάλαι
πρόρριζον, ὡς ἔοικεν, ἔφθαρται γένος.   *Ibid.* 764–5

Alas, alas! The entire race of our master's ancient line
has fallen, as it seems, and is destroyed root and branch.

The next important link in the evolution of the theme comes from a long consolatory decree of A.D. 242, a prose inscription from Arkesina in Amorgos commemorating men killed in battle. The style is simple, the spelling indifferent, and the ideas expressed – the desertion of parents by their children, the sorrow left behind, the inescapable death fixed by fate, the crown of glory that will be theirs – are all traditional. Its value as evidence here lies in its closeness to popular tradition. The death of one Kronios is described in the following terms, directly associated with the workings of fate:

ὥσπερ | δένδρον εἵμερον, εὐθαλές, ὑπὸ πνεύματος ἐκρει|ζωθέν,
ἐπὶ τῆς γῆς ἔπεσεν, οὕτως καὶ ὁ Κ[ρ]όνιο[ς] | μοιριδίως ἔπεσεν ἐπὶ
τὴν πεπρωμένην αὐτῷ | εἱμαρμένην, πένθος ἄτλητον καταλιπὼν
| γονε[ῦ]σιν αὐτοῦ.   *BCH* (1891) 586.9

Just as a cultivated, thriving tree falls to the ground, uprooted
by the wind, so too Kronios fell doomed, according to his
destiny, leaving unending grief to his parents.

The simile recurs, in strikingly similar form, in Michael Psellos' lament
for Skleraina, written in verse in learned and rhetorical style (eleventh
century):

ὡς δένδρον ἀνθοῦν ἐκ νοητῶν κοιλάδων,
φεῦ, φεῦ, πρὸ ὥρας, ἐτρυγήθη ριζόθεν.   Cantarella 166.2.20–1

like a tree blossoming from the valleys of the mind,
alas, alas, she has been harvested, uprooted before her time.

Nor was it restricted to learned poetry. A Pontic mourner laments her
dead husband with the same image:[47]

Τὸ δένδρον ντ' ἐπεκκούμπιξε ἀπὸ κορφᾶς ἐτσάλωσεν καὶ
σύρριζα ἐρροῦξεν.   *ArP* (1946) 68.2, 5

The tree he leant upon rotted from its peak and
fell from its roots.

And a mother from Naxos cries out over the body of her dead daughter:

Γιὰ ἰδέστε τη, πῶς κείτεται, σὰ λεμονιὰ κομμένη!   Theros 750.6

Look at her, how she lies, like a felled lemon tree!

The relevance and vitality of this image among the Greek peasantry
is beautifully illustrated from an account recorded by Elli
Papadimitriou from the Civil War of 1945–9: seeing her husband
brought in dead, a woman cries out Πεύκο μου! (My pine tree!).[48]
Imagery is often most forceful when it is stark, spontaneous and
unadorned.

But popular imagination is irrepressible, and has also elaborated the
theme in countless ways. In a seventeenth-century manuscript written
in vernacular Greek, we find an interesting and early example of the
extended image of Charos as uprooter of trees and vintager of grapes:
Ὁ κόσμος δένδρον γάρ ἐστι, καὶ ἡμεῖς τὸ πωρικόν του, καὶ ὁ Χάρος εἶναι
τρυγητής, μαζώνει τὸν καρπόν του. (For the world is a tree, and we

are its fruit, and Charos is the vintager who gathers the fruit).[49]
The lines are almost indistinguishable from a modern couplet from
Epiros:

Γιατὶ ὁ κόσμος εἶν' δεντρί, καὶ μεῖς τ' ὀπωρικό του,
κι ὁ Χάρος, ποὺ εἶν' ὁ τρυγητής, μαʒώνει τὸν καρπόν του.

Aravantinos 254

For the world is a tree, and we are its fruit,
and Charos, who is the vintager, gathers its fruit.

The full significance of allusion to spring, harvest and trees in popular
tradition, then, is that the whole world is nothing but a garden, and the
people are flowers, fruit and trees for Charos to pluck and uproot. In
a Maniot lament, all the threads developed separately elsewhere are
brought together with a fine sense of detail. The allusion in the last line
is to the old men – the bare posts, which Charos makes his fence:

Ὁ Χάρος ἐβουλήθηκε νὰ φτιάση περιβόλι . . .
Βάνει τὶς νιὲς γιὰ λεμονιές, τοὺς νιοὺς γιὰ κυπαρίσσια,
βάνει καὶ τὰ μικρὰ παιδιὰ γαρούφαλα καὶ βιόλες,
ἔβαλε καὶ τοὺς γέροντες στὸν τοῖχο του τρογύρω.

Pasayanis 9.1, 3–5

Charos decided to make a garden . . .
he puts young girls as lemon trees, young men as cypresses,
and he puts small children as carnations and gillyflowers,
and he put old men all round on his fence.

The identification of the dead man with an uprooted tree was sufficiently
well established in Homeric tradition to be freely elaborated in similes.
Herodotos extended it to include the divine agency in a man's fate. In
tragedy, it became part of the actual lament. Meanwhile, as the prose
inscription from Amorgos shows, it had lived on in vigorous form in
popular tradition, and probably continued to do so until it gave rise
to a new interpretation in Byzantine vernacular poetry: no longer a
jealous god on behalf of Díke, threatening to uproot the wealthy, but
Charos, arbitrarily picking on the just and unjust alike. Nor has the
image degenerated into a perfunctory formula: the cry ξεριʒώθη! (he
has been uprooted!) over the dead man has its counterpart in the blessing
καλορίʒικο! (good rooting!) on the newly married couple when they
set up their new home together. Finally, ριʒικό and μοῖρα are now
synonymous, meaning *fate*. The ancient association of the two concepts
has been completed by their actual identification.

Water and thirst

One of the inscribed tablets of the fourth century B.C. contains the following detailed instructions for the journey of the dead man in the Underworld:

Εύρήσσεις δ' Ἀΐδαο δόμων ἐπ' ἀριστερὰ κρήνην,
πὰρ' δ' αὐτῆι λευκὴν ἑστηκυῖαν κυπάρισσον·
ταύτης τῆς κρήνης μηδὲ σχεδὸν ἐμπελάσειας.
εὑρήσεις δ' ἑτέραν τῆς Μνημοσύνης ἀπὸ λίμνης
ψυχρὸν ὕδωρ προρέον· φύλακες δ' ἐπίπροσθεν ἔασιν.
Εἰπεῖν . . .
"δίψηι δ' εἰμ[ὶ] αὐὴ καὶ ἀπόλλυμαι· ἀλλὰ δότ' αἶψα
ψυχρὸν ὕδωρ προρέον τῆς Μνημοσύνης ἀπὸ λίμνης."
καὐτοί σοι δώσουσι πιεῖν θείης ἀπ(ὸ κρή)νης.   Kern *OF* 32a

You will find to the left of Hades' halls a spring,
and standing by its side, a white cypress tree.
Do not go near this spring.
But you will find another spring by the Lake of Memory,
with cool water flowing from it. There are guardians in front.
Say . . .
'I am parched with thirst and I perish. Give me quickly
the cool water flowing from the Lake of Memory.'
And of their own accord they will give you to drink from the
holy spring.

W. K. C. Guthrie has drawn attention to the white cypress tree, not elsewhere known to be associated with the sacred spring or with the dead in antiquity, and possibly to be explained as an assimilation with the white poplar.[50] Whatever its origins, the association of spring and cypress tree in the Underworld is still known to this day, as in the following lament from Mani:

Ὁ Χάρος στὸ περιβόλι του ἔχει ἕνα κυπαρίσσι,
στὴ ρίζα τοῦ κυπαρισσιοῦ εἶναι μιὰ κρύα βρύση.

Pasayanis 103.1–2

Charos in his garden has a cypress tree,
at the roots of the cypress there is a cool spring.

It is not an isolated reference. Allusion to the dead man as a tree whose foliage shaded his house and family may be further extended to include a reference to the cool spring at its root.[51]

In the ancient tablets, the sacred spring was important to the Underworld traveller to quench his thirst as well as to guide him. Similarly, the cool spring to refresh the thirsty traveller was a traditional image of praise addressed to a good man.[52] By an extension of the same image, the dead man is praised in the modern laments as a cooling spring during his lifetime, like the immortal water itself (Theros 686). In a lament from the Peloponnese, the dead man says 'I am running water, who goes and does not return' (Tarsouli 211.5), and a Maniot mourner complains that her spring has run dry, leaving her parched and unprotected (Pasayanis 58.1). The association of thirst with the dead is still so close that οἱ διψασμένοι (the thirsty ones) is synonymous with οἱ πεθαμένοι (the dead) (Aravantinos 255).

The ancient tablet refers to two springs, one of Lethe and one of Mnemosyne. Today, 'the pain-killing draught of Lethe' has evolved, by a process traceable through Byzantine tradition, into 'the water of forgetfulness', connected with the familiar 'plant of forgetfulness' of the love songs.[53] As for Mnemosyne, tradition is more confused. But the idea found in one of the Alexandrian epigrams and in Bion's *Epitáphios*, that the tears of the living can flow down to Hades to greet the dead is elaborated in some of the Byzantine vernacular laments in the form of tears so boundless that they make a river or lake to reach the dead.[54] In the modern laments, it is sometimes expressed as the mourner's duty to weep sufficient tears to make a lake or spring to quench the thirst of the dead:

Τί στέκεστε, ὀρφανὰ παιδιά, σὰν ξένοι, σὰ διαβάτες...
καὶ δὲν τρέχουν τὰ μάτια σας σὰ σιγαλὸ ποτάμι,
τὰ δάκρυα λίμνη νὰ γενοῦν, νὰ βγῆ μιὰ κρύα βρύση,
γιὰ νὰ νιφτοῦν οἱ ἄνιφτοι, νὰ πιοῦν οἱ διψασμένοι;

Aravantinos 255

Why do you stand there, orphaned children, like strangers,
 like passers-by?...
Why do your eyes not run like a quiet river,
so that your tears become a lake and make a cool spring,
for the unwashed to be washed, for the thirsty ones to drink?

It is this river, lake or spring which makes possible the contact between living and dead, and hence the function of ancient Mnemosyne has been preserved in a new form. In a fine lament from Epiros this theme is developed, not for its religious or ritual connotations, but for complex allusion, designed to express by means of poetic hyperbole the over-whelming grief of a mother for her dead child, and hence implicitly, the ritual importance of tears and lamentation:[55]

Τί νὰ σοῦ στείλω, μάτια μου, αὐτοῦ στὸν κάτω κόσμο;
Νὰ στείλω μῆλο – σήπεται, κυδώνι – μαραγκιάзει,
σταφύλι – ξερογίзεται, τριαντάφυλλο – μαδιέται.
Στέλνω κι ἐγὼ τὰ δάκρυα μου, δεμένα στὸ μαντήλι.
Τὰ δάκρυα ἤτανε καφτερά, καὶ κάηκε τὸ μαντήλι,
καὶ τὸ ποτάμι τὰ 'ριξε σὲ χήρας περιβόλι,
ὅπου τὰ δέντρα δὲν ἀνθοῦν, τὰ μῆλα δὲ μυρίзουν,
τὰ κόκκινα τριαντάφυλλα ροδόσταμα δὲ χύνουν.
Καὶ βγῆκε ἡ περβολάρισσα καὶ τὰ μυριοχουγιάзει:
– Ποιὸ εἶναι τὸ κακορίзικο, πού 'ρθε στὸ περιβόλι;
– Κυρά μου περβολάρισσα, μὴ μὲ μυριοχουγιάзης.
Ἄχ, νά 'ξερες ἡ μάνα μου, πῶς καίγεται γιὰ μένα!   Giankas 911

What shall I send you, my dear one, there in the Underworld?
If I send an apple, it will rot, if a quince it will shrivel,
if grapes they will fall away, if a rose it will droop.
So let me send my tears, bound in my handkerchief.
But the tears were burning, and the handkerchief was scorched,
so the river washed them up in the garden of a widow,
where the trees have no blossom and the apples no fragrance,
where the red roses give no rose-water.
And the woman gardener comes out and jeers at the tears.
– What is this ill-fated thing which has entered my garden?
– My lady gardener, do not jeer at me so.
Ah if only you knew how my mother burns with grief for me!

The imagery of the cypress tree, the spring and the thirsty dead are therefore interrelated, rooted in eschatological beliefs of great antiquity. Besides the survival of poetic images, however, there has also been a continuation and evolution of its religious significance. In the lament from Epiros for Zafeiris, discussed at the end of chapter 4, the out-stretched spirit of nature is mourned as a cypress tree, its roots cut, its branches withered. The same comparison is elaborated at a more conscious level and in Christian form in an early and popular Cypriot version of the Virgin's lament, where Christ is the sacred tree, whose branches, the Twelve Apostles, spread their shade over the whole world, and the cool spring at its roots is the Virgin herself.[56]

This analysis, although far from exhausting all the images and ideas, illustrates the importance of the allusive method throughout Greek tradition. The continuity, both in form and content, rests not so much in the static conservation of ancient poetic forms as in the constant rehandling of traditional beliefs and practices. The means of transmission and evolution was complex, dependent sometimes on the assimilation of eastern elements through Christian tradition and sometimes on incorporation into learned writing, especially rhetoric and erotic literature. But there is a sufficient number of specific images, found only in the modern laments outside ancient Greek, to suggest an independent transmission through popular tradition. Here, the evidence of the funerary inscriptions of late antiquity would seem to suggest a link. Finally, while the importance of the allusive method in the modern laments may be explained as a universal feature of folk poetry, the richness, complexity, and above all the interrelation of the different themes can be appreciated more fully and precisely when related to their long evolution.

Notes

Modern works are abbreviated according to the initials of their titles. For abbreviations of ancient authors and works, see Liddell–Scott–Jones *Greek Lexicon*, xvi–xxxviii (9th edition).

Chapter 1

1 *Il.*23.9. See also Lattimore *TGLE* 221.
2 A. *Ch.*429–33. Cf. *ibid.* 8, *Ag.*1541–6, *Th.*1002–3, 1058–9, 1066–71, *Pers.*674, S. *Ant.*26–9, 203, 876, *Aj.*924, *Ph.*360, E. *IT* 173–4.
3 See also S. *EL.*1126–70, *Ant.*883–4, E. *Alk.*526, *Hek.*678–9, A. *Pers.*1077.
4 Pl. *Phd.*60a.
5 *Ibid.* 118a. ψυχορραγεῖ: E. *Alk.*20, 143.
6 Pl. *Phd.*108a–b.
7 E. *Alk.*1 Sch.: ἡ διὰ στόματος καὶ δημώδης ἱστορία.
8 *Ibid.* 1139–42.
9 Pl. *Phd.*107d. For a Christianised form of this unusual ancient tradition, surviving in Byzantine and modern Greek, see p. 25, and Politis *Laog* (1909) 190.
10 Dem. 43.62: τὸν ἀποθανόντα προτίθεσθαι ἔνδον. This may mean *within the household*, i.e. in the courtyard or before the porch, rather than in the house, see Boardman *JRS* (1955) 51–66. The evidence of the Dipylon vases (eighth century) has been analysed by Reiner *RTG* 37–8.
11 Closing of the eyes and mouth: *Od.*11.426, 24.296, *Il.*453, Pl. *Phd.*118a. Preparation of the body: *Il.*18.343–55, 19.212, S. *EL.*1138–42. Type of garments: *Il.*24.580, *LGS* 93A p. 260. Wedding attire: Peek 1238.3.
12 *LGS* 93A p. 260, 74C p. 217. For the position of the dead, see *Il.*19.212, Hsch. s.v. πρόθυρον and δι᾽ ἐκ θυρῶν. It was believed that this facilitated the departure of evil spirits, see Ti.Lokr. 102a.
13 Strewing of herbs: Arist. *HA* 4.8.534b.22, Plin. 10.195 (origanon); Plu. 2.676d, *Tim.*26, Ar. *Ec.*1030 (celery). Use of evergreens: Ar. *Ec.*1031 (vine); Plu. *Lyk.*27 (olive); and Boardman *JRS* Pl. 4 (laurel). Garlands: Ar. *Lys.*602, Bion 1.75–8, Artem. 1.77, Plu. *Tim.*26.
14 Ar. *Ec.*1033, E. *Alk.*99–100.
15 Thphr. *Char.*16, Serv. on *Aen.*3.680.
16 Kurtz and Boardman 104.

17 Louvre 905, Brussels Inv.A 3369 (Boardman *JRS* Pl. 28, 33).

18 Louvre 905, *CVA* 80.1–2, 81.1–2, 82.1, 84.1–2.

19 Women: Athens 450, *CVA* 80. Men: *CVA* 80, Kerameikos Inv. 677, Louvre 905 (Boardman *JRS* Pl. 19, 28).

20 Zschietzschmann *AM* (1928) 17–36, B 8–18.

21 Athens 12960, 2410–17, 450, *CVA* 80.3.

22 *CVA* 80.1–3, 81.1–2, 84.1.

23 Louvre 575 (Zschietzschmann B 9.17).

24 Vermeule *JHS* (1965) 123–48 and Iakovidis *AJA* (1966) 43–50 discuss the evidence of a group of painted *lárnakes* recently excavated from Tanagra in Boiotia. The problem of the origin of the gesture is considered by Zschietzschmann ch. 1 and by Hausmann *GW* 22 ff., who considers its possible relation to the ecstasy gesture of the Minoan goddess (see his Pl. 6). S. Alexiou, however, stresses that the lamentation gesture and the ecstasy gesture were quite distinct, *KCh* (1958) 248–9.

25 *Il.*24.724, 18.317.

26 A. *Ch.*8–9.

27 Literary examples include A. *Ch.*423–8, 22–31, *Pers.*1054–65, S. *El.*89–91, E. *Supp.*71, 826–7, 977–9, 1160, *Alk.*86–92, 98–104, *Ph.*1485–92, *Andr.*825–35, *Il.*10.78, 406, 24.711, Sa. 140a L–P, Pl. *Phd.*89b.

28 For a discussion of the use of music at funerals, see Reiner *RTG* 67 and Hausmann *GW* 14. A dance associated with Hades and with funerals is referred to in E. *Supp.*74–5 and *HF* 1025–7.

29 *Il.*24.784–7. The body of Achilles was not burnt until the eighteenth day, *Od.*24.63–5.

30 Dem. 43.62: ἐκφέρειν δὲ τὸν ἀποθανόντα τῇ ὑστεραίᾳ ᾗ ἂν προθῶνται, πρὶν ἥλιον ἐξέχειν. If the *ekphorá* took place early in the morning on the day after the *próthesis*, then it would have been on the third day after death, since the *próthesis* normally lasted for one whole day. The sources are not always explicit on this point, and it would be wise to infer that the duration of the *próthesis* varied at different times and in different parts of the Greek world. In Athens, and more generally in later antiquity, the evidence indicates that the *ekphorá* and burial were normally held on the morning of the third day: Thuc. 2.34, Sch. Ar. *Lys.*612, Pl. *Lg.*959a, Klearch. ap. Procl. *in R.*2.114 Kroll, Plut. *Num.*22, Philostr. *VA* 3.88, Antipho *Chor.*34. See Rohde *Psyche* ch. V n. 50, 51.

31 Athens 806 (large sepulchral crater showing procession of chariots and mourners, c. 750 B.C.), 803 (large sepulchral amphora of same period, showing the dead man on a horse-drawn, two-tiered chariot, followed by mourners), 10862 (geometric amphora showing hoplite procession, c. 750–700 B.C.).

32 Berlin 93 (Zschietzschmann B 2), cf. Kurtz and Boardman Pl. 34–5. The lamentation gesture also figures frequently on scenes depicting the funeral cortège from paintings of the Mycenean period.

33 ὀτοτύζειν *LGS* 74C, φθέγγεσθαι Pl. *Lg.* 959e, 960a.

34 Sokolowski *EFA* (1955) no. 16, 5–6.

35 Kurtz and Boardman Pl. 36, cf. Pl. 37–8.

36 *LGS* 74C p. 218.

37 Rites held on the thirtieth day after death were known as τριηκόστια, *LGS* 93A, and as τριακάδες, Harpokration and Photios s.v.: τοῖς τετελευτηκόσιν ἤγετο ἡ τριακοστὴ ἡμέρα διὰ θανάτου καὶ ἐλέγετο τριακάς. For the annual rites, see Pl. *Lg.*717d–e, *LGS* 73C, Is. 1.10, 2.46, 6.51, 65, 7.30, 32, 9.7, 36. Further references are

given by Wyse *SI* 269 n. Other annual festivals for the dead include the second day of the Athenian festival of Anthesteria, known as *Choaí*, when it was believed that the souls of the dead rose to haunt the living, Photios s.v. μιαρὰ ἡμέρα, cf. E. *IT* 958–60, Ath. 7.2, 10.49; and also the *nekýsia*, Cic. *Leg*.2.22, 23, 35, Hsch. s.v. ὡραῖα· νεκύσια. The *nekýsia* is frequently associated with the *genésia*, Hsch. s.v. *genésia*, Ammon. *Diff*. s.v. γενέθλια· γενέθλια καὶ γενέσια διαφέρει, Poll. *Onom*.3.102, Hdt. 4.26, Antiatticista p. 86. 20. Jakoby rightly stresses that the *genésia*, which was held in Athens on the fifth day of Boedromion, has nothing to do with the birthday of the dead, *CQ* (1944) 64–75.

38 *Tríta*: Ar. *Lys*.611–13, Is. 2.36. *Énata*: Is. 2.36, 8.39, Aeschin. 3.225. Rohde's view that they were celebrated on the third and ninth days after burial, which has been widely accepted, is based on two arguments: first, that it is 'against all evidence' to suppose that the *tríta* coincided with the *ekphorá* (no evidence is cited); and second, that the Roman *novemdiale*, which was 'clearly modelled on Greek custom', definitely took place on the ninth day after burial, Porph. on Hor. *Epod*.17.48: nona die quam sepultus est, *Psyche* ch. v n. 83. The fullest discussion of the problem is by Freistedt *AT* 90–126, who demonstrates convincingly that both *tríta* and *énata* were more likely to have been reckoned from the day of death, basing his argument on a detailed analysis of the sources within their context, and making use of some inscriptional evidence. More recently Kurtz and Boardman have put forward the view that the *tríta* were reckoned from death and not from burial – rather surprisingly, without reference to Freistedt's study – but their arguments are not entirely convincing, since none of the sources cited in their notes are as explicit as they suggest (145–6, 360n.): most mention offerings at the grave without reference to third-day rites, and only in Ar. *Lys*.611–13 are *tríta* and burial mentioned together. Further, it is strange that the authors should so categorically affirm the dating of *tríta* from the day of death, and yet adhere, without comment, to the traditional dating of *énata* from the day of burial (147): since *tríta* and *énata* are twice mentioned together (Is. 2.36–7), they can hardly have been reckoned from different days, see also Freistedt 119–26. Complete certainty is perhaps precluded by the nature of the evidence, nor should we forget that ancient practice may have varied: the legislation of the Labyadai from Delphi specifically forbids lamentation 'on the next day' (after burial) 'and on the tenth day and after one year': μηδὲ τᾶι hυστεραίαι, μηδ' ἐν ταῖς δεκάταις, μηδ' ἐν τοῖς ἐνιαυτοῖς, μήτ' οἰμώζεν μήτ' ὀτοτύζεν (see Freistedt 124–6 for the possible interpretations of this passage). Some further points may be made in support of Freistedt's view of *tríta* and *énata*: first, nothing conclusive can be argued from the Roman *novemdiale*, since it differed from what is known of the Greek *énata*, and cannot be assumed to be derived from it, *RE* s.v.; second, the thirtieth-day rites are explicitly said to have been reckoned from the day of death (see n. 37 above), and it is likely that the *tríta* and *énata* were similarly reckoned; third, both rites have survived in Byzantine and modern Greek tradition, with remarkably little change in the terminology, and there can be no doubt that they are reckoned from the day of death, not burial, see ch. 2 n. 39 (p. 214) and ch. 3 n. 40 (p. 217).

39 See Kurtz and Boardman 100–2, 203–13.

40 Lock of hair: A. *Ch*.6–7, S. *El*.51–3, 448–58. Libation: A. *Ch*.129–31, 149–51, 164, 166, 486–8, E. *IT* 158–69, Edmonds *FAC* 1.708, Peek 428, 1157, 1422, 1970, *CIL* 8.27331a, *LGS* 93A.

41 Honey-cake: *Il*.23.170, *Od*.11.27, E. *Or*.115, A. *Pers*.612, Ar. *Lys*.601. Fish: Ath. 344c. *Kóllyba*: Thuc. 3.58.4, Ar. *Pl*.678 Sch., Hsch. s.v., cf. *CVA* 38, 43. The *kóllyba* were sometimes offered in a special three-compartment vessel called a *kérnos*, with a lighted candle in the centre, Nilsson *GPR* 28 and Xanthoudidis *ABSA* (1905–6) 9–23.

42 Kb. 461, Paus. 50.43.3. For general references to animal sacrifice, see *LGS* 93A p. 260: προσφαγίωι χρέσθαι κατὰ τὰ πάτρια, Thuc. 5.11 and Plu. *Sol*.9. Sheep are mentioned in E. *El*.92, lambs and kids in Plu. *Cat.Ma*.15. The archaeological evidence is summarised by Kurtz and Boardman 215–16.

43 Paus. 10.4. 7, Aristid. 21, Pi. *O* 1.90 Sch., cf. Nilsson *GGR* Tab. 11, 3–4.

44 A. *Ch*.483: δαῖτες ἔννομοι, cf. Kb. 646b. Ἐναγισμοί are defined in the Lexica as ὁλοκαυτώματα. Costly banquets burnt to the dead became more frequent in later antiquity, and are satirised by Lucian, *Luct*.19, *Charid*.22.

45 *Aulós* and lyre: *CVA* 43, cf. Reiner *RTG* 67. Ribbons and garlands: *CVA* 34, 35, 38, 41, 42, 43, 82. Robes: Thuc. 3.58.4, *CVA* 98.1. Torches and lamps: *SEG* 3.774.14, cf. Athens 17310, 1927, 1946, 1815, 12794.

46 Athens 1982, 1825, 12959.

47 *CVA* 86, 43, 96.8, Boardman *JRS* Pl. 7.

48 *CVA* 43, 46.

49 Boardman *JRS* Pl. 7, *CVA* 97, 43. In Athens 1880 the mourner appears to be quite naked, but this may be due to the poor preservation of the painting. Many white-figure *lékythoi* also show two figures, one seated by the stele (apparently receiving offerings and in earnest conversation, sometimes caressing a child which is held out to him, sometimes playing the *aulós* or lyre), and the other standing beside the stele, *CVA* 35, 43, 48, 96, 98. The traditional interpretation of this scene as a depiction of the dead man in conversation with the living is disputed by Kurtz and Boardman 104–5, but they do not offer any alternative explanation of the two figures.

50 A. *Ch*.37–46. See Harrison *PGSR* 69, 74.

51 Cf. Kb. 606.4, and in tragedy E. *fr*.757 Nauck: εἰς γῆν φέροντες γῆν, *Supp*.531–6, *Hel*.906–8, A. *Th*.477–9.

52 This is how the Chorus of Elders succeeded in raising Dareios' ghost, A. *Pers*.623–32, 639–42. See also *Ag*.1538–40, *Ch*.123–8, 398–9, 489–90, E. *IT* 160–1, 170, *Ph*.682–8, *Tr*.1301–9, Kb. 569.5.

53 Cf. *AP* 7.476.8–10 (Meleager): ἀλλά σε γουνοῦμαι, Γᾶ παντρόφε, τὰν πανόδυρτον | ἠρέμα σοῖς κόλποις, μᾶτερ, ἐναγκάλισαι.

54 At Gambreion in Aiolis the law prescribes that mourning should not exceed three months for men and four for women, Sokolowski no. 16.11–13: τῶι δὲ τετάρτωι λύειν τὰ πένθη τοὺς ἄνδρας, τὰς δὲ γυναῖκας τῶι πέμπτωι. Kurtz and Boardman interpret as four months for men and five for women (*GBC* 201); but the Greek implies an exclusive means of reckoning. In Sparta, Lykourgos is said to have restricted the period of mourning to eleven days, Plu. *Lyk*.27; while in Athens it was limited to thirty days, and in Ioulis apparently to three, *LGS* 93A.

55 It was normally held at the house, immediately after burial, on the third day after death, *RE* 720 s.v. *perídeipnon*, cf. Photios s.v. *kathédra*. See Nehring *SSGIG*.

56 *Il*.18.339.

57 Hdt. 6.58, Tyrt. *ALG* 1.9.5, cf. Paus. 4.14.5.

58 Ath. 259e.

59 A. *Ch.*733, Pl. *Lg.*800e 1–3, cf. Sch.: Καρικὴ μούση· τῇ θρηνῳδεῖ· δοκοῦσι γὰρ οἱ Κᾶρες θρηνῳδοί τινες εἶναι καὶ ἀλλοτρίους νεκροὺς ἐπὶ μισθῷ θρηνεῖν, and Luc. *Luct.*20.

60 See *RLV* s.v. Klageweiber, *RLIGA* s.v. Bestattungsgebräuche, and Bartók and Kodály *CMPH* 5.81, 91, 109–12. For the use of hired mourners in Greece today, see ch. 3.

61 Nilsson *UT* 78.

62 Willetts *PCPS* 191 (1965) 50–61, *LCG* 18–19 where among other references are cited Antipho 6.12, Isokr. 10.43, Ar. *Th.*74, 210, Dem. 19.118, E. *Hek.*834, And. 1.50, Lys. 13.1, Is. 6.27, Dem. 30.12, Timai. 84. For the use of the term generically, see Pl. *Lg.*773b, and Willetts *JHS* (1972) 184–5; and as *mother's brothers*, *Leg.Gort.*4.24, 5.9, cf. Hdt. 4.115.

63 Willetts *LCG* 18–19.

64 *IC* 4.46B, 12: αἱ δ' ἰάττας ὁδῶ | διαπέροιεν οἱ καδ|[εσται]... 76B, 1–4: θανάτōι, αἴ κ' οἱ ἐπιβάλλ[οντες καθαίρ]εν μὲ λείōντι, διδάκσα|ι τὸν δικαστὰν καθαίρε[ν.... | ....νσι. Erinna uses *kedestés* for the bridegroom's father who lights the funeral pyre for the dead bride, *AP* 7.712 (Willetts *LCG* 19).

65 Among the Iroquois, members of the same *gens* are mourners at the funeral of a dead *gentilis*, but the address at the grave, the preparation of the grave and the burial of the body are performed by members of other *gentes*, Morgan *AS* 84. Among the Tlingit Indians, all duties of undertaker at funerals are performed by members of the opposite group or phratry; and among the Tsimshians of north-west Canada a burial is attended by members of the clan of the deceased's father (the opposite clan, since descent is reckoned in the female line), whose services are paid, Frazer *TE* 3.275, 316. More recent evidence collected from the Malankuravans of India shows that the nephew (a member of the opposite clan according to their system of relationship) is invariably involved in the funeral ceremony, Krishna Iyer *TTC* 1.89–90, 33–4, 125–6, 152–5, 185–7, 220–1 (Willetts *LCG* 19).

66 The possibility cannot be excluded of a similar connection between πένθος meaning *grief*, especially *mourning for the dead*, and πενθερός, which originally denoted *father-in-law* and was later extended to *parents-in-law*, *relations by marriage*. Homer uses πενθερός twice, once in the context of the obligation of a father-in-law to avenge his son-in-law's adultery, and once for Odysseus, whose bitter lamentation on hearing Demodokos' lay of the wooden horse leads Alkinoos to suppose that he must be the father-in-law or son-in-law of one of the Trojan heroes (*Il.*6.168–70, *Od.*8.581–3). The first non-literary occurrence of the word is in the Drakonian law code, as quoted by Demosthenes, for the father-in-law's obligation to take part in the legal prosecution in a trial for homicide, the implication being that he had previously taken some part in the execution of revenge, Dem. 43.57. Like κηδεστής, πενθερός seems to have been used in connection with the specific obligation both in death and marriage owed by the relations-in-law to the opposite group. It is true that Frisk traces the words to two distinct IE roots (*GEW* s.v.); but his derivation is only speculative, and before there has been a full investigation of both the historical and the linguistic evidence the possibility remains open that πενθερός was an adjectival form related to πένθος/πενθέω as κρατερός το κράτος/κρατέω.

67 See Reiner *RTG* 72–100, Smyth *GMP* introd. 120–4, Harvey *CQ* (1955) 168–9.

68 *Il.*6.499–500, 18.51, 316–17, 22.430, 476, 23.10, 24.665, 723, 761 *et pass.* For the distinction between *góos* and *thrénos*, see Nilsson *UT*76–7, n. 21, Reiner *RTG* 8–9.

69 *Po.*12.1452b, cf. Nilsson *UT* 85–7.

70 Jeremias *HAOG* 320: 'Es wehklagten die Gattinen, es respondierten die Freunde' (fragment from the verso of a Babylonian burial ceremonial of the Asurbanipal period). In an exhaustive study of the music of primitive peoples, Wallaschek distinguishes antiphony and the use of hired groups as belonging to early stages of development, suggesting their origin in the two divisions of the tribe, *PM* II, VI.

71 See Bruck *TSGR* 231, Rohde *Psyche* 166, 193 n. 64, Nilsson *HM* 217, 241, 247.

72 *Leg.*2.25.63.

73 Plu. *Sol.*12b.

74 *Ibid.* 21.

75 Dem. 43.62.

76 *LGS* 93A, and pp. 261–2.

77 See Thomson *SAGS* 1.229 n. 146, who cites the following references: A. *Ch.*98 Sch., Ar. *Pl.*596 Sch., Poll. 5.163, Harpokr. s.v. ὀξυθύμια, Plu. *Mor.*708–9, Ath. 325a, Thphr. *Char.*16.7.

78 The law specifies thorough washing in fresh water or sea water, *LGS* 93A p. 261.

79 *LGS* 74C.

80 ἐν ταῖς στροφαῖς: the meaning is disputed, and has been interpreted variously as *turnings in the song* (a reference to the antiphonal performance of the lament), *BCH* (1895) 5–69, *doorways* and *turnings in the street*, i.e. 'at street corners', *LGS* 73C *ad loc.*, and *RE* s.v. *Labyadai*. Although there is no exact parallel to this use of στροφαί the latter would appear to be the most natural interpretation of the Greek; see ch. 3 n. 32 (p. 217) for the survival of the custom and for more recent attempts to prohibit it.

81 Sokolowski no. 16.

82 *Ibid.* no. 83 = *LGS* 2 p. 204, *SIG* 3.1221, 1227, cf. Paus. 2.27.1.

83 Plu. *Lyk.*27.

84 D.S. 11.38.

85 *Leg.*2.25, 64–7.

86 Stob. *Florileg.*44.40.

87 Hdt. 6.58.

88 *RIJ* 1.12. This view was challenged by Jevons *CR* (1895) 247–50.

89 *Pol.*1319b.

90 Stob. *fr.*4.6d, Aristid. 1.127.

91 Nilsson *UT* 81.

92 Porph. *Abst.*4.22, see also Rohde p. 115.

93 Rohde p. 124, 146 n. 49–52 and Bruck *TSGR* 231 f.

94 Jakoby *CQ* (1944) 65–75, see especially 69–70.

95 Willetts *CCF* 311–12, cf. Solon *fr.*1.5, 1–4 D, Plu. *Sol.*12.

96 Thomson *SAGS* 1.125 draws attention to an inscription relating to the Mysteries of Demeter at Andania, which decrees that the clan chief Mnasistratos be appointed first hierophant under the new regime, surrendering the administration of the Mysteries to the state, *SIG* 736.3, 9. Onomakritos is said to have held an official post at the court of the Peisistratidai as editor and arranger of the sayings and writings of Musaios, Hdt. 7.6.

97 Hdt. 5.66–9.

98 *Ibid.* 5.67, see also Dieterich *DFG* 33 f. Similarly the Labyadai, whose restrictions on funeral rites have already been considered, were a religious phratry founded

in the fifth century, whose members (numbering between 101 and 182 persons) were admitted not by birth as in the old, aristocratic clans, but by special adoption rites from the community as a whole, see *BCH* 19 (1895) 5–69 and *RE* s.v. *Labyadai*.

99 Rohde pp. 133, 135, 137, 149 n. 79.

100 *TSGR* 183, see also Childe *Man* (1945) 16–18.

101 A detailed analysis of this aspect of Solon's legislation has been made by Asheri, *Hist* 12 (1963) 1–21.

102 *Ibid.*, see also Seebohm *SGTS* III.

103 Plu. *Sol.*21: καὶ τὰ χρήματα κτήματα τῶν ἐχόντων ἐποίησεν.

104 Is. 4.19, 8.32, Aeschin. 1.13. See Thomson *SAGS* 1.109–10 and Seebohm *SGTS* 47–8.

105 Willetts *LCG* 48 col. 10.40–8.

106 Evidence from outside Athens is too fragmentary to present a complete picture, but some important details point to similar trends elsewhere: first, in the laws from Katana the restrictions on funeral rites appear to have been introduced in close connection with laws on family and property, Stob. *Florileg.*44.40; second, it is implied that in Syracuse the restrictions had a popular and democratic character, D.S. 11.38.2–5; finally, Pittakos is known to have carried out anti-aristocratic reforms in Lesbos, Arist. *Pol.*1285a.35.

107 The prominence of women in funeral lamentation is attested from earliest times in archaeology, epigraphy and literature. In Homer the ritual *góos* is sung by women unless there are none present, or unless the lament is a spontaneous expression of grief or a promise of revenge (as in *Il.*22.10–23, 65–100, 314–42). As professional singers comparable to Phemios and Demodokos the θρήνων ἀοιδοί of *Il.*24 are also men. In tragedy most of the laments are sung by women, except where there is a male chorus; men's solo laments tend to remain distinct from the women's more ritual lamentation, frequently containing a vow or a resolve to avenge the death of the lamented person. See Reiner *RTG* 53–6.

108 The laws from Gambreion point to a close connection between restrictions on funeral rites and encouragement of the Thesmophoria. Harrison *PSGR* 143 suggests that the reason for the particularly heavy legislation against women there may be due not to their more conservative and lugubrious nature, but to the survival of matriarchal conditions.

109 421, cf. *Th.*181–202 for the undesirable effects of lamentation on the soldiers' morale. One may also note that both Antigone and Elektra appeal to the women of their cities in calling for justice for the dead, S. *Ant.*694–8, *El.*954, 1090; cf. 86–91, 103–9, 145–6, 231–7, 806–14, 854–7, 951–7, 975–85, E. *El.*135–49, 181–7 for Elektra's own determination to maintain her passionate lamentation.

110 Plu. *Sol.*12. For laws on homicide see Dem. 43.57, 23.24, 51–5, Arist. *Ath.*57.2–3, and MacDowell *AHL*.

111 Pl. *Lg.*959e, 800e, Luc. *Luct.*10 f.; even Epicurus observed tradition, Usener *Epic.*258.14, 20, Cic. *ND* 1.30.85, D.L. 10.18.

112 Weber *SSAG* 65–6 suggests that one important and possibly intentional result of Solon's legislation was that in Attica the *thrênos* was eventually superseded by the *epitáphios lógos*.

113 See Paus. 2.13.3, 3.15.3, 26.5, 8.4.9, 35.8.

Chapter 2

1 See Laurent *BZ* (1936) 300–15, and Brown *WLA* 54–6.
2 Io. Malalas, Migne 97.344, 324, see also Browning *GAM* 8.
3 Gregorovius *GSA* 1.35, Brown *WLA* 50–7, 72, Browning *GAM* 8.
4 *SEC* p. 892.33 (Spyridakis *EEBS* (1950) 89).
5 Cf. Migne 59.198, 60.726, 767 (Loukatos *ELA* (1940) 43, nos. 4, 1, 2, 5), and Pl. *Phd.*108a–b.
6 Loukatos 43 no. 3.
7 Migne 34.224–30 (Spyridakis 89).
8 *Comm. ad Hom. Il.*699.42 (Koukoules *BBP* 4.152).
9 Migne 46.985d, cf. *Thrak* (1929) 131 (Spyridakis 97, 99).
10 Cont.Theoph. 548.5 (Koukoules 154). See also Rush *DBCA* 105–7.
11 δανάκη, Koukoules 158.
12 *Paid.*2.7, 8, cf. Hklt. 98: αἱ ψυχαὶ ὀσμῶνται καθ' ᾅδην. For the washing of the corpse in milk and wine, see Rush *DBCA* 115.
13 The word σάβανον is derived from Latin *sabanum, savanum*, Du Cange 1313, Korais *At.*2.422–3, and it is found in Greek as early as Clement of Alexandria. For φᾶρος, see *Il.*23.352, *Od.*2.97, 19.138, 24.132 (Politis *LS* 3.326 n. 5 and 327 n. 1).
14 Loukatos 50 nos. 1–4.
15 Migne 46.992c.
16 Spyridakis 102–3, cf. Migne 60.725 (Loukatos 52).
17 Politis comments on the medieval character of this custom and its explanation, *LS* 3.333 and 2.268–83; but there can be no doubt that it is related to the practice of pouring out water (ὕδωρ ἐκχέν), which was forbidden in the legislation from Keos in antiquity, *LGS* 93A.
18 Migne 46.497a–537b.
19 *Ibid.* 46.878–92.
20 βλασφήμους λόγους, *ibid.* 61.791.
21 *Ibid.* 59.346, cf. 57.374: Σὺ δέ, ὥσπερ αὐξῆσαι τὸ ἔγκλημα σπεύδων, καὶ θρηνῳδοὺς ἡμῖν ἄγεις Ἑλληνίδας γυναῖκας, ἐξάπτων τὸ πάθος..., 63.44: Εἰ οὖν οὗτος (*sc.* ὁ θάνατος) συμβαίη, καί τινες τὰς θρηνούσας ταύτας μισθώσαιντο...πολὺν αὐτὸν χρόνον τῆς ἐκκλησίας ἀπείρξω ὡς εἰδωλολάτρην, and also 62.811, 60.726, 61.390, 59.467, 348, 52.576, 62.203 (Loukatos 62–3). It is probable that Chrysostom, writing in the fourth century, was using *Hellene* in the religious sense, i.e. Hellene as opposed to Christian; but in any case it did not have the generalised, pejorative sense of *pagan*, i.e. any non-Christian, which it acquired in the fifth century and afterwards. See Browning *GAM* 15.
22 Reference is made frequently to the wild dancing of mourning women, see Migne 63.811, 61.390, 52.576, 59.467.
23 *Ibid.* 63.44: ἡμεῖς δὲ οὐκ ἀνεχόμεθα ἔθη τοιαῦτα ὀλέθρια τῇ ἐκκλησίᾳ ἐπεισαγαγεῖν.
24 Greg.Nyss. *ibid.* 46.868a–b: ἣν ἐν ἡδονῇ τοῖς ἀνθρώποις τὸ δάκρυον, Bas. *ibid.* 31.224–5, Io.Chrys. *ibid.* 153.785.
25 Pl. *Lg.*947b–c: κορῶν δὲ χορὸν πεντεκαίδεκα καὶ ἀρρένων ἕτερον.
26 They were known as δεκανοί, κοπιαταί, ἀσκήτριαι, κανονικαί, ἀκόλουθοι. Justinian, legislating on their number and payment in the Church of Constantinople, mentions that Anastasios had limited their number to 1,100, *Nov.*43 (Spyridakis 135–6); see also Rush *GBCA* 203–8. Horses were sometimes used to convey the coffin from house to tomb, see Migne 49.52 (Loukatos 67–8 no. 5).

Notes to pages 30–32

27 Migne 63.811: Ποῦ πορεύεται ὁ πολὺς ὄχλος ἐκεῖνος; τί γέγονεν ἡ κραυγὴ καὶ ὁ θόρυβος;
...Τί δὲ καὶ ἐγένοντο αἱ βοαί; ποῦ τὰ στόματα τὰ πολλὰ ἐκεῖνα, τὰ κραυγάζοντα...θαρρεῖν
ὅτι οὐδεὶς ἀθάνατος, cf. *ibid.* 809, 807, 42; 62.203; 61.697, 702, 707, 48.1020
(Loukatos 70–1).

28 Migne 46.993c–d. Riots are said to have threatened to break up several imperial
and sacred funerals, *ibid.* 18.463, 46.868a–b, 153.516–18, Io. Kantakouzenos
*Hist.*2.17.

29 φῶς τὸ ἀληθινόν, Migne 60.725 (Loukatos 74), cf. *V.Thom.Alex.*, SEC 603
(Spyridakis 143). Rush points out that before the third century, Christian
fathers opposed the use of candles and torches because of their association with
pagan cults, *GBCA* 224–5.

30 Ath. 442a: λύχνων ὀσμὰς οὐ φιλοῦσι δαίμονες, cf. Anton. *V.Sym.Styl.* (Spyridakis
143–4).

31 The similarity was such that the author of the Christian tragedy *Christòs
Páschon* was able to give the actual words of Medea's farewell to her children
to Mary as she greeted her son for the last time, *CP* 1315, 1318 ~ E. *Med.*1070.
See chapter 4 n. 25 (p. 219) on the question of date and authorship of this
play.

32 Spyridakis 149, cf. Migne 3.556d.

33 Again in the *Christòs Páschon*, the myrrh-bearing women perform a long
invocation at the tomb, which by implication is essential to Christ's Resurrection,
2020–6. The Church's disapproval of the practice among the people is expressed
by Chrysostom, Migne 63.803–4: Ἐν τῷ τάφῳ πρὸς τὸν πλησίον ἕκαστος ὧδέ πη
φθέγγεται, – ῏Ω τῆς ταλαιπωρίας! ῏Ω τῆς οἰκτρᾶς ἡμῶν ζωῆς! ῎Αρα τί γινόμεθα;, 50.551:
οἱ ἅμα τε τοῖς τῶν τεθνηκότων τάφοις ἐφίστανται, καὶ ὥσπερ ἀντὶ τῆς θήκης, τοὺς ἐν τῇ θήκῃ
κειμένους ἐστῶτας ἰδόντες, οὕτως αὐτοὺς ἀπὸ τῶν προθύρων εὐθέως ἀνακαλοῦσι, cf. 48.606. For
some of the more literary funerary epigrams, see Cantarella 22, 35, 40, 121, 154, 175.

34 Migne 47.343, 48.1038, 61.235.

35 *Ibid.* 57.348, 55.512, 59.348, 60.598, 147, 148.

36 Politis *LS* 3.349–51, cf. Sym. *OS* Migne 155.670–96.

37 Migne 35.776: ἐρρέτωσαν...ὅσα διὰ χοῶν τε καὶ ἀπαργμάτων...ἀφοσιοῦνται νόμῳ πατ-
ρίῳ μᾶλλον ἢ λόγῳ δουλεύοντες, cf. 37.871: χοὰς τοῖς δαίμοσιν, ἃς προσφέρουσιν οἵ γε
δεισιδαίμονες, 36.377: ἀγόνων χοῶν καὶ ἀπαργμάτων ὡρίων, ὧν τοῖς νεκροῖς χαρίζονται
νόμον ποιησάμενοι τὴν συνήθειαν (Koukoules 212).

38 Planudes 105, cf. Politis *Paroim.*1.571 (Koukoules 211–12).

39 *Trita* and *énata*: Leont.Neapol., p. 55.2 ed. Gelzer: εἰς τὰ τρίτα τοῦ παιδός;
Pachym. 1.19, p. 55 Bonn; Nikeph.Gregor. 1.3, p. 65 Bonn; Io.Kantakouzen.
III.1, p. 14 Bonn: μετὰ δὲ τὴν ἐνάτην τῶν ἐπὶ τοῖς τετελευτηκόσι συνήθως γεγενημένων
ἱλασμῶν; *Apokálypsis Theotókou*, Vassiliev *Anecd.graec.-byzant.* p. 133: ταῖς
λειτουργίαις τὰ τρίτα καὶ τὰ ἐννέα καὶ τὰ λοιπά, *V.S.Theod.* 20, p. 12 Arsenij: τελέσασα
τὰ τοῦ ἀνδρὸς τρίτα καὶ ἔνατα. See also Du Cange, s.v. *eniaúsia*, *énnata* (387),
mnemósynon (940), *trita* (1612–13). These and other references are cited by
Politis, *LS* 3.348 n. 2. See also Freistedt *AT* 4–6, 78–89 for a discussion of
third- and ninth-day rites in the early Greek Christian communities. For legislation, sacred and secular, see *Apostolische Konstitutionen* VIII 42.1, pp. 552 ff.
ed. Funk, and Justin. *Nov.*133.3.1, p. 671 ed. Schoell.

40 On the origin of the fortieth-day rites, and their relation to the thirtieth-day
rites of Greek antiquity, see Freistedt *AT* 6–15, 161–71, 172–8. He argues that
the Hebrew origin of the custom, which the early Church fathers insist upon
(see Migne 1.1145 ff.), is questionable, and that in fact the custom was most

214

widespread not among the Jews but among the early Oriental Christian communities of Armenia, Syria, Egypt, Palestine and Greece. In the western Church, on the other hand, the most important commemoration rites were held on the third, seventh and thirtieth days (51). The earliest reference in Greek to fortieth-day rites is found in a pagan inscription, probably to Hermes, of uncertain date but before the fourth century A.D. (Wünsch *JKPh* 27 Suppl. (1902) 121). For the use of hymns, psalms and prayers in the Greek Church, see Migne 63.43, 50.634.

41 Rallis–Potlis 4.387–8: Εἰ τῷ ἱερεῖ ἔξεστιν περιστερὰς ἐν τοῖς τάφοις τῶν τεθνεώτων καὶ τοῖς μνημοσύνοις αὐτῶν σφαγιάζειν (Koukoules 211).

42 Migne 155.670–96.

43 *AS* Maii 5.413a (Spyridakis 162).

44 Migne 115.437c, 31.232c, 155.670–96, Greg.Theol. *ibid.* 35.928a–b.

45 Io.Chrys., Migne 47.409: Πολλοὺς δ᾽ ἔγωγε οἶδα, μετὰ τὴν τῶν φιλτάτων ἀποβολήν, τοὺς μὲν τὴν ἐν ἀγροῖς δίαιταν τῆς πόλεως ἐναλλαξαμένους καὶ τῶν ἐν ταύτῃ καλῶν, τοὺς δὲ παρὰ τὰ μνήματα τῶν ἀπελθόντων τὰς οἰκίας δειμαμένους καὶ τὸν βίον ἐκεῖ καταλύσαντας, cf. 50.551. Sometimes, images of the dead were made and lamented, together with surviving articles of their clothing, 57.403: Εἰ γὰρ καὶ νῦν εἰκόνας διαπλάττοντες ἄνθρωποι, ἐπειδὴ τὸ σῶμα κατασχεῖν οὐκ ἔχουσιν...προσηλωμένοι ταῖς σανίσιν ἐκεῖ, cf. 59.366: Τί δέ; τῶν πολλῶν τὰς εἰκόνας ὅταν ἴδωμεν ἀνακειμένας ἐν ταῖς οἰκίαις, οὐχὶ μᾶλλον θρηνοῦμεν; (Loukatos 102, 99).

46 Cf. Zoras 65.3, 5: Γῆν ἔσχηκα προμήτορα, γῆ μὲ καλύψει πάλιν. The idea is not exclusively Greek, see Ps. 146.4.

47 See *AB* 18.256, Migne 31.232 ff., 35.928a, 61.236, 791, 792, 59.347, 114.313a, 115.1156a–c.

48 C. Bondelmontius, *Descriptio Cretae* ed. Legrand *DIA* 116–17 (Morgan *CPSI* 146). This account may be compared with a description by Michael Apostolis in a letter written in 1467 of a funeral he witnessed near Skutari on the Albanian coast: Συνειλέχθησαν οἱ τοῦ νεκροῦ ἀγχισταὶ καὶ τουτονὶ περιστάντες τῆς θρηνῳδίας ἀπήρχοντο, τῶν μὲν ἀνδρῶν ἱσταμένων, καθημένων δὲ τῶν γυναίων· καὶ τῶν μὲν ἀρχομένων, τῶν δὲ διαδεχομένων, οἵῳ τῷ τρόπῳ Κρῆτες ἐχρῶντο περί τε γάμους ἡρώων καὶ πανηγύρεις θεῶν· ὅθεν καὶ ἐς ἡμᾶς τουτὶ τὸ πρᾶγμα διαμεμένηκε, τοιουτότροπα ἐς χόρους (*sic*) ᾀδόντων τῶν Κρητῶν τε καὶ τῶν Κρησσῶν, Noiret *LIMA* 80, cf. Schirò *ZBa* (1963–4) 145–60. Particularly noteworthy is the mention of antiphonal singing, which he compares with ancient and contemporary practice in Crete. The death of the young man occurred, apparently accidentally, during a sword contest held annually within the precincts of the Church of St Laonikos on Palm Sunday, in preparation for Holy Week. It is not clear why Apostolis should refer to these people by the name of Taulantioi, as the ancient Illyrian tribe of that name was of no historical significance after the third century B.C. As for the sword contest, the nearest modern equivalent which I have come across is the custom, still observed in northern Epiros, on 'Lazarus' Saturday' (the day before Palm Sunday), when the young boys masquerade through the village in strange costume, brandishing spears, sabres and bells, and threatening the villagers, Megas *EE* 142–3. Ancient parallels which might usefully be investigated include the warlike dances and contests associated with the rites celebrating the death and rebirth of the god, see Ath. 139d–f.

Chapter 3

1 Cited by Lekatsas *Psyche* 126, cf. Theros 783, Michaelidis-Nouaros 315, Passow 154.10–12, Politis *LS* 3.323.
2 *Il.*24.44–5, cf. Migne 60.726 (Loukatos 43.2–3), Politis 65B 1.
3 *Laog* (1934) 390, *ArP* (1964) 161.
4 *ArP* (1951) 181–2, *Laog* 389.
5 Politis 92, cf. Pl. *Ph.*118a.
6 *ArP* (1951) 182.
7 Peek 632.4: Ἄιδης⟨ο⟩ἶ σκοτίας ἀμφέβαλεν πτέρυγας (fourth century B.C.). The modern concept of Charos as winged probably derives in part from the fusion of Charos and the Archangel Michael, which goes back to vernacular poetry of the late Byzantine period, see Moravcsik *SBN* (1931) 45–61, Zoras *Parn* (1970) 420–38.
8 *Laog* (1934) 389.
9 See Vlastos *SS* 166 s.v. πεθαίνω and Vostantzoglou *Antilexikon* 503.
10 *Laog* (1934) 388, *ArP* (1964) 161.
11 *Ibid.* 390.
12 Schmidt *GMSF* 38 (Lawson *MGF* 108–14).
13 *ArP* (1951) 182, *Laog* (1934) 391, see also Politis *LS* 3.327, Lekatsas 348.
14 Politis cites evidence of the use of the garland at funerals of the young and newly married in Macedonia, Chios and Laconia, *LS* 3.327 n. 7, cf. Tournefort *VL* 1.99 for the dressing of a dead woman in bridal attire in Crete.
15 The complete text of this lament is published in *ET* (May 1963) 436.
16 Politis *LS* 3.328.
17 Pasayanis *prologue*, cf. Loukatos 64, who cites similar evidence for Laconia, Pylia and his native Kephallonia, where he recorded the following couplet: Τὸ ξόδι θέλει συντροφιά, θέλει γενιὰ μεγάλη, | νὰ τ' ἀρχινᾷ ἡ μιὰ μεριά, νὰ τὸ ἀφίν' ἡ ἄλλη *ibid.* 55.
18 Politis 197, Pasayanis 13, 63.
19 *Laog* (1911) 475.
20 Cited by Spanakis *KCh* (1955) 401 n. 58, in a detailed commentary on the stipulation in the Testament of Andreas Kornaros (1611) that no *moiroloítres* be permitted to enter the church or his house, or to lament at his graveside, as was customary among the *gentili et etnici* in Crete; cf. Tournefort *VL* 1.99, where payment seems to have been in the form of money. An edict from Zakynthos of 1622 legislates against lamentation and funeral rites, and more recently the Church has legislated against the use of hired mourners in Sinope and Alagonia, Loukatos 63–4.
21 Patriarcheas *NK* (1939–40) 1044.
22 See Kyriakidis *GL* 57–9, Lioudaki 413.2, *NK* (1939–40) 1040.
23 Pasayanis *prologue*, *Laog* (1911) 547, Lioudaki 407, Baud-Bovy 1.350.
24 A liturgical dance at the wake of a priest has been recorded from Crete within living memory, Lioudaki 409.
25 *ArP* (1951) 185–6, (1964) 164–5, Politis 220, *Laog* (1934) 396.
26 *ArP* (1951) 186, cf. Lioudaki 403, Politis *LS* 3.330, Loukatos 55.
27 *Laog* (1911) 473 n. 1.
28 Politis *LS* 3.333, 2.268–83.
29 *Laog* (1934) 399.
30 The women come last in Anaselitsa, Thrace (*Laog* (1934) 401), but are more prominent in Mani (*ibid.* (1911) 475).

31 Politis *LS* 3.335 n. 1, Loukatos 69.

32 *Laog* (1911) 475, *ArP* (1941) 112–13. Politis cites an edict of 1365 from Crete which forbids the custom of taking the procession round by the main streets, *LS* 3.334 n. 3, see also Jegerlehner *BZ* (1904) 467; but the same custom is described in Crete by Tournefort *VL* 1.107. In recent times, the following custom was recorded from Arachova: Μετὰ τὴν ἐκκλησία τὸν περνοῦν βόλτα κι ἀπ' τὴν ἀγορά *LA* 1153 Α39 (Loukatos 71).

33 *Laog* (1911) 475, Kanellakis 339.

34 Politis *LS* 3.336, 346, *Laog* (1934) 401–2.

35 Lioudaki 406. See chapter 1 p. 9.

36 Politis *LS* 3.337, *Laog* (1934) 401–2.

37 *Luct.*24. See Loukatos 90, Politis *LS* 3.342–4, 353, Akoglou *LK* 225.

38 *Laog* (1934) 404–5, Politis *LS* 341–2.

39 Cf. Pasayanis 115, Tarsouli 227.3–6.

40 See Politis *LS* 3.345, 346 n. 4, *Laog* (1934) 408–9.

41 See Dawkins *FL* (1942) 131–47, Politis *LS* 3.346–7, *Laog* (1934) 409. For the Roman *Rosalia* as one of the occasions prescribed for offerings at the graves of relatives and friends, see Toynbee *DBRW* 64 n. 253.

42 Καθ' ὃν χρόνον ἐν τῷ οἴκῳ παρασκευάζονται τὰ πρὸς μνήμην νεκρῶν κόλλυβα, ἡ τοῦτα ποιοῦσα θέτει χωριστὰ μέρη ὠνοματισμένα εἰς τὸν καθένα, προφέρουσα ἑνὸς ἑκάστου τὸ ὄνο-μα (Crete), Zografakis *LA* 895 (Loukatos 98).

43 Apollon. *Mir.*3, see Lawson *MGF* 487, 540.

44 Politis *LS* 3.355 n. 6, and for antiquity, see Hdt. 1.67–8, A. *Pers.*405.

45 See Passow 162.3–7, Petropoulos 238.45.

46 From a private collection of folk songs recorded before World War II by Despoina Mazaraki, kindly made available to me by Nikephoros Rotas. Cf. Petropoulos 42.3.

47 Wolf *Peasants* 88 cites a paper by Gearing 'Religious ritual in a Greek village' on how commonality is asserted at village funerals: even the dead man's enemies attend, and are welcomed by the household.

Chapter 4

1 Cf. *fr.*168 L–P: ὦ τὸν Ἄδωνιν. The Sapphic fragments are discussed by Atallah *ALAG* 93–7.

2 The earliest reference to the *Adónia* in comedy indicates that it was already established as a popular, if not highly respected, festival of the time, Kratin. *fr.*15, ed. Edmonds *FAC* 1.28: (*sc.* Gnesippos)...ὃν οὐκ ἂν ἠξίουν ἐγὼ | ἐμοὶ διδάσκειν οὐδ' ἂν εἰς 'Αδώνια. Other comic poets known to have written plays about Adonis or his festival include Plato *fr.*1–8 (Edmonds 1.491–2), Arar. *fr.* 1 (Edmonds 2.13), Antiph. *fr.*13–15 (Edmonds 2.167), Philippid. *fr.* 1–3 (Edmonds 3a.168). For references to Adonis which indicate the popular character of his festival, see Eub. *Astytoi fr.*14 (Edmonds 2.88) and Diph. *Zographos fr.*43, 38–41 (Edmonds 3a.116). Atallah suggests that the reason for the lack of earlier literary evidence from Athens may lie in the popular, non-official character of the festival, *ALAG* 104. Plutarch's account of the *Adónia* in fifth-century Athens, although of later date, agrees substantially with the evidence from comedy: 'Αδωνίων γὰρ εἰς τὰς ἡμέρας ἐκείνας καθηκόντων, εἴδωλά τε πολλαχοῦ νεκροῖς ἐκκομιζομένοις ὅμοια προὔκειντο ταῖς γυναιξί, καὶ ταφὰς ἐμιμοῦντο κοπτόμεναι καὶ θρήνους ᾖδον, *Alk.* 18.5.

3 Wilamowitz *Adonis* 10, Smyth *GMP* lxviii.

4 See Theok. 3.48 Sch., Jer. *in Eʒek.*8.14, Amm.Marc. 19.1.11, Eus. *PE* 3.11.9, Sall. *de diis et mundo* in *FPG* 3.32 ed. Mullach, *EM* s.v. For further discussion, see Frazer *AAO* 129–31, and Atallah *ALAG* 320–4.

5 See Theok. 15.113, Hsch. s.v. Further evidence is cited by Atallah *ALAG* 211–28, who disputes the view advanced by Frazer *AAO* 137 ff. and others that the custom originated in a fertility rite, arguing that the ancient sources explicitly emphasise the ephemeral quality of these seed plants (pp. 227–8).

6 Atallah *ALAG* 269.

7 Jerem.22.18. See Frazer *AAO* 7–8, Atallah *ALAG* 305–6.

8 For the Homeric song to Linos, see *Il.*18.570, and for Egyptian song to Maneros, see Hdt. 2.79. The custom of lamenting the first sheaves of corn to be reaped in the summer while invoking the name of Isis survived in Egypt until the first century B.C., D.S. 1.14.2. See Frazer *AAO* 237.

9 Pausanias says that Sappho confused the songs of Adonis and of Linos in her poetry, 9.29.8, cf. Sa. *fr.*140b L–P, Pi. *fr.*126 ed. Bowra. See Reiner *RTG* 110–13. A version of the Linos song is cited, with comments, in *Il.*18.570 Sch.(B) (Page *PMG* 880), cf. *ibid.* Sch.(T) 279 Maass, Eust. *Il.*1163.59.

10 For *ailinon* as a cry of grief, see E. *Or.*1395; and as a cry of joy or victory, see A. *Ag.*121, S. *Aj.*628, E. *HF* 348–9, *Hel.*172, cf. Ath. 619b–c: ἐν δὲ γάμοις ὑμέναιος· ἐν δὲ πένθεσιν ἰάλεμος· λίνος δὲ καὶ αἴλινος οὐ μόνον ἐν πένθεσιν, ἀλλὰ καὶ "ἐπ' εὐτυχεῖ μολπᾷ", κατὰ τὸν Εὐριπίδην. Like the song for Lityerses, it was also a farmer's song, Poll. 138: λίνος καὶ λιτυέρσης σκαπανέων ᾠδαὶ καὶ γεωργῶν. The Greek *ailinon* may be derived from the Phoenician *ai-lanu* (woe is us!), and the cry may be compared with others found in many parts of the world, e.g. Egyptian *lulululu*, Greek *eleleû*, Latin *ululare*, Basque *Lelo* (also personified), Vlachic *lele*, and Irish *olagón*.

11 *Il.*18.493, Hes. *Sc.*274, Sa. *fr.*111 L–P, Pi. *P.*3.17, *fr.*126 ed. Bowra, cf. Pi. *P.*3.313 Sch., ed. Boekh pp. 362–3.

12 See Daremberg–Saglio, s.v. *Hymenaios.* The connection between marriage and death in Greek tradition is discussed by Alexiou and Dronke *SM* (1971) 825–41. See also chapter 6, pp. 120–2.

13 For the song of Lityerses in relation to Mariandynos, see Hsch. s.v. Μαριανδυνὸς θρῆνος, Poll. 1.38. Mariandynos is described as the dying corn god in Photios and the Suda s.v., and the story of his death is told by Athenaios 619–20, cf. *FHG* 3.13, A.R. 2.780 Sch., A. *Pers.*937 Sch.(A).

14 Anon. *Paraphr.* 784–93 and Eust. *Comm. in Dionys.* 787 ff., both cited by Müller *GGM* 2.420, 355. George Pachymeres describes the condition of the Mariandynoi under Roman subjection as being Μαριανδυνοῦ θρηνητῆρος ἀξίως τἀκεῖ θρηνήσαντος *de Mich. Palaeolog.*, Migne 143.4.311. Possinus refers to the saying as 'adagium vetus', tracing its origins not to Aeschylus but to ancient customs, and confirming its survival in later tradition, *Obs.Pachym.*2, Migne 143.1111, 653. Eustathios quotes the saying in a slightly different form, adding that it was proverbial, and that the Carians, Phrygians and Mysians were no less famous for their lamentation. It is also listed as a proverb, with reference to Aeschylus and Eustathios, by Andreas Schottus in Leutsch *Paroemiogr.*, *Stromat.*686.

15 The verb is used in the context of the lament for a god in a wide variety of sources, see Bion 1.94, Diod.Sic. 1.14, Ath. 619.

16 See Hes. *fr.*305 ed. Merkelbach–West, and Konon *Narr.*19 in *FGH* 1.95 ff. There is a similar tradition about Olen of Lykia, Paus. 10.5.7.

17 Konon *Narr.*19 (Argos); Paus. 9.29.6, *Il.*18.570 Sch.(BT) ed. Dindorf (Thebes). Cf. Pi. *fr.*126 ed. Bowra.

18 Plu. *Apophth.Lac.*228e (Leukothea); Philostr. *Her.*20.22 (Achilles); E. *Med.*1379 Sch., Paus. 2.3.7, Philostr. *Her.*20.24 (ἑορτὴ πένθιμος for Medea's children); Zen. 5.8 in Leutsch *Paroemiogr.*1.117 (antiphonal lament in Megara and Corinth). In the latter, at least fifty people were involved, and the cult was an annual event, see Bekker *Anecd.Graeca* 1.281.30. Special honours for the Bakchiadai are mentioned in Pi. *N* 7.155 Sch. ed. Boeckh p. 485. See Reiner *RTG* 103–4, Nilsson *GF* 633.

19 Kern *OF* 227.209 = Prokl. *in R.*1.94 Kroll: ὥσπερ δὴ καὶ 'Ορφεὺς τοῖς Διονυσιακοῖς εἰδώλοις...καὶ...τοὺς θρήνους προσῆψεν ἀπὸ τῶν προηγουμένων ἅπαντα ταῦτα ἐκείνοις ἀναθείς, C.A. *Protr.*2.12: Δηὼ δὲ καὶ Κόρη δρᾶμα ἤδη ἐγενέσθην μυστικόν, καὶ τὸ πένθος αὐταῖν 'Ελευσὶς δᾳδουχεῖ, cf. *ibid.* 15; Eus. *PE* 15.1: ὡς εἰσέτι καὶ νῦν τῶν θεῶν γάμους καὶ παιδοποιίας, θρήνους τε καὶ μέθας. See Farnell *CGS* 3.173–9.

20 John 19.25–7, 20.11. Lamentation is mentioned in Luke 22.27–8, but without reference to Mary.

21 Khouri-Sarkis *OS* (1957) 203, cited by Grosdidier de Matons *RM* 4.144–5. The suggestion made by Solomos that Romanos was drawing on popular Passion Plays of his time is not supported by any evidence, *AB* 164.

22 Besides similarities in structure and theme, and the use of the same refrain, υἱέ μου καὶ Θεέ μου, there are some verbal echoes of Romanos: *MMB* 5.168 no. 4, lines 4, 6 and 8 ~ Romanos 19.2, 8 *proem* 2; 1, 8.

23 *MMB* 5.168 no. 4, 4–8: Τί ἔδυς ἐξ ὀφθαλμῶν μου | ὁ "Ηλιος τῆς δόξης; | Οἴμοι οὐ φέρω ὁρᾶν σε ἀδίκως ἐπὶ ξύλου, | τιτρώσκεις γὰρ τὴν καρδίαν μου | τῆς σῆς πλευρᾶς ἡ λόγχη, *MMB* 5.186 no. 16, 1–2, 9–10, 16–18: 'Αρχίφωτον ἀπαύγασμα | τῆς πατρικῆς σου δόξης,|...πῶς πέπονθας; ῥομφαία γὰρ δεινή με διακόπτει...

24 Θρῆνος τῆς ὑπεραγίας Θεοτόκου εἰς τὴν Σταύρωσιν τοῦ Δεσπότου Χριστοῦ (*Thrênos Theotókou*), Cod. Athous 4655 (Iberon 535) and 1309 (Laura 22), ed. Manousakas in *MM* (1956) 65–9, and reprinted by Zoras 60–2. For a discussion of the text, see Manousakas 60–4, Zoras 21. In the seventeenth century, Diakrousis composed a rhymed version of it, which passed into popular tradition in Crete, see Manousakas 63, Amarioti *EEKS* (1939) 131–5.

25 *GNPC* 11–74. Tuilier's argument, briefly summarised, is as follows: the grounds on which earlier critics rejected the attribution to Gregory are largely subjective; all manuscripts, some of which are certainly old, contain the attribution; passages in the play taken from Euripides are closer to the earlier manuscript tradition of Euripides (where this can be checked with the evidence of papyrus fragments) than to later Byzantine manuscript tradition; the similarity of lines 454–60 to Romanos 19.1, 4–8 is more readily explained if we accept the earlier date, since borrowings from homilies and other works of the Church fathers are characteristic of the early melodists; although no specific reference to the play is made by biographers of Gregory, theatrical works are mentioned; finally, the clearly diphysite standpoint of the play coincides with the general movement in Gregory's time, when classical models were also commonly Christianised. A similar view, less cogently argued, was advanced earlier by Solomos, *AB* 77–85. Grosdidier de Matons, in his recent edition of Romanos, adheres to the later dating of the play, *RM* 4.161. See Doering *TC*, Krumbacher *GBL* 746–8.

26 *CP* 454–60 ~ Romanos 19.1, 4–8. The superiority of Romanos' version cannot be used as a criterion for dating, as was attempted by Solomos *AB* 80–1 and by Cottas *TB* 226. The absurd claim made by Cottas that the *Christòs Páschon*

was the source of all later passion plays, Italian as well as Greek, has found few adherents, see *TB* 244–9.

27 *CP* 1548–52. See *Protevangelium Iacobi* 13–16 (Tischendorf 24–30), where Joseph is convinced of her chastity only by a miracle. In Mt. 1.18–19, one word from the angel allays his suspicions; but they recur in some of the later hymns, see Wellesz *BMH* 282.

28 *CP* 754–60, cf. Symeon Metaphrastes *S. Mariae Planctus*, Migne 114.213b, and *Thrênos Theotókou* 75–6, Zoras 61. Similar motifs occur elsewhere in homiletic tradition, see S. Germani Patriarchae *In dominici corporis sepulturam*, where the Virgin, lamenting Christ at the tomb, wishes she could have died with him (Migne 98.272a); and also Georgii Nicomediensis *In SS. Mariam assistentem cruci*, where, in an imagined dialogue with Christ at the Cross, she wishes she could relieve his pain by dying in his stead (Migne 100.1472b). For the suicide wish in the modern ballads, see *Laog* (1934) 252.120.

29 *CP* 266–346. For the curse formula, see 298–9 and Politis 128A 10–11.

30 See Tomadakis *BY* 2.76–9, who suggests that it was compiled over a long period by several hands. Trembelas refers to Theodore the Studite (ninth century) as a possible author, *MEE* s.v. *epitáphios thrênos*; but there seems little evidence to support this view. Similarities with other works include: *Epit.thr.*2.14 ~ *MMB* 5.180.11, 1; 2.5 ~ Sym.Metaphr. *Planctus* 216; 1.12 ~ *MMB* 5.186.16, 12–13 and Sym.Metaphr. *Planctus* 209a.

31 The pagan origins of this symbolism, and its incorporation into early Christian doctrine, are discussed in detail by Rahner *GMCM* 89–176.

32 The motif is used by Varnalis in his poem Ἡ Μάνα τοῦ Χριστοῦ from Τὸ Φῶς ποὺ Καίει: Καθὼς κλαίει σὰν τῆς παίρνουν τὸ τέκνο ἡ δαμάλα | ξεφωνίζω καὶ νόημα δὲν ἔχουν τὰ λόγια.

33 See Tischendorf *EA* 266–300. On the dates of the two recensions, see Tischendorf's prologue and Schneemelcher–Henneke *NT Apocrypha* 1.448.

34 Tischendorf 282–3 ~ *Epit.Thr.*1.8 and Sym.Metaphr. *Planctus* 209a; Tischendorf 285 ~ *Thrênos Theótokou* 83–90.

35 Jacopone da Todi *Laude* ed. Mone *LH* 2.147, 446. The difference in the treatment of the theme of the Virgin's grief is more remarkable in view of other parallels between Greek and Latin hymns cited by Mone, 150 ff. In western tradition, both Latin and vernacular, the Virgin's lament emerges in the second half of the twelfth century, when it was elaborated in the Passion Plays and as a separate lyrical piece, see Sticca *CM* (1966) 296–309, and also Dronke *PIMA* 28–31 on lyrical *planctus* with biblical themes before Abelard. Dr S. P. Brock has pointed out to me that there are striking parallels to the Virgin's lament in the Greek *Acta Pilati* in a long lament preserved in two manuscripts (Mingana syr. 87 and 127, *c*. 1450 and 1683), written in the combination of Arabic language and Syriac script known as Garshūni. In the introduction to his edition and translation, Mingana indicates that the real author of the document is Gamaliel, and that it constitutes a further link in the chain of *Acta Pilati*, being a translation or close imitation of a Coptic document, which has survived only in fragments, dealing with the history of Pontius Pilate, *WSt* 2.166–82. The Virgin's lament is introduced by a series of rhetorical questions, justifying her sorrow by reference to the lamentation of the Patriarchs: 'The weeping of Jacob, the head of the Patriarchs, has been renewed today, O my beloved; why then should not the Virgin Mary weep over her Son whom she conceived in virginity?' (*ibid.* 182–3).

36 *EEBS* (1953) 491–506, *ArP* (1954) 188–225, *MCh* (1948) 217, Sakellarios 2.84, 28. A bibliography, with other versions, is listed in *Laog* (1934) 253.

37 Sakellarios 2.84, 28 and 49, cf. Romanos 19.3–5 and *CP* 730–3. But the parallel between the ballad and the *Christòs Páschon*, close as it is, does not prove the direct dependence argued by Cottas, *TB* 246–8. On the antiquity of the Virgin's lament in Cyprus, and especially on the Cyprus Passion Play (MS *c.* 1260–70), see Mahr *CPPC*.

38 *Laog* (1934) 249–53.70–2, 86–7, 107–9; and for suicide wish, see 116–18, *ibid.* 256.95–6, *DIEE* (1892) 722γ *et passim.* For the two swoons in the apocryphal gospel, see Tischendorf 282. Swooning in association with lamentation appears to be a feature of medieval literature, not found in classical or biblical sources, see Gierden *AFA* 52.

39 Cf. Tischendorf 285, *Thrênos Theotókou* 89–90: τὸ στόμα τὸ γλυκύτατον ἵνα καταφιλήσω. For the gesture of a mother kissing her dead son, common in medieval literature, Gierden cites a possible biblical precedent in Gen. 50.1, where Joseph kisses his dead father, adding that the gesture was unknown in classical literature, *AFA* 54–5. But Aphrodite more than once kisses the dead Adonis in Bion's *Epitáphios*, 13–14, 41–5; and, if it be objected that their relationship was not one of kinship, a closer parallel probably existed in Euripides *Ba.*1329 ff. Unfortunately, there is a lacuna in the text of Agave's lament for Pentheus at this point, but if we accept the postulated restitution from *CP* 1311–13, 1315, 1256–7, 1466–72, 1122–3, she lamented and kissed each limb of Pentheus' body in turn by way of a last farewell. The general content of these lines is independently confirmed by Apsines in *Rhet.Gr.*9.590, ed. Walz, see *Ba.* ed. Dodds (1960) pp. 234, 245.

40 Cf. *Laog* (1934) 255.42–4. The bloodstained moon during the Crucifixion is mentioned in *Anaphora Pilati*, Tischendorf 417A: σελήνη δὲ τὸ φέγγος ὡς αἱματίζουσα διέλιπεν. In the ballads, the theme is adapted to the familiar formula of questions, with the effective addition of the silence of the birds, cf. Politis 92.42.

41 Megas *EE* 157. For the expression of this belief in the laments, see Theros 697.12, *Laog* (1934) 257.103–9, Politis 206.1.

42 *ArP* (1954) 195–6. Romaios cites a version from Chios which he claims to have preserved the 'original' form: Πάρε, Γιάννη, τὴ μάννα σου, καὶ μάννα μου, τὸν ὑγιό σου, Kanellakis 96.

43 *Ibid.* 194, where Romaios comments on *DIEE* (1892) 722γ. It is interesting to note that the same thought is expressed by the angels when they bring the news to Mary in the Arabic lament referred to above, n. 35: 'O Mary, what are you doing sitting, while your Son is standing before the Governor and is being judged and insulted by the High Priest of the Jews?... O dove of Hannah, what are you doing sitting, while your Son is being crucified in the place of the *Kranion*?' *WSt* 2.184.

44 The origins of 'Saint Kalé' have been analysed by Romaios, *ArP* (1954) 197 ff. See also Politis *Laog* (1909) 350, Lawson *MGF* 164.

45 Hsch. s.v. *Kallíste.* It is believed that on 1 September, male and female Καλοὶ τῶν Ὀριῶν (Good people of the mountains) come out and seek their sister Kalé to the four corners of the earth, *Laog* (1909) 347–9, cf. Politis *Parad.* 661.

46 The weeping of the ancient Nereids is mentioned in *AP* 9.151.5–8. Just as Demeter appealed to the sun for help in her search for Persephone (Hom. *Hm.*2.64–73), so too, in a modern lament, a mother asks: Ἥλιε μου καὶ τρισήλιε μου καὶ κοσμογυριστή μου,| ψὲς ἔχασα μιὰ λυγερή, μιὰ ἀκριβοθυγατέρα·| νὰ μὴ τὴν εἶδες πουθενά, νὰ μὴ τὴν ἀπάντησες; Politis 221.1–3.

47 In his sermon *De deitate filii et spiritus sancti*, Gregory of Nyssa includes a lyrical *planctus* for Isaac, although he is careful to point out that Abraham,

being a just man, did not actually speak these words, Migne 46.568d. As Mercati has demonstrated, Gregory's *planctus* is closely modelled on a similar one in a sermon of Ephraem, *In Abraham et Is.*, *ESO* 1.9–30. The tradition of this fictitious lament is continued by later Church fathers, see Mercati pp. 4 ff., and Grosdidier de Matons *RM* 1.132. Romanos, in his *kontákion On Abraham and Isaac* (no. 41), follows patristic tradition by introducing the lament with the words " πῶς οὐκ εἶπας;", but continues with another lament from Sarah, and a tense dialogue between Abraham and Sarah, which is no longer imagined, but real. It is possible, though by no means certain, that this *kontákion* was known to the author of the Cretan Θυσία τοῦ 'Αβραάμ, see Baud-Bovy *Byʐ.* (1938) 217–26.

48 The parallels have been collected by Lioudaki *EEKS* (1939) 412 ff., and are cited by Megas in his edition of the play, p. 118.

49 Megas *EE* 160–1 and plate 1.

50 When asked why villagers were so anxious on Good Friday, an old woman from Euboia is reported to have replied, 'Of course I'm anxious; for if Christ does not rise tomorrow, we shall have no corn this year', Lawson *MGF* 573. See also Martino *MPR* 343–4.

51 Kakouri *HC* (1956) 6–22, *PAA* (1952) 223, where she notes also the survival in Aigina of the custom of planting 'gardens of Adonis', known as *arakiá*.

52 Kakouri *HC* (1956) 9–10, 18–19.

53 On 14 September in Lemnos, housewives make new dough which is blest in church and taken round the streets in procession with the Cross; in Naxos, farmers place beside the sanctuary a bundle of barley, beans, peas etc., which are blest by the priest and sown with the crop for the following year; in Karpathos and Pylia, there are similar associations between reaping and the Feast of the Cross, Megas *EE* 236–9.

54 Kakouri *PAA* (1952) 224, Megas *EE* 189–90. Similarly, on 1 May in Kastania, a figure called *Fouskodéntri* is mourned, while in Mykonos, another figure called *Kratonéllos* is dressed with sea flowers and plants, and then lamented, Megas *EE* 190–1.

Chapter 5

1 E. *Tr.*582, cf. 98 ff., 600, 1317–32, A. *Ag.*321–9, 1167–72.

2 *ALG* 1.76.1, Plu. *Pel.*1.

3 A. *Pers.*956–77.

4 Cf. Peek 1880 for the same structure. Kallimachos' lament for Queen Arsinoe refers to dirges sung by the whole city: θρῆνοι πόλιν ὑμετέρ[αν κατέχοντι πᾶσαν·] οὐχ ὡς ἐπὶ δαμοτέρων δ' ὀλέθρῳ κέκοπται χθών...*fr.* ed. Pfeiffer 1 (Pap. Berol. 1.13417a. 70).

5 18.8 ed. Keil, cf. Philostr. 2.9.582.

6 Malalas, Migne 97.235, 243, 419a–421c, cf. 486, 491.

7 Similar rhetorical figures, and even identical phrases, occur in Niketas Choniates' rhetorical lament for the sack of Constantinople in 1204 and in Michael Doukas' lament for its fall in 1453; yet both claim to be based on eye-witness accounts, see Choniates *Hist.*763–7 (Bonn 1835) and Doukas *Hist.Byʐ.*11.305d–311a (Bonn 1834).

8 *Hist.*365.9–11.

9 *Ibid.* 763–7. The lament is preceded by an account of the pillage and massacre, and of the universal lamentation of the people, 757.18, 760.5–9.

10 Ed. Lambros 2.397–8, cf. 1.93–106. Similar phrases occur in Demetrios Kydones, *Oratio de non reddenda Callipoli* Migne 154.1013a–c.

11 Anagnostes, *de Thessalonicensi excidio* 481–528 (Bonn 1838). Two anonymous *thrênoi* in learned style for the fall of Thessaloniki are published by Lambros *NE* (1908) 372–91. Both belong to the fifteenth century, and, though independent, show common features. Another verse chronicle in *politikòs stíchos* but learned language is published by Sathas *MB* 1.245, see also *BZ* (1889) 421.

12 Lambros *NE* (1908) no. 1, 206.20, cf. Mich. Choniates ed. Lambros 2.398.19–20: Ποῦ νῦν τὰ σεμνά, τλημονεστάτη πόλις; | ὡς φροῦδα πάντα καὶ κατάλληλα μύθοις.

13 Lambros no. 2, 219.20 – 226.9 and no. 6, 249. Cf. Politis *Laog* (1909) 127–9, *LS* 1.14–27.

14 For a catalogue of all *thrênoi*, learned and popular, see Zoras *AK* 157–283. For texts, see Lambros *NE* (1908) 190–271, Zoras *BP* 177–221, *ED* (1950) 851–62, *SBN* (1935) 239.

15 See Zoras *SBN* (1935) 239, Kriaras *Anakálema* 12–20.

16 On the provenance and authorship of the *Álosis*, see Hadzidakis *BZ* (1894) 581–98, Knös *Ell* (1967) 311–37; and on the *Anakálema*, see Kriaras 1–19, Morgan *KCh* (1960) 394–404. Other articles, and a complete list of editions of the two poems, are cited by Beck *GBV* 164–6, who considers both the Cretan and the Cypriot origin of the *Anakálema* hard to prove.

17 Kriaras 19.

18 *Anakal.*96: τὴν Πόλην τὴν ἐξάκουστην, cf. *Al.*668 (Kriaras 17–18). Other parallels, equally close, include *Thrênos of the Four Patriarchates* 59, Politis 5.10, 6.8, Giankas 27.12, 29.9, 24, 38.17. *Anakal.*57–60: Ἥλιε μου, ἀνάτειλε παντοῦ, σ' ὅλον τὸν κόσμον φέγγε | ...κι εἰς τὴν Κωνσταντινόπολην...|...δὲν πρέπει πιὸ νὰ φέγγης, cf. *Al.*406, 118 (Kriaras 18). This invocation is extremely common in historical laments, see Politis 3, *Laog* (1957) 381.
*Anakal.*3: ἐχάσασιν τὸ σπίτιν τους..., cf. *Al.*134, 236, 644 (Kriaras 17). *Anakal.* 46: μὲ τὴν τρεμούραν τὴν πολλήν..., cf. *Al.*201 (Kriaras 17). *Anakal.*89: Εἴπω καὶ τίποτε μικρὸν ἀλληγορίας λόγον, cf. *Al.*5 (Kriaras 18). The formula is very common, especially in long poems. *Anakal.*47: καὶ θέση πόδαν ἄτακτο εἰς τὸν ἐμὸν αὐχένα, cf. *Al.*874.
But the phrase 'may Turks not trample upon you' is a proverbial expression. A closer parallel to *Al.*874, where the poet asks Venice to 'lay her foot' on the enemy's neck, might be argued to be found in E. *Tr.*1131–2, where the Trojan women beg Troy to lay her foot on the Achaians' backs! Finally, the only parallel between *Anakal.*90–1 and *Al.*35, 37 is in the use of the second person indefinite (Kriaras 17–18).

19 1019–25, 14–17, 441–9.

20 See Knös *HLNG* 159–65.

21 The language of the poem is predominantly, but not uniformly, archaising. For popular forms and words, see 215, 218, 278, 305–6. The use of rhyme is analysed by Krumbacher *SBAW* (1901) 329.

22 Ed. Krumbacher *SBAW* (1901) 329–61, reprinted by Zoras 204–7. Also in dialogue form, between Constantinople and Venice, is the Θρῆνος τῆς Κωνσταντινουπόλεως, ed. Papadopoulos-Kerameus *BZ* (1903) 267–72, cf. Zoras 200–3.

23 One historical lament in the vernacular which belongs to the beginning of the fifteenth century is the Θρῆνος περὶ Ταμυρλάγγου (*Thrênos for Timur Lenk*), ed. Wagner *Carm.*28–31. Spyridakis considers it probable that the modern folk songs about Tataris refer to the same event, *ELA* (1953–4) 41–53.

24 See *Anakálema* 5–21, 57–60, 75, 87–8, *Thrênos for Constantinople* 34, 39–44, 108–11, 118–21, 123–4, *Thrênos of the Four Patriarchates* 21, 47, 59, 65.

25 Διήγησις εἰς τὸν θρῆνον τοῦ αἰχμαλωτισμοῦ τῆς εὐλογημένης Κύπρου, a long poem of 906 rhymed verses of unknown authorship, but written by someone who witnessed the events himself. It is edited in *KyCh* (1925) 56–82.

26 'Ανάλωσις 'Αθήνας, ed. *BZ* (1903) 273–5, cf. Zoras 221–2; Μάλτας Πολιορκία by Cretan poet Antonios Achelis, ed. Pernot in Legrand, *CM* (1910); Λεηλασία τῆς Παροικίας τῆς Πάρου by anonymous Cretan poet, ed. Kriaras *Ath* (1938) 127; Θρῆνος εἰς τὴν 'Ελλάδος καταστροφήν by Corfiot poet Antonios Eparchos, in ancient Greek and elegiac couplets, and based in parts on Moschos' *Epitaph.Bion*, see Kournoutos *LT* 4.150–4; Πόλεμος τῆς Κρήτης by Athanasios Skleros, again in learned style and archaising language, ed. Sathas *EA* 2; Θρῆνος τῆς Κρήτης by Gerasimos Palladas, *EEKS* (1939) 348.

27 Georgillas, ed. Legrand *BGV* 1.203–25, cf. Zoras 223–35; Sklavos, ed. Wagner *Carm.*53–61. Cf. anonymous Ποιημάτιον περὶ τοῦ ἐν ἔτει 1508 Σεισμοῦ τῆς Κρήτης in hexameters and pseudo-Homeric Greek, ed. Lambros *NE* (1914) 441–8.

28 Both poems are inscribed Διήγησις διὰ στίχων τοῦ δεινοῦ πολέμου ἐν τῇ νήσῳ Κρήτῃ γενομένου; Diakrousis' work appeared in Venice in 1667, Bounialis' in 1681. See edition by Xirouchakis *KP*.

29 Diakrousis 108.11–111.4; Bounialis 216.10–27, 220.1–25.

30 Cf. Bounialis 570.3–24, Diakrousis 112.3–14.

31 *Introd.*7. The historian Kordatos argues in particular against the authenticity of the famous *Song of Saint Sophia* (Politis 2, Passow 196), suggesting that it was made up at the time of 1821 for propaganda purposes, *INL* 44–6. His reasons are as follows: the linguistic form belongs to the nineteenth century, not earlier, nor is the poem referred to in earlier sources; St Sophia is not a 'large monastery', and no Orthodox Christian, especially of the fifteenth century, would appeal to Franks to take away the sacred things, because of dogmatic differences between them; the Patriarch did not chant on the right, nor the Emperor on the left; the line 'it is the will of God that the City should become Turkish' derives from a prophecy of those monks who were most hostile to union, and it is therefore out of place in the context of an appeal to the Franks; finally, if this was the will of God, the Virgin should have known and had no reason to weep. Some of Kordatos' reasons are plausible; but on the whole I do not think they are conclusive, and certainly they do not invalidate all the songs of this type which were first published in a variety of sources, see Passow 194–8.

32 Politis 1 (note) points out that the capture of the city by the Russians was regarded by the people as a liberation from the Turkish yoke, and that the song refers to its fall in 1362 and to the previous invasions, one of which in 1205 is known to have taken place during Easter Week. This is hard to prove.

33 McPherson *JHS* (1889) 86–8. Her argument is that the explicit reference to Thessaloniki, together with the fact that the Patriarchate was vacant in 1453 but not in 1430, points to its original composition for Thessaloniki (where there is also a church of St Sophia), and to the later transference of these lines to a lament for Constantinople. The only objection to her argument is that in folk poetry, so far as I am aware, ἡ Πόλη always refers to Constantinople. Perhaps the song can be understood as a reference to both Thessaloniki and Constantinople.

34 *F* 170. Again, the authenticity of some of the songs he published has been questioned, especially where the source given is not the original singer, but the school teacher who claimed to have collected it from his village.

35 *Laog* (1957) 379–80, cf. two other songs said to refer to Trebizond, 378–9, 381.
In fact, they appear to lament the fall of Constantinople when news of the
catastrophe was brought to Trebizond, as is more explicit in another related
Pontic song published by Zoras, *ED* (1950) 851–62.

36 Giankas 19–66.

37 Cf. 22, 28, 39, 45; other variations include ἕνα πουλάκι ξέβγαινε ἀπὸ τὸ κακοσούλι
32, cf. 41, 44, 57.

38 Cf. 38, Politis 16; other variations include Giankas 61, *Laog* (1915) 368.1.

39 See Zoras *SBN* (1935) 239.35: μαῦρα πουλιὰ ἐφάνησαν ἀπὸ τὴν ἑσπερίαν, and Politis 1.

40 Giankas 12.5–6, 49.4–5, 60.5–6, Politis 4.4–5, 6.33–4, 13.3–5, 15.12–13 (κλαῖνε);
Giankas 21.7, 32.7–8, 38.5, 58.18, 66.5–6, Politis 13.1–2 (πῆραν). For the use of
these structures in laments for earlier events, see Politis 1, Passow 193–6, *Laog*
(1957) 379–80.

41 Some are analysed by Herzfeld in an article to be published shortly in *KCh*.

42 See *Laog* (1957) 74.5, 1–4, cf. Giankas 63 (lament for Battle of Spelaion in
1854), and *Thrênos for Constantinople* 3–5, Zoras 200.

Chapter 6

1 See Wilamowitz *TGL* 7, 42, 57–8, Smyth *GMP* cxx–cxxv, Harvey *CQ* (1955)
159–62.

2 Frisk *GEW* s.v.

3 Maas argues that before Attic tragedy, the *thrênos* was 'die unliterarische
teilweise vielleicht sogar unartikulierte Totenklage, die als barbarisch...galt',
RE s.v. But his view is not in accordance with evidence cited by Nilsson *UT*
76–85 and by Reiner *RTG* 4. Some support may be offered by Sa. *fr.*150 L–P,
οὐ γὰρ θέμις ἐν μοισοπόλων θρῆνον ἔμμεν'· οὔ κ' ἄμμι τάδε πρέποι. Although this is thought
to be a fragment of a lament composed by Sappho for her own daughter (Maxim.
Tyr. 18.9), the possibility cannot be excluded that there is an implied contrast
in the second phrase: it was not for *them* to sing dirges (rather, for the Muses
themselves). Further, the girl may have been dying and not actually dead,
therefore lamentation would be inappropriate, as in the other example cited in
the same passage by Maximus. Finally, two important instances of *thrênos* as
a more formal lament are dismissed by Maas as exceptions (*Od.*24.60 and Pi.
I 8.63–4).

4 *Od.*24.60, *Il.*24.720, Plu. *Sol.*21.5, Pi. *I* 8.63–4, *P* 12.6–8, Pl. *R.*388d, 398e.

5 *Thrênos*: Pi. *fr.*114–23 ed. Bowra, Simon. Page *PMG* 520–31. See Harvey *CQ*
(1955) 169–70. *Góos*: see chapter 1, n. 68 (p. 210), and Reiner *RTG* 8–18.

6 A classification of the use of *thrênos* and *góos* in tragedy indicates that some
distinctions were sometimes made, but that there was a tendency, more perceptibly
in the plays of Euripides, to treat the terms as synonymous. *Thrênos* is found (1)
as the ritual lament for the dead: A. *Th.*863, 1064, *Ag.*1541, *Ch.*335, 342, S.
*El.*94, 1469, *OC* 1751, 1778, E. *El.*215, *Tr.*609; its formal character is suggested
in S. *Aj.*924, *El.*88, E. *Rh.*976 and perhaps A. *Ag.*992; (2) together with other
words of lamentation, including *góos*, apparently without distinction: S. *El.*103,
232, E. *Andr.*92, *Supp.*87–8, *IT* 144, 182, *Hel.*164–6, 174, *Hek.*297–8, 434;
(3) as a general term for lament, not necessarily for the dead: A. *Pr.*388,
*Ag.*1322–3, E. *Or.*984; (4) in the verbal form in proverbial phrases expressing
the idea of fruitless lamentation: A. *Ch.*926, S. *Aj.*852, E. *Ph.*1762. *Góos* is
found (1) as the ritual lament for the dead, usually passionate and ecstatic:

A. *Th.*854, 967, *Pers.*541, 545, 947, 1050, 1077, S. *El.*81, 139, 243, 291, 870, *Ant.*427, 1247, *OC* 1609, 1622, 1668, E. *Andr.*1159, 1198, *El.*1211, *Supp.*71, 79, 977, *Tr.*316, *HF* 110, 488, *Ion* 769, 1459, *Or.*1121, *Rh.*260; and more specifically, with the function of rousing the spirit of the dead: A. *Pers.*687, 697, *Th.*917, 964, *Ch.*321, 330, 449, E. *Supp.*1143, *El.*59, 141, 144, 125; (2) in phrases of a set type, such as 'cease lamentation' or 'leaving lamentation for kinsfolk': A. *Pers.*705, S. *Aj.*579, 973, 319, *El.*353, 375, 379, *Tr.*1199, E. *Supp.*287, 111, *Hel.*321, *Ph.*883, 1309, 1057, *Med.*59, 1211, *Or.*1022, *Hi.*1181; (3) with the implication of being ill-omened for the living: A. *Supp.*116, *Th.*657, S. *Ant.*883, E. *Hel.*339; (4) together with other words for weeping and wailing, apparently without distinction: S. *OT* 30, E. *Alk.*88, *HF* 1026, *Or.*204, 320, 959, *IT* 860; (5) in a more general sense, as being characteristic of women, or opposed to joy: E. *Supp.*82, *Alk.*922, *Ph.*1672, *IT* 832.

7 Aristokl. ap. Ammon. *de diff. verb.*, p. 54 ed. Valck.: θρῆνος δ' ἐστὶν ᾠδὴ τῆς συμφορᾶς, οἰκεῖον ὄνομα ἔχουσα· ὀδυρμὸν ἔχει σὺν ἐγκωμίῳ τοῦ τελευτήσαντος. . . τὸν θρῆνον ᾄδεσθαι παρ' αὐτῇ τῇ συμφορᾷ πρὸ τῆς ταφῆς καὶ μετὰ τὴν ταφὴν καὶ κατὰ τὸν ἐνιαύσιον χρόνον, Prokl. *bibl.Phot.*321a: (in contrast to the *epikédeion*) ὁ δὲ θρῆνος οὐ περιγράφεται χρόνῳ. For glosses in the Lexica, see Hsch., *EM*, Suda s.v. *góos*.

8 *RE* s.v. *kommós*. For the *iálemos* in tragedy, see A. *Supp.*115, E. *Ph.*1033, *Tr.*1304, *Or.*1390, *Rh.*895. The *kommós* is discussed in detail by Nilsson *UT* 85–7.

9 See Bion 1.97. The lexicographers appear more familiar with *kommós* as a ladies' hair style, although it is stated in the Suda that the word is also thought to mean the lament of hosts of women. In view of this apparent decline in usage, its survival in Epiros today for the lament of Zafeiris is the more remarkable, see Kyriakidis *EL* 37.

10 E. *IT* 146, *EM* 327, Didymos ap. Orion 58.7, Prokl. *Chr.*6, Dionys. Thrax in Bekker *Anecdota Graeca* 2.750. From the fifth century, it was used in poetry as a synonym for *thrênos*, E. *Hel.*185, *Tr.*119, *IT* 146, 1091, A.R. 2.780, *AP* 11.135.3, see also Page *GPL* 206–9. Bowra has suggested a possible derivation of *élegos* from Armenian *elegn* = flute, *EGE* 6; but the antiquity of the connection between the *aulós* and elegiac couplets and the soundness of his evidence are disputed by Campbell *JHS* (1964) 63–8.

11 Paus. 10.7.5–6; see also Page *GPL* 206–30, who contrasts Euripides' elegiacs in *Andr.*103–16 with non-funereal elegiacs. But these verses contain no 'storm of passion', or even an address to the dead; on the contrary, they are remarkable for their careful structure. The difference between them and other elegiacs is not therefore so great as he suggests.

12 See Harvey *CQ* (1955) 171–2.

13 In an unpublished paper *Wisdom and the Common Meal in the Seventh Century*, kindly made available to me by the author, J. S. Morrison suggests that the common meal was a widespread institution of archaic life with important political, social and educative functions for the whole community (Sparta: Hdt. 1.65, X. *Lac.*5.2; Crete: Arist. *Pol.*1271a.21), surviving in classical times as a private institution among aristocratic families (Pl. *La.*179b, *Smp.*176a, Ar. *fr.*153), with the exception of Sparta where it remained public (Hdt. 1.65). Basing his discussion on an examination of the extant work of elegiac poets in the archaic period, and of the evidence of later writers about them, he argues that the elegiac couplet was one form through which the traditions and wisdom of the common meal were handed down, and that this is indicated by the common purpose, tone and method of early elegiac poetry, despite differences

in time and place of composition. Finally, there is evidence in Homer for the significance of songs and speeches at meals, *Il.*1.473, 2.404, 9.65, 22.492, *Od.*1.325; cf. X. *Lac.*5.6. On the general significance of after-supper songs, see Thomson *SAGS* 1.494–8.

14 Poll. 6.202: εἴποις δ' ἂν ὅτι τὸ γυναικεῖον γένος ἐστὶ θρηνῶδες καὶ φιλόθρηνον, cf. Plu. *Sol.*21.5, Thuc. 2.34.4. For elegiac couplets improvised at table, see Ar. *Ve.*1219, Pl. *G* 451e.

15 Cf. Zen. 5.28: εἰώθεσαν οἱ παλαιοὶ ἐν τοῖς περιδείπνοις τὸν τελευτήσαντα ἐπαινεῖν, καὶ εἰ φαῦλος ἦν.

16 Cagnat *RP* (1889) 51–65 and Armstrong *AELI* 239–42 put forward a strong case for the existence of such manuals in Latin. More recent opinion is summarised by Lattimore *TGLE* 16–17, cf. 19–20.

17 See Thuc. 2.35–46, Gorg. *Epit.*, Pl. *Mx.*236b. For the *epitáphios épainos*, see Plu. 2.218a; and for the *epitáphios sophistés*, the man who composed such speeches, see Ach.Tat. 3.25, Luc. *Luct.*20.

18 Cf. *ALG* 1.76.1, Ael. *NA* 5.34, D.S. 17.115.

19 Plu. *Pel.*1.6, *Mor.*1030a, Prokl. *bibl.Phot.*321a = *EM* 454.48, *Et.Gen.* AB, Serv. on *Ecl.*5.14 (Reiner *RTG* 2). Plutarch mentions an *epikédeion* for the loss of Spartans (*Pel.*1) and another on the death of Pindar (*ibid.* 1020a).

20 A. *Pers.*621, 657–63, E. *Hel.*966, *HF* 717, cf. Pi. *fr.*119 ed. Bowra, Plu. *Rm.Qu.*23: τοὺς κατοιχομένους ἐπὶ τὰς χοὰς ἀνακαλοῦνται.

21 *EM* s.v., Paus. 1.43.2. For a full discussion of this verb in ancient and modern Greek, see Romaios *KR* 374–5.

22 *MMB* 5.168.4: ἡ Παρθένος σὺν δάκρυσιν θερμοῖς ἀνεκαλεῖτο. Romaios suggests that the word *Anakálema*, as used in the fifteenth-century lament for the fall of Constantinople, implies, in addition to the meaning *lament*, the people's invocation to their Emperor to rise and save them from the enemy, *KR* 385.

23 *Hist.Lex.*2.51, B3 s.v. This and the previous example are cited by Romaios *KR* 371.

24 *IGF* (1901) 6–13. The spelling *myrológi* still persists, however, see Dimitrakos. The form *moiriológi*, widely current today, can be traced back to the fourteenth century, see *Belthandros and Chrysantza* 128.

25 Stephanus s.v. cites μοιρογένεσις vox haec perperam degeneravit ap. Firmicum in μυριογένεσις in quo nempe tractabat de genituris partilite collectis. Under *mýromai*, he cites: aeque vitiosa forma schol. Hom. *Il.*A L. 2, 8: μυρία, τινὲς θρηνητικὰ παρὰ τὸ μυριᾶσθαι, καὶ ἐπίθετον αὐτὸ τῶν ἀλγέων ἥκουσαν, ἐφ' οἷς μυριᾶσθαι καὶ τὸ κλαῦσαι. The scholiast is mistaken, but his comment implies the existence of a verb μυριᾶσθαι = κλαῦσαι. In the Suda we find: μυρομένη· ὀδυρομένη, θρηνοῦσα.

26 Buck *GD* 24. In Attic, there are signs of confusion from the fourth century B.C., cf. Danov *BIAB* 11.2 (later).

27 Buck *GD* 29, Hatzidakis *ENG* 28, Bachtin *ISMG* 20–30.

28 I have followed the text and translation of George Thomson.

29 See A. *Supp.*116, *Ag.*1136–46, *Pr.*637, S. *Aj.*823–65, *OT* 1241–50, 1307–66, *Ant.*806–82, 891–943, *Tr.*917–22, *Ph.*796–8, E. *Alk.*244–72, *Med.*96–8, 111–14, 143–7, *Hipp.*669–79, *Andr.*384–6, *Hel.*212–13, *Or.*1537–9, *Ba.*1368–87, *IA* 1279–1337, 1505–8, *Rh.*728. That this tradition had some connection with the popular belief that the dying swan sang her own lament is suggested by Aelian, *NA* 5.34.

30 *Il.*4.517, 19.409–10, 23.119.

31 *Il.*19.287–302, 315–39, *Od.*4.722–34, 7.213–14. See also Dieterich *DFG* 72 ff.

32 *Ibid.* 77 ff., cf. Mayer *MGI* Anhang, from which most of the inscriptional evidence quoted in this context is taken.

33 Kallin. *ALG* 1.3.1, Mimn. 1.39.1, A. *Pr.*103–5, *IG* 12.7.396, 401.13.

34 Mayer *MGI*. For *moira* in impersonal sense, see Peek 1695, *AP* 7.472. It is found also as *wretched fate, death,* see Peek 9, 2039.9.

35 Mayer cites Kb. 511b: ἀλλά με Μοῖρ' ἐδάμασσεν, 714: ὤλεσεν...θανάτῳ Μοῖρα κραταιή, *ibid.* suppl. 479a = *IG* 5.2.178: Μοῖρ' ἐπέδησε λυγρά. Other examples include Wilhelm *GEK* x, Peek 232, 546, 774, 935, 945, 1282, 1300, 1374, 1576, 1664, 1698, 1783, 1981, 2035.7–8.

36 Cf. Peek 1555: Τίς μοιρῶν μίτον...ἐκλώσατο;, Kb. 372c: Τίς (σ)ε κιχήσατο Μοιρῶν;, *AP* 7.439: ἄκριτε Μοῖρα, | πρώϊον ἐξ ἥβας ἔθρισας..., *ibid.* 468: Ἰὼ κακοπάρθενε Μοῖρα..., *ibid.* 602:...ἅ μέγα νηλειής...(Μοῖρα), Peek 684: ὡς ἀδίκως Μοῖρα τόδ' εἰργάσατο, *ibid.* 1122: Μοῖρα...ἄγε με βαμέναι εἰς 'Αΐδαν.

37 An interesting parallel is the old English popular song *Fortune my Foe,* first referred to in written sources in 1565, and alluded to by Shakespeare in *The Merry Wives of Windsor* II.3, also by Beaumont and Fletcher, Jonson and many others. One reason for its popularity was that 'the metrical lamentations of extraordinary criminals have been usually chanted to it for upwards of two hundred years', and it was therefore known as the *hanging tune,* since criminals would sing their stories to it on their way to the gallows. It gained wide currency in this form through the Broadsides, especially those of the Roxburghe Collection, where ballads to this tune are all founded on murders, dying speeches or grievous misfortunes, Chappell *PMOT* 1.162–4. The parallel is significant because it provides independent evidence of the inherently popular character of the theme, and of its relation to literary tradition, especially to drama and tragedy.

38 See Ach.Tat. 1.13, 5.7, and Greene *Moîra* 331–98.

39 Books 1–4, 7, 10, 14; and for *Moîra,* see 1.492–3, 7.75, 10.97, 109, 14.97–100.

40 Eugenianos *Drosilla and Charikles* 6.207: ὡς γὰρ μοῖρα μέλαινα δυσώνυμος ἀμφεκύκλωσεν ..., *ibid.* 214–15: τόν ρα φάους ἀπέμερσε, κακώνυμος, αἰὲν ἀτειρὴς | Μοῖρα μέλαινα, φέραλγος, ἀπ' ἔγχεος 'Αραβίοιο, Manasses *Aristandros and Kallithea* 3.9: "Αν ζῶντα γάρ τινα καλῶς ἡ Μοῖρα προαρπάσῃ, in Hercher *ESG.* Cf. *AP* 7.574.3–5: Μοῖρα...ἀρπάξασα ...ἤμερσε θεμίστων.

41 μοιρογράφημα: *Kallimachos and Chrysorrhoe* 250, 735 *et passim, Belthandros and Chrysantza* 438, μοιρογράφος: *ibid.* 442, μοιρογράφομαι: *ibid.* 732.

42 Cf. 615, 703–22, 841–2, 1443, 1665–8, 2043–54, 2366–7, *Belthandros* 36, 738–9, *Florios and Platziaflora* 400–32, 465–84, 998–1037.

43 Note the preservation of Moîra's traditional verb λαγχάνειν, cf. Peek 2035.7–8. Moîra was associated with absence from home from as early as the fifth century B.C., see Peek 1209.23. Other instances of addresses to Moîra in the modern laments include *Laog* (1911) 266.5, *ibid.* (1921) 543.94, Giankas 210, and a lament from Mandraki, Nisyros, recorded in April 1972 from Maria Kapite by Mr M. F. Herzfeld, and kindly made available to me: ὄχου μοῖρα μου καμένη, ὄχου μοῖρα μου κακή, | τὸ παιδί μας ἐσκοτώθη κάτω στὴν 'Αμερική. For an appeal to one's own *moîra* in connection with marriage, see Politis *LS* 3.106–8.

44 Many instances, primarily connected with the division of property by lot, have been collected and discussed by C. Alexiou *STC* 73–81.

45 Schmidt *VNG* 212, 216, Schmitt *DIEE* 3.291–308, Politis *Parad.*916–22, Loukatos *KG* 1271, 1272. A particularly striking example quoted by Schmidt is the following proverb, τάχ' ἡ μοῖρα στὸ χαρτί, πελέκας δὲν τὰ κόβει.

46 Cf. Peek 716, 1029, 1098, 1374, 1667, 1555, Kb. 372, Geffcken 214. The concept can be traced back to Homer, *Il*.20.128, 24.210, *Od*.7.198. See Mayer *MGI* C2.

47 *Od*.7.496–7, cf. 10.368. See Schmitt *IGF* (1901) 11: μοιρολογῶ = λέγω τὴν μοῖραν μου, κλαψομοίρης = κλαίω τὴν μοῖραν μου (Dossius 55).

48 *Od*.19.119, *Il*.18.234, Hes. *Sc*.132, Theok. 16.31, Bion 1.68, Mosch. 3.90, 4.605, Peek 1704: μὴ μύρου...με. The same formula is expressed with a different verb, however, in Cumont *Syr*.15.298: μὴ θρήνει με, and in Samm. 6133: μὴ στέναζε.

49 Hsch. 728, 1753, 642. The verb is not frequent in Byzantine literature, but it does occasionally appear in the modern laments, see Passow 336.3: Κ' ἐγὼ σὲ κλαίω, σὲ μύρομαι, στὰ μαῦρα φορεμένη.

50 Καταλέγω = recount, recite: *Od*.7.496–7, 10.368, Hdt. 4.50 *et passim*. In Attic, it occurs only once in the specialised sense of *recite*, X. *Smp*.6.3. Καταλογή = *recitation* (as opposed to singing): *IG* 9.2.531, 12, Hsch. s.v. Numerous examples of κατάλεγμα = *lament* in ecclesiastical and early Byzantine sources are cited by Stephanus s.v.

51 Καταλογή = *love song*: *Lybistros and Rhodamne* 1541, 2870, 3397; καταλέγω = μοιρολογῶ *Kall*.2378. See Schmitt *IGF* (1901) 11, Korais *At*.2.182. For modern usage, see Kyriakidis *IADP* app. 11, Hatzidakis *MNE* 2.65.

52 See Bachtin *ISMG* 48–9, Browning *MMG* 79–81. Examples of variant forms in the romances include τραγοῦδιν (*Lyb*.1529), τραγούδημαν (*ibid*. 3497), κατάλογος (*ibid*. 2870), καταλόγιν (*ibid*. 1543), καταλογίτσιν (*Achilleid* 1222), καταλόγιασμα (*ibid*. 969), μοιριολόγιν (*Belth*.128), μοιρολόγημαν (*Imberios and Margarona* 187). A modern analogy is the coexistence in one village of Chios of two forms, περλόγι and περιλογή, Pernot *ELNH* 2.124.2.

53 See Kyriakidis *IADNP* 11. The antiquity of the form *paralogé* is suggested by the text of Ath. 636.6: Φοίνικες...ἐν οἷς δὲ παρελογίζοντο (⟨παρακατελογίζοντο⟩ Hermann) τὰ ἐν τοῖς μέτροις κλεψιάμβους. Athenaios also refers to the *Ionikológos* or *kinaidológos* as among the most popular singers of his time, 620e. They performed *Ionikà ásmata*, obscene pieces recited rather than sung, which, although without much literary merit, formed part of a distinctively Ionian minstrel tradition of considerable antiquity, see Wilamowitz *NGWG* (1896) 2.209–32.

54 Kyriakidis *IADNP* 11.

55 See Joannidu *UFNK* 45, 60–8.

56 *Od*.4.718–20, cf. 707–10, 1.231–48, 2.363–70, 13.219–20, 14.121–30, 16.142–5, 19.361–74. Returning home after ten years of absence to announce the safe arrival of Agamemnon, the Herald greets his native Argive soil, glad that his bones can be laid there to rest, and addresses the palace as φίλαι στέγαι, A. *Ag*.518.

57 The poet begins with an address, full of praise, to his home, then he takes leave: Τούτοις ὅλοις με, πατρική, θέλγεις, στέγη · | τούτοις με κάμπτεις καὶ κατακλᾷς, φιλτάτη (32–3, cf. 43), calling her his second mother: Ὅμως δὲ χαῖρε, χαῖρε, μῆτερ δευτέρα (45). Finally, he bids farewell to the neighbourhood and to his neighbours: Σῴζου δέ, σῴζου καὶ σύ, πιστὴ γωνία, | ...Ὑμεῖς τε, χρηστοὶ γείτονες, σῴζοισθέ μοι...(52, 54), Cantarella 162–5. A similar formula of farewell to house and family is found in the modern laments for absence from home (Politis 166), for the departure of a bride (Giankas 760, 761, 763), and for the dead (*Laog* (1938) 183.8).

58 Cod. Vindob. th. gr. 244 (ed. Sathas *Pand* (1872) 472–8 and Wagner *MGT* 203–20), cod. Athen. 701 (ed. Bouboulidis *KL* 31–4), cod. Athen. 535 (ed. Zoras *NEst* (1943) 913–19), cod. Iberon 751 Athous 4871 (Lambros *CGM* 2.219), cod. Iberon 1203 Athous (Bouvier *DTMI* 10, 16–21), cod. Berolin.

263. The last is discussed by Bees *BNJ* (1937) 57–66, who concludes from the name and other details that it is Epirot in origin and not Cretan, as Krumbacher supposed, *GBL* 817–18. See Beck *GBV* 191–2. For comparable laments in the vernacular romances, see *Belth.*129–33, *Fl.*1042–8.

59 Giankas 648, Passow 324a.

60 Giankas 659, 660.

61 Modern examples include Aravantinos 218, Politis 6, *Laog* (1938) 488, Giankas 12. On the origins of the practice of *paidomázoma*, see Finlay *HG* 3.476–8, Runciman *FC* 34–5.

62 See Lawson *MGF* 554–60, Politis *LS* 3.232–362.

63 E. *Tr.*1219–21, Peek 1238.3. The custom is frequently referred to in modern laments for the unmarried, as in Politis 217.14–20. See also van Gennep *RP* 133, 152.

64 This line must refer to the twelve extracts from the Gospels read during Holy Week, and to the Apocalypse, see also Sakellaridis 185.5–6. Other bridal farewells include Giankas 760–5; for their relation to funeral laments, see Joannidu *UFNK* III. I am grateful to the folklorist A. L. Lloyd for providing me with much valuable information on comparable parallels between bridal farewells and funeral laments in the folk tradition of other Balkan countries, notably Hungary, Bulgaria and Romania: in Romania it is still customary in many parts to erect at the grave head of a young unmarried person a pine tree similar to those erected outside the house of newly-weds. One of the oldest motifs found in some versions of the pastoral ballad *Miorița* (*The Little Lamb*) concerns the marriage in the other world of a young shepherd to a 'shining bride of the sky'. In a funeral lament for a young girl, the mourner asks: 'Who in the world has seen | a great wedding without a tree? | a wedding with a black crowd? | a wedding without gipsy minstrels, | and a bride in a coffin?' (Gulian *SVFR* 232, reference and translation kindly provided by A. L. Lloyd). The ritual function of the death-and-marriage imagery and the simulation-wedding funeral is, in essence, one of appeasement: by creating the illusion that those who die unmarried have married in the next world, the grief of the mourner is allayed and the wrath of the dead averted. The motif is general; what appears to be characteristically Greek is the idea of death as marriage in the Underworld, to Hades or Charos in the case of a girl, and to the earth or the tombstone in the case of a man. See also Mușlea, *MM* 3–32.

65 For a fuller discussion of the evidence in ancient Greek, and of its influence on later tradition, see Alexiou and Dronke *SM* (1971) 819–63.

66 See Politis 186.8–12, 187, 195.4–6, 204.1–5, *Laog* (1911) 267.12, (1917) 573.6, (1929) 23.81, 26.86, (1934) 275.1. Some 'set openings' are listed in *Laog* (1960) 385–6, cf. Pasayanis 66–70, 80–2, 87–9.

67 Cf. *Laog* (1912) 183.8, 4–7, (1917) 573.8, 1–12, (1953) 276.5, (1960) 370.12, Pasayanis 85.

68 See Peek 1590, 1599, Kb. 371: ἀπλήρωτ' Ἀΐδα, τί με νήπιον ἥρπασες...;, *AP* 7.671: πάντα Χάρων ἄπληστε, τί τὸν νέον ἥρπασες αὕτως...; Modern couplets of this type are frequent, see *Laog* (1934) 190.5: Ἀνάθεμά σε, Χάροντα, σὰν ἔβγης τσαὶ (γ)υρίζης, | ἕξι μηνῶν ἀντρό(γ)υνο νὰ πάης νὰ χωρίσης, Sakellaridis 185.199, 25–7.

69 Cf. *Il.*23.10, E. *El.*125–6, A. *Pr.*637–9. Further examples of the same sentiment in modern laments include *Laog* (1911) 490.8, 1–2, 269.33, 1–2.

70 On the modern distich and its possible relation to the ancient elegy, see Soyter *Laog* (1921) 379–426. Frequently competitive, it may be improvised by each

of the company in turn after the meal is over, see Romaios *KR* 386–417. Many of the longer Underworld ballads are explicitly stated to be sung in the context of a meal, Politis 215, 214, 217, Passow 426–33. Sometimes, Digenis is named as the hero whose exploits are recounted, Politis 78b. The relation of the ballads on the death of Digenis to other folk songs is discussed and illustrated by Politis *Laog* (1909) 169–275.

71 Motifs from the Underworld ballads (Politis 207, 213, 217–22) are sometimes found in women's ritual laments from many parts of Greece, see *Laog* (1929) 21.82, (1960) 369.8, 10, 19.

72 Giankas 96, 98, 220, Politis 39.

73 Cf. *Laog* (1921) 547. The Maniot tradition that the Spartans did not lament those fallen in war is correct (X. *HG* 6.4.16, Plu. 241b), although of course it proves nothing about their alleged descent from the Spartans.

74 Cf. *Laog* (1911) 268.17–33, (1921) 542, (1926) 192, (1934) 184–8, 190, (1953) 275, 291, 443–4, (1957) 185, (1960) 383–6, Sakellaridis 164.1–2.

75 See Mimn. *ALG* 1.40–1.2, Alk. 38, 347 L–P, *AP* 11.56: ὡς δύνασαι, χαρίσαι, μετάδος, φάγε, θνητὰ λογίζου· | τὸ 3ῆν τοῦ μὴ 3ῆν οὐδὲν ὅλως ἀπέχει, Peek 1367: φροντί3' ἕως 3ῆς, πῶς καλῶς ταφήσεε, | καὶ 3ῆσον ὡς 3ήσοις· κάτω γὰρ οὐκ ἔχις, | οὐ πῦρ ἀνάψε, οὐδὲ διπνῆσε καλῶς.

Chapter 7

1 *Il*.18.51, 316, 23.12, 17, 24.721, 723, 747, 761. See Thomson *AA* 185, Nilsson *UT* 76, Reiner *RTG* 30. Thomson points out that the same word is also used for leading the dithyramb, Archil. *ALG* 1.233.77, Arist. *Po*.4.14.1449a, Ath. 145a (*AA* 169).

2 *Il*.24.723–46, 747–60, 761–76. See Thomson *AA* 185, *SAGS* 1. 467.

3 *ALG* 2.279–81, Page *PMG* 871.

4 See Reiner *RTG* 71–100.

5 Examples include S. *Aj*.974–1039, *El*.1126–70, E. *Tr*.740–81, 1158–1208, *El*.54–81.

6 See Thomson *SAGS* 1.465, and *OA* 1.34–6 for an analysis of the complex structure of the *kommós* in A. *Ch*.315–479.

7 See chapter 1, pp. 11–12 and *Il*.19.287–302, 315–39. In answer to Briseis' lament for Patroklos, which is followed by a refrain of cries from the women, comes Achilles' lament, which is also followed by a refrain of cries from the old men; but the cries of the women, as those of the men, should not, I think, be seen as merely perfunctory, nor as a pretence to conceal their real feelings, but as a spontaneous expression of their own grief, touched off by the laments of Briseis and Achilles. For comparable sentiments expressed by the strange mourners today, see chapter 3, pp. 40–1.

8 These divisions in the Homeric laments were first noted by Peppmüller, who compared them with the ἀρχή, ὀμφαλός and σφρηγίς of the *nómos*, see Leaf's edition of the *Iliad*, 2.589n. Other laments which show a similar construction include *Il*.19.287–300, 22.477–514, A. *Pers*.532–97, 852–906, *Ch*.306–478, S. *Aj*.992–1039, *El*.86–120, 1126–70, *Ant*.891–928, E. *HF* 451–96, *IT* 143–235, 344–91, *Ph*.1485–1538, *Med*.1021–80.

9 See Thomson *SAGS* 1.452–5 for an analysis of the structure of this ode and of its function and significance.

10 *Ibid*. 467–8. In Theokritos' second idyll, the epode is repeated by the deserted girl like a magic incantation after each verse, designed to make her loved one return: Ἰυγξ, ἕλκε τὺ τῆνον ἐμὸν ποτὶ δῶμα τὸν ἄνδρα.

11 *Il.*18.315, 22.429, 515, 24.722, 746, cf. 6.499, 18.65–6, 23.14, 24.760, 776.
12 A.   *Supp.*114–15/125–6,   *Pers.*268/274,   550–2/560–2,   568–73/576–81,
    651/656,   663/671,   931/941,   955/967,   974–7/987–91,   985/1000,   1002–5/
    1008–10,   1019/1031,   1043–5/1051–3,   *Sept.*875/881,   966/978,   994–9/1000–4,
    *Ch.*382/396, S. *Aj.*891–914/937–60, *El.*134–6/150–2, *OT* 1313–16/1321–4,
    *Ant.*839–44/862–9, 850/869, 1306–11/1328–32, E. *Tr.*159–73/182–93.
13 The first three strophic pairs contain only three cries, Orestes' initial ὤ, balanced
    by Electra in the first antistrophe and the chorus in the third (315, 332, 372). As
    the tension rises, cries are used to reinforce the appeals of Orestes and Elektra
    (382, 396), until Orestes calls on the Curse of the House of Atreus with repeated
    cries (405–9). The metrical *stretto* of the seventh to ninth strophes, analysed by
    Thomson (*OA* 1.36–7), is combined with a further increase of cries (429–33,
    434–8, 461–2), until the climax of three cries within a single strophe, as the
    Curse is once more remembered and appealed to (466–70). A similar technique
    is used in part of the final *kommós* from the *Persians*, 931–1077.
14 A general address, like 'my child', is frequently preferred, see *Il.*19.315, 22.431,
    725 *et passim*. At Hector's wake, the name is three times repeated, once by each
    mourner (742, 748, 762). Among primitive peoples, it was believed that mention
    of the dead man's name would cause the return of his spirit, and it was therefore
    avoided, see Frazer *TPS* 349–58.
15 Cf. *Pers.*251–2, 590, 1002–3, S. *Aj.*979, *El.*1150–2, E. *Supp.*1139–40, *HF* 880,
    1187, *Tr.*173, 289, 582, 1071, 1084, 1294–5, *Alk.*394, *Rh.*747.
16 Cf. *Ch.*106–64, S. *Aj.*866–78, 891–914, *Tr.*863–95, E. *Alk.*86–111, *Supp.*598–
    633.
17 For the use of this type of dialogue in verse inscriptions, see Peek 1831–72,
    1881–8.
18 Geffcken 17–18 (seventh century), Peek 1831 (sixth/fifth centuries). See Lattimore
    TGLE 131–2.
19 Kb. 120, *MAMA* 6.138, Peek 755, 1214, 1399, 1871 *et passim*. See Lattimore
    TGLE 50, 57, 236.
20 Peek 1873–80.
21 Peek 1214, 1389, 1486, 1561, *IPE* 4.317, 5.
22 *GPL* 211.
23 *TGLE* 230–1. On the antiquity of the dialogue between living and dead, see
    ARW 24, Rohde 257, 366, 381, Boehm *NGT* 37. Nilsson cites evidence from
    Rome, though not from Greece, of mimetic dialogues between the ancestors
    and relatives of the dead, and emphasises the antiquity of the dialogue form in
    the lament, *UT* 101–10.
24 Reiner *RTG* 35.
25 1.13, 3.16, 5.7.
26 Cantarella 28–9, 31–2. It occurs, perhaps fortuitously, in Quintus' *Fall of Troy*,
    1.100–14, 3.435–50, 5.532–57, and it survived in somewhat more structured
    form in the *epitáphios lógos*, as in Eustathios' elaborate funeral oration for the
    Emperor Manuel Komnenos, Migne 135.974–1032.
27 See Maas *GM* 25. For hymns in this metre, see Cantarella 94–5, 123–4.
28 See Cantarella 58.4, 65.4, 175.1–5.
29 *AP* 9.524, Abel *Orphica* 284, Powell *CA* 199.37, Dieterich *RM* (1901) 77. For
    a summary of the objections to the theory that the *kontákion* was derived
    exclusively from Syriac forms, see Zuntz *JTS* (1965) 512–13.
    See Wellesz *BMH* 108–9. Interesting evidence of antiphonal singing in the

sixth century in Greek and Latin is cited from the *Vita* of St Caesarius of Arles (†c. 542) by Dronke, *BGDSL* (1965) 54–5: in order to put a stop to the gossip of the congregation during the liturgy, he made the congregation take part by learning psalms and hymns, and by singing proses and antiphons, alternating a versicle in Greek with one in Latin, *S. Caesarii episcopi Arelatensis Opera omnia* 2.303 cap. 19 (ed. Morin).

31 Zoras 60–2: *A.* 1–6 (proem), *B.* 7–111 (Virgin's lament), *A.* 112–24 (epilogue). Virgin's lament: *A.* 7–19 (address), *B.* 20–60 (predominantly narrative section), *A.* 61–111 (renewed address and lament). For the use of the cry 'my son and God' in the *stavrotheotókia*, see *MMB* 5.168.4.

32 Runciman *FC* 113, 161.

33 Zoras 200.3.

34 *Ibid.* 204.5, cf. *AP* 9.28, where Mycene contrasts her present obscurity with her past greatness.

35 Cf. Theros 687: *A.* 1, *B.* 2–8, *A.* 11 = 1, Pasayanis 135: *A.* 1–8, *B.* 9–49, *A.* 50–4, Petrounias B 15b: *A.* 1–5, *B.* 6–30, *A.* 31–5. In the latter, the intervening narrative describes the manner of death, and so reinforces the cry for revenge in the final appeal. Petrounias defines this structure as characteristic of the vendetta ballad, p. 15.

36 Reiterated cries and commands: Baud-Bovy 2.171, Giankas 867, 868 (the opening three commands are balanced by three commands at the end), Pasayanis 115, 98, 101, Tarsouli 227, 232. Appeals by name: Pasayanis 97.8–9, 98.3–10, 100.6–9, 171.1–8, Giankas 868, 907, 910, 914, *Laog* (1912–13) 7, (1953) 33.54. See also the Cretan tragedy *Erofíle* 5.525.

37 μερзανένιος = κοραλλένιος. I am indebted to Dr D. Vayakakos, director of the Editorial Centre of the Historical Lexicon of the Academy of Athens, for the interpretation of this word.

38 Cf. Tarsouli 232, Psachos 150, Theros 686, 694, 707, 713, 728, 730, 733, 745, Politis 184, 185, 205, 209.

39 Theros 700, cf. 726, 743, Pasayanis 35, 53 *et passim.*

40 Politis 183, Theros 776.19–22.

41 *Laog* (1909) 229.18, (1911) 489.6 (dead to the sun), (1929) 27.90 (dead to coffin), (1953) 281.26 (dead to his departing good looks), Theros 705.

42 Tarsouli 249, cf. Pasayanis 109, *Laog* (1912–13) 182.6.

43 Cf. Politis 214.9–12, 221.15–19, 222.16–22, Theros 678.5–10, 679.3–5, 680.15–18.

44 Cf. A. *Pers.*955–73, *Thebaid fr.*5 ed. Evelyn White (Loeb 1936) 486.

45 Examples include A. *Pers.*550–3, 560–3, 800, 1023, *Th.*876, 884–5, 933–6, *Ch.*319, 398, 436–7, 461, *Ag.*441–4, 1504, S. *Aj.*394, *El.*1158–9, *Ant.*916–20, 1344–6, *Tr.*950–2, *OC* 1670–6, E. *Alk.*141, *Supp.*778–83, 826–7, 972–4, 1125–6, 1130–1, *Hel.*185, 198–9, *Ph.*1290–2. See Thomson *SAGS* 2.134–5, Reiner *RTG* 26–7.

46 Alliteration and assonance: A. *Pers.*227, 280–1, *Th.*961–74, *Ag.*1485–6, 1494–5, *Ch.*43, 152–6, 423, 425, S. *El.*129, 849–63, *Aj.*866–87, *Ant.*1261–6. Parallelism and asyndeton: A. *Pers.*861–3, 865–7, 925, *Th.*917–20, *Ag.*1410, S. *El.*164–5, 850–2, *OT* 1312–15, E. *Tr.*1186, *Or.*1405–6, *IA* 1327–9, *IT* 220. Oxymoron: A. *Th.*941, *Ag.*1545, *Ch.*42, S. *El.*1144–5, *Ant.*923–4, *OC* 1692–3, E. *HF* 1060–1, *Tr.*1223, 1316, *Hipp.*821, 868.

47 Ar. *Ra.*1331–55.

48 A. *Th.*975, 829–31, *Ag.*687–90, 1080–2, S. *Aj.*904, 923, E. *Ba.*367.

49 For the importance of the *kôlon* in Greek metre, see White *VGC* 664.

50 Cf. A. *Ch.*327–8: ὀτοτύζεται δ' ὁ θνήσκων, | ἀναφαίνεται δ' ὁ βλάπτων, S. *El.*197: δόλος ἦν ὁ φράσας, ἔρος ὁ κτείνας, A. *Pers.*694–6, 700–2, *Th.*989–99, *Ch.*436–7, S. *OT* 1320, 1340–1, E. *Supp.*833–4, *Alk.*141, *Or.*1404–6, *Tr.*102, 502. Sometimes a similar, if more rhetorical effect is achieved by the repetition of pronouns and conjunctions, as in E. *IA* 1327–9: τοῖσι δὲ λύπαν, τοῖσι δ' ἀνάγκαν, | τοῖσι δ' ἐξορμᾶν, τοῖσι δὲ στέλλειν, | τοῖσι δὲ μέλλειν, cf. A. *Ch.*436–7, E. *Supp.*777. For antithetical *kôla* in the rhetorical *epitáphios lógos*, see examples analysed by Thomson *JHS* (1953) 80. Other examples in mystic fragments, popular songs and the early philosophers are cited by Norden *AK* Anhang 1.

51 Norden *AK* 816–19, cf. *AT* 3.2b.

52 See Thomson *JHS* (1953) 79–81, Ioannidou *HGS*.

53 For a similar style in the funeral oration, see Migne 135.1026c, 46.884b–c, 114.216c–217d.

54 For antithetical style in the liturgy, see *Lit.Alex.* cod. Ross. 49b, ed. Swainson 33–4. It is interesting that most of the surviving fragments of Herakleitos have been preserved by Hippolytos of Rome (third century A.D.) in his *Elenchos* 9.7–10; in spite of his polemic against Herakleitos, his own doctrine of truth is formulated by means of antitheses, *ibid.* 10.32–3 (*CGS* 242–3, 288–92).

55 *BMH* 124.

56 See especially 15.8–11, 16–19 (ed. Wellesz, *MMB* 9 p. LXXV): χαῖρε θεοῦ ἀχωρήτου χώρα· | χαῖρε σεπτοῦ μυστηρίου θύρα· | χαῖρε τῶν ἀπίστων ἀμφίβολον ἄκουσμα· | χαῖρε τῶν πιστῶν ἀναμφίβολον καύχημα· | ... A brilliant analysis of the complex structure of this hymn, and of its relation to the double cursus, is given by Dronke *BGDSL* (1965) 62, 65–8.

57 Ed. Bonner, *Studies and Documents* (1940), cf. Wellesz *JTS* (1943) 41–52, Kahle *ibid.* 52–6.

58 See *Hymn to Physis*, Cantarella 31–2.8–9, 15, 27, Apollinarios *ibid.* 10.84–94, Greg.Naz. *ibid.* 14.2. Further, a striking parallel to the lament in Achilles Tatius 1.13, quoted on p. 152, can be found in one of the funeral services: Ἀλλ' ὁμοῦ ὁ γάμος ὁμοῦ καὶ ὁ τάφος, | ὁμοῦ ζεῦξις ὁμοῦ καὶ διάζευξις, | ὁμοῦ γέλως ὁμοῦ θρῆνος, Pitra *AS* 1.257.

59 ἀντὶ μὲν ἱμερτοῦ θαλάμου τάφον, ἀντὶ δὲ νύμφης | στήλην, ἀντὶ γάμου δ' αἰνὸν ἄχος γενέταις, Peek 710.5–6, cf. 1263.9, 1330.5–6, 1437.5, 1584.5–6, *AP* 7.649. Οὐ γά[μον] οὐδ' ὑμ|έναιον ἐσέδρακον, | ἀλλά με Μοῖρα | ἄγαγε..., Peek 1826.1–2, cf. 658.9, 667.3, 683.3–5, 804.5–6, 811.5–6, 1162.7–8, 1243.5–6, 1810–30, 1833.7–8, 1853.1, 2026.9–13, 2038.12–13, 19.

60 Cf. Peek 1113.1–8, 1416, 1785–1801, 1913.5–6. For the repetition of the same formula to introduce contrasting ideas, cf. Peek 1759, 1988, *AP* 7.371.

61 Cf. Peek 1249 (θνήσκει 19, 20; θνήσκω 30), 1508 (ὤλετο 3, 5), 1576 (ἄρτι 5, 6), 1584 (που; 1, 2), 1680 (κλαύσατε 13, 16), 2038 (ἄρτι 1, 3), 2039 (ἄρτι 7, 8), 2040 (αὐτή μοι...αὐτὴ καὶ...27–8), *AP* 7.476 (δάκρυα 1, 3; αἰάζω, αἰαῖ 6, 7, ἅρπασεν 7, 8).

62 Peek 120: αὐτὴ ἡ γενήσασα καὶ κηδεύσασα ἐπέγραψα, cf. 789, 1016, 1264.4.

63 *De Hysmines et Hysminiae Amoribus*, ed. Le Bas in Hirschig *ES* 556, cf. 558, 564, 566.

64 Ed. Bouvier *DTMI* 5–6 no. 1.

65 Cf. Giankas 73, 878, Passow 395, 415, Politis 1. Variations of this formula include Giankas 912, Passow 351, 362, 399; they can also be found in ancient poetry, see Moschos 3.26, 37–44, 58, Bion 1.32–5, 68.

66 Cf. Peek 1810–30.

67 This device is also common in the historical laments, as in the Cretan song for the siege of Rhodes of 1520: Οὖλες οἱ χῶρες χαίρονται κι οὖλες καλὴν καρδιά 'χουν, | μὰ ἡ Ρόδο ἡ βαριόμοιρη στέκει ἀποσφαλισμένη (Kriaris 44). For a discussion of its frequency and variability in both historical songs and *moirológia*, see Herzfeld *KCh* (forthcoming). Word play on the name of Charos is found in the form Πές μου, Χάρε, νὰ χαρῆς, with which we may perhaps compare Ar. *Ra.* 184: Χαῖρ' ὦ Χάρων, χαῖρ' ὦ Χάρων, χαῖρ' ὦ Χάρων.

Chapter 8

1 Some of these have been pointed out by Thomson, *JHS* (1953) 79–83.

2 A. *Ag.*645, 1474, *Ch.*151, 386, 475, *Pers.*625–7, E. *Hel.*177, *IT* 179, *Tr.*578.

3 Pl. *Mx.*236e, *Symp.*180d, 194e, Dem. 60.1, Isokr. 10.12–13, Thuc. 2.35.2, Gorg. 6, Lib. *Laud.Const.*5 (Thomson *JHS* 81) cf. Hyp. *Epit.*2. The idea is also frequent in the laments of tragedy, see A. *Pers.*694–7, 700–2, *Ch.*89–91, S. *Tr.*947–9, *OC* 1556–8, 1710–12, E. *HF* 1378–82.

4 Dem. 60.15, Pl. *Mx.*236e, Lys. 2.1–2, A. *Ag.*785–7, *Ch.*855, Theok. 17.11, Lib. *Laud.Const.*3.1, and hymns cited by Norden which open with the singer questioning his ability to find the right name to invoke the god, *AT* 144–7 (Thomson *JHS* 81–2). Cf. Ael.Arist. 18.8.

5 Cf. *Ag.*1505–7, 1541–50, *Ch.*87–90, 93–9, 315–19, 418–19, *Th.*825–8, 851–2, 1057–9, S. *Aj.*1185–91, E. *Tr.*110–11, 792–3, *HF* 1025–7, 1146–52, *Hel.*164–6, 217–18, *Ph.*1289–95, 1310–12, *Hipp.*826–7, *Hek.*154–64, 176–94, 695–6.

6 Cf. S. *Aj.*879–86, 1185, 1215–16, *Ant.*839, 908, 921, 1284–92, 1307, *Tr.*984–1016, *OT* 1309, E. *Hipp.*840–3, 856–9, *Andr.*841–60, *Ph.*1498–1538, *Alk.* 863, 879, 897, 941, Bion 1.60, Mosch. 3.50, 112, Ach.Tat. 1.13.

7 Cf. 920–1, 1034–6, E. *HF* 485–9, *Med.*1040–50.

8 See Ael.Arist. 18.20, Kb. 344, 371, 372, Peek 1880.

9 Greg.Nyss. *in Funere Pulcheriae*, Migne 46.864c: Οὐκ οἶδα ὅπως τῷ λόγῳ χρήσωμαι· ...Ἄ τίς ἀδακρυτὶ διεξέλθοι;, cf. 865b–c, Eust. *Manuelis Comneni Imp. Laudatio Funebris*, Migne 135.974a; Meletios *Thrênos* for Patriarch Jeremiah II, *DIEE* (1883) 65 : Πόθεν τανῦν τοῦ θρήνου ἀπάρξομαι; ... Πῶς μου ἡ γλῶττα τῷ λόγῳ ἐξυπηρετήσειεν ἀμογητί; Quintus 1.100, 645, 4.465, Eustath. *Hysm.*10.384.

10 Cf. anonymous *káthisma*, Cantarella 76.1.4: Ποῖόν σοι ἐγκώμιον προσαγάγω ἐπάξιον; Τί δὲ ὀνομάσω σε; Ἀπορῶ καὶ ἐξίσταμαι. Konstantinos Akropolites *Hymn to Virgin*, *DIEE* (1892) 43.5 : Τίς σε πρὸς ἀξίαν αἰνέσειε; τὴν ἀμώμητον ἀμηχανοῦντες, δυσωποῦμεν ὑπὲρ ἡμῶν τῷ τόκῳ σου πρέσβευε...For initial questions in the Virgin's lament, see *CP* 1121, 1306–9, Sym.Met. *Planctus*, Migne 114.212d: Ποίους θρήνους ἐπιτυμβίους, καὶ τίνας ὕμνους ἐπικηδείους σοι ἄσομαι;, *MMB* 5.166.2, 168.4.

11 *Kall.*1443–6, *DA* (G) 8.211–12, *Álosis* 225–8 (Zoras 181), *Anakálema* 26–7 (Kriaras 30), *Thrênos for Timur Lenk* 1–10 (Wagner *Carm.*28).

12 Cf. Sym.Met. *Martyrium S. Sebastiani et Sociorum*, Migne 116.796d.

13 Cf. Michaelidis-Nouaros 314.3.1–2, 4.1–2.

14 Cf. Pasayanis 94.1–2. Examples of questions intensifying the lamentation are too numerous to cite.

15 Cf. Politis 8, 11, 127.6, Theros 705. A similar device, but without the final contrast, is found in one of the ancient epigrams, *AP* 9.57: Τίππε παναμέριος, Πανδιονὶ κάμμορε κούρα, | μυρομένα κελαδεῖς τραυλὰ διὰ στομάτων; | ἦ τοι παρθενίας πόθος ἵκετο, τάν τοι ἀπηύρα | Θρηΐκιος Τηρεὺς αἰνὰ βιησάμενος;

16 See Pl. *Hp.Ma.*282a: εἴωθα μέντοι ἔγωγε τοὺς παλαιούς τε καὶ προτέρους ἡμῶν πρότερόν τε καὶ μᾶλλον ἐγκωμιάζειν ἢ τοὺς νῦν, εὐλαβούμενος μὲν φθόνον τῶν ζώντων, φοβούμενος δὲ

μῆνιν τῶν τετελευτηκότων, cf. Pl. *Lg.*802a, Gorg. 6, Dem. 60.14, Thuc. 2.35.2, Hdt. 1.32, Bakchylides 3.67, 5.187, 12.199, Pi. *O* 8.54, A. *Ag.*894 (Thomson *JHS* 81–2).

17 Thomson *SAGS* 1.453 cites *Il.*1.39–42, 394, 450–6, 503, 5.116, 16.236, *Od.*4.763, Pi. *O* 1.75, *I* 6.42, Bakchyl. 11.2, A. *Ag.*149, 525, S. *OT* 164, Ar. *Ach.*405, *Eq.*592, *Th.*1157.

18 See *Il.*18.333–5, 19.287–90, 315–20, 22.434–6, 477–83, 500–8, 24.749, 757, S. *Aj.*1000–1, *El.*1126–30, 1145–50, *Ant.*901–3, E. *Supp.*790–3, 918–24, 963–7, *IT* 203–8, 229–31, 344–8, *Alk.*915–25, Bion 1.50–3, Mosch. 3.71–5, Peek 747.3, 1300, 1710, 1880, 2040.

19 For contrasts of this type which are similarly extended beyond the fate of one individual, see A. *Pers.*858–905, S. *Aj.*1185–1222.

20 See *Il.*19.315, 22.500, S. *Aj.*1211, E. *IT* 344, *Alk.*915, Mosch. 3.71.

21 See *Il.*18.324, 333, 19.288, 22.435, 477, 482, 24.749, S. *Aj.*1001, *El.*1126, 900–4, E. *Supp.*964, *IT* 344, 348, *Alk.*915, 922.

22 See Greg.Nyss. *Enkómion for St Ephraem*, Migne 46.844d; *Epitáphios Lógos for Empress Plakilla*, ibid. 878c; *Vita* of St Makrina, ibid. 988b; Eust. *Man. Comn. Imp. Laudatio Funebris, ibid.* 135.992d–997d; Euthymios *Laudatio Funebris Eustathii, ibid.* 136.765; Meletios *Thrênos* for Patriarch Jeremiah II, *DIEE* (1883) 66, Greg.Naz. *Carmina Epitaphia*, Migne 38 nos. 23–6.

23 Quintus 1.108–11, Psellos *On the Death of Skleraina*, Cantarella 166.2.1–7.

24 According to James, the *Testament of Job* belongs to a large class of apocryphal books, but is unique in the number of hymns and poetical speeches it contains. The author may have been a Christianised Jew, writing in Greek and paraphrasing, though not translating, a Hebrew original, ed. cit. pp. 88–94. Of particular interest stylistically are the use of balanced clauses, followed by a constant refrain, and the reiteration of νῦν, contrasted with εἴχε, since these are recurrent elements of the lament throughout Greek tradition, see n. 42 below.

25 Cf. *MMB* 5.169.4; Sym.Met. *Planctus*, Migne 114.216, *Ep.Thrênos* stasis 2.5; *CP* 1315–17.

26 Cf. popular acclamations for Easter, Cantarella 83.8, 7–8.

27 It seems probable that Romanos introduced this particular convention into Greek from Ephraem, see his homily *To Good Friday, the Robber and the Cross*, ed. Assemani 3.471: Πρώην 'Ρεβέκκας ἐπιθαλάμιον εἶπον· σήμερον τὸν ἐκ 'Ρεβέκκας ἐπιτάφιον ᾄδω.... σήμερον ἐπάγει σταυρός, καὶ ἡ κτίσις ἀγάλλεται. It also occurs, together with the reiteration of *now*, in a Syriac Letter purporting to be from Dionysios the Areopagite to Timothy, lamenting the death of Peter and Paul. The lament is written in elaborate and sustained *Kunstprosa*, similar to that of Melito's Paschal Homily: Nunc adimpleta est vox Jacobi dicentis: 'Joseph non est super et Simeon non rediit ad me.' Jam non est Paulus ille, lux Ecclesiae fideliumque confidentia, neque amplius exstat Simon fundamentum Ecclesiae christianorumque decus. Hodie adimpletum est quod dixit propheta: 'Quomodo dispersi jacent lapides sancti!' Hodie adimpletum est verbum David dicentis: 'Posuerunt morticina servorum tuorum escam volatili coelorum, et carnem justorum tuorum bestiis terrae.' Ubi nunc cursus Pauli? Jam a labore itinerum quieverunt pedes illius sancti; neque amplius catenis obstringuntur in carceribus. Pitra *AS* 4.264 (Syriac and Armenian texts pp. 241–54). I am indebted to Dr S. P. Brock for drawing my attention to this Letter.

28 See Grégoire *DA* 204.1–2, 241.35.

29 Cf. Giankas 883, 886, 897, Baud-Bovy 2.137.4, Petrounias в 1a.

30 Cf. Politis 208, 212, Pasayanis 146.
31 See *Il*.22.477–83: ἰῇ ἄρα γεινόμεθ᾽ αἴσῃ | ἀμφότεροι, σὺ μὲν ἐν Τροίῃ ... | αὐτὰρ ἐγὼ Θήβῃσιν... | νῦν δὲ σὺ μὲν ᾽Αΐδαο δόμους ὑπὸ κεύθεσι γαίης | ἔρχεαι, αὐτὰρ ἐμὲ στυγερῷ ἐνὶ πένθεϊ λείπεις, cf. 500, 18.333, 19.287, 315, S. *Ant*.900–3, Bion 1.50.
32 Norden *AT* 182–3, 220–3.
33 See Kühner *AGGS* 2.40–1, 354; and, for use of pronoun and copula together for special emphasis, *ibid*. 32, 352.
34 Pi. *N* 10.80: ἐσσὶ μοὶ υἱός (cf. Mark 1.11: σὺ εἶ ὁ υἱός μου), *P* 5.5–20, 1.87, *O* 6.87–94, *I* 2.12, Bakchyl. 3.92, 7.1, 9.45–50, 10.1, 11.9, 17.28. Examples of σύ with ἐσσί not cited by Norden include Hom. *Hm*.3.267–8, 364–7. In general, these instances point to ἐσσὶ γάρ as a prayer formula, parallel to δύνασαι δέ see Norden *AT* 154.
35 Cf. *Il*.24.749, E. *IT* 344–8, *SEG* 4.107. For the repetition of σύ in the lament, as in the hymns, see E. *Alk*.460, *Hel*.1107–20, 1144, *Hipp*. 840–50, *HF* 460–72: σοὶ μὲν.... σὺ δ᾽ ἦσθα..., σοὶ δ᾽ ἦν.
36 See Norden *AT* 163–76.
37 See Peek 2040: ...αὐτή μοι καὶ παῖδας ἐγείναο πάντας ὁμοίους, | αὐτὴ καὶ γαμέτου κήδεο καὶ τεκέων, | ...καὶ κλέος ὕψωσας ξυνὸν ἱητορίης (cf. Pi. *P* 4.281–2, 289) and *IG* 1.923 (ed. minor): καλὸς μὲν ἰδεῖν, τερπνὸς δὲ προσειπεῖν (cf. Peek 2008, 2030.17).
38 Examples are cited and discussed by Schwyzer *EE* 14–15, 27–9; comparing the use of this formula in the religion of Greece and Rome before syncretism with its use in other religions of the ancient near east, he concludes that it is comparatively rare in AG. But he discounts *Od*.11.252: αὐτὰρ ἐγὼ τοί εἰμι Ποσειδάων ἐνοσίχθων...purely because the pronoun is separated from the verb, included 'nur aus rhythmischen Gründen' (p. 14); nor, to my knowledge, does either he or Norden refer to the outstanding example in Hom. *Hm*.3.480: εἰμὶ δ᾽ ἐγὼ Διὸς υἱός, ᾽Απόλλων δ᾽ εὔχομαι εἶναι, cf. Archil. *Eleg*. *ALG* 3.2.1: εἰμὶ δ᾽ ἐγὼ θεράπων... His conclusions on the use of *egò eimí* in the LXX may be correct; but in my opinion, the discussion so far has tended to attach too much importance to a rigid, structural analysis of the external features of the formula, and insufficient attention has been paid to the content and to the complexities of the linguistic factors.
39 Peek 1171–1208, 1959.
40 See Hom. *Hm*.5.109, 145, 185–7.
41 Andreas Cret. *Mégas Kanón*, Cantarella 103.77–9: Σὺ εἶ ὁ ποιμὴν ὁ καλός· ζήτησόν με τὸν ἄρνα... | Σὺ εἶ ὁ γλυκὺς ᾽Ιησοῦς, σὺ εἶ ὁ πλαστουργός μου, cf. Romanos 19.17, 7–8.
42 See *Thrênos* of Father Synadenos of Serrai, Lambros *NE* (1909) 254.104–16; *Thrênos for Constantinople*, Zoras 201.36–45:...γιατ᾽ ἤσουν ξενοδόχισσα, κυρὰ τῶν αἰχμαλώτων, | ...ὁπού ᾽χες χίλιες ἐκκλησιὲς καὶ χίλια μοναστήρια, | ...εἶχες νερὰ τρεχάμενα, εἶχες πανώριες βρύσες... | εἶχες καὶ τὴν ῾Αγιὰν Σοφιάν, τὸ κήρυγμα τοῦ κόσμου, |ἀπ᾽ ὅπου ἐσοφίσθηκε τοῦ κόσμου ἡ σοφία.
43 Cf. *ArP* (1951) 188–9, Petrounias A 10.1–10, 23–4, 51–4, Theros 714, Lioudaki 415.5.
44 See *Akáthistos Hýmnos*, ed. Wellesz *passim*.
45 Cf. Georgios Akropolites *On the Death of Irene Comnena*, Cantarella 213.50: Αὐτὸς πνοή μοι καὶ γλυκὺ φῶς ὀμμάτων...; *Anakálema* 101: ᾽Εκείνη ἦταν ἥλιος, κι ἡ Πόλις ἡ σελήνη...
46 See *Il*.22.481: ὡς μὴ ὤφελλε τεκέσθαι..., 24.764, A. *Pers*.915–17, *Pr*.747–51, S. *Aj*.1192–8, *OC* 1689–93, E. *Supp*.786–8, 821, 829–31, *Hipp*.836–8, *Andr*.523–5,

861–5, 1190–6, *Hel.*169–73, *Or.*982–1000, *IA* 1291–1312. See also Reiner *RTG* 12, 16.

47 A. *Ch.*345–53, cf. *Il.*22.426, 24.729, A. *Pr.*152–9, S. *El.*1131–5, *OT* 1347–8.

48 A. *Ch.*354–62, 363–71, cf. S. *Ant.*925–8, *El.*126–7, *OT* 1349–55, E. *Tr.*766–72, *IA* 1319–29, *Hel.*1110–17.

49 See *AP* 7.22, 282, 735, 746, *IG* 12.8.449, 12–14. On the decline of the optative, see Meillet *AHLG* 274–80, Bachtin *ISMG* 55.

50 See Cumont *Syr.* (1933) 385: Ἥλιε, τὴν μοῖραν ϫητήσῃ ἐμήν...cf. *SIG* 1181, *SEG* 6.803, *MAMA* 1.339 (Lattimore 116–18).

51 *Il.*3.104. For modern Greek material, see Loukatos *SE* (1960) 4.2.

52 Lier *Phil.* (1903) 456–60 argues in favour of the derivation of the Latin formula from the Greek, drawing on substantial epigraphic and literary evidence; but Lattimore does not accept the case as proved, *TGLE* 189–91.

53 Many other parallels are cited by Lattimore 188.

54 Ael.Arist. 18.9: Νῦν ἔδει μὲν πάντας οἰωνοὺς εἰς πῦρ ἐνάλλεσθαι...

55 For classical form, see *AP* 8.176, Quintus 5.465, 468, 3.464–5, Greg.Naz. *Carmina Epitaphia*, Migne 38.23–4, *CP* 1 (= E. *Med.*1), 898, 1022–3, 1316–18. The form with ἔδει is found in Greg.Nyss. *in funere Pulcheriae*, Migne 869b: ἀλλ' ἔδει αὐτὴν εἰς μέτρον ἡλικίας ἐλθεῖν, καὶ νυμφικῷ θαλάμῳ ἐμφαιδρυνθῆναι, cf. Eust. *Man. Comn. Imp. Laudatio Funebris, ibid.* 1025b–c: Οὐκ ἔδει τοιαύτην τῷ βασιλεῖ ἀποτελευτηθῆναι αὐτῶν πόνων μακρῶν ἀνάπαυλαν. Ἔδει τοὺς μακροὺς καμάτους παύσαντα καθ' ἡσυχίαν μεῖναι.

56 For this formula in the *thrênoi* for Constantinople, see Lambros *NE* (1909) 190, *Anakálema* 59. Other examples in modern laments include Passow 371, Politis 175, 195, 196, Baud-Bovy 2.39, Pasayanis 24, 66, 67: Δὲ σοῦ 'πρεπε, δὲ σοῦ 'μοιαϫε χάμου στὴ γῆ νὰ πέσῃς, | μόν' σοῦ 'πρεπε καὶ σοῦ 'μοιαϫε στ' 'Αμάη τὸ περιβόλι. It is significant that it is especially common in the laments for those who die young, and expresses the same idea as in antiquity, that it was wrong for them to die before their parents, or before marriage.

57 Cf. *Laog* (1929) 25.84, 17–20, Baud-Bovy 2.172, Voutetakis 8.1–2, 118.

58 Sakellaridis 181 p. 166, cf. Pasayanis 113, 114, Baud-Bovy 2.174, Michaelidis-Nouaros 313 B4, Theros 717, 730, 758, Tarsouli 20 (wish reversed and uttered as if by the dead), 215, Giankas 900.5–7, Petropoulos 223.19B.

59 I wish to thank Mr P. G. Tuffin, who is completing a Ph.D. thesis on the *adynaton* in Greek tradition, for providing me with references to the *adynaton*. Other examples include Giankas 890, Passow 364, 387–9, Pasayanis 70, Petropoulos 22B, 23B, *Laog* (1915) 575D. Although the *adynaton* was an established convention in ancient Greek, it does not appear in the context of lamentation. At the end of the long Romanian lament *Tradafir* (*Rose tree*), it is the mourner who expresses to the dead the impossibility of his return: 'And now, you'll return when the deer will plough, when the pike fish sows, when the plough-share blossoms, when the ploughshaft puts forth leaves. Then you'll come again.' I am grateful to A. L. Lloyd for this text.

60 *Il.*19.287–8, 295–300, 315–20, 24.729–30, 749–50, 771–2, A. *Pers.*647–56, 709–12, *Ch.*345–62, S. *Aj.*921–4, 996–7, Bion 1.71. Examples in modern laments include Theros 773, Pasayanis 100.7, 107.8–13, 169.

61 Lattimore, who cites this inscription among others with a similar theme, comments that the translation of the last clause is uncertain, ἡμῶν being apparently intended for ὑμῶν, *TGLE* 188 n. 125. According to Thumb, the pronunciation of υ was already divided between ν and ι in the fifth century A.D., although the

process did not become general until the tenth century, *CQ* (1914) 187. In papyrus letters, however, confusion between ὑμῶν and ἡμῶν, and between υ and η in other words, is found from the Ptolemaic period, see Mayser *GGP* 85 (οὐκ ἔφυ for οὐκ ἔφη), 86 (ἡμῶν for ὑμῶν and ἡμῖν for ὑμῖν are cited as especially frequent, also the reverse confusion of ὑμῶν for ἡμῶν). Salonius mentions an example of ὑμῶν for ἡμῶν in a letter written by a Persian between 130 and 121 B.C., *SSF* 2.3 (1927) 17, 7; and several further examples from the third century A.D. are referred to by Zilliacus *SSF* 13.3 (1943) 14 (ἡμῶν for ὑμῶν), 20 (ἡμεῖν for ὑμῖν), 21 (ἡμῶν for ὑμῶν). Unfortunately, Mendel gives no date for the inscription. It is probably of the first century A.D. but may well belong to the late Hellenistic period (first century B.C.). It provides interesting and early epigraphic evidence for the confusion. I wish to thank Miss Gillian Hart for advice on the phonological question and for the papyrological references, and Mr A. G. Woodhead for suggesting a date for the inscription.

62 Cf. Pasayanis 101.7–11, 107.14–20, 115, *Laog* (1911) 269.30, Michaelidis-Nouaros 314, Petrounias A 10.8.
63 See *Il.*5.156, S. *Aj.*972–3, Sol. *ALG* 1.33.22,6, Kb. 406.13, Peek 697.5–6, 2002.7–8.
64 Cf. Michaelidis-Nouaros 314, Petrounias A 10.3–4, *ArP* (1951) 187.5–8, 189.1–4, 20.
65 Cf. Tarsouli 227.6, Petrounias A 10.53–4, *ArP* (1951) 187.4: καὶ 's σὰ παιδόπα τ' ἔρημα ἕναν λογόπον 'κ' εἶπες. Other ancient examples include *Il.*22.482–6, E. *Supp.* 918–24, Bion 1.50–3.
66 *Luct.*13. See Migne 114.313a, 115.1156a, 116.796d–797a; and on this aspect of the lament in general, see Reiner *RTG* 11, 15.

Chapter 9

1 See Wells *BT* 85.
2 See Hom. *Hm.*8.28, Pl. *Smp.*197d–e, Samm. 343; magic incantation from papyrus text, Cantarella 28–9.9; Orphic *Hymn to Physis, ibid.* 31–2.11; Ioannes Geometres *Hymn to Virgin, ibid.* 150.68, 1.
3 Cf. A. *Ag.*895–902, Hom. *Hm.*8.3–7.
4 Cf. Tarsouli 223, 224, Pasayanis 13, 82.5, 98, 116, 117, Theros 755, 763.
5 See *Il.*18.56–60, Kb. 719.7, *RM* (1879) 313a, *MAMA* 1.102, Ramsay *CBP* 684.3, Peek 736.3, 1079.5, 1938.
6 See Andreas of Crete *Mégas Kanón*, Cantarella 103.50, 103; Michael Psellos *Lament for Skleraina, ibid.* 166.2, 20; Στίχοι θρηνητικοὶ 'Αδὰμ καὶ Παραδείσου, Zoras 64.73; *Thrênos for Constantinople, ibid.* 201–2.72–94; *The Plague of Rhodes*, Wagner *Carm.*32–52.
7 A wide range of parallels in similes from Homer and from modern folk songs has been collected and analysed by Petropoulos *Laog* (1959) 366. Other similes in modern laments include *Laog* (1911) 266.4, Tarsouli 232.9–10, Giankas 879.6, Pasayanis 62.2–5, 73, 88.8, Politis 209.5.
8 See Bultmann *Phil.* (1948) 1–36, from whom the references in notes 8–12 are taken: *Il.*1.605, *Od.*19.35, Hes. *Op.*339, Pi. *fr.*114, A. *Ag.*4, S. *Ant.*944, *El.*86, E. *Ion* 1550, Ar. *Ra.*455.
9 *Od.*16.15, 17.39, 19.417, Pi. *O* 2.8–9, A. *Pers.*150, *Eum.*1025, S. *Ant.*879.
10 *Il.*5.47, 6.11, 24.558 *et passim*, A. *Th.*403, *Ch.*319, *Eum.*522, E. *Alk.*269, Pl. *Smp.*219a.

11 S. *Aj.*856, *Ant.*809, *OC* 1549, E. *IA* 1281, 1506.

12 Cf. *Od.*17.41, Simon. *ALG* 2.88.76, A. *Pers.*299–301, *Ag.*602, S. *Aj.*395.

13 Cf. A. *Pers.*979: τὸν σὸν πιστὸν πάντ᾽ ὀφθαλμόν.

14 Cf. Peek 736.3, 945.3, 1097.5–6, Kb. 262.6.

15 See Ps.27.1, Mt. 8.12, Jn. 1.5, Ephraem ed. Assemani 3.417e. For the sun as symbol of justice in OT, see Ps. 84.11, Mal. 42, cf. Mt. 5.45. Light symbolism is, however, found extensively in early Byzantine hymn writers using classical rather than eastern forms, see Clement *Hymn to Christ*, Cantarella 3.2, 35–7; Apollinarios *Translations of Psalms*, *ibid.* 8.4, 3; Greg.Naz. *Evening Hymn*, *ibid.* 15.3, 3–9 and 13–21.

16 See Quintus 3.563–4; Georg.Akropolites *On the Death of Irene Comnena*, Cantarella 213.50–1; Διδασκαλία παραινετικὴ τοῦ Σπανέα ed. Lambros *DIEE* (1900) 105.13, Eust. *Manueli Comn. Imp. Laudatio funebris*, Migne 135.1025b.

17 Cf. *Anakálema* 101–2, *Thrênos for Constantinople* Zoras 201.23–4, *The Plague of Rhodes* 158–6 Wagner *Carm.*37, *Erofile* 5.4.505, 5.5.575–6. Other modern parallels include Politis 194, 197.5–6, 186.10–11, Theros 763.9, 772.15–16, Giankas 879.6, Pasayanis 169.13–15, Baud-Bovy 1.316, *ArP* (1946) 68.2, 1.

18 See Kern *OF* 32, 4f, 5c, Pl. *Ti.*44b, *R.*586a, Hklt. B 59, 60, 71, Parm. B 1.2, Demokr. B 230.

19 Peek 701, 1209.3, 1539.2. See Lattimore *TGLE* 169.

20 *MAMA* 3.347.5, cf. Antiphanes Edmonds *FAC* 2.186.53: εἶτα χήμεῖς ὕστερον εἰς καταγωγεῖον αὐτοῖς ἥξομεν κοινῇ τὸν ἄλλον συνδιατρίψοντες χρόνον.

21 *AP* 10.65, cf. Ar. *Ra.*136–8, S. *Ant.*1284.

22 Cf. E. *Andr.*891, Pl. *Smp.*187d–e, and a curious *Lament for Pet*, preserved in a papyrus fragment of the first century A.D., Grenfell and Hunt 2.40.219: [ἀπορο]ῦμαι ποῦ βαδίσω, ἡ ναῦς μου ᾽εράγη.

23 The way of justice is a common biblical theme, see Dt.26.17, Jn.14.6; but the idea of wandering or straying seems to have originated in Greek, see Pl. *R.*586a, *Phd.*81d.

24 *Lit.Alex.* ed. Swainson 34.49b, cf. Ephraem ed. Assemani 3.471e–f, *Akath. Hm.* ed. Wellesz 205–9.

25 Theros 665, 769, Pasayanis 102. See also Romaios *KR* 229.

26 Hesseling *BZ* (1929–30) 186–91 postulates Italian and Slavonic influence on the figure of Charos the horseman, which dates from the eleventh century, accepting Verrall's rejection of κλυτόπωλος = *famed in horses* as an epithet of Hades (*Il.*5.654), *JHS* (1898) 1–14. Some evidence for the antiquity of the idea in Greek has, however, been collected by Schmidt *VNG* 222 ff.

27 S. *El.*1126–8, 1145–50, E. *Supp.*964–7, 918–24, 790–3, 1132–8. Cf. Hom. *Hm.*8.3–4, Pi. O 2.7.

28 *Trag.fr.adesp.*427 Nauck. See Thomson *OA* 2.73.

29 Eustath.Makr. *Hysm.*6.12.213f, Sym.Met. *Martyrium S. Sebastiani et Sociorum* Migne 116.796d, *Thysia* 767–8. More archaising forms appear in Quintus 3.435 (= *Il.*1.284, 3.284, 6.5). The *Akath.Hm.* includes the idea of support, pillar, roof, door, gate, wall in the address of praise, see 132–3, 175, 184, 222, 276–7, cf. Ephraem ed. Assemani 3.471.

30 *Thrênos for Crete EEKS* (1939) 348.9: Μὰ τώρα σὰν πύργος ἔπεσε | σὰν φῶς ἀπ᾽ ἄνεμον ἔσβησε... Cf. *Od.*11.556.

31 Cf. *Laog* (1909) 176–201. The theme is also common in the modern laments, as in the following example I collected from Rhodia in 1963: Βάζω, φκιάνω τὸ σπίτι μου ψηλότερ᾽ ἀπὸ τὰ ἄλλα· | βλέπω τὸ Χάρο πού ᾽ρχεται τὸ μαυροκαβαλάρη.

Romaios *KR* 237 points out that Charos may sometimes build his own tower, with young men for the floor, old men as the foundations, and children as the turrets.

32 *ArP* (1946) 69.3: 'Απανωθύρ', χαμέλυνον, καὶ κατωθύρ', ἐλ' ἄνθεν, | καὶ σεῖς, στυλάρα τοῦ σπιτί', ἐλᾶτε καὶ ἁρμοθέστεν, | μὴ ἐβγάλωσι τὸν Ἕλλενον, τὸ νέον παλληκάριν.

33 Mimn. *ALG* 1.40–1.2. See Verrier *VF* 49–55.

34 Cf. A. *Ag*.536, *Supp*.637, *AP* 7.439.

35 See Peek 658.8, 678, 683.5, 878.1–2, 968.1, 1151.11, 1249.5–7, 1551.7–8, 1553. 3–4, *SEG* 8.484, Wilhelm *GEK* ii–iv, *AP* 7.490, 8.182.7.

36 Cf. Peek 942, 1541.2, 1891, 1997, 2005, Samm. 7288.4–5, *MAMA* 1.102. Other parallels are listed by Wilhelm *Byẕ*. (1931) 461. See also Alexiou and Dronke *SM* (1971) 836–7.

37 See Eustath.Makr. *Hysm*.10.381; Anon. *Monodia for Constantinople, NE* (1908) 240.4, 16; Sym.Met. *Martyrium S. Varii*, Migne 115.1156b–c; Greg.Nyss. *in funere Pulcheriae, ibid.* 46.865b–c; Prodromos *Rhod*.6.291–302 (258).

38 Politis 130.1, 135.5, 2; cf. Sa. 122 L–P.

39 Politis 83.12, 209.5; cf. *DA* 181 (Esc.).

40 It does occur in the more popular versions of the Virgin's lament and in the *Epitáphios Thrênos*, see chapter 4 pp. 67–8. In Romanos' *kontákion On the Nativity II*, imagery of spring and harvest pervades his whole conception of the salvation of Adam and Eve, and it is brought to a climax when the Virgin hears of the necessity of the Crucifixion and exclaims to Christ, 'Ὢ βότρυς μου, μὴ ἐκθλίψωσί σε ἄνομοι· | βλαστήσαντός σου μὴ ὄψωμαι τέκνου σφαγήν ed. Grosdidier de Matons 2.108.17, 6–7.

41 See Politis 187, 193, 205, 212, Theros 726, 755. References to Charos with a scythe are frequent in Byzantine and post-Byzantine vernacular poetry, and the scythe or scythe-bearing chariot is commonly portrayed in contemporary illustrations, see the discussion by Zoras of Πένθος θανάτου in *Parn* (1970) 279–313, 420–38.

42 Another variation of this simile is found in Politis 128a 6–9.

43 See A. *Ag*.966–7, *AP* 9.87. Modern extensions of this theme include Politis 187, Theros 726, Pasayanis 62, Giankas 873, *ArP* (1946) 68.2, 4.

44 *Laog* (1911) 266.5, 7–8. See also Romaios *KR* 237–8.

45 Cf. *Il*.11.155–9. Perhaps the same idea underlies the famous but obscure lines on the fallen Achilles, *Od*.24.39–40: σὺ δ' ἐν στροφάλιγγι κονίης | κεῖσο μέγας μεγαλωστί, λελασμένος ἱπποσυνάων.

46 Cf. E. *Hipp*.683–4 (part of a curse), Ar. *Ra*.586–8.

47 Cf. Politis 187.1, 5.

48 Referred to by Eleni Ioannidou in her introduction to the second, as yet unpublished, volume of Papadimitriou, *Martyríes* (vol. 1 Athens, 1964).

49 Cod. Paris. suppl. grec. 680 f. 73v, ed. Moravcsik *SBN* (1931) 48. Cf. *Dialogue between Charon and Man*, written in the form of an alphabetical acrostic, Cod. Roman. Bibl. Nat. gr. 15 (fifteenth century), ed. Moravcsik *ibid.* iii. 35–8: Ἴτα δεντρὸν εὑρίσκομαι κι ἦρτες νὰ μὲ τρυγήσης, | κι ἦρτες μὲ πόθο εἰς ἐμὲ καὶ δὲν πᾶ νὰ μ' ἀφήσης;

50 Guthrie *OGR* 182 rejects Comparetti's view that it is the white poplar that is intended here, and draws attention to Cook's suggestion that the white cypress is an assimilation of the two, *Z* 2.467.

51 See *ArP* (1946) 70.4, where parallels from Mani and Thrace are also cited. In the Romanian lament *Tradafir* (also referred to in chapter 8 n. 59, p. 238), the

dead man receives detailed and elaborate instructions for his journey to the next world, after his soul has departed and his flesh has left his bones: he is to travel on a long road until he comes to a parting of ways... 'Be careful which path you take. Do not turn off to the left, for that's the dark road... Turn off to the right, for that's the bright road...' Further on he will come to a meadow, where he is to pick flowers to ease his heart's pain, and give them to the dead. Going onwards again he will find a red willow tree 'its tops among the stars, its roots in the sea... And under the roots is a cool fountain... The Holy Mother is there, with a glass of clear water, and whoever drinks it, his heart's grief passes; and she gives it to the traveller.'

52 See A. *Ag.*901: ὁδοιπόρῳ διψῶντι πηγαῖον ῥέος, *AP* 5.168: ἡδὺ θέρους διψῶντι χιὼν ποτόν (Thomson *OA* 2.73).

53 See Kyriakidis *EL* 205–6, Boehm *NGT* 14–15, Moravcsik *SBN* (1931) 50–1.

54 *AP* 7.476.1–4, Bion 1.64–6; cf. *Thrênos* by Father Synadenos of Serrai, *NE* (1908) 251.37–8: "Ὢ καὶ νὰ εἶχα δάκρυα ἄπειρα σὰν ποτάμι | νὰ 'κλαιεν ἡ καρδία μου ὥστε ποὺ ν' ἀποκάμη. Modern examples include Pasayanis 55.2–9, Tarsouli 202, Petropoulos 217.

55 The same kind of hyperbole is used with extraordinary power in some of the love songs, where the lover's kiss has the force to transform nature itself, see Politis 126.

56 Sakellarios 2.84, 28.

Bibliography

Abbreviations for reference works, epigraphical publications and periodicals are listed at the end of the bibliography. All references in the bibliography are to page numbers, except in the case of some collections of folk songs, where (no.) after the item indicates that references are to numbered texts and not to pages.

Abbott, G. F. *Macedonian Folklore*, Cambridge, 1903
Abel, E. *Orphica*, Leipzig, 1885
Akoglou, X. Λαογραφικὰ Κοτυώρων, Athens, 1939
Alexiou, C. 'Survivals of Tribal Custom in Ownership and Division of Property in Modern Greece', 73–81. *Antiquitas Graeco-Romana ac Tempora Nostra*, Prague, 1968
Alexiou, M. and Dronke, P. 'The Lament of Jephtha's Daughter: Themes, Traditions, Originality', *SM* 12.2 (1971) 819–63
Alexiou, S. "'Η Μινωϊκὴ θεὰ μεθ' ὑψωμένων χειρῶν", *KCh* 12 (1958) 179–299
Allen, W. S. *Vox Graeca: a guide to the pronunciation of classical Greek*, Cambridge, 1968
Amarioti, M. "'Η 'Περισταμένη'", *EEKS* 2 (1939) 313–23
Ambrosch, J. A. *De Charonte Etrusco*, Bratislava, 1837
Anderson, W. D. 'Notes on the Simile in Homer and his Successors', *CJ* 53 (1957) 81–7
Antoniadis, S. *Place de la liturgie dans la tradition des lettres grecques*, Leiden, 1939
Apostolakis, I. Τὰ δημοτικὰ τραγούδια, Athens, 1929
Τὰ τραγούδια μας, Athens, 1934
Τὸ Κλέφτικο τραγούδι, Athens, 1950
Aravantinos, P. (Aravantinos), Συλλογὴ δημοτικῶν ᾀσμάτων τῆς 'Ηπείρου, Athens, 1880
Argenti, P. P. and Rose, H. J. *Folklore of Chios*, Cambridge, 1949
Armstrong, H. H. *Autobiographical Elements in Latin Inscriptions*, Baltimore, 1910
Asheri, D. 'Laws of Inheritance, Distribution of Land and Political Constitutions in Ancient Greece', *Hist* 12 (1963) 1–21
Assemani, J. S. *S. Ephraemi Opera Omnia*, vol. 3, Rome, 1732–46
Atallah, W. 'Adonis dans la littérature et l'art grecs', *Études et Commentaires* 62, Paris, 1966
Athanasiadis, E. "'Εθιμα Σάντας", *ArP* 11 (1941) 112–13

Bibliography

Aubry, P. *Le rythme tonique dans la poésie liturgique*, Paris, 1903
Bachmann, L. *Anecdota Graeca*, Leipzig, 1829
Bachtin, N. *Introduction to the Study of Modern Greek*, Cambridge, 1935
Bartók, B. *Hungarian Folk Music*, English edition, London, 1931
Bartók, B. and Kodály, Z. (ed.), 'Laments', *Corpus Musicae Popularis Hungaricae*, Budapest, 1966
Baud-Bovy, S. (Baud-Bovy), *Chansons du Dodécanèse*, 2 vols., Athens, 1935
'Sur le "Χελιδόνισμα"', *ByzMet* 1 (1946) 23–33
'Sur un "Sacrifice d'Abraham" de Romanos', *Byz* 13 (1938) 321–34
Études sur la chanson cleftique, Athens, 1958
Baumstark, A. *Liturgie comparée*, Prieuré d'Amay, 1939
Beck, H. G. *Kirche und theologische Literatur im byzantinischen Reich*, Munich, 1959
Geschichte der byzantinischen Volksliteratur, Munich, 1971
Bees, N. Νεοελληνικὰ δημοτικὰ ἄσματα ἐκ χειρογραφικῶν κωδίκων, Athens, 1911
'Vulgärgriechische Verse aus einem Berliner Palimpsest über das Leben im Fremde', *BNJ* 13 (1937) 57–66
Bekker, I. *Anecdota Graeca*, Berlin, 1814; repr. Graz, 1965
Bergson, L. *Der griechische Alexanderroman, Rezension B*, Acta Universitatis Stockholmensis, Studia Graeca Stockholmensia III, Uppsala, 1965
Blum, R. and Blum, E. *The Dangerous Hour*, London, 1971
Blume, C. *Liturgische Prosen des Übergangsstiles*, Leipzig, 1915
Boardman, J. 'Painted Funerary Plaques and Some Remarks on Prothesis', *JRS* 50 (1955) 51–66
Boardman, J. and Kurtz, D. *See* Kurtz, D. and Boardman, J.
Boehm, F. *Die neugriechische Totenklage*, Berlin, 1947
Bonner, C. *The Homily on the Passion by Melito*, Studies and Documents 12, Baltimore, 1940
Bouboulidis, F. K. Κρητικὴ λογοτεχνία. Βασικὴ Βιβλιοθήκη 7, Athens, 1955
Bouvier, B. Δημοτικὰ τραγούδια ἀπὸ χειρόγραφο τῆς Μονῆς τῶν Ἰβήρων, Athens, 1960
Bouvy, E. *Poètes et Mélodes*, Nîmes, 1880
Bowra, C. M. *Greek Lyric Poetry*, Oxford, 1961
Early Greek Elegists, London, 1938
Bradbrook, M. C. *The Growth and Structure of Elizabethan Comedy*, London, 1963
Brambs, J. G. (ed.), *Christus Patiens*, Leipzig, 1895
Brand, J. *Popular Antiquities*, London, 1849
Brown, P. *The World of Late Antiquity*, London, 1971
Browning, R. *Greece, Ancient and Medieval*. Inaugural lecture, London 1967
Medieval and Modern Greek, London, 1969
Bruck, E. F. *Totenteil und Seelgerät im griechischen Recht*, Munich, 1926
Buck, C. D. *The Greek Dialects*, Chicago, 1955
Bultmann, R. 'Zur Geschichte der Lichtsymbolik im Altertum', *Phil* 97 (1948) 1–36
Buresch, C. 'Die griechischen Trostbeschlüsse', *RM* 49 (1894) 424
Buschor, E. *Grab eines attischen Mädchens*, Munich, 1941
Cagnat, R. 'Sur les manuels des graveurs d'inscriptions', *RP* 13 (1889) 51–65
Cairns, F. *Generic Composition in Greek and Roman Poetry*, Edinburgh, 1972
Calder, W. M. 'The Dithyramb – an Anatolian Dirge', *CR* 36 (1922) 11–14
Campbell, D. A. 'Flutes and Elegiac Couplets', *JHS* 84 (1964) 63–8
Campbell, J. K. *Honour, Family and Patronage: A Study of Institutions and Moral Values in a Greek Mountain Community*, Oxford, 1964
Cantarella, R. (Cantarella), *Poeti Bizantini*, vol. 1, *Testi*, Milan, 1948

Bibliography

Chadwick, H. M. *The Growth of Literature*, 3 vols., Cambridge, 1925–39
Chambers, E. K. *The Medieval Stage*, Oxford, 1903
Chambers, G. B. *Folksong and Plainsong*, London, 1956
Chappell, W. *Popular Music of the Olden Time*, New York, 1893; repr. 1965
Chevalier, C. 'Le Mariologue de Romanos', *RSR* 28 (1938) 46–9
Child, F. J. *English and Scottish Popular Ballads*, 5 vols., New York, 1882–98; repr. 1957
Childe, V. G. 'Directional Changes in Funerary Practices during 50,000 Years', *Man* 45 (1945) 13–19
Christ, W. von, *Die Parakataloge im griechischen und römischen Drama*, Munich, 1875
Christ, W. von and Paranikas, M. K. *Anthologia Graeca carminum Christianorum*, Leipzig, 1871
Cook, A. B. *Zeus*, 3 vols., Cambridge, 1914–40
Cottas, V. *Le théâtre à Byzance*, Paris, 1931
"Περὶ τῆς εἰκονογραφήσεως τοῦ Ἐπιταφίου", *BNJ* 13 (1937)
Croon, J. H. *The Herdsman of the Dead*, Utrecht, 1952
'The Mask of the Underworld Demon', *JHS* 75 (1955) 129–40
Danckert, W. 'Mythen vom Ursprung der Musik', *Antaios* 7 (1965–6) 365–79
Dawkins, R. M. 'The Process of Tradition in Greece', *ABSA* 37 (1940) 48
Forty-five Stories from the Dodecanese, Cambridge, 1950
'Soul and Body in the Folklore of Modern Greece', *FL* 53 (1942) 131–47
Deissman, A. *Licht vom Osten*, Tübingen, 1909
Deville, G. *De popularibus cantilenis apud recentiores Graecos*, Paris, 1886
Diels, H. (ed.), *Die Fragmente der Vorsokratiker*, Berlin, 1912
Dieterich, A. *Nekyia*, Leipzig, 1893
Mutter Erde, Leipzig/Berlin, 1905
Dieterich, K. *Geschichte der byzantinischen und neugriechischen Literatur*, Leipzig, 1902
Dietrich, B. C. *Death, Fate and the Gods*, London, 1965
Doering, A. *De tragoedia Christiana, quae inscribitur* ΧΡΙΣΤΟΣ ΠΑΣΧΩΝ, Barmen, 1864
Dölger, F. J. *Die byzantinische Dichtung in der Reinsprache*, Berlin, 1948
Dreves, G. M. *Ein Jahrtausend lateinischer Hymnendichtung*, Leipzig, 1909
Dronke, P. 'The Beginnings of the Sequence', *BGDSL* 87 (1965) 43–69
Medieval Latin and the Rise of the European Love-Lyric, 2 vols., 2 ed. Oxford, 1968
Poetic Individuality in the Middle Ages, Oxford, 1970
Dronke, P. and Alexiou, M. *See* Alexiou, M. and Dronke, P.
Duval, R. *La littérature syriaque*, Paris, 1903
Edmonds, J. M. (ed.), *Lyra Graeca*, vol. 1. Loeb class. lib., London/New York, 1922–7
(ed.), *Fragments of Attic Comedy*, 3 vols., Leiden, 1957
Eisler, R. *Orphisch-Dionysische Mysteriengedanken in der christlichen Antike*. Vorträge der Bibl. Warburg 1922–3 III. Leipzig/Berlin, 1925
Farnell, L. R. *Cults of the Greek States*, 5 vols., Oxford, 1896–1909
Greek Hero Cults, Oxford, 1921
Fauriel, C. (Fauriel), *Chants populaires de la Grèce moderne*, 2 vols., Paris, 1824
Felouki, E. "Νεκρικὰ ἔθιμα ἀπὸ τὴν Ἀλεξανδρούπολη", *Laog* 10 (1929) 459–63
Festugière, A. M. J. *Personal Religion among the Greeks*, California, 1954
Finlay, G. *History of Greece*, 7 vols., Oxford, 1877

Bibliography

Fischer, W. *Das Grablied des Seikelos*, Amman Festgabe 1.153–65
Follieri, E. *Initia hymnorum Ecclesiae Graecae*, 5 vols., Vatican City, 1960–6
Frazer, J. G. *Totemism and Exogamy*, London, 1910
    The Golden Bough. Taboo and the Perils of the Soul. The Dying God. Adonis,
    Attis and Osiris. London 1923–7
Freistedt, E. 'Altchristliche Totengedächtnistage', *LQF* 24 (1928)
French, A. 'The Economic Background to Solon's Reforms', *CQ* 6 (1956) 11–25
    'Land Tenure and the Solon Problem', *Hist* 12 (1963) 242–7
Frisk, H. *Griechisches etymologisches Wörterbuch*, Heidelberg, 1954–70
Funk, A. *Apostolische Konstitutionen*, Tübingen, 1893
Ganszyniec, R. 'Zwei magische Hymnen aus florentiner Papyri', *BNJ* 3 (1922) 120
Gedeon, M. Βυζαντινὸν Ἑορτολόγιον, Constantinople, 1899
Georgiadis, G. "Δημοτικὰ τραγούδια Μεσοχωρίου Καρπάθου", *DAr* 2 (1956) 278–90
Georgiadis, T. *Greek Music, Verse and Dance*, New York, 1956
Giankas, A. (Giankas), Ἠπειρώτικα Δημοτικὰ Τραγούδια (no.), Athens, n.d.
Gierden, K. *Das altfranzösische Alexiuslied der Handschrift L. Eine Interpretation*
    unter der Gesichtspunkt von Trauer und Freude. Untersuchungen zur Romanischen
    Philologie, 1, Meisenheim am Glan, 1967
Gillman, I. 'Conflict of Religions after Constantine', *JRS* 111 (1964) 80–4
Giophylli, F. "Θιακὰ μοιρολόγια", *IME* (1926) 257–73
    Ἡ γλώσσα τῆς Ἰθάκης, Athens, 1950
Glotz, G. *La solidarité de la famille en Grèce*, Paris, 1904
Goossens, R. 'Grec ancien et grec moderne', *ByzMet* 1 (1946) 135–65
Gow, A. S. F. *Bucolici Graeci*, Oxford, 1952
Grant, F. C. *The Hellenistic Religions, Age of Syncretism*, New York, 1953
Greene, W. C. *Moira*, Cambridge, Mass., 1944
Grégoire, H. *Les sources historiques et littéraires de Digénis Akritas.* Actes du iiie
    Congrès Int. d'études byzantines. Athens, 1932
    'Nouvelles chansons épiques des ixe et xe siècles', *Byz* 14 (1939) 235
Gregorovius, F. *Geschichte der Stadt Athen im Mittelalter*, Stuttgart, 1889
Griessmair, E. *Das Motiv der Mors Immatura in den griechischen metrischen Grab-*
    inschriften, Innsbruck, 1966
Grondijs, L. H. *L'iconographie byzantine du Crucifié mort sur la croix*, Brussels, 1941
Grosdidier de Matons, J. *Romanos le Mélode*, 4 vols., Sources Chrétiennes nos. 99,
    110, 114, 128, Paris, 1964–7
Gulian, C. I. *Sensul Vieţii in Folclorul Romînesc*, Bucarest, 1957
Guthrie, W. K. C. *Orpheus and Greek Religion*, London, 1952
    Tradition and Personal Achievement in Classical Antiquity, London, 1960
Hahn, J. von, *Albanesische Studien*, Jena, 1854
Haldane, J. A. 'Musical Instruments in Greek Worship', *GR* 13 (1966) 98–107
Hammer, S. *Neograeca*, Poznan, 1920
Harrison, J. E. *The Religion of Ancient Greece*, London, 1905
    Prolegomena to the Study of Greek Religion, Cambridge, 1922
    Themis, Cambridge, 1927
Harvey, A. E. 'The Classification of Greek Lyric Poetry', *CQ* 5 (1955) 157–74
Hasiotis, G. H. Συλλογὴ τῶν κατὰ τὴν Ἤπειρον δημοτικῶν ᾀσμάτων, Athens, 1866
Hatzidakis, G. N. *Einleitung in die neugriechische Grammatik*, Leipzig, 1892
    Μεσαιωνικὰ καὶ νέα ἑλληνικά, 2 vols., Athens, 1905
    'Zur neugriechischen Wortlehre', *Gl* 2 (1909–10) 287–99
Hausmann, U. *Griechische Weihreliefs*, Berlin, 1960

Bibliography

Heinische, P. *Die Totenklage im alten Testament*, Biblische Zeitfragen 13 (1932), Münster

Heitman, K. 'Orpheus im Mittelalter', *AKG* 45 (1963) 253–94

Hercher, R. *Erotici scriptores Graeci*, vol. 2, Teubner ed., Leipzig, 1858

Herzfeld, M. F. '"The Siege of Rhodes". A Cretan folksong in its cultural context' *KCh* 25 (1973) *forthcoming*

Hesseling, D. C. *Charos*, Leiden/Leipzig, 1897

'Charos rediens', *BZ* 30 (1929–30) 186–91

Høeg, C. 'Les rapports de la musique chrétienne et de la musique de l'antiquité classique', *Byẓ* 25 (1955) 383–412

Iakovidis, S. E. 'A Mycenaean Mourning Custom', *AJA* 70 (1966) 43–50

Ioannidou, E. Ἡράκλειτος: γλῶσσα καὶ σκέψη, Athens, 1962

Jakoby, F. 'ΓΕΝΕΣΙΑ: A Forgotten Festival of the Dead', *CQ* 38 (1944) 65–75

James, M. R. *Apocrypha Anecdota*, Texts and Studies 5 (1897), Cambridge

Jegerlehner, J. 'Beiträge zur Verwaltungsgeschichte Kandias im 14. Jahrhundert' *BZ* 13 (1904) 435–79

Jeremias, A. *Handbuch der altorientalischen Geisteskultur*, Berlin/Leipzig, 1929

Jevons, F. B. 'Greek Burial Laws', *CR* 9 (1895) 247–50

Joannidu, M. *Untersuchungen zur Form der neugriechischen Klagelieder*, Munich, 1938

"Ὁ Χάρος καὶ τ' ἀδέλφια του", *ELA* 3–4 (1941–2) 38–59

Kakouri, K. "Λαϊκὰ δρώμενα Εὐετερίας", *PAA* (1952) 223–5

'*Dromena*' champêtres. Le '*Leidinos*', Athens, 1956

Διονυσιακά, Athens, 1963

Kakridis, I. T. 'Caeneus', *CR* 61 (1947) 77–80

Kallinikos, K. I. "Ἡ φροντὶς τῶν νεκρῶν ἐν τῷ χριστιανισμῷ", *EK* 4 (1914) 200

Kalonaros, P. P. Βασίλειος Διγενὴς Ἀκρίτας, 2 vols., Athens, 1941

Kanellakis, K. N. (Kanellakis), Χιακὰ Ἀνάλεκτα, Athens, 1890

Karmiris, I. N. "Περὶ τῆς καθόδου τοῦ Χριστοῦ εἰς τὸν Ἅδην", *BNJ* 14 (1937–8) 274

Karouzos, S. "Ἐπιτύμβια στήλη τίτθης στὸ Ἐθνικὸ Μουσεῖο", *Hell* 15 (1915) 312

Kern, O. *Orphicorum fragmenta*, Berlin, 1922

Kirpichnikov, A. "Πόθεν ληπτέον τὸ ὑλικὸν τῆς ἱστορίας τῆς βυζαντινῆς φιλολογίας", *DIEE* 3 (1889) 536–46

'Reimprosa im 5. Jahrhundert', *BZ* 1 (1892) 527–30

Knös B. *L'histoire de la littérature néo-grécque*, Acta Universitatis Upsaliensis, Studia Graeca Upsaliensia 1, Uppsala, 1962.

Korais, A. *Atakta*, Paris, 1828–35

Kordatos, I. Ἱστορία τῆς νεοελληνικῆς λογοτεχνίας, 2 vols. Athens, 1962

Kosmas, N. B. "Τὰ μοιρολόγια τῶν Πραμαντῶν", *Laog* 19 (1960) 366–78

Koukoules, F. Βυζαντινῶν βίος καὶ πολιτισμός, 6 vols., Athens, 1948–55

"Βυζαντινῶν νεκρικὰ ἔθιμα", *EEBS* 16 (1940) 3–80

"Λαογραφικαὶ εἰδήσεις παρὰ τῷ Εὐσταθίῳ", *EEBS* 1 (1924) 5–40

Koulourioti, M. Οἱ πρῶτες μακρυνὲς ρίζες τῆς νεοελληνικῆς λογοτεχνίας, Athens, 1952

Kournoutos, G. Λόγιοι τῆς Τουρκοκρατίας, 1. Βασικὴ Βιβλιοθήκη 4, Athens, 1955

Kretschmer, P. 'Mythische Namen. Lityerses und Hylas', *Gl* 14 (1925) 33–6

Kriaras, E. Ἀνακάλημα τῆς Κωνσταντινόπολης, Thessaloniki, 1956

Kriaris, A. Κρητικὰ δημοτικὰ τραγούδια. Πλήρης συλλογή, 3 ed. Athens, 1969

Krishna Iyer, L. A. *The Travancore Tribes and Castes*, Trivandrum, 1937

Krumbacher, K. *Geschichte der byzantinischen Litteratur*, 2 ed. Munich, 1897

'Ein dialogischer Threnos auf den Fall von Konstantinopel', *SBAW* (1901) 329–62

Kühner, R. *Ausführliche Grammatik der griechischen Sprache*, Hanover, 1890–1904

Bibliography

Kurtz, D. and Boardman, J. *Greek Burial Customs*, London, 1971

Kyriakidis, S. P. Αἱ γυναῖκες εἰς τὴν λαογραφίαν, Athens, 1921

Ἑλληνικὴ λαογραφία, Athens, 1922

Αἱ ἱστορικαὶ ἀρχαὶ τῆς δημώδους νεοελληνικῆς ποιήσεως, Thessaloniki, 1934

Lambrechts, P. 'La résurrection d'Adonis', *AIPhO* 13 (1953) 207–40

Lambros, S. Μιχαὴλ 'Ακομινάτου τοῦ Χωνιάτου τὰ σωζόμενα, 2 vols., Athens, 1879–80;
repr. Groningen 1968

Collection de romans grecs, Paris, 1880

"Μονῳδίαι καὶ θρῆνοι ἐπὶ τῇ ἁλώσει τῆς Κωνσταντινουπόλεως", *NE* 5 (1908) 190–271

"Δεκατρία δημώδη ᾄσματα μετὰ μουσικῶν σημείων", *NE* 11 (1914) 423–32

Catalogue of the Greek Manuscripts on Mount Athos, Cambridge, 1895

Lattimore, R. *Themes in Greek and Latin Epitaphs*, Illinois, 1962

Laurent, V. 'Amulettes byzantines et formulaires magiques', *BZ* 36 (1936) 300–15

Lawson, J. C. *Modern Greek Folklore and Ancient Greek Religion*, Cambridge, 1909;
repr. New York, 1964

Le Bas, P. (ed.), 'De Hysmines et Hysminiae amoribus' in *Erotici Scriptores*,
G. A. Hirschig, Paris, 1856

Legrand, E. *Recueil de chansons populaires grecques*, Paris, 1874

Bibliothèque grecque vulgaire, Paris, 1881–1913

Collection de monuments pour servir à l'étude de la langue néo-hellénique, first series,
19 vols., Paris, 1869–72

'Description des îles de l'Archipélago', Paris, 1897

Lekatsas, P. Ἡ ψυχή, ἡ ἰδέα τῆς ψυχῆς καὶ τῆς ἀθανασίας της καὶ τὰ ἔθιμα τοῦ θανάτου,
Athens, 1957

Διόνυσος. Καταγωγὴ καὶ ἐξέλιξη τῆς Διονυσιακῆς θρησκείας, Athens, 1971

Lelekos, M. Δημοτικὴ ἀνθολογία, Athens, 1868

Leumann, M. *Homerische Wörter*, Basel, 1950

Leutsch, E. L. and Schneidewin, F. G. *Corpus Paroemiographorum Graecorum*, 2 vols.,
Göttingen, 1839–51; repr. Hildesheim, 1958–61

Lianidis, S. "Νεκρικὰ καὶ ταφικὰ στὴ Σάντα τοῦ Πόντου", *ArP* 26 (1964) 159–76

Lier, B. 'Topica carminum sepulcralium Latinorum', *Phil* 62 (1903) 445–77

Lioudaki, M. (Lioudaki), "Ἡ τελευτὴ στὴν Κρήτη", *EEKS* 2 (1939) 403–27

Λαογραφικὰ Κρήτης. Α' Μαντινάδες, Athens, 1936

Lloyd, A. L. *Folk Song in England*, London, 1967

Lord, A. B. *The Singer of Tales*, Cambridge, Mass., 1960

Loukatos, D. S. "Λαογραφικαὶ περὶ τελευτῆς εἰδήσεις παρὰ 'Ιωάννῃ Χρυσοστόμῳ", *ELA* 2
(1940) 30–118

Κεφαλλονίτικα γνωμικά, Athens, 1952

"'Απὸ τὰ λαογραφικὰ τοῦ ἡλίου: παροιμίες", *SE* 1.4 (1960)

"Ἡ σημασία τοῦ ἡλίου στὴν ἑλληνικὴ ζωή", *SE* 2 (1961)

Lueddeckens, E. *Untersuchungen über religiösen Gehalt, Sprache und Form des
ägyptischen Totenklage*, Berlin, 1943

Maas, P. 'Echoverse in byzantinischen Epitaphien', *BZ* 13 (1904) 161

'Die Chronologie der Hymnen des Romanos', *BZ* 15 (1906) 1–44

'Das Kontakion', *BZ* 19 (1910) 285–306

Greek Metre, English ed., Oxford, 1962

Maas, P. and Trypanis, C. A. (ed.), *S. Romani Melodi Cantica. Cantica Genuina*,
Oxford, 1963

(ed.), *S. Romani Melodi Cantica. Cantica Dubia*, Berlin, 1970

MacDowell, D. M. *Athenian Homicide Law*, Manchester, 1963

Bibliography

McPherson, F. 'Historical Notes on Certain Modern Greek Folksongs', *JHS* 10 (1889) 86–9

Mahr, C. A. *The Cyprus Passion Play Cyclus*, Indiana, 1947

Mango, C. 'Byzantinism and Romantic Philhellenism', *JWCI* 28 (1965) 29–43

Manousakas, M. I. Ἑλληνικὰ ποιήματα γιὰ τὴ σταύρωση τοῦ Χριστοῦ, *Mélanges Merlier* 2 (1956) 49–74

Marshall, F. H. *Three Cretan Plays*, London, 1929

Martino, E. *Morte e pianto rituale nel mondo antico*, Turin, 1958

Mavrogordato, J. 'Modern Greek Folk-Songs of the Dead', *JHS* 75 (1955) 42–53 *Digenes Akrites*, Oxford, 1956

Mayer, A. *Moira in griechischen Inschriften*, Giessen, 1927

Mayser, E. *Grammatik der griechischen Papyri aus der Ptolemäerzeit*, vol. 1, Leipzig, 1906

Megas, G. "Ὁ λεγόμενος κοινὸς βαλκανικὸς πολιτισμός", *ED* 3 (1950) 747–60 Καλλιμάχου καὶ Χρυσορρόης ὑπόθεσις. *Mélanges Merlier* 1 (1952) "Οἱ Τραπεζουντιακοὶ θρῆνοι ἐπὶ τῇ ἁλώσει τῆς Κωνσταντινουπόλεως", *ELA* 8 (1953–4) 12–23

Megas, G. (ed.), Ἡ Θυσία τοῦ Ἀβραάμ, Athens, 1954 Ἑλληνικαὶ Ἑορταί, Athens, 1956

Meillet, A. *Aperçu d'une histoire de la langue grecque*, 4 ed. Paris, 1935

Melachrinos, A. Δημοτικὰ τραγούδια, Athens, 1946

Mercati, S. I. S. *Ephraem Syri Opera*, vol. 1, Rome, 1915

Merkelbach, R. 'Βουκολισταί. Der Wettgesang der Hirten', *RM* 99 (1956) 97–133

Merkelbach, R. and West, M. L. (ed.), *Fragmenta Hesiodea*, Oxford, 1967

Merlier, M. Τραγούδια τῆς Ρούμελης, Athens, 1931 *Études de musique byzantine*, Paris, 1935

Meyer, W. *Anfang und Ursprung der lateinischen-griechischen rhythmischen Dichtung*, Munich, 1866

Michaelidis-Nouaros, M. (Michaelidis-Nouaros), Δημοτικὰ τραγούδια Καρπάθου, Athens, 1928

Mingana, A. 'Christian Documents in Syriac, Arabic and Garshūni', *WSt* 2 (1928) 163 ff.

Mirambel, A. *Études de quelques textes maniotes*, Paris, 1929

Mitsakis, K. *The Language of Romanos the Melodist*, Munich, 1967

Mone, F. H. *Lateinische Hymnen*, Freiburg, 1854

Moravcsik, G. 'Il Caronte bizantino', *SBN* 3 (1931) 45–68

Morgan, G. 'Cretan Poetry: Sources and Inspiration', *KCh* 14 (1960)

Morgan, L. H. *Ancient Society*, 2 ed. Chicago, 1910

Mossé, C. 'Classes sociales et régionalisme à Athènes au début du vie siècle', *AC* 33 (1904) 401–3

Muşlea, J. 'La mort-mariage, une particularité du folklore balkanique', *Mélanges de l'école roumaine en France*, 3–32, Paris, 1925

Muth, R. 'Hymenaios und Epithalamium', *WS* 67 (1954) 5–45

Mylonas, G. E. 'Homeric and Mycenaean Burial Custom', *AJA* 52 (1948) 56–81

Nehring, A. *Seele und Seelenkult bei Griechen, Italikern und Germanen*, Diss. Breslau, 1917

Nilsson, M. P. 'Der Ursprung der Tragödie', *Opuscula Selecta* 1.61–110, Lund, 1951; *NJK* 27 (1911) 609–96 'Immortality of the Soul in Greek Religion', *OS* 3.40–55, Lund, 1960 *Homer and Mycenae*, London, 1933

Bibliography

Nilsson, M. P. *Greek Popular Religion*, New York, 1940
 Griechische Feste von religiöser Bedeutung, Leipzig, 1906.
Nock, A. D. *Hellenistic Mysteries and Christian Sacraments*, London, 1964
Noiret, H. *Lettres inédites de Michel Apostolis*, Paris, 1889
Norden, E. A. *Die antike Kunstprosa*, 2 vols., Leipzig, 1898
 Agnostos Theos, Leipzig/Berlin, 1923
Page, D. L. 'Elegiacs in Euripides' *Andromache'*, *Greek Poetry and Life* 206–30, Oxford, 1936
 (ed.), *Poetae Melici Graeci*, Oxford, 1962
Pandelakis, E. G. "Αἱ ἀρχαὶ τῆς ἐκκλησιαστικῆς ποιήσεως", *Theol* 16 (1938) 5–31
Papadopoulos, D. "Ἔθιμα καὶ δοξασίαι περὶ τοὺς νεκροὺς τοῦ χωρίου Σταυρίν", *ArP* 16 (1951) 179–90
Papadopoulos-Kerameus, A. Ἀνάλεκτα Ἱεροσολυμιτικῆς Σταχυολογίας, 5 vols., Petrograd, 1891–8
 "Θρῆνος τῆς Κωνσταντινουπόλεως", *BZ* 12 (1903) 267–72
 "'Ανάλωσις 'Αθήνας", *BZ* 12 (1903) 273–5
Parlangeli, O. 'Il "Canto della Passione" presso i Greci del Salento', *EEBS* 23 (1953) 491–507
Parry, M. *Les formules et la métrique d'Homère*, Paris, 1928
Pasayanis, K. A. (Pasayanis), Μανιάτικα μοιρολόγια καὶ τραγούδια (no.), Athens, 1928
Passow, A. (Passow) *Popularia carmina Graeciae recentioris* (no.), Leipzig, 1860
Paton, W. R. 'Sacrifices to the Dead', *FL* 5 (1894) 275–8
Patriarcheas, B. "Λαϊκὴ ποίησις καὶ ἱστορία: ὁ ἔμμετρος λόγος ἐν Μάνῃ καὶ τὰ μοιρολόγια", *NK* 25 (1939–40) 469–78
 "Ὁ θρῆνος τοῦ νεκροῦ", *NK* 25 (1939–40) 1040–9
Pavolini, P. E. *Lamenti funebri greci*, Naples, 1916
Peek, W. *Attische Grabinschriften*, Berlin, 1954
 Griechische Grabgedichte, Berlin, 1960
Peppmüller, R. H. *Über die Composition der Klagelieder im vierundzwanzigsten Buch der Ilias*, Halle, 1872
Pernot, H. *Phonétique des parlers de Chio*, Paris, 1907
 Études de littérature grecque moderne, Paris, 1916
 D'Homère à nos jours, Paris, 1921
 Chansons populaires grecques des xve et xvie siècles, Paris, 1931
Petrakakos, D. *Die Toten im Recht*, Leipzig, 1905
Petropoulos, D. A. "Αἱ παρομοιώσεις εἰς τὰ δημοτικὰ ἄσματα καὶ παρ' Ὁμήρῳ", *Laog* 19 (1960) 353–87
 (Petropoulos), Ἑλληνικὰ δημοτικὰ τραγούδια, 2. Βασικὴ Βιβλιοθήκη 47, Athens, 1959
Petrounias, B. (Petrounias), Μανιάτικα μοιρολόγια (no.), Athens, 1934
Pfeiffer, R. (ed.), *Callimachi fragmenta*, Bonn, 1921
Picard, C. 'Le repas nuptial chez Hadès', *RHR* 34 (1947–8) 113–19
Pitra, J. B. (ed.), *Analecta Sacra*, Paris, 1876–; repr. 1966
Politis, N. G. (Politis), Ἐκλογαὶ ἀπὸ τὰ τραγούδια τοῦ ἑλληνικοῦ λαοῦ (no.), Athens, 1914; repr. 1966
 Μελέτη ἐπὶ τοῦ βίου τῶν νεωτέρων Ἑλλήνων, Athens, 1871
 "Δημώδεις κοσμογενικοὶ μῦθοι", *DIEE* 4 (1892) 579–625
 'On the Breaking of Vessels as a Funeral Rite in Modern Greece', *JAI* 23 (1894) 28–41

Bibliography

Μελέται περὶ τοῦ βίου καὶ τῆς γλώσσης τοῦ ἑλληνικοῦ λαοῦ,
  I. Παροιμίαι, 4 vols., Athens, 1899–1902
  II. Παραδόσεις, 2 vols., Athens, 1904
"'Ακριτικὰ ᾄσματα. Ὁ θάνατος τοῦ Διγενῆ", *Laog* 1 (1909) 169–275
"Ὁ γάμος παρὰ τοῖς νεωτέροις Ἕλλησιν", Λαογραφικὰ Σύμμεικτα 3.232–322, Athens, 1931
"Τὰ κατὰ τὴν τελευτήν", *ibid.* 323–65
Pouqueville, F. C. H. L. *Voyage dans la Grèce*, Paris, 1820
Powell, J. U. *Collectanea Alexandrina*, Oxford, 1925
Psachos, K. A. (Psachos), Δημώδη ᾄσματα Γορτυνίας (no.), Athens, 1923
Quasten, J. 'Musik und Gesang in den Kulten der heidnischen Antike und christlichen Frühzeit', *LQF* (1930), Münster
Rahner, H. *Greek Myths and Christian Mystery*, English ed., London, 1963
Rallis, G. A. and Potlis, M. (Rallis–Potlis) Σύνταγμα τῶν θείων καὶ ἱερῶν κανόνων, 6 vols., Athens, 1852–9
Ramsay, W. M. *Cities and Bishoprics of Phrygia*, Oxford, 1895–7
Reiner, E. *Die rituelle Totenklage der Griechen*, Tübingen, 1938
Richmond, I. A. *Archaeology and Afterlife in Pagan and Christian Imagery*, London, 1950
Richmond, V. B. *Laments for the Dead in Medieval Narrative*, Pittsburgh, 1966
Riezler, H. 'Die homerische Gleichnisse und die Philosophie', *Ant* 12 (1936) 253–71
Robert, L. Collection Froehner 1, *Inscriptions grecques*, Paris, 1936
Rohde, E. *Psyche: the cult of souls and belief in immortality among the Greeks*, Freiburg, 1898; English ed. London, 1925
Romaios, K. "Τὸ μοιρολόγι τῆς Παναγίας", *ArP* 19 (1954) 188–225
  Κοντὰ στὶς ρίζες, Athens, 1959
"Ὁ Ξάντινον ὁ͵παντολαλεμένο", *ArP* 27 (1965) 150–206
Runciman, S. *The Fall of Constantinople*, Cambridge, 1965
Rush, A. C. *Death and Burial in Christian Antiquity*, Washington, D.C., 1941
Sakellaridis, K. O. (Sakellaridis), Τὸ Νισυρικὸ δημοτικὸ τραγούδι (no.), Athens, 1965
Sakellarios, A. (Sakellarios), Τὰ Κυπριακά, 2 vols., Athens, 1890–1
Sale, W. 'Callisto and the Virginity of Artemis', *RM* 108 (1965) 11–35
Salonius, A. H. 'Zur Sprache der griechischen Papyrusbriefe', *SSF* 2.3 (1923)
Samter, E. *Geburt, Hochzeit und Tod*, Leipzig, 1911
Sartori, P. *Die Speisung der Toten*, Progr. Dortmund, 1903
Sathas, K. Μεσαιωνικὴ βιβλιοθήκη, 7 vols., Venice, 1872–94
  Ἑλληνικὰ ἀνέκδοτα, Athens, 1867
Schiro, G. 'Visita a Scutari di Mich. Apostolio nel 1467', *ZBa* 2 (1963–4) 145–60
Schmid, W. *Geschichte der griechischen Literatur*, Munich, 1929
Schmidt, B. *Das Volksleben der Neugriechen*, Leipzig, 1871
  Griechische Märchen, Sagen und Volkslieder, Leipzig, 1877
'Totengebräuche und Gräberkultus im heutigen Griechenland', *ARW* 24 (1926) 281–5, 25 (1927) 52
Schmitt, J. 'Myrolog oder Moirolog?', *IGF* 12 (1901) 6–12
  "Ποίημα ἀνέκδοτο τοῦ Μαρίνου Φαλιέρη", *DIEE* 4 (1892) 291–308
Schwyzer, E. *Ego Eimi: die religionsgeschichtliche Herkunft und theologische Bedeutung der johanneischen Bildreden*, Göttingen, 1939
Seebohm, H. E. *The Structure of Greek Tribal Society*, London, 1895
Seyrig, H. 'Scène d'offrande funèbre sur un lécythe blanc', *Mélanges Merlier* 2 (1956) 351–3

Bibliography

Shepard, L. *The Broadside Ballad*, London, 1962

Smyth, H. W. *Greek Melic Poets*, London, 1906

Sokolowski, F. *Lois sacrées de l'Asie mineure*, Paris, 1955

Solomos, A. Ὁ ἅγιος Βάκχος, Athens, 1964

Soteriou, M. "Χρυσοκέντητον ἐπιγονάτιον μετὰ παραστάσεως τῆς εἰς Ἄδην καθόδου", *BNJ* 11 (1934–5) 284–96

Soyter, G. *Byzantinische Dichtung*, Athens, 1938
'Das volkstümliche Distichon bei den Neugriechen', *Laog* 8 (1921) 379–426

Spanakis, S. G. "Ἡ διαθήκη τοῦ Ἀντρέα Κορνάρου (1611)", *KCh* 9 (1955) 379–478

Spandonidi, E. (Spandonidi), Τραγούδια τῆς Ἀγόριανης (no.), Athens, 1939

Spyridakis, G. "Τὰ κατὰ τὴν τελευτὴν ἔθιμα ἐκ τῶν ἁγιολογικῶν πηγῶν", *EEBS* 20 (1950) 75–171
"Τὸ τραγούδι τῶν αἰχμαλώτων τοῦ Τάταρη, μοιρολόϊ ἢ ᾆσμα ἱστορικόν; ", *ELA* 8 (1953–4) 41–3

La siège de Malte et la prise de Chypre, Athens, 1955–6

Stafford, A. *The Female Glory. Life of the Blessed Virgin*, London, 1635; ed. O. Shipley, London, 1869

Stavrou, T. Νεοελληνικὴ μετρική, Athens, 1930

Sticca, S. 'The Literary Genesis of the Planctus Mariae', *CM* 27 (1966) 296–309

Strehlein, H. *Die Totenklage des Vaters um den Sohn in der sophokleischen und euripideischen Tragödie*, Munich, 1959

Stroud, R. S. *Drakon's Law on Homicide*, California, 1968

Struve, K. L. *Der politische Vers der Mittelgriechen*, Hildesheim, 1839

Swainson, C. A. *The Greek Liturgies*, Cambridge, 1884

Synkollitis, S. "Ὁ νεκρὸς εἰς τὴν Ἀνασελίτσα", *Laog* 11 (1934) 387–414

Tarsouli, G. (Tarsouli), Μωραΐτικα τραγούδια (no.), Athens, 1942

Theros, A. (Theros), Τὰ τραγούδια τῶν Ἑλλήνων, 2 (no.), Βασικὴ Βιβλιοθήκη 47, Athens, 1942

Thompson, W. E. 'The Marriage of First Cousins in Athenian Society', *Phoenix* 21 (1967) 273–82

Thomson, G. *Greek Lyric Metre*, Cambridge, 1929; 2 ed. 1960
Aeschylus and Athens, London, 1941; 3 ed. 1966
Studies in Ancient Greek Society. Vol. 1: *The Prehistoric Aegean*, London, 1949; 2 ed. 1954
Studies in Ancient Greek Society, Vol. 2: *The First Philosophers*, London, 1955; 2 ed. 1961
'From Religion to Philosophy', *JHS* 73 (1953) 77–83
Aeschylus, The Oresteia and the Prometheus Bound, translated into English verse, New York, 1965
The Oresteia of Aeschylus, 2 vols., Prague, 1966

Thumb, A. *Handbook of the Modern Greek Vernacular*, Eng. ed. Edinburgh, 1912
'On the Value of Modern Greek for the Study of Ancient Greek', *CQ* 8 (1914) 181–203

Tillyard, H. J. W. 'Quantity and Accent in Byzantine Hymnody', *Laud* 4 (1926) 285–386

Tischendorf, L. P. C. *Evangelia Apocrypha*, Leipzig, 1853; repr. Athens, 1959

Tomadakis, N. Ἡ βυζαντινὴ ὑμνογραφία, 3 ed. Athens, 1965

Tournefort, M. *A Voyage into the Levant*, Eng. ed. London, 1718

Toynbee, J. *Death and Burial in the Roman World*, London, 1971

Bibliography

Tozer, H. F. 'The Greek-speaking Population of Southern Italy', *JHS* 10 (1889) 11–42

Trenkner, S. *The Greek Novella in the Classical Period*, Cambridge, 1958

Triandafyllidis, M. Νεοελληνική γραμματική, Athens, 1941

Triandafyllidis, P. Οἱ φυγάδες, Athens, 1870

Trypanis, C. A. 'Metres of Early Byzantine Religious Poetry', Atti del 8 Congresso di Studi Bizantini (1938) 233

'Byzantine Oral Poetry', *BZ* 56 (1963) 1–3

Trypanis, C. A. and Maas, P. *See* Maas, P. and Trypanis, C. A.

Tuilier, A. *Grégoire de Nazianze: La Passion de Christ, tragédie*, Sources chrétiennes no. 149, Paris, 1969

Tziatzios, E. Τραγούδια τῶν Σαρακατσαναίων, Athens, 1928

Usener, H. *Epicurea*, Leipzig/Bonn, 1887

Valetas, G. (Valetas), Ἀνθολογία τῆς δημοτικῆς πεζογραφίας, Athens, 3 vols. 1947–9

Van Gennep, A. *The Rites of Passage*, Eng. ed. London, 1960

Vasiliev, A. A. *History of the Byzantine Empire*, 2 vols., 2 ed. Madison, 1961

Vassiliev, A. V. *Anecdota Graeco-byzantina* (pars prior), Moscow, 1893

Vendryes, J. *Traité d'accentuation grecque*, Paris, 1931

Vermeule, T. 'Painted Mycenaean Larnakes', *JHS* 85 (1965) 123–48

Verrall, A. W. 'Death and the Horse', *JHS* 18 (1898) 1–14

Verrier, P. *Le vers français*, Paris, 1931

Vilborg, E. *Achilles Tatius: Leucippe and Clitophon*, Göteborg/Stockholm, 1955

Vlastos, P. (Vlastos), Ὁ γάμος ἐν Κρήτῃ, Athens, 1893

Συνώνυμα καὶ συγγενικά, Athens, 1931

Voutetakis, D. Τραγούδια Κρητικά, Chania, 1904

Wace, A. J. B. and Thompson, M. S. *The Nomads of the Balkans*, London, 1914

Waern, I. 'Greek Lullabies', *Er* 58 (1960) 1–8

Wagner, W. *Medieval Greek Texts*, London, 1870

Carmina graeca medii aevi, Leipzig, 1874; repr. Athens, n.d.

Wallaschek, R. *Primitive Music*, London, 1893

Weber, L. *Solon und die Schöpfung der attischen Grabrede*, Frankfurt, 1935

Wellesz, E. (ed.), *Ancient and Oriental Music*, London, 1957

(ed.), 'The Akathistos Hymn', *MMB* 9 (1957), Copenhagen

A History of Byzantine Music and Hymnography, 2 ed. Oxford, 1961

'The Nativity Drama of the Byzantine Church', *JRS* 37 (1947) 145–51

'Melito's Homily on the Passion', *JTS* 44 (1943) 41–52

Wells, E. K. *The Ballad Tree*, New York, 1950

Werner, E. 'Hellenism and Judaism in Christian Music', *HUCA* 20 (1947) 408–70

White, J. W. *The Verse of Greek Comedy*, London, 1912

Wilamowitz-Moellendorff, U. von 'Des Mädchens Klage. Eine alexandrinische Arie', *NGWG* 2 (1896) 209–32

Textgeschichte der griechischen Lyriker, Göttingen, 1900

Bion von Smyrna. Adonis, Berlin, 1900

Wilhelm, A. *Griechische Epigramme aus Kreta*, Oslo, 1950

Willetts, R. F. *Aristocratic Society in Ancient Crete*, London, 1955

Cretan Cults and Festivals, London, 1962

'Marriage and Kinship at Gortyn', *PCPS* 191 (1965) 50–61

The Gortyn Code, Berlin, 1969

Winnington-Ingram, R. P. *Mode in Ancient Greek Music*, Cambridge, 193ᶜ

Witowski, S. *Epistulae privatae graecae*, Leipzig, 1906

Bibliography

Wolf, E. R. *Peasants*, New Jersey, 1966

Woodhead, A. G. *The Study of Greek Inscriptions*, Cambridge, 1959

Wyse, W. (ed.), *The Speeches of Isaeus*, Cambridge, 1904

Xanthoudidis, S. A. "Κρητικοὶ κέρνοι", *ABSA* 12 (1905–6) 9–23

Xirouchakis, A. (ed.), Κρητικὸς πόλεμος, Trieste, 1908

Young, A. M. 'Of the Nightingale's Song', *CJ* 47 (1951) 181–4

Zafeirakopoulos, D. K. "Έθιμα τῆς κηδείας ἐν Μάνη", *Laog* 3 (1911) 473–7

Zambelios, S. Ἄσματα δημοτικὰ τῆς Ἑλλάδος, Kerkyra, 1852

Zilliacus, H. 'Zur Sprache griechischer Familienbriefe des III. Jahrhunderts n. Chr.', *SSF* 13.3 (1943)

Zoras, G. (Zoras), Βυζαντινὴ ποίησις. Βασικὴ Βιβλιοθήκη 1, Athens, 1956

'Un Θρῆνος inedito sulla caduta di Constantinopoli', *SBN* 4 (1935) 237–48; revised ed. Athens, 1955 (in Greek)

"Πόνοι καὶ ἐλπίδες τῶν ὑποδούλων", *ED* 3 (1949) 415–19, 472–6, 619–21

"Ἡ ἅλωσις τῆς Κωνσταντινουπόλεως", *ED* 5 (1950) 851–62

Περὶ τὴν ἅλωσιν τῆς Κωνσταντινουπόλεως, Athens, 1959

"Ὁ Χάρος καὶ ἡ ἀπεικόνησις αὐτοῦ ἐν τῷ στιχουργήματι 'Πένθος θανάτου'", *Parn* 12 (1970) 420–38

Zotos, D. A. Ἡ ξενητεία τῶν Ἠπειρωτῶν, Athens, 1935

Zschietzschmann, W. 'Die Darstellung der Prothesis in der griechischen Kunst', *AM* 53 (1928) 17–36, B8–18

Zuntz, G. Review of Maas/Trypanis *Sancti Romani Melodi Cantica. Cantica Genuina*, *JTS* 16.2 (1964) 511–17

Opuscula Selecta: Classica, Hellenistica, Christiana, Manchester, 1972

Abbreviations

I. Reference works and epigraphical publications

AB   *Analecta Bollandiana*, Brussels, 1882

ALG   *Anthologia Lyrica Graeca*, E. Diehl. 2 vols. Teubner, 2 ed., Leipzig, 1925

AP   *Anthologia Palatina*, ed. H. Beckby (Anthologia Graeca), Munich, 1957

AS   *Acta Sanctorum*, J. Bolland, Paris, 1863–

Bonn   *Corpus Scriptorum Historiae Byzantinae*, Bonn, 1829–97

CGL   *Corpus Glossariorum Latinorum*, G. Loewe and G. Goetz. Leipzig, 1888; repr. Amsterdam, 1965

CIL   *Corpus Inscriptionum Latinarum*, Berlin, 1862–

CVA   *Corpus Vasorum Antiquorum*, vols. 1–2 (Grèce. Athènes, Musée Nationale). Union Académique Internationale, Paris, 1954

Du Cange   *Glossarium ad scriptores mediae et infimae Graecitatis*, C. du Fresne, Lugduni, 1688; repr. Paris, 1943

FGH   *Fragmente der griechischen Historiker*, F. Jakoby, Berlin, 1922

FHG   *Fragmenta Historicorum Graecorum*, C. Müller, Paris, 1841–70

FPG   *Fragmenta Philosophorum Graecorum*, F. W. A. Mullach, Paris, 1860–81

GCS   *Die griechischen christlichen Schriftsteller der ersten drei Jahrhunderte*, Leipzig, 1916

Geffcken   *Griechische Epigramme*, J. Geffcken, Heidelberg, 1916

GGM   *Geographi Graeci Minores*, C. Müller, Paris, 1855–61

Grenfell and Hunt   *The Oxyrhynchus Papyri*, B. P. Grenfell and A. S. Hunt, London, 1898

Hist.Lex.   Ἱστορικὸν Λεξικὸν τῆς Ἀκαδημίας Ἀθηνῶν, Athens, 1933–

IC   *Inscriptiones Creticae*, M. Guarducci, Rome, 1935

IG   *Inscriptiones Graecae*, Berlin, 1873–

IGML   *Inscriptions grecques du Musée du Louvre*, A. Dain, Paris, 1933

IPE   *Inscriptiones orae septentrionalis Ponti Euxeni*, B. Latyschev, Petrograd, 1885–1916

IS   Ἱερὰ Σύνοψις καὶ τὰ Ἅγια Πάθη, Athens

Kb.   *Epigrammata graeca ex lapidibus conlecta*, G. Kaibel, Berlin, 1878

LA   Λαογραφικὸν Ἀρχεῖον τῆς Ἀκαδημίας Ἀθηνῶν (Archives)

255

Abbreviations

Le Bas–Wadd. *Inscriptions grecques et latines*, P. Le Bas and W. H. Waddington, vol. 3, Paris, 1837
LGS Leges Graecorum Sacrae, J. de Prott and L. Ziehen, Leipzig, 1896, 1906
L–P Poetarum Lesbiorum Fragmenta, E. Lobel and D. L. Page, Oxford, 1955
MAMA Monumenta Asiae Minoris Antiqua, London, 1928–
MEE Μεγάλη Ἑλληνικὴ Ἐγκυκλοπαίδεια, Athens, 1926–
Migne *Patrologiae cursus completus*, ser. Graeca, J. P. Migne, Paris, 1855
MMB Monumenta Musicae Byzantinae, C. Høeg, H. Tillyard and E. Wellesz, vol. 5, Transcripta 3–5, Copenhagen, 1936
Nauck *Tragicorum Graecorum Fragmenta*, A. Nauck, Leipzig, 1889
Peek *Griechische Vers-Inschriften*, Berlin, 1955
RE Realencyclopädie der klassischen Altertumswissenschaft, A. Pauly, G. Wissowa and W. Kroll, Stuttgart, 1894–
RIJ Recueil des inscriptions juridiques, R. Dareste, B. Hassoullier, T. Reinach, Paris, 1891–5, 1898–1904
RLIGA Reallexikon der Indo-germanischen Altertumskunde
RLV Reallexikon der Vorgeschichte, Berlin, 1924–32
Samm. Sammelbuch griechischer Urkunden aus Ägypten, F. Preisigke and F. Bilabel, Strassburg/Heidelberg, 1915–
SEC Synaxarium Ecclesiae Constantinopolitanae, H. Delehaye, Brussels, 1902
SEG Supplementum Epigraphicum Graecum, Leiden, 1923–
SIG Sylloge Inscriptionum Graecarum, W. Dittenberger, 3 ed. Leipzig, 1915–
Stephanus *Thesaurus Linguae Graecae*, H. Stephanus, London, 1816–18
Stud.Pont. Studia Pontica, Brussels, 1903

II. Periodicals

ABSA Annual of the British School at Athens, London
AC L'Antiquité Classique, Louvain
AIPhO Annuaire de l'Institut de Philologie et d'Histoire Orientales, Brussels
AJA American Journal of Archaeology, Princeton
AKG Archiv für Kulturgeschichte, Münster
AM Mitteilungen des deutschen archäologischen Instituts, Athenische Abteilung, Stuttgart
Ant Die Antike, Berlin
Antaios, Stuttgart
ArP Ἀρχεῖον Πόντου, Athens
ARW Archiv für Religionswissenschaft, Freiburg
Ath Ἀθηνᾶ, Athens
ATL Ἀρχεῖον τοῦ Θρακικοῦ λαογραφικοῦ καὶ γλωσσικοῦ θησαυροῦ, Athens
BCH Bulletin de Correspondance Hellénique, Paris
BGDSL Beiträge zur Geschichte der deutschen Sprache und Literatur, Halle
BIAB Bulletin de l'Institut Archéologique, Académie Bulgare des sciences, Sofia
BNJ Byzantinisch-neugriechische Jahrbücher, Athens/Berlin
Byz Byzantion, Brussels
ByzMet Byzantina-Metabyzantina, New York
BZ Byzantinische Zeitschrift, Munich
CJ Classical Journal, Chicago
CM Classica et Mediaevalia, Copenhagen
CP Classical Philology, Chicago

Abbreviations

CQ   *Classical Quarterly*, London
CR   *Classical Review*, London
DAr   Δωδεκανησιακὸν 'Αρχεῖον, Athens
DIEE   Δελτίον τῆς ἱστορικῆς καὶ ἐθνολογικῆς ἑταιρείας τῆς 'Ελλάδος, Athens
ED   'Ελληνικὴ Δημιουργία, Athens
EEBS   'Επετηρὶς τῆς 'Εταιρείας Βυζαντινῶν Σπουδῶν, Athens
EEKS   'Επετηρὶς τῆς 'Εταιρείας Κρητικῶν Σπουδῶν, Athens
EK   'Εκκλησιαστικὸς Κῆρυξ, Athens
ELA   'Επετηρὶς τοῦ Λαογραφικοῦ 'Αρχείου, Athens
Ell   'Ελληνικά, Thessaloniki
EO   *Échos d'Orient*, Paris
EPh   'Επτανησιακὰ Φύλλα, Athens
Er   *Eranos*, Uppsala
Est   'Εστία, Athens
ET   'Επιθεώρηση Τέχνης, Athens
FL   *Folk-Lore*, London
Gl   *Glotta*, Göttingen
GR   *Greece and Rome*, Oxford
HC   *L'Hellénisme Contemporain*, Paris
Hist   *Historia*, London
HSCP   *Harvard Studies in Classical Philology*, Cambridge, Mass.
HThR   *Harvard Theological Review*, Cambridge, Mass.
HUCA   *Hebrew Union College Annual*, Cincinnati
HZ   *Historische Zeitschrift*, Munich
IGF   *Indo-germanische Forschungen*, Strassburg/Berlin
IME   'Ημερολόγιον τῆς Μεγάλης 'Ελλάδος, Athens
JAI   *Journal of the Anthropological Institute*, London
JHS   *Journal of Hellenic Studies*, London
JKPh   *Jahrbücher für klassische Philologie*, Leipzig
JOAI   *Jahresheft des österreichischen archäologischen Instituts*, Vienna
JRS   *Journal of Roman Studies*, London
JTS   *Journal of Theological Studies*, Oxford
JWCI   *Journal of the Warburg and Courtauld Institutes*, London
KCh   Κρητικὰ Χρονικά, Iraklion
KyCh   Κυπριακὰ Χρονικά, Larnaka
Laog   Λαογραφία, Athens
Laud   *Laudate*, London
LQF   *Liturgiegeschichtliche Quellen und Forschungen*, Münster
Man,   London
MCh   Μικρασιατικὰ Χρονικά, Athens
NE   Νέος 'Ελληνομνήμων, Athens
NEst   Νέα 'Εστία, Athens
NGWG   *Nachrichten der kaiserlichen Gesellschaft der Wissenschaften zu Göttingen*
NJK   *Neue Jahrbücher für das klassische Altertum*, Leipzig
NK   Νέον Κράτος, Athens
OS   *L'Orient Syrien*, Paris
PAA   Πρακτικὰ τῆς 'Ακαδημίας 'Αθηνῶν, Athens
Pand   Πανδώρα, Athens
Parn   Παρνασσός, Athens
PBSR   *Papers of the British School at Rome*, London

Abbreviations

PCA   *Proceedings of the Classical Association,* London
PCPS   *Proceedings of the Cambridge Philological Society,* Cambridge
Phil   *Philologus,* Berlin
Pl   Πλάτων, Athens
RA   *Revue Archéologique,* Paris
REA   *Revue des études anciennes,* Bordeaux
REG   *Revue des études grecques,* Paris
RF   *Rivista di Filologia,* Turin
RHR   *Revue de l'histoire des religions,* Paris
RM   *Rheinisches Museum für Philologie,* Frankfurt
RP   *Revue de Philologie,* Paris
RSR   *Revue des sciences religieuses,* Strasbourg
SBAW   *Sitzungsberichte der bayerischen Akademie der Wissenschaften,* Munich
SBN   *Studi bizantini e neoellenici,* Naples/Rome
SE   *Solar Energy,* Ἡλιακὴ Ἐνέργεια, Athens
SIF   *Studi italiani di filologia classica,* Florence
SM   *Studi medievali,* Spoleto
SSF   *Societas Scientiarum Fennica,* Commentationes Humanarum Litterarum, Helsinki
Syr   *Syria,* Paris
TAPhA   *Transactions and Proceedings of the American Philological Association,* Boston
Theol   Θεολογία, Athens
Thes   Θησαυρίσματα, Venice
Thrak   Θρακικά, Athens
WS   *Wiener Studien,* Vienna
WSt   *Woodbrooke Studies,* Cambridge
ZBa   *Zeitschrift für Balkanologie,* Wiesbaden
ZVk   *Zeitschrift für Volkskunde,* Berlin

Glossary of transliterated words

This glossary includes only those words which are used in the text more than once, and which are not readily comprehensible to readers with no Greek. The definitions given apply to the words as used in this book, and are not intended to be general.

AG = Ancient Greek, BG = Byzantine Greek,
MG = Modern Greek.

anakálema (*BG, MG*)   invocation, lament

aulós (*AG*)   reed-pipe

choaí (*AG*)   libations

ekphorá (*AG*)   carrying-out of the corpse from house to tomb

énata (*AG*)   funeral rites held on the ninth day

eniaúsia (*AG*)   funeral rites held after one year

ephýmnion (*AG*)   refrain in choral odes, usually placed between antistrophic pairs, or between strophe and antistrophe

epikédeion (*AG*)   lament, usually in verse

epitáphios lógos, epitáphios (*AG, BG*)   funeral oration

Epitáphios (*BG, MG*)   holy cloth with embroidered representation of Christ in the Tomb, which is laid in the *kouvoúklion*, or wooden likeness of Christ's Tomb

Epitáphios Thrênos (*BG, MG*)   lament for Christ's death and burial chanted in the Orthodox service on the evening of Good Friday and the morning of Easter Saturday

epodé (*AG*)   song chanted over someone, spell

epodós (*AG*)   refrain in choral odes, usually placed at end

éxarchos (*AG*)   leader of choral performance

Glossary

genésia (*AG*)   funeral rites, probably held originally on anniversary of death; later transformed in Attica into public festival for dead on fixed day of calendar

génos (*AG*)   *gens*, clan

góos (*AG*)   dirge, lament

gynaikonómos (*AG*)   supervisor of women's affairs

kanón (*BG*)   hymn of Byzantine church

kedestés, also *kadestás* (*AG*)   relation-in-law

kommós (*AG*)   lament in tragedy sung alternately by one or more chief characters and chorus

kontákion (*BG*)   hymn of early Byzantine church, made up of 18–30 *tropária*, or stanzas, which are composed on pattern of model stanza, or *hirmus*

koukoúlion (*BG*)   proem to *kontákion*

mnemósyna (*BG, MG*)   memorial services for dead

moîra (*AG, BG, MG*)   fate

moirológi (*BG, MG*)   lament

oîkos (*AG*)   family unit centred on household

parádosis (*MG*)   mythical folk story believed to be true, which is connected with natural phenomena, geographical regions, historical events or persons

paregoriá (*MG*)   funeral feast

perídeipnon, also *sýndeipnon* (*AG, BG*)   funeral feast

politikòs stíchos (*BG, MG*)   fifteen-syllable accentual verse, the metre of Byzantine and post-Byzantine vernacular poetry and of modern folk songs

próthesis (*AG*)   laying-out, wake

Stavrotheotókion (*BG*)   hymn for Mary at the Cross

Theotókos (*BG, MG*)   Mother of God, title given to Mary after Council of Ephesos (A.D. 431)

thrênos (*AG, BG*)   lament

triekóstia, also *triakóstia* (*AG*)   funeral rites held on the thirtieth day

tríta (*AG*)   funeral rites held on the third day

tropárion (*BG*)   see *kontákion*

týche (*AG, BG, MG*)   fortune

Indexes

I. General Index

Indexes

food, as offering 8, 32
Fortune my Foe 228 n. 37
Frazer, J. G. 210 n. 65, 218 n. 5 *et passim*
Freistedt, E. 208 n. 38, 214 nn. 39–40
fruit,¹ as offering 45, 47, (apples, grapes, quinces) 7–8, 9, 32, 42–3
funeral: meal 10, 31, 45–6, 71, 105, 127; oration 162, 166, 180, see also *epitáphios lógos*; procession 29–31, 34, 43–4, 49, lamentation at 123–4, see also *ekphorá*; service 26, 31, 44

Gambreion, laws from 7, 16–17, 209 n. 54, 212 n. 108
garlands 5, 58, 77, 120
Gelon of Syracuse 17
genésia 19, 208 n. 37
Genoa 145
génos 11, 13–14, 18–21, 210 n. 65
Georgillas, Emmanuel 87; *Plague of Rhodes* (Θανατικὸν τῆς Ρόδου) 90
Georgios of Nikomedia 220 n. 28
Germanos, Patriarch of Constantinople 220 n. 28
Germans 98–9; German Occupation 99–100
Gierden, K. 221 nn. 38, 39
gipsy nail-maker 65, 73
gnomic laments (γνωμικὰ μοιρολόγια) 126–8
gods, laments for 55–6, 60–2, 68, 69
Good Friday ballads 68–75
góos 11–13, 102–3, 106, 225–6 n. 6
Gorgias of Leontinoi 151
Gortyn, laws from 11, 20–1
Great Idea (Μεγάλη 'Ιδέα) 94
Gregory Nazianzen: author of *Christòs Páschon?* 64; epigrams 196; homilies 30, 32–3
Gregory of Nyssa 27–9, 31, 153, 221–2 n. 47
grief, violent 5, 27–8, 34, 46, 68–9
Grosdidier de Matons, J. 219 nn. 21, 25
Groto, Luigi, *Lo Isach* 77
Guthrie, W. K. C. 202, 241 n. 50

Hades: and Christ 71, 153–4; fusion with Charos and Thanatos 49, 153; marriage to 230 n. 64; scales of 26;

snatching of 195–7, 230 n. 68; winged 216 n. 7
Hades (Underworld) 49, 84–5, 92, 144; dead in 36, 41–3, 147; descent to 62, 63, 66, 71–2; journey to 190–2, 202–3; as Paradise 50; return from 72, 181, 192; river or spring in 39, 202–4
hair: cutting of 8, 27–8, 41; for dead 7; grown long 32; tearing of 6, 28, 29, 33, 91, 96, 163; wetting of 41–2; worn loose 8, 41–2
Halikarnassos, inscription from 106
Harmodios 105
harvest, associated with ritual death 56–60
Hebrew 63, 86, 152–5, 172–4, 177, 188; *see also* Jews; Semitic
Hekate 16, 76, 173
Hell 26, 48, 49
Hellenistic age 23, 24, 108, 118, 179; Greek 116–18, 172
Helots 10
Herakleitos 27, 153–4, 213 n. 12, 234 n. 54
herbs, strewn on dead 5, 7, 27, 39
Hermes 89, 99
Herodotos 19, 57, 61, 198–9, 201
heroes, laments for (ancient) 55, (modern) 100, 126
Hesiod 58, 117
Hesychios 110–11
hexameter 59, 104
Hippolytos of Rome 234 n. 54
historical songs and laments 83, 90–101, 126, 145
Homer, 5, 57–8, 113, 118, 131, 135, 179; *moîra* in 113–14; similes in 186, 194, 198; terms for lamentation in 11–13, 102–3, 107; *Epigrams* 173; *Hymns* 133, 173, 221 n. 46, 237 nn. 34, 38, 40; *Il.* (6) 4–5, (14) 198, (18) 10, (19) 132, 165, 231 n. 7, (22) 162, 173, 237 nn. 31, 46, (23) 139, 186, (24) 6, 12, 36, 132–3, 178, 183; *Od.* (5) 229 nn. 56, 75, (11) 4, (16) 187, (24) 11–12
homéstioi 16
homicide 22, 212 n. 110
homilies: evidence for funeral ritual in 25, 27–34; lament for Isaac in 77; Paschal 153; Virgin's lament in 65, 70

265

Indexes

smell: of corpse 48; of soul 27
Smyrna, earthquake mourned 85, 166, 179
soloist, part in lament 12–13, 131–3, 137, 150
Solon 6, 8, 12, 14–17, 19–20, 21, 199
Sophokles; *thrênos* and *góos* in 225–6 n. 6; *Aj.* 151, 162; *Ant.* 113, 136, 212 n. 109; *El.* 22, 199, 212 n. 109, 234 n. 50; *OC* 178; *OT* 113, 166; *Ph.* 113; *Tr.* 113, 137
soul: journey of 30, 32, 202–3; pies for (ψυχόπιττες) 47; released from Hades 37, 47, 71–2; snatching of 5, 25–7, 38; struggle of (ψυχορραγεῖν) 5, 25–6, 37–8; weighing of 26
Souli 96–8
Spain 10
Sparta 17; Spartans 126, 199, 231 n. 73
spirits, evil 5, 16, 27, 30–1, 39, 44
Spyridakis, G. 213–15 *passim*, 223 n. 23
Stabat Mater 68
Stavrotheotókion 63–5, 70, 144, 219 n. 23, 220 n. 30
stichomythia, *see* dialogue
strophic form 132–4, 141–4
sweeping of house 16, 25
Symeon, Archbishop of Thessaloniki, *de ordine sepulturae* 25, 32
Symeon Metaphrastes; *Planctus Mariae* 65, 68, 70, 114; *Vita S. Euphrosynes* 163; *Vita S. Xenophontis* 163–4
Synesios of Cyrene 63
Syracuse: legislation from 212 n. 106; loss lamented 84
Syriac 63, 142, 155, 188, 232 n. 29, 236 n. 27

table songs (*epitrapézia tragoúdia*) 125
Tartara 48
Tenedos 98, 144
Teos, inscription from 155–6
tetrameter, trochaic 137
Thanatos 5, 38, 196
Thebes 60, 61
Theodore the Studite 220 n. 30
Theokritos 56, 59, 231 n. 10
Thesmophoria 17, 21, 212 n. 108
Thessaloniki, siege and sack (1430) lamented 86, 93–4

Thessaly: ancient 61; funeral customs from 38, 40–1; laments from 127–8
thíasoi 19
Thomson, G. 211 nn. 77, 96, 227 n. 28, 231 n. 1, 234 n. 50, 235 n. 1
Thrace: funeral customs 37–8, 42; laments 71–4
three-part form 132–4, 139–40, 142–5, 150, 166
thrênos: in Byzantine Greek 61, 87–92, 94, 110; choral 13, 18, 19, 23, 61, 103, 132; decline of archaic form 23, 106; distinguished from *góos* 11–13, 102–4, 106, 108, 225–6 n. 6; prohibited 12, 18
Thrênos for Constantinople (Θρῆνος τῆς Κωνσταντινουπόλεως) 145, 169, 233 nn. 22, 24, 237 n. 42
Thrênos for Cyprus (Θρῆνος τῆς Κύπρου) 90
Thrênos of Four Patriarchates (Θρῆνος τῶν Τεσσάρων Πατριαρχείων) 89, 145, 223 nn. 21, 24
Thrênos Theotókou (Θρῆνος τῆς ὑπεραγίας Θεοτόκου εἰς τὴν Σταύρωσιν τοῦ Δεσπότου Χριστοῦ) 64–5, 68, 70, 144, 219 n. 24, 221 n. 39, 233 n. 31
Thrênos for Timur Lenk (Θρῆνος περὶ Ταμυρλάγγου) 223 n. 23, 235 n. 11
tomb 14; lamentation at (*AG*) 8, 15–16, 23, 103, 106, 108–10, (*BG*) 31, (*MG*) 44–5, 47, 124, 109–10; mourner's desire to live at 28, 33, 38; ritual at (*AG*) 7–9, 14–17, 20–3, (*BG*) 32–3, (*MG*) 44–5, 47; tombstone, address by 138–9, 147, address to 45, 147, marriage to 220 n. 64; *see also* offerings
torches: apotropaic properties 30–1; in funeral procession 15, 30, 77, 214 n. 29; at graves 8; at weddings 56, 58, 120
Tournefort, M. 216 nn. 14, 20, 217 n. 32
Trebizond, alleged laments for 94–6, 225 n. 35
triadic form 132
triekóstia, triakósta 16, 32, 47, 207 n. 37
trimeter, iambic 118
tríta 7, 208 n. 38, 214 n. 39
Troy, fall lamented 84
Tsakonian laments 122, 149–50
Tuilier, A. 64, 219 n. 25
Turks 48–50, 76, 126; in historical laments 90, 93, 95, 96, 100

270

Indexes

týche 113–15
tyrants, tyranny 10, 18–19

Underworld *see* Hades
Underworld ballads 38, 125–6, 164–5, 231 n. 70

Varnalis, K. 220 n. 32
vase-paintings 5–8, 14, 15, 22, 206 n. 10, 207 *passim*, 209 *passim*
vendetta 22; ballads 124–5, 171
vengeance 21–2, 124–5, 139, 171, 179, 181–2, 186, 199
Venice 144–5
Venizelos, E. 126
vernacular language, use in medieval poetry 63, 87–90
vessels: breaking of 27, 42, 45; for offerings 5, 7–8; removal of 15
vigil: for Christ 70, 77; laments at 127; during wake 34, 42
Virgin Mary: appeals to 77, 145; bath of 74; curse of 65, 75; death of 25; in Hades 49; and Kalé 75–6; lament of 62–78, 109, 120–1, 142–4, 168, 174, 204
Vlachs 100
vow unfulfilled 5, 37

wailing 18, 21–2, 57; at funeral procession 7, 16, 29, 43–4; as origin of lament 102; at tomb 15, 16, 34; at wake 11–13, 38, 40
wake: customs at 27, 39; duration of 6, 15; lamentation at 28, 34, 40–2, 49, 50,

108, 122–3, 127, 149; preparation of corpse for 5, 27, 39–40; see also *próthesis*
washing: of bride and groom 120; of clothes 46; of corpse 5, 27, 39; of mourners 10, 11, 45
water: of life 75–6; as offering and for purification 5, 7, 10, 32, 39, 42, 45–6
weapons 41, 147
wedding attire 5, 27, 39, 120
wedding laments 120–2, 230 n. 64; songs 58
Wellesz, E. 154
white 5, 16–17, 27, 47
Willetts, R. F. 11
wine: for mourners 45–6, 71; as offering 7, 8, 32, 45–6; for washing dead 27, 39, 44, 48, 58
women: condemnation of 28–9; cults exclusive to 56; duties of elderly 39, 44; lamentation of 34, 108, 122–5, 128, 212 n. 107, 216 n. 30; restrictions on 15–18, 21–2; separated from men 15, 29, 42–3, 47
word play 151, 156, 233 n. 48
World War I 99; II 99–100

The Young Girl and Charos (Ἡ Λυγερὴ κι ὁ Χάρος) 148, 164

Zafeiris 78–82, 108, 204
Zeus 134
Zoras, G. 219 n. 24, 241 n. 41

II. Index of motifs and images

This index is selective, relating to motifs and images in the laments discussed in the book.

acceptance of death 128, 147, 181
address to dead: modes of 171–7; and structure of lament 133–4, 140, 142–5
adýnaton 181, 238 n. 59
aeroplanes 100
agón, death as 26
animals: join lamentation, (bears and bulls) 141, (ewe, heifer) 67, 141, (horses) 94–5, (lion) 141
apple, dead as 196

beauty in death 60, 65–8, 70, 141
bee 159
birds: asked not to sing (cuckoo, nightingale) 97; dead as (eagle, dove) 120–1, 177, (nightingale) 185–6, (partridge) 177, (peacock, swallow) 185–6; as harbingers of spring (swallow) 81–2; join lamentation (cuckoo, halcyon, nightingale, swallow, turtle-dove) 93, 95, 97, 158; as